AF251425

The Sacred in Twentieth-Century Politics

The Sacred in Twentieth-Century Politics

Essays in Honour of Professor Stanley G. Payne

Edited by

Roger Griffin

Robert Mallett

and

John Tortorice

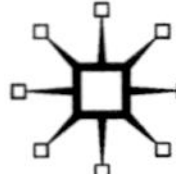

First published 2008 by
PALGRAVE MACMILLAN

Palgrave Macmillan in the UK is an imprint of Macmillan Publishers Limited,
registered in England, company number 785998, of Houndmills, Basingstoke,
Hampshire RG21 6XS.

Palgrave Macmillan in the US is a division of St Martin's Press LLC,
175 Fifth Avenue, New York, NY 10010.

Palgrave Macmillan is the global academic imprint of the above companies
and has companies and representatives throughout the world.

Palgrave® and Macmillan® are registered trademarks in the United States,
the United Kingdom, Europe and other countries.

ISBN-13: 978–0–230–53774–3 hardback
ISBN-10: 0–230–53774–X hardback

This book is printed on paper suitable for recycling and made from fully
managed and sustained forest sources. Logging, pulping and manufacturing
processes are expected to conform to the environmental regulations of the
country of origin.

A catalogue record for this book is available from the British Library.

Library of Congress Cataloging-in-Publication Data
The Sacred in Twentieth-Century Politics: Essays in Honour of Professor
   Stanley G. Payne
   Edited by Roger Griffin, Robert Mallett, and John Tortorice.
      p.   cm.
   Proceedings of a conference held in May 2004 at the University of
   Wisconsin–Madison.
   Includes bibliographical references and index.
   ISBN 978–0–230–53774–3 (alk. paper)
   1. Religion and politics–History–20th century–Congresses.
   I. Payne, Stanley G.   II. Mallett, Robert, 1961–   III. Griffin, Roger.
   IV. Tortorice, John S.
   BL65.P7S23 2008
   322'.10904—dc22   2008020795

10   9   8   7   6   5   4   3   2   1
17   16   15   14   13   12   11   10   09   08

Printed and bound in Great Britain by
CPI Antony Rowe, Chippenham and Eastbourne

This volume is dedicated to Prof. Stanley G. Payne in recognition of his enormous contributions to scholarship. The genesis of this volume lies with a conference in honour of Prof. Payne held at the University of Wisconsin-Madison in May 2004. In preparing the book the editors owe a great debt to Prof. Juan Linz and Prof. Emilio Gentile, who provided many invaluable insights and commentaries that helped shape the final work.

The Editors
22 April 2008

Contents

List of Illustrations

Notes on Contributors

Chip Berlet, Senior Analyst, Political Research Associates in the Boston area, US. c.berlet@publiceye.org.

Robert E. Frykenberg, Professor Emeritus of History and South Asian Studies, University of Wisconsin-Madison, US. refryken@wisc.edu.

Roger Griffin, Professor in Modern History, Oxford Brookes University, UK. rdgriffin@brookes.ac.uk.

Kemal H. Karpat, Professor Emeritus in History, University of Wisconsin-Madison, US.

Anatoly M. Khazanov, Ernst Gellner Professor of Anthropology, University of Wisconsin-Madison, US. khazanov@wisc.edu.

Eric Langenbacher, Visiting Assistant Professor, Department of Government, Georgetown University, US. langenbe@georgetown.edu.

Robert Mallett, Lecturer in Modern European History, Departments of Medieval and Modern History, University of Birmingham, UK. r.mallett@bham.ac.uk.

Rana Mitter, University Lecturer in Modern Chinese History and Politics, University of Oxford, UK. rana.mitter@chinese.ox.ac.uk.

Eusebio Mujal-León, Professor in the Department of Government/ Director of the Cuba XXI Project, Georgetown University, US. mujalleo@georgetown.edu.

Stanley G. Payne, Hilldale-Jaume Vicens Vives Professor of History Emeritus, University of Wisconsin-Madison, US. sgpayne@wisc.edu.

John Tortorice, Director of the George L. Mosse Program, Department of History, University of Wisconsin-Madison, US. jtortori@wisc.edu.

Werner Ustorf, Director of Department of Theology & Religion, University of Birmingham, UK. w.ustorf@bham.ac.uk.

Klaus Vondung, Professor Emeritus in German Studies (Germanistik), Universität Siegen, Germany. vondung@germanistik.uni-siegen.de.

1
Introduction: The Evolutions and Convolutions of Political Religion

Roger Griffin

Joined at the hip

Johann Goethe once claimed that 'great events throw their shadow before them'. Perhaps it is the instinct of scholars in the human sciences to work where the light is strongest that explains why some of the major, formative processes of modern history have been added so belatedly and hurriedly to the repertoire of legitimate research topics. It was only towards the end of the nineteenth century that the pioneers of sociology engaged intelligently with the impact of industrialisation and what has come to be known as 'modernity', long after countless writers and artists had started investigating its ominous spiritual fallout with visionary clarity. Subsequently, such epoch-forming phenomena as the rise of socialism and 'the masses', nationalism, Bolshevism, fascism, anti-colonialism, the counter-culture of the 1960s, and ecologism have entered the West's historical consciousness by stealth rather than in the full glare of academic analysis.

'Political religion' (PR) seems destined to be regarded one day as yet another phenomenon which should have engaged the collective attention of the Western human sciences more promptly and urgently. Perhaps some of the intellectual resources needed for this could have diverted from what was, for decades, too often a sterile, unimaginative, and highly politicised preoccupation with 'totalitarianism' and 'extremism' – both of which ironically turn out to be fully intelligible only once their relationship to PR has been grasped. The latter's continued neglect by many mainstream historians, political scientists, and sociologists may have been encouraged by the difficulty Western academia has experienced in breaking out of centuries of Enlightenment rationalism that underestimated the power of the irrational and mythic.

Its grasp on the concept of religion may also have been weakened by even more centuries of Eurocentrism, which made the sophisticated parallel universes of cognition and human science bound up with the world's major non-Judeo-Christian religions – notably the rich intellectual traditions of Buddhist, Islamic, and Hindu thought – practically invisible except to specialists in 'Oriental Studies'.

The genesis of this book lies in the conference 'Political Religions in the Modern Era', held in May 2004 at the University of Wisconsin-Madison in honour of Professor Stanley Payne's retirement. It is here that most of the chapters collected in this volume were first presented in embryonic form.[1] The three that constitute Part I 'problematise' the concept political religion and underline the need for definitional and taxonomic clarity in applying it to particular ideological phenomena. At the same time, they demonstrate how much the understanding of the modern world would be impoverished if it – or some close equivalent – was not used. Part II then offers four examples of the sacralisation of politics under secular political regimes of the right and left, while Part III consists of three case studies in what at first sight may appear the politicisation of religious cosmologies. However, it turns out to deal with considerably more complex compounds of 'this worldly' and suprahistorical, metaphysical constructions of reality. Overall, the book reveals the multifaceted, heterogeneous nature of PR in the modern world, as well as its power literally to change the course of history.

The term 'political religion' is, of course, only one of several with which academics have sought to capture and interpret the presence of the 'sacred in politics', a phenomenon first engaged with in a systematic way by Eric Voegelin and Raymond Aron in the late 1930s, even though the 'religious' aspect of Bolshevism, Fascism, and Nazism had been widely commented on before their groundbreaking works. Since 1945, the subject has occupied some formidable – sometimes impenetrable – minds and, by the dawn of the twenty-first century, had developed a sizable specialist literature,[2] as well as its own dedicated academic journal in English.[3] Since 9/11 it now finds itself a fashionable topic, much as nationalism became suddenly 'in' as a theme for book proposals and conferences after the collapse of the Soviet Union caused repressed nationalisms to spring out of the ground like mushrooms.

This book joins a stream of would-be major contributions to the task of understanding how far the religious can be disentangled from the political in the modern age, and how far attempts to do so reveal them in some cases to be as organically inseparable as Siamese twins. Yet the renaissance of PR as a concept has not been welcomed by all historians. Ian Kershaw, for example, had occasion – in the course of his reflections on the uniqueness of Nazism – to dismiss its renaissance as a field of studies 'as the "voguish revamping of an age-old notion"' which could contribute nothing to the understanding of the Third Reich.[4] Hopefully this book, dedicated to one of the most eminent modern historians of the Anglophone world, will give other historians pause if they are tempted to echo such summary dismissals of the term's value. On the other hand, those already predisposed to recognise PR's heuristic potential should have no difficulty identifying several features that make this volume a particularly valuable contribution to fostering the maturation of a specialism which, though well out of its infancy, is still undergoing a somewhat turbulent adolescence. It is a specialism, moreover, that finds itself having to grow up fast against the background of a political and social world being daily reshaped by the very forces with which it is grappling in a Laocoon-like embrace.

The first 'special feature' is that in several of the essays the author emphasises the thorny taxonomic problems raised by the concept of 'the sacred in politics' and suggests ways of resolving them in a way that invites intelligent debate and a process of convergence rather than ghettoisation into hostile 'camps' of thought. Second, the case studies range from the well-trod territory of the two interwar fascist regimes, Soviet communism, and the US 'religious right' to several phenomena with which few readers are likely to have more than a nodding acquaintance: Maoism, Castroism, 'democratic' Islam in Turkey, and Hindutva. Third, taken together the chapters demonstrate the powerful contribution that this field of studies can make to understanding major episodes in the unfolding of modern and contemporary political history when an equilibrium is achieved between two dynamic 'moments' of analysis: the first subsumes the particular 'nomothetically' within generic concepts associated with PR; the second is an 'idiographic' concern with the uniqueness of particular movements in all their complexity and individual 'personality'.

Fourth, rather than implicitly condemning the 'extremism' and 'fanaticism' of PR in the name of democracy, reason, and moderation, these essays cumulatively call into question simplistic equations of the intrusion of the sacred into politics regarded as extremist. Instead they invite a more sober, more forensic examination of the phenomenon. This means carrying out research 'in depth' in a way that subsumes not just more attention to empirical detail, but a more methodologically and culturally self-questioning examination of the irrational, and – from a liberal humanist perspective – dangerous 'religious' forces that can embed themselves not just in movements openly opposed to democracy, but within democracy itself. When hosted by democratic processes, PR can set about corroding even the best entrenched 'liberal' systems from within. These general points can be grasped more fully if we briefly consider the chapters in sequence.

Part I: Conceptualising political religion

Stanley Payne's article, written shortly after the 2004 Madison conference and first published in an issue of *Totalitarian Movements and Political Religions*, sets the analytical, exploratory tone of much of the book by considering the problems of refining 'political religion' as an ideal type to the point where it becomes of significant heuristic value to historians. Having highlighted crucial ambiguities in the core term 'religion', it proceeds to use the distinction proposed in Emilio Gentile's groundbreaking *Politics as Religion* between 'political' and 'civic' religion in considering the interpenetration of religious and political projects under Christianity, Islam, the French Revolution, and American democracy. The scope of the discussion is then widened by considering the religious component intrinsic to revolutionary movements and regimes of the left and right, notably Anarchism, Marxism–Leninism, Fascism, and Nazism.

The vast remit of the topic is further highlighted when Payne dwells on the importance of the *Juche* cult (originally an offspring of Marxism–Leninism and the specific political situation of North Korea), the charismatic politics of new African states, Islamism, Basque nationalism, and 'multiculturally diverse political correctness', which he dubs 'MDPC' to indicate that it has assumed traits of a civic religion. What emerges from such a panoramic vista is the indispensability of the concept 'political religion' in order to make sense of a wide range of diverse political phenomena that have arisen as a response to a globalising and secularising modernity. Yet it also throws into relief the considerable pragmatic difficulties involved in extricating the sacred from the secular, let alone mapping their respective zones of competence. It also demonstrates the need for comparative studies in this area of the human sciences to cast their empirical net as widely as possible to avoid the risk of generalising from a handful of familiar Western paradigms of both politics and religion – thereby falling back into the trap of Eurocentrism.

Werner Ustorf adds a fresh angle to understanding the religious dimension of PR with his presentation of the sophisticated response to sacralised politics formulated in interwar Europe by two Christian intellectuals acutely conscious of the gulf between the metaphysical foundations of their religious belief and their commitment to any worldly creed, above all Nazism. It is noteworthy that both Paul Schütz and Hans Ehrenberg – in tune with an existentialist theological reading suspicious of the institutionalisation and external trappings of Christianity – sanctioned the application of the term 'religion' to political ideologies so long as it was not confused with the *faith* that sustains a metaphysical and genuinely redemptive, 'soteriological' worldview. The particular interest of Schütz's thesis today is that it was formulated partly as the reaction of a Christian missionary to his encounter with Islam outside the haven of European religious constructions.

Even greater heuristic mileage for contemporary historians is implicit in Ehrenberg's theory, however. It held that the increasingly global crisis provoked by modernity in the interwar period was leading some forms of ultranationalism to promote a symbolic return to a largely mythic and artificially constituted 'original religion' in order to satisfy the primordial human need for roots and meaning. At the same time, he recognised that the resulting PR also embraced technological advance in a resolutely anti-reactionary, anti-conservative spirit, producing a 'post-religious' situation whose complexity defies crude categories of 'modern' and 'anti-modern', 'religious' or 'secular'. This is a model with considerable potential for understanding not only a number of the most powerful 'totalitarian' regimes of the twentieth century, but contemporary forms of religious politics as well. Indeed, the relevance of this theory to Frykenberg's later essay on Hindutva is particularly striking. In short, Ustorf's essay underlines the value of looking beyond the pioneering work of Voegelin or Aron to analyse the role played by *theological* thinkers, past and present, in pioneering political religious studies when contemporary academics first set out to refine their understanding of the key concepts and phenomena involved. (Perhaps the voices of non-Christian theologians and clerics on such matters could also prove illuminating.)

The essay by Eusebio Mujal-León and Eric Langenbacher has been included in the section on 'Conceptualising Political Religion' because of the sustained methodological concern they demonstrate with the task of constructing a taxonomic framework appropriate to answering the question 'Is Castroism a political religion?' Their reflections cause them to propose their own typological schema based on the intersection of two axes, running from ideology to PR and from traditional to non-traditional religion. They also lead to the identification of a cluster of criteria by which to assess the strength of a PR in a given regime. Castroism is then evaluated according to these criteria, principally totalitarianism, the leader principle, the aspiration to create a 'new man' as the embodiment of Cuba's moral regeneration, the creation of a new calendar and a new political liturgy, as well as extreme nationalism. This points to a growing pocket of consensus within the human sciences, for their approach has an obvious resonance with the taxonomic scheme illuminating the linkages between PR, totalitarianism, and palingenetic myth proposed in *Politics as Religion* – the scheme that also forms the starting point to Stanley Payne's chapter.

What Mujal-León and Langenbacher's chapter indirectly highlights is not only the irreconcilable tension between political and revealed religion, but the way propaganda and coercion are born to varying degrees from the totalising thrust of all fully fledged political religions, however idealistic and benign the original 'cause'. It also shows that putative PR 'isms' like Castroism are to be approached as complex developmental processes and continually mutating phenomena rather than static, homogeneous entities easily lending themselves to straightforward classification within rigid categories.

Part II: The sacralisation of politics

The analysis of Castroism serves as a suitable prelude to Part II of this book, which is concerned with the 'sacralisation of politics'. This part opens with Robert Mallett's analysis of the attempted Fascistisation of Italy under Mussolini as a sustained attempt to infuse a nebulous sense of the 'sacred' into all aspects of social existence and consciousness. The strategies it employed to achieve this end shows that it clearly operated – in terms of a distinction later applied in Vondung's chapter – simultaneously as a *Ersatzreligion*, a substitute religion, and a *Religionsersatz* [a substitute *for* religion], or rather – in Schütz's terminology – as a *Glaubensersatz* [a substitute *for* a metaphysical faith], despite the National Fascist Party's (PNF) sustained attempt to paper over the cracks between the regime and the Vatican. Rather than adopting the conventional tack of seeking evidence for this in written texts, Mallett uses a series of images drawn from painting, posters, and media art to project the Fascist vision of the leader, the new man, the nation, the Militia, *Romanità* ('Romanness'), the new Empire, and the new Europe. It is clear that the 'spirituality' underpinning the vision of aviation, war, and the new Italy they convey was neither Christian nor 'pagan', but rooted in a cultic reverence towards the transformative, redemptive power of the modern state itself. In other words, they are products of what Ehrenberg implies should be seen as a 'post-Christian' religion which combines the cult of an imagined past with the embrace of technology in a spirit that is to be seen as fundamentally *modernist* instead of reactionary.

Klaus Vondung's consideration of the value in seeing Nazism as a form of PR focuses on a point reinforcing the groundbreaking analyses of the Third Reich put forward by Voegelin, Raymond, Mosse, and Vondung himself, notably his study of the 'ideological cult and political religion of Nazism'.[5] In their different ways, they all stress the importance of recognising a genuine element of belief in a suprapersonal – but not suprahistorical – 'immortality' as crucial to explaining events in Germany between 1933 and 1945. The first of three important inferences to be drawn from this chapter is the conviction that Nazism's mission was to intensify the spirituality of the 'eternal' German *Volk*, one not coterminous with the direct transposition of a Christian cosmology, soteriology, and philosophy of history into secular terms in the way suggested by Claus-Ekkehard Bärsch. Nor does it vindicate Richard Steigmann-Gall's thesis propounded in *The Holy Reich*[6] that Nazism represented the 'positive Christianity' claimed by Nazi propaganda. Instead, we are dealing with a sacralisation of politics clothed in a blend of Christian and pagan religiosity which is ultimately an attempt to apotheosise the nation and wean Christians from their 'true' faith.

Second, Vondung attaches considerable weight to the value of 'apocalypticism' as a generic historical narrative of imminent renewal from decadence or societal collapse. He suggests that the radicalisation of the Nazis' 'holy' war to achieve racial purity and historical redemption – a war which culminated in genocide on an unparalleled scale – is unintelligible without appreciating the central role played by the eschatological master narrative embedded in the Nazi understanding of the crisis of contemporary society. It is an approach which highlights the importance of its readiness to demonise the Jews and other alleged racial enemies to the point of seeing their destruction as a cathartic event, the precondition for national rebirth. The third point implicit in Vondung's analysis is that Nazism actually involved elements of the two processes that purists would like to keep apart: the politicisation of religion and the sacralisation of politics, another reminder of the ideal typical – and hence necessarily *utopian* – nature of water-tight taxonomic categories in this area of study.

It might be expected that, in contrast to fascism, Marxism–Leninism represented a refreshingly unambiguous, 'one-way' process of 'the sacralisation of politics'. However, apart from challenging the terminology adopted elsewhere in the book by recommending Aron's concept of 'secular religion' rather than 'political religion' for communism's more comprehensive, totalising implications, Anatoly Khazanov soon disabuses the reader of such naïve assumptions. He shows that Bolshevism 'faithfully' followed the template of Christianity both as a total creed and a social practice profoundly with respect to a series of phenomena – the 'sacrality' of the new political order and historical dispensation, the proselytism and messianism of Marxism–Leninism, the deification of leaders, the treatment of canonical ideological writings as 'Holy Scriptures', the pervasive sense of evil, and the expectation of the 'new Soviet man'. Indeed, readers might infer at times that they are reading about a radically secularised form of religion rather than an extreme example of the sacralisation of politics. Certainly, Khazanov shows that, in functional terms at least, Bolshevism set out to 'substitute' the religious role of the Church by offering a source of social cohesion, identity, salvation, rituals, and rites based on an all-embracing cosmology and iconography.

Another feature of Khazanov's analysis is that it addresses an important aspect of all regimes whose praxis is based on a totalising PR, whether of the right or left, by stressing the utter utopianism of its vision of the ideal society and highlighting the fatal human consequences of the Bolsheviks' ruthless attempt to realise Marxism–Leninism as a total worldview within a few years of historical time. That said, by the 1980s the Bolshevik system had become a hollow shell, no less devoid of social, affective, and existential substance for the subjugated masses than the Tsarist regime it had replaced.

The far-reaching implications of Khazanov's analysis for understanding the political history of communism are emphasised when read in conjunction with Rana Mitter's study of the Maoist Cultural Revolution from the perspective of PR. Demolishing stereotypes of Maoism's essential 'Otherness' forged during the Cold War, the key role played by European modernity in its genesis is thrown into sharp relief. When modernisation started conspicuously devastating the foundations of the millennial feudal system of Imperial China, a new generation of intellectuals became exposed to 'Western' brands of utopianism. As a result, the subjective 'crisis of civilisation' triggered by the First World War and the ensuing period of anti-liberalism, authoritarianism, and mass movements in Europe were able to have a formative impact on the political climate within which both Kuomintang nationalism and Chinese communism emerged. This provided fertile soil for a tradition of utopian radicalism launched by Maoism that was not abruptly terminated in 1945 as it was in Europe with the defeat of Fascism and Nazism. At its height, the 1960s Cultural Revolution was mass-producing programmatic declarations of the need for cleansing violence that recall the cult of creative destruction promoted by earlier generations of 'Nietzschean' revolutionaries such as Mikhail Bakunin, Filippo Marinetti, or Ernst Jünger. Striking too is Maoism's intrinsically futural (and modernist) dimension as a radical attempt to create a new nation and a 'new man' on the basis of an agrarian society in order to transcend the social chaos and ideological void of post-imperial China.

Another important point for the comparative study of PR in Mitter's chapter is the largely spontaneous emergence in China of 'religious' forms of political ideology and ritual – notably the 'salvationist' aura of Mao himself as a redeemer figure and the 'scriptural' connotations of his thought for the Red Guard. These are deeply familiar from European history to Western historians, even though Maoist China's proportionally minute intelligentsia had no Christian role models upon which to base its ideas, and despite the profound gulf separating Confucianism and Christianity as belief systems. This implies that the roots of modern PR need to be sought in the more primordial strata of human belief and psychology than is suggested by much existing work on Fascism, Nazism, and Bolshevism, whose collective focus rarely extends beyond the Christian millenarianism of early modern Europe. Another intriguing parallel with the Western experience of the sacralisation of politics worth exploring in this context is what Mitter portrays as the ritualisation of the 'Long March' to become a secular pilgrimage – another example of primordial rather than Christian symbology at work. This is highly reminiscent of the re-enactment of the 'Great Trek' by Boer nationalists in 1936, which became such a major feature of their self-invention as a homogeneous 'Volk' within Ossewabrandwag cosmology.

Given the spectacular achievement of communist China in making the transition from the Cultural Revolution to a capitalist boom economy, the staggering percentage of the world's population and economic resources directly involved in this transition, and the causal link between Maoist 'fundamentalism' and the Pol Pot regime, Mitter's chapter underlines the urgent need for comparative PR studies to include Maoism alongside Fascism, Nazism, and Bolshevism – all of which are paradigmatic examples of PR's ability to inspire both modern revitalisation movements and totalitarian regimes within the unique conditions of the twentieth century. The lack of an established Church in China, to be replaced or aped by Maoism, also makes it one of the 'purest' examples of PR unaffected or undistorted by the 'Politicisation of Religion', which is the theme of Part III.

Part III: The politicisation of religion

11 September 2001 inaugurated a climate of debate in the Western media dominated by ill-conceived talk of 'religious fundamentalism', 'clashes

of civilisation', and 'Islamo-fascism'. The present book deliberately goes against the grain of populist discourse by offering an essay on political Islam in its democratic rather than extremist guise. This is particularly fitting, given that it has been published in honour of an academic whose life has been dedicated to deepening the historical understanding of modern political extremism by looking, as William Blake puts it, 'not with but through the eye', and has never allowed the intrinsic emotiveness of his subject to overwhelm the intellectual rigour and moderation demanded by the 'Enlightenment project'.

In fact, Kemal Karpat's case study in 'political Islam' becomes an oasis of serenity and hope when set against the subject matter of the other essays. His analysis of the achievement of Turkey's *Adalet ve Kalkinma Partisi* (AKP – or Justice and Development Party) in becoming integrated within a pluralist party system demonstrates that it is possible to marry Islamic religion with the commitment to democracy, reformism, gradualism, pluralism, and social radicalism on behalf of poor and marginalised ethnic and faith communities. Its achievement is a reminder of the potential power of *un*-spectacular, *non*-charismatic permutations of radical politics whose cohesion is drawn from a *civic* religion. When the sacred in politics is kept compatible with Enlightenment values the quest for suprapersonal values does not centre on the attempted renewal of an 'organic nation' or the defence of a 'sacred' community of 'true believers', but on the no less mythic, and anti-anomic 'human rights' and respect for the 'sanctity' of individual life promoted by the secular faith of humanism, whether it assumes a liberal or religious rationale.

Karpat's essay offers a glimpse of an alternative to the utopianism, fanaticism, and 'active nihilism' bred by totalising political religions, and to the unstable and unsustainable regimes based on them that are condemned to mass-produce crimes against humanity in order to fulfil unrealisable dreams of national homogeneity, the eradication of decadence, and the creation of a new society and the 'new man'. In a utopian scenario, the quiet voice of moderation audible in this chapter would be heard by all those concerned with bringing about the transition from a world rent by conflicts between anti-democratic and pseudo-democratic forces, to a sustainable, pluralistic world community based on global, interlocking systems of representative government underpinning a humane society.

By contrast, the last two chapters of the book plunge the reader once more into the turbulent world of PR in its dehumanising, racist aspect. Their contrast with the analysis of the AKP is perhaps all the more disturbing because, in both cases, the political religion under examination operates not in an open 'terroristic' war with liberal democracy, but in a guise that corrupts and destroys it from within. Robert Frykenberg's detailed dissection of Hindutva as a PR reveals a force as social, cultural, and philosophical as it is political. At certain points in its evolution, Hindutva has exhibited remarkable parallels with the *völkisch* movement that emerged in Germany in the late nineteenth century to provide an important precondition for the rise of Nazism. In this respect, the chapter is thus another reminder of the need for PR studies to abandon Eurocentric and Christianity-centric assumptions if it is to move beyond the parochial and culture-specific in order to grapple with *global* responses to globalisation, whose original vehicle in this case was British colonialism.

Frykenberg's analysis may be all the more disconcerting for those who rarely stray from the familiar mountain pastures and deep ravines of European political history. In contrast to Hitler's National Socialist German Workers Party (NSDAP) and Mussolini's Partito Nazione Fascista (PNF), politicised Hindu parties, notably the Bharatiya Janatha Party (BJP), formed in 1980, have not attempted to establish the totalitarian regime that – in the context of interwar Europe – would have been the natural expression of their profoundly racist equation of Hinduism with 'Indianness'. Instead, an astute blend of fanaticism with pragmatism has allowed them to marry the apocalyptic politics of a totalising PR at the level of mass mobilisation and charismatic politics with the constitutional pluralism of India's axiomatically secular state.

By operating as a form of *civic* religion within the parliamentary process, rather than as a terrorist extra-parliamentary movement, the BJP has been able to become India's governing party *constitutionally*. This is a success unparalleled in Europe, where populist racist parties like Le Pen's Front National, which otherwise display some intriguing parallels with Hinduist parties, have never come close to achieving power, despite the waves of moral panic they regularly trigger among left-wing activists. Yet Frykenberg's analysis adds something new to PR studies in another way. Hinduism turns out, no less than *völkisch* nationalism or the Romanian nationalism of the Legionaries of the Archangel Michael, to be an elaborately *invented* tradition. In fact, it is a modern construction so far removed from the spirit of genuine Hindu religious traditions that it is tempting to reverse the common-sense categorisation and approach Hindutva as a *sacralised* form of secular politics *masquerading* as a religious orthodoxy. As such it is a composite substitute *for* religion rather than a 'genuine' politicised religion.

If this were accepted, then the legions of Hindu clerics, priests, and 'holy men' involved in Hindutva would be the contemporary counterparts of the many Christian clergy who became 'clerical Fascists' under Mussolini or who, like the 'German Christians', attempted to create a hybrid of Christianity with Nazism.[7] In this sense they are 'believers', but ones who at a deep level of consciousness have somewhere along the line traded in 'faith' for 'religion'. The open-ended spiritual quest to experience the numinous and metaphysical in their earthly existence has thus been bartered for the false security of a heightened sense of racial and historical belonging and *power* that represents a disturbing travesty of a sacred tradition, one which – for those it designates enemies of Hindu India – is often a lethal travesty.

Chip Berlet's final chapter on the influence of messianism, apocalypticism, and PR on US politics, with its dense mesh of theoretical taxonomic considerations and empirical data, is a suitable chapter with which to conclude this foray into the dense jungle of 'political religion'. It stresses once more the unresolved definitional issues raised by the concept, and locates it within a cluster of other, no less problematic, generic terms such as 'fascism', 'apocalypticism', and 'palingenetic myth'. It also adds further elements of methodological refinement, such as the concept of the 'metaframe', and the visual metaphor taken from one of Escher's series of psychedelic drawings to evoke the dynamic relationship between totalitarianism and the sacralisation of politics. The whistle-stop tour which follows of the key 'totalitarian groups' characterising US politics, each with its idiosyncratic relationship to Christianity (politicised religion) or secular racism (sacralised politics), again underscores the challenging taxonomic problems posed by particular phenomena in this field of study.

Berlet adds another significant dimension to this multi-layered analysis with his account of the linkage between the Christian Right, neo-conservatism, and George W. Bush's Republicanism. By this point it is clear that, no less than in contemporary India, the boundaries between civic and PR are fuzzy to say the least. This is a particularly unsettling inference, since it means that the domestic and foreign policies of the world's only superpower are being partly shaped – especially in times of national or international crisis – by a cosmology which is, however familiar, at bottom no less bizarrely 'religious' in its core axioms than is Hindutva.[8]

Work in progress

Political scientists and contemporary historians are living in what the Chinese call 'interesting times'. If the first 50 years of the twentieth century were a laboratory for new types of authoritarian *regime* unclassifiable with the political vocabulary of Greek antiquity, then the last 50 have created a habitat breeding ever new permutations of totalitarian *movement*, which are no less challenging to conventional terminology and taxonomy. 'Totalitarian movements' are ones whose ideological principles, if translated into the praxis of a political system, would create an autocratic regime with its full quota of liturgical politics, charismatic energies, propaganda, coercion, and social engineering directed to the creation of a 'new order', a 'new man', and a 'new woman'.

The renaissance in the comparative study of PR is one response to this situation. It has created an academic environment in which no one volume can hope to be truly 'groundbreaking'. However, some inference about fruitful strategies for future research in this area can be drawn from the ten essays collected here. The first is that however much an advance the taxonomic scheme elaborated in Emilio Gentile's *Religion in Politics* may be on many previous ones, it is still in need of considerable refinement, especially in terms of disentangling 'political' from 'civic' forms of PR and of delimiting the sphere of the sacred from the secular. It will soon become clear to the reader that each author is approaching the topic with a different vocabulary and level of terminological self-consciousness. Moreover, the very term 'political religion' is problematic in so far as it can be used to describe the name of the overall subject area, a 'totalising' form of PR that contrasts with civil religion (a distinction central to Gentile's schema), and the ritual, theatrical, aesthetic, spectacular, liturgical style of politics spawned by totalitarian regimes. 'Civic religion' may also be a more limiting term than 'secular religion', though defining 'secular' poses thorny issues of its own.

Second, these chapters emphasise the need to clarify the core notions of 'religion' and the 'sacred', as well as refining the demarcation between what can variously be called established/revealed/scriptural/institutionalised/traditional religion, and religion in a weaker sense that simply (and simplistically) equates it with any belief system that provides social cohesion and communal values. One way of giving focus to this 'cosmic' area of enquiry is perhaps to concentrate on resolving the ambiguities of the concept of 'transcendence'. Leaving aside the idiosyncratic connotations given the concept by Ernst Nolte in his 1965 *Three Faces of Fascism*, which makes it something fascism 'resisted' rather than aspired to provide, it is surely crucial to distinguish between suprahistorical, supratemporal (metaphysical) transcendence, and one which occurs suprapersonally but *within* secular historical time, through the medium of such mythic entities as the nation, the race, or the international proletariat.

Whatever tack is adopted, it is self-evident from the essays collected here that progress in the understanding of PR will be impeded as long as narrow Christian preconceptions about what constitutes religion, faith, immortality, and the 'end of history' persist, while the cosmological schemes found in 'pre-Christian', 'primitive', 'pre-scientific' cosmologies – and the primordial human needs they satisfy – are ignored. Certainly terms such as 'fundamentalism', 'salvation', 'prophet', 'orthodox', and 'secular' acquire new connotations as social scientists extend the focus of their enquiry to include non-Western phenomena. It is also important not to overlook the profound role religion has always played not just in legitimising the overthrow of 'traditional regimes' but also in underpinning their stability.

The chapters also suggest more work needs to be done to illuminate the seemingly obvious distinction between the 'sacralisation of politics' by those committed to the secular transformation of society, and the 'politicisation of religion' by those who derive a political agenda from their ultra-orthodox faith in a revealed or traditional faith. Such research may reveal that a complex process of hybridisation sometimes takes place that makes the two processes different aspects of the 'same' phenomenon, and that politicised and civic religion can also conjoin in ways that defy even complex pigeon-holing.

Finally, the chapters on Maoism and Hindutva in particular offer a tantalising glimpse of another perspective from which to consider the genesis and dynamics of PR – namely as the product of modernity. In turn this opens up the prospect that there may be an as yet largely unrecognised heuristic value in seeing political religions as permutations of socio-political *modernism*.[9] In other words, such movements embody attempts to counteract the nomic crisis resulting from modernity by erecting a canopy of total meaning to replace the one being gradually worn away by increasingly global processes of modernisation. Much has been understood, but much remains to be done.

The *Festschrift*

Last but not least it is important to stress that the academic analyses contained in this book are not its sole *raison d'être*. As the appendix containing an interview with Stanley Payne as well as his curriculum vitae (CV) to August 2006 make clear, it also serves a celebratory purpose. Given the nature of its subject matter, there is a particular, if benign, irony in the fact that this volume has a subtext of a ritualistic nature, one that points to a transcendent rather than a chronological concept of time. Of course, any academic publication is an act of defiance in the face of *chronos*, to the extent that its authors and publishers hope it will leave its 'mark' on a specialism or even on an entire discipline. But the conference that served as the genesis of this book was held as a tribute to the 'life-time achievement' of Professor Stanley Payne. The publication of the chapters deriving from the papers given on that occasion (supplemented with two others commissioned to make coverage of the topic more comprehensive) thus constitutes his *Festschrift*. They not only take their place within the growing literature on 'political religion', but partake in what is sometimes known as 'festive time'. As anthropologists will confirm, celebration is itself an act of commemoration, one with echoes of the primordial, *nomos*-generating, 'world-creating' rituals of premodern societies.

At first sight, a book on PR may seem a curious choice for such a purpose. After all, as Stanley Payne's CV eloquently shows, the outstanding achievements of his extraordinarily prolific and influential career have been made firstly as one of the world's most eminent Hispanicists outside Spain, and secondly as a scholar who has, for a quarter of a century, maintained his position as the foremost theorist and historian of generic fascism. Yet in some respects it is singularly appropriate that this volume serves as the testimony, though not the testament, to such an egregious career. This becomes clear if we dwell for a moment on his article exploring the heuristic value of the term 'political religion' opening this volume. It may seem far removed from the first book he published in 1961 on the Spanish Falange, yet its kinship with his established areas of expertise becomes apparent when we consider its historiographical qualities.

Unlike some other well-known historians, Payne has always recognised the need to supplement expert empirical knowledge of a topic with three components. The first is the understanding of the broader historical context of recurrent patterns and kindred phenomena within which every unique set of events can be located. He has instinctively written the history of twentieth-century Spain from the perspective that drove Tim Mason at a 1988 conference to attack the tendency of seeing the history of the Third Reich in isolation from the wider context of interwar history, thus obscuring the fact that Nazism was part of 'something much larger'. There is therefore an organic connection between Payne's study of the Falange in the late 1950s and the work that culminated in his *The Spanish Civil War, the Soviet Union, and Communism 1931–1939*, published four decades later, that earned him the 2005 Marshall Shulman Prize. It should be noted that this was awarded not by Hispanicists, but by the American Association for the Advancement of Slavic Studies.

The second point is a sustained concern with key generic terms and political science debates pertinent to a given historiographical topic. An interest in the Falange and Franco's regime thus inevitably led Payne to engage proactively in refining the concepts of 'fascism' and 'authoritarianism'. Not only did this lead him to highly productive friendships with major historians in related fields of research who shared this approach – notably Juan Linz, George Mosse, and Emilio Gentile – but to formulate his own taxonomy of fascism, published in 1980 as *Fascism: Comparison and Definition*, which eclipsed all other currently available theories of fascism conceptual sophistication and the range of examples covered.

The third is the instinctive grasp of the way not just history but historiography itself is a phenomenon in constant evolution, with new topics and issues coming into view, new theoretical debates forming on the horizon – sometimes evaporating like storm systems as quickly as they appeared – and a steady flow of publications in many languages that incrementally increase the secondary literature on any topic – and hence total wealth of empirical knowledge, only a fraction of which is available to any one researcher. To 'keep up with' a specialism embedded in such a dynamically evolving world of knowledge requires not just an extraordinary industry, but a profound openness and adaptability to an ever-changing academic environment. It was these qualities that have enabled Payne not only to stay in the forefront of the specialist history of Franquism and its many subtopics, but to successfully undertake the history of Spain and Portugal and to update his first book on generic fascism with *A History of Fascism: 1914–1945* (1995). This he did with such consummate skill that it re-established his position at the cutting edge of comparative fascist studies and remains unrivalled as an overview of the subject to this day. It was also these qualities that enabled him to have such a formative influence on shaping the understanding of modern history through his energetic editorial work on numerous journals, notably *The Luso-Brazilian Review* and *The Journal of Contemporary History*.

I would also like to mention a fourth quality which cannot be inferred from the printed page, but which Stanley Payne, again in marked contrast to several eminent contemporary historians, has in abundance. It may even provide the secret mainspring of his glittering career. I am referring to an instinctively passionate, collaborative, and collegial approach to his profession, one that eschews Lorenzian territorial imperatives, seeking instead fruitful points of convergence and synergy rather than conflict and litigation. His blend of modesty with the drive to know more, learn from others, and share his insights has made him not just an outstanding research academic, but a teacher and colleague of rare distinction. My own laconic testimony must stand for many pages of tributes that could be written by those whose academic careers have been all the richer for his presence in their field.

It is within this context that the opening chapter on the heuristic value of 'political religion' should be read: not just as a contribution to the topic, but also as a sample of Payne's qualities. It displays a concern with comparative frameworks of analysis, an openness to theory, and an urge to find a balance between the idiographic and nomothetic – all hallmarks of his life's work. It subsumes wide-ranging reading in secondary literature, but also concludes with a characteristically original thesis by evoking not the clash between liberalism and Islam, but between religious and cultural exclusiveness and the fanatically 'multi-cultural political correctness', which he construes as a form of civil religion in its own right. His text has been written in a spirit of Enlightenment humanism that will have no truck with wishy-washy sentiments or intellectual laziness. It embraces the concept PR, but only on condition that it is used as an ideal type whose heuristic value is constantly tested by application to properly researched empirical examples.

This book has been published in a spirit of Stanley Payne, and its chapters will hopefully be read in that spirit too. Cumulatively, it encourages historians to turn away from the more extreme contortions of the 'cultural turn', away from 'reading' the past in a way that reduces facts to texts, and the curiously dematerialising effects of 'deconstructing' historical phenomena without the countervailing drive towards interpretive reconstruction. (In political religious studies as elsewhere, explanatory narratives, even grand ones, are not just in order but essential as long as they are reflexive, heutristic and not 'totalising' ones). At the same time it simultaneously appeals to historians to abandon narrow and ultimately sterile conceptions of 'empiricism' that disdains a serious concern with generic concepts, conceptual frameworks, and substrata of irrational motivation. By the same token, it encourages a movement *towards* intelligent engagement with general patterns intrinsic to unique political and historical products of modernity as it continues to globalise itself, spawning events that originate in cosmologies and myths but are all too tragically physical in their real impact on individual human lives.

The conference in Madison upon which this volume is based was, by all accounts, held in a sustained spirit of conviviality. It was a fitting tribute to the life-asserting mode of liberal humanism that for four decades has informed Payne's engagement with some of the most momentous historical events and processes of the twentieth century, many of which contained a dark core of repression, hatred, and violence. The temperamental reaction to fanaticism implicit in his vast *oeuvre* has been a living expression of a type of humanism that in a utopian scenario would become hegemonic in the new century. Without undermining religious faith, its dissemination would enable prejudice to be replaced by knowledge and fear of the Other would give way to curiosity and respect, dissolving the hatreds and fears that feed the terrorism of secular states as much as that of religious *guerrillas*. However, in the mid-noughties when this book was conceived history was still being decisively shaped by those who bear out the dictum of a poet writing at the height of the Cold War which dominated the second half of the last century: 'And you never ask questions with God on your side.'[10]

Notes

1. The exceptions are Stanley Payne's chapter which first appeared as the article 'On the Heuristic Value of the Concept of Political Religion and its Application', *Totalitarian Movements and Political Religions* 6/2 (September 2005), pp. 163–74, and those of Chip Berlet and Kemel Karpat, which were specially commissioned for this volume.
2. For a bibliographical and historical review of the concept of political religion, see Emilio Gentile, *Politics as Religion* (Princeton, NJ: Princeton University Press, 2006). It was first published in Italian in 2001 as *Le religioni della politica* (Bari: Laterza).
3. *Totalitarian Movements and Political Religions* was founded by Robert Mallet and Michael Burleigh in 2000.
4. Ian Kershaw, 'Hitler and the Uniqueness of Nazism', *Journal of Contemporary History* 39/2 (2004), p. 247.
5. Klaus Vondung, *Magie und Manipulation: Ideologischer Kult und politische Religion des Nationalsozialismus* (Göttingen: Vandenhoeck & Ruprecht, 1971), pp. 159–71. The thrust of Vondung's argument is summarised in 'Spiritual revolution and magic: speculation and political action in National Socialism', *Modern Age* 23/4 (1979).
6. Richard Steigmann-Gall, *Holy Reich: Nazi Conceptions of Christianity, 1919–1945* (Cambridge: Cambridge University Press, 2003).
7. See Matt Feldman and Marius Turda (eds), *Clerical Fascism in Interwar Europe* (London: Routledge, 2008).
8. A powerful exposure of the crucial role played by Christian faith in shaping the policies of Bush's administration since 9/11 is Emilio Gentile, *La democrazia di Dio: La religione americana nell'era dell'impero e del terrore* (Bari: Laterza, 2006), which appeared in English as *God's Democracy. American religion after September 11* (New York: Praeger, 2008).
9. For a full exposition of this thesis concerning modernism see Roger Griffin, *Modernism and Fascism. The Sense of a Beginning under Mussolini and Hitler* (London: Routledge, 2007).
10. Bob Dylan, 'With God on Our Side', *The Times They Are A-Changing* (1964).

Part I

Conceptualizing Political Religion

2
On the Heuristic Value of the Concept of Political Religion and Its Application

Stanley G. Payne

The usefulness of the concept of Political Religions (PR) in the modern world depends first of all on the definition of the term 'religion'. Over a century ago Emile Durkheim established among sociologists and anthropologists the concept that religion consists essentially of the organisation of rites and rituals formed around a belief system aimed at buttressing social solidarity and morality. Thus, any strong ideology that was fully articulated and expressed socially might be considered a religion. This is the definition most commonly employed by those who use the concept of PR.

A more traditional definition is used by the sociologist Rodney Stark, who concludes that 'religion consists of explanations based on supernatural assumptions and including statements about the nature of the supernatural and about ultimate meaning'. More simply, religions are based on belief in a God or Gods who have revealed themselves in revelations believed to come from God or the Gods themselves.[1] This is the traditional definition of transcendental, supernatural or theistic religion (or what Eric Voegelin called *überweltliche Religion*), obviating any valid concept of purely world-immanent or secular religion.

Proponents of the Durkheimian approach point to 'Godless' Asian religions, such as élite forms of Buddhism, Taoism or Confucianism, which do not embrace the concept of a God or Gods but instead posit a kind of general mystical essence which underlies reality and gives it meaning. Stark's response is that the Godless forms of Asian religions are merely the exception which proves the rule, being elitist doctrines based on rarified meditation and mysticism, whereas the ordinary forms of these religions as practiced by the vast majority of their adherents are elaborately polytheistic – religions based on Gods.[2]

Yet it cannot be denied that, as Emilio Gentile has pointed out so clearly,[3] the revolutionary ideologies and regimes of the twentieth century sacralised politics in a special and elaborate manner, albeit with varying degrees of exclusiveness that made different kinds of accommodation with 'real' religion. Can quite different forms of sacralised politics and theistic religions all be termed religions? None of the putative PRs have ever claimed officially to be religions (as Gentile notes), but is it analytically, conceptually and heuristically useful or advantageous to think of them as such? Eric Voegelin was one of the first analysts to use this approach with precision, but later changed his mind, concluding that religion and PR were distinct and should not be conflated. The concept of political religion, like generic fascism, does not refer to an absolutely existing empirical entity but is simply an analytical concept and heuristic device, whose validity and utility depends on the care and precision with which it is employed.

The divine monarchies of the ancient Middle East derived their authority from transcendent Gods, in most cases more than one. Such state systems should, however, be more properly called caesaropapist than theocratic. Ancient Jews lived under a variety of systems; the early form tended towards theocracy, the monarchies either towards caesaropapism or the politicisation of established religion. Rome subsequently exhibited broad religious tolerance, but the notion advanced by some that it developed the more limited form of civil religion is exaggerated, though Rome did anticipate certain aspects of the latter.

The growth of Christianity and Islam brought further differentiation. Late in the fourth century Christianity became the official religion of the Roman state, a relationship that would continue in predominantly Christian societies until the American Republic disestablished church and state 14 centuries later. Christianity has been perhaps the most 'transpolitical' of religions, having more or less flourished amid the widest variety of political forms (sometimes even including Islamic and other oriental despotisms). The Catholic West tended generally towards constantly mutating forms of caesaropapism (with an occasional effort at theocracy), but soon introduced the doctrine of the two spheres, with dual – though by no means fully separate – sovereignties of church and state. This division, though at no time intended to be absolute, provided one key to the subsequent development of Western pluralism and, eventually, of more limited and representative government.[4] The Orthodox East tended towards caesaropapism. A peculiar kind of caesaropapism was introduced in Protestant kingdoms by the sixteenth-century Reformation, but by then Western institutions of pluralism, the rule of law and partially representative government mediated or limited the power of the ruler.

Islam, conversely, recognised no difference between church and state, having no distinct institutionally organised church. There was no concept of *ecclesia*, while the Western notion of a purely spiritual, non-secular and distinct *religio* was apparently developed by medieval Christian monks. All of life in Islam came theoretically to be governed by Sharia, which might have provided the potential for theocracy, but the authority that imposed religious observance de facto was the state and/or society, which only in exceptional circumstances was led by a religious official as distinct from the state ruler. Eventually the chief of state in some of the major Muslim polities became caliph, the representative of God and head of Islam. Yet in a religion without an ecclesiastical establishment equivalent to that of Christianity, Judaism or some other religions, the caliph was not a pope nor even a caesaropope like some Byzantine emperors or Russian tsars. Islamic teachers, in turn, have frequently dissociated themselves from those whom they regard as evil or erroneous Islamic rulers and state.

Religion played an important role in all traditional regimes in terms of legitimisation of the state and ruler, and frequently in affirming the special identity of the society. Very many different kingdoms or ethnic groups held some variant of the concept of 'chosen people', sometimes with a special mission for territorial expansion or conversion. In somewhat different ways nearly all the major world religions (and many minor ones) became politicised after this manner. They helped to produce a wide variety of imperial, royal or ethnic cults of politicised religion, but this involved the politicisation of the traditional or established religion, not a new secular cult of sacralised politics.[5]

All agree that modern sacralised politics emerged with the Jacobin phase of the French Revolution and its accompanying 'Cult of Reason', which went beyond the notion of 'civil religion' that Rousseau had defined earlier. The Jacobin cult was, in fact, the only putative form of PR that tried directly to take the form of an overtly organised religion, perhaps because it antedated the broader secularisation of society. As the nineteenth century advanced, however, successors of the Jacobins would abandon any ambition to create a direct substitute religion.

What is generally understood as modern secularism introduced varying alternatives, substitutes and supplements for theistic religion. These would eventually take a bewildering variety of forms whose taxonomy is entirely beyond our scope and space. Their ubiquity is due to the fact that, as Mircea Eliade put it, 'the great majority of the irreligious are not liberated from religious behaviour, from theologies and mythologies'.[6] The numerous objects of fetishism and personal adoration, which are particularly common in the twenty-first century, should be distinguished from the structured ideologies which Voegelin regularly terms modern 'gnosticisms'. These things serve as substitutes for religion, but most cannot be termed substitute religions, and our concern is only those involved in politics.

Since Jacobinism was at least to some degree inspired by the earlier American Revolution, the character and relationship of the concurrently emerging American Civil Religion (ACR) quickly arises. Gentile's taxonomy clearly and convincingly distinguishes between the arbitrary and totalising nature of PR, contrasted with the limitations and tolerance of CR, which renounces any claim to control theistic religion. The main putative PRs have all greatly expanded the state's power and sought to atomise society, while CRs have often encouraged voluntary associations. In the United States the disestablishment of church and state was designed at least in part to preserve the freedom of the religious.

In fact, CRs are quite diverse and some have been quite intolerant. During the late nineteenth and early twentieth centuries aggressively anti-Catholic CR, or incipient CR, in countries such as France, Spain, Portugal and Mexico engaged in overt persecution. In Spain and Mexico this involved widespread violence; the former case featured the most extensive persecution of Catholicism in a Western country since the Reformation. CRs may be informed by various kinds of broader ideological values, even if they do not specifically sacralise politics. They are not at all immune to such concepts as chosen people, messianism or a transcendent mission, but may thrive on them. In modern times, these latter concepts simply take more secular form in CR.

Hence the tendency for many of the millions of communicants of the ACR to employ such concepts, which in their earliest forms commenced with the very founding of the republic,[7] even though sometimes fuelled by the spirit of toleration. This stemmed especially from the great moral, cultural and spiritual influence of the New England Puritans, but milder versions of it have been found in southern states, as well. Belief in a special American mission is not a complete constant, and has not been shared by all Americans; rather, it waxes and wanes, particularly in time of crisis. Its four major expressions took place in the Civil War, the First World War,[8] the Second World War and the Cold War, and it has to some extent re-emerged in the war on terrorism, its two last major avatars being Ronald Reagan and George W. Bush.[9]

Potent as the ACR has sometimes been, it did not sacralise political functions per se. Neither did it originally establish the shibboleth 'separation of church and state', which only began to enter the American lexicon in the mid-nineteenth century. The Constitution and Bill of Rights only prohibited the establishment of a federal American church, and this alone was enough to make the fledgling republic a total anomaly. Established churches in the individual states were not prohibited, and in some cases continued for several decades. The principle of separation of church and state only developed gradually over an entire century, fuelled by anti-Catholicism first and by growing secularism and liberalism second, until it began to be entered into judicial rulings by fiat starting in the mid-twentieth century. It has never become an article of constitutional legislation.[10]

Secular cults, which emerged in the eighteenth century, multiplied and flourished much more in the century that followed, taking such forms as St Simonianism and Comptism, and very many others. The most important form of political cult at first was nationalism, more than social revolutionism, the two between themselves laying the seeds for the future sacralisation of politics.[11] In differing ways, both nationalism and left revolutionary movements generated their own 'religion of the people', but the relationship of these two types of movement to traditional religion tended to differ. Whereas the left revolutionary movements were hostile, sometimes to the point of violence, even extremist nationalist movements took a different approach, either seeking to embrace or otherwise gain the support of the nation's churches, at worst avoiding conflict with them. This foretold the different approach towards religion of the only major new early twentieth-century revolutionary movement – fascism – when contrasted with the left revolutionary movements. The politicisation of religion was absolutely fundamental to nationalism, constituting a fundamental step in a kind of prelude to the sacralisation of politics, as in the case of German *Kulturprotestantismus*. Such developments would lead some German Christian commentators to refer to the formation of what they called political religion in Germany, and some other Western countries even before the emergence of National Socialism, seeing this as a unique feature of modern Western secular, or semi-secular, culture.

The ways in which all revolutionary movements, left or right, as well as some of the extremist nationalisms, adopted the characteristics of religion, are clear. These include development of a salvation myth, expressed in holistic socio-political and cultural terms; creation of elaborate ceremonies and liturgies; canonisation of saints and martyrs; the development of a cultural and spiritual revolution to resocialise human beings and create a new man, accompanied by public modes of contrition, repentance and expiation; and the projection of messianic and universalist goals. The revolutionary movements projected new cosmologies, demonologies and versions of the apocalypse.

Anarchism is the one major form of left revolutionism which never developed its own state or society, and is sometimes said to have been so opposed to all religion – which it sought to destroy completely – that it could never be more than a substitute for religion, rather than a substitute religion. Nonetheless, anarchism possessed most of the same prerequisites in this regard. It developed its own cultic anti-religious (normally anti-Catholic) forms, such as a salvation myth, ceremonies and liturgies (even if never organised by a centralised state), saints and martyrs, a cultural and spiritual revolution designed to create the new man, and messianic and expansionist goals, which sought to win the world for anarchism. In the anarchist utopia, the central state would wither away, and some have held that this would have made it impossible for a hypothetically successful anarchism to have established any fully articulated PR. This, however, simply overlooks the fact that anarchism projected itself as a kind of secular 'congregationalism', without pope or bishops. There are many religious groups without a dominant central organisation. For that matter, the anarchist utopia posited a kind of confederal council in lieu of a central state. If successful, the former would presumably have officially propagated the anarchist cult.

The dominant version of twentieth-century revolutionism, Marxism–Leninism, was, like anarchism, aggressively atheist and utterly opposed to all traditional religion, though in the Soviet Union's first decade Protestantism was favoured in order to weaken the formerly established religion. Though Soviet practice did not develop as many cultic forms specifically mimetic of theistic religion as would National Socialism, it developed forms of replacement for virtually every single feature of Orthodox Christianity, while, at least from 1929 on, repressing and persecuting all forms of theistic religion more or less equally. The Soviet regime would have always rejected indignantly any claim that it was developing a new 'religion'. Like anarchism, communism was supposed to be the ultimate in anti-religion, though leaders of both ideologies argued that each was offering the perfect substitute for religion. Later, during the Second World War, Stalin entered into a temporary and partial truce with the Orthodox Church. All this raises the question of whether the proper conceptualisation of the problem would be that of *religionsersatz* (religion substitute), rather than an *ersatzreligion* (substitute religion), as Hans Buchheim has suggested.[12]

The relationship of the two major fascist regimes to traditional religion was different. Though Italian Fascism began as a left nationalist, strongly anticlerical movement, Mussolini eventually grasped that it would be desirable and possible to come to terms with the Catholic Church. By comparison, German National Socialism, even in its origins more virulent than Italian Fascism, avoided attacking the churches from the start. Two factors were at work here. One was the nature of the fascist rise to power, which could not be through the Communist tactic of insurrection or conquest, as Hitler found to his discomfort in 1923. It was not possible to overthrow the governments of institutionally stable European countries in peacetime; legalist tactics and the acquisition of allies were essential, requiring the avoidance of conflict with religion.

The second factor was the character of nationalism, and of fascist ideology itself. This required a certain inclusiveness with regard to historic national institutions that still enjoyed support but might be manipulated, while the fascist emphases on idealism, vitalism and antimaterialism made fascism appear to be compatible with religion in a way that Marxism–Leninism could never be. In Germany, the earlier liberal Protestant development of *Kulturprotestantismus* had already paved the way for Christian compromise with radical nationalism. Certainly there were millions of Christians – some of them merely nominal, others at least partially devout – in Italy and Germany who also considered themselves full and convinced members of the state parties.[13] All the major revolutionary movements 'immanentised the eschaton', in Voegelin's phrase, but the fascist regimes – during their brief history – only demanded the loyalties of Christians in this world, and largely left them free to practice and believe whatever they wished about the next one. That this was an acceptable compromise from a Christian point of view is most debatable, but for the time being it was adequate for Hitler[14] and Mussolini.

No other putative PR went so far to develop its public forms in imitation of religious symbols and ceremony than did the Third Reich.[15] As Klaus Vondung points out, however, that was not the principal reason that Voegelin applied to it in 1938 the label of PR. Voegelin was referring especially to its existential core of faith and totally reordered perception of reality, which identified it as one of what he called the modern *innerweltliche Religionen* as distinct from the traditional *überweltliche Religionen*. Hitler, and other Nazi leaders, constantly referred to the need for *Glaube* in a creed based on blood. Hitler often spoke publicly of 'God', 'the Almighty', 'the creator of the universe' or 'Divine Providence', though there is no indication that he ever used these terms in a Christian sense. National Socialists presented numerous personal 'testimonies' and had an explicit *Heilsgeschichte*. In internal discussions, Catholic Church leaders seriously speculated that all this amounted to a new political religion, or religion of politics.

In a different way, Italian Fascist leaders seemed to provide a place for Catholicism itself within their synthesis of the *nuova civiltà*. The cult of *Romanità* grounded this synthesis, which remained incomplete, within which Roman Catholicism might in some respects be celebrated because it was Roman, not because it was Catholic or Christian. Fascist leaders sometimes advanced the idea that the Catholic sense of order had helped to form the new Italian state, and there was willingness to foster Catholic missionary work in the new Fascist empire. It is not clear how much was known about the unpublished papal encyclical of 1938 that denounced racism and totalitarianism.

The ultimate intentions of the two regimes must remain speculative. Both parties harboured aggressively atheist, anti-Christian minorities, though these were to some extent kept under wraps by the leadership. Certainly religion would have been subjugated much more under both regimes had the Axis won the war. In 1942 Mussolini talked privately about getting rid of the monarchy and the papacy, but no firm conclusions can be drawn from the private wartime expostulations of the two dictators.

The fascisms, or quasi-fascisms, that maintained specific religious identities of their own constitute quite different cases, and the three principal examples – Spain, Romania and Croatia – differed considerably among themselves. The Spanish movement insisted on its Catholic orthodoxy, though it was occasionally anti-clerical in practice. The Franco regime, which it helped to inform, became a strongly Catholic state, eventually more thoroughly identified with religion than any other in Europe. It did not create a PR, but thoroughly politicised the existing religion, and was later satirised by its enemies as practising 'national Catholicism'. The Romanian Iron Guard made a peculiar form of Romanian Orthodox mysticism the core of its doctrine, though a few of its assassins and theorists occasionally recognised the heterodoxy of its violent practices, as apparently was also the case among a few of the Croatian *Ustashi*. Ferenc Szalasi's Hungarist or Arrow Cross movement had no specific religious identity in a country, like Germany, divided between Catholicism and Protestantism. It recognised a subordinated Christianity as essential to national life, more specifically and overtly than did National Socialism. It encouraged church membership, the denomination of which was deemed irrelevant. Thus the Romanian movement politicised religion in a bizarre and extreme way but did not create a distinct PR (in a manner somewhat parallel with Islamism), while Szalasi seemed nearer Hitler and Mussolini, even though more insistent on the positive role of religion than either of them.

Imperial Japan presents yet a different case. The Shintoism that was expanded in the late nineteenth century, and practiced as a special state cult until 1945, represented the nationalisation and politicisation of an existing religion, something hardly unprecedented, even though its state-cult form was in itself unique. It sacralised certain aspects of politics, yet it did not exactly create a new PR. Unlike Communist states and certain other regimes, it was not exclusive, but in its general functioning rather similar to the Roman empire, permitting its communicants to practice other transcendant religions, mainly different forms of Buddhism and Christianity.

The totalitarian regime that has created something of a new synthesis for an ideology and practice, that, in its sacralisation of politics deserves the label of PR more than any other, is North Korea and its *Juche* cult. Like Communist China, the North Korean regime strongly emphasises nationalism. Korean culture was traditionally very Confucianist, and prior to Communism Korean society was also more responsive to Christianity than any other in Asia. In a manner different from Imperial Japan, North Korea has developed its own form of post-Confucianist 'family state', with the leader the divine (or in the Korean case superhuman) head of a tightly identified 'family nation', for whom he is the centre of a cult that offers collective transcendance.

Juche means 'self-reliance' or 'independence', and in its earliest form was announced by Kim Il Sung in December 1955. It was originally used to buttress the political and ideological independence of North Korea from the Soviet Union, but gradually developed to replace Marxism–Leninism itself. 'The North Korean Constitution of 1998 under Kim Jong Il does not mention anything about Marxism and Leninism', but simply states that the Democratic People's Republic of Korea (DPRK) is officially guided by the *Juche* idea.[16]

Juche doctrine underwent its final development during the 1980s, when it was expanded beyond being the special version of Marxism–Leninism appropriate for North Korea, to a new proclamation as a universal truth for all mankind. *Juche* ideology stresses the importance of consciousness, creativity and self-determination. Consciousness relies on 'brain', 'spirit', will-power and learning the right knowledge, which inevitably leads to collectivism. Creativity, moreover, leads inevitably to change and higher goals, which are transcendental. Truth is eternal, and thus leads to 'eternal life', though not in the Christian sense. 'God' simply represents the higher goal of collective life, which will achieve the ultimate being, the perfection of man. *Juche* doctrine represents the ultimate deification of human beings, and, technically, may be said to be a form of 'transcendental atheism'.[17] It also provides theoretical justification for maintaining the most militarised state system in the world through its priority doctrine of 'military-first politics', the only guarantee of the 'independence' which is the very meaning of *Juche* itself. The *Juche* idea also provides theoretical justification for political and ideological survival after the demise of the Soviet Union, for *Juche* doctrine purports to uphold the only true socialism, in which the people are already the collective masters and have nothing to learn from Western democracy.

Kim Il Sung was the perfect leader who revealed the sacred scripture of the *Juche* and its mission. Through his word and his example, the DPRK offers salvation to the entire human race. For North Koreans this represents a superior nationality with a special messianic and apocalyptic mission. The Workers Party of Korea numbers 15 per cent of the total population, and administers the most thorough system of mass indoctrination to be found anywhere in the world. *Juche* is expressed in music, art, architecture, medicine and virtually every walk of life. Individual identity is much more thoroughly repressed than in any other Communist system, but there are constant group competitions in all areas of life.

In some ways, Kim Il Sungism represents a return to the ancient divine monarchies of the Middle East, having developed the most extreme and elaborate leader-cult in modern history. The North Korean state is the only one in the world with a dead man as official president, and the only Communist regime to establish a genuine familial dynastic succession.[18] Some South Korean and Japanese commentators have labelled the DPRK a 'religious state', the site of an extremist PR.

A new phase in the development of PR began in the 1960s, with the emergence of newly independent Middle Eastern and African states, which began to form their own national cults. The largest new democracy, India, created a more limited CR, as had the protodemocratic Kemalist Turkey before it. Some of the African states, by contrast, attempted to develop their own new PRs, seeking more elaborate ritual and ceremonial forms, syncretistically incorporating aspects of traditional religions, as well.[19] Perhaps the only ones to achieve full-scale incipient new PRs, however, were the new Afro-Communist regimes of the 1970s, which followed variations on the Marxist–Leninist forms, to the complete subordination of traditional religion.

Anthony D. Smith has pointed out that in the Introduction to his *Nationalism in Asia and Africa* (1971), Elie Kedourie seemed to suggest that the new nationalisms might be divided into three categories: (1) Secular modernist (which presumably might form CRs); (2) Neo-traditionalist, involving the extreme politicisation of existing religions; and (3) Those tending to form new PRs.[20] This is one possible approach to the taxonomy of the new states of the latter part of the twentieth century.

The extreme new politicisation of religion in the Muslim world only came to the fore after the decline of the secular revolutionary Arab regimes. This was not accidental, for the failure of 'Arab socialism' and of the Soviet invasion of Afghanistan combined to provide both space and momentum for the expansion of Islamism. In this regard, frequent references to 'Islamofascism' merely reflects the standard careless use of pejoratives. Saddamist Baathism had genuinely fascist characteristics, but Islamism differs considerably, except in the banal sense that all violent, authoritarian movements resemble each other in certain ways at an appropriate level of abstraction. Gentile is undoubtedly correct when he says that Islamism represents an extreme politicisation of traditional religion rather than a new PR.

Islamism is often confusingly labelled 'Islamic fundamentalism', but this is only slightly less confused than 'Islamofascism'. Islam has always been the most basically fundamentalist of the monotheist religions, given its intense formalism and simple theology. Nearly all living Muslims are more fundamentalist than the great majority of Christians and Jews, extremely few of them belonging to any liberal or modernised version of their religion. To confuse Islamists with Islamic fundamentalists would theoretically make most Muslims Islamists, and this is simply not the case.

Islamism has developed as a uniquely radical and, paradoxically, modern version of Islam due to its revolutionary and totalitarian policies, which go far beyond any mere religious fundamentalism. It should also be remembered that there are various different schools of Islamism, some of which are more moderate and amount to little more than a politicising and modernising mobilisation of fundamentalists. The ones who have captured world attention are the revolutionary totalitarians who should not be confused with pious fundamentalists. Their calls for maximally violent Jihad obviously have roots in Islamic history. Sugarcoating the nature of Jihad in history falsifies the latter and, morally, is not far removed from Holocaust Denial. But the historic Jihad was not synonymous with the current call for Islamic world revolution, which in key characteristics also represents a call to revolution within Islam. The extreme forms of Islamism have developed a revolutionary totalitarian creed that shows little interest in traditional Islamic fundamentalist spirituality or even in theology per se, ignoring most of the higher achievements of Islamic culture. It represents a politicisation of religion in some respects for non-religious purposes.

Hindutva in India also represents a new modern extreme politicisation of religion. It is nationalist and national-imperialist (and in this regard differs from Islamist universalism), but thus far the proportion of its followers who call for terrorist, revolutionary imperialist policies have not become dominant.

Hindutva, however, may be more typical of new extremist ideologies in the early twenty-first century, which are generally parochial and nationalist rather than universalist. The thrust towards globalisation has had the effect of partially fragmenting or deconstructing some of the older centers of power, while paradoxically encouraging new parochial identities and collectivities. The Western country in which this process is most acute is Spain, which is currently full of frenzied and multiple efforts to develop new micronations and parochial identities.

The most extreme Spanish case, that of Basque nationalism, has involved both intense politicisation of religion on the one hand, as well as, according to some students, the parallel development of a new PR cult among its most extreme organisations. In the first instance, various observers have pointed to what they sometimes call the 'apostasy' of part of the Basque clergy, who abandon their spiritual priorities and values to provide systematic support for extremist nationalism.[21] In the second, a recently published dissertation insists that the secular extremist sectors of Basque nationalism have simply constituted a 'substitute religion'.[22]

In the early twenty-first century, there are two new universalist ideologies. Islamism is confronted by the Western ideology of multiculturally diverse political correctness (MDPC), which, as the direct opposite of the former, proclaims pacifism. MDPC is married to a doctrine of globalisation which pretends to transcend all cultures, while theoretically showing the utmost respect for all non-Western cultures. It is the principal creed of Western Europe and dominates the educational institutions, the media and much of politics in the United States.[23] Yet it remains no more than a 'candidate PR', for several reasons. One is that it lacks any universally agreed canonic definition, and is accepted by different individuals and groups in varying degrees. There are extremists and moderates, the fully converted true believers and the mere conformists who only pay lip service. It may be observed, of course, that this is characteristic of the expansionist and mobilisational phase of all religions and PR.

Another problem is that, unlike nearly all preceding candidate PRs, MDPC is based not merely on equality but also on political democracy, which somewhat limits the potential for establishing and enforcing a central cult. Moreover, MDPC is a sort of stealth ideology, normally not expressed in its full and extreme form for fear of alienating the unconverted. This leaves most people in confusion or partial ignorance regarding its creed, which operates more as a general orientation than as an explicit ideology. Its forms of coercion are soft rather than hard. Its tactics are Gramscian, not directly revolutionary, seeking to establish first a cultural hegemony that can then be translated into full political power. It is an ideological movement adjusted to the institutions and political practices of Western democracy, but is inevitably somewhat diluted thereby. Moreover, it affects to be deconstructive and postmodernist, which creates great formal cognitive dissonance that may be impossible to overcome. Thus the capacity of MDPC to establish itself eventually as a full PR remains problematic.

The concept of PR has proven useful not as an absolute definition of a *ding an sich* but simply as a heuristic device for the analysis of strong ideology and its cultic practices. It helps to explain the character and function of the major new ideologies in a largely secular era. Gentile's conclusion that PR has little future in the twenty-first century is, however, probably mistaken. Organised creeds show little sign of disappearing, but assume new forms and undergo new mutations. Even the secular west has generated a new kind of secular religion, though one not fully formed, while the nationalisms we have ever with us.

Notes

1. R. Stark, *For the Glory of God: How Monotheism Led to Reformations, Witch-Hunts and the End of Slavery* (Princeton: Princeton University Press, 2003), pp. 4–5.
2. Ibid., pp. 4–6, pp. 367–76.
3. E. Gentile, *Le religioni della politica. Fra democrazie e totalitarismi* (Rome-Bari: Laterza, 2001), 'The Sacralization of Politics: Definitions, Interpretations and Reflections on the Question of Secular Religion and Totalitarianism', TMPR, 1 (2000), 18–55; and 'Fascism, Totalitarianism and Political Religion: Definitions and Critical Reflections on Criticism of an Interpretation', TMPR, 5:3 (Winter, 2005), 326–75.
4. For one of the most recent discussions, see R. P. Kraynak, *Christian Faith* and *Modern Democracy: God and Politics in the Fallen World* (South Bend: Notre Dame, 2001).

5. The best approach to the broad phenomenon of 'chosen peoples' and sacred mission is A. D. Smith, *Chosen Peoples: Sacred Sources of National Identity* (Oxford: Oxford University Press, 2003).

6. M. Eliade, *The Sacred and the Profane: The Nature of Religion* (New York: Harper & Row, 1961), pp. 205–06.

7. J. H. Hutson, ed., *Religion and the New Republic: Faith in the Founding of America* (Lanham, MD and Oxford: University Press of America, 2000).

8. R. Gamble, *The War for Righteousness* (Wilmington: ISI Books, 2003).

9. There is a long literature on this. Among recent publications, see R. T. Hughes, *Myths America Lives By* (Champaign-Urbana: Illinois, 2004); S. Webb, *American Providence: A Nation with a Mission* (New York: Continuum, Illinois, 2004); and D. Gelernter, 'Americanism–and its Enemies', *Commentary* (January, 2005), 41–48.

10. The basic study is P. Hamburger, *Separation of Church and State* (Cambridge, MA-London: Harvard, 2002).

11. J. H. Billington, *Fire in the Minds of Men: Origins of the Revolutionary Faith* (New York: Basic Books, 1980), reminds us that for most of the nineteenth-century nationalism, not social revolutionism, was the more dominant revolutionary creed.

12. H. Buchheim, 'Despotie, Ersatzreligion, Religionsersatz' in H. Maier, ed., *'Totalitarismus' und 'Politische Religionen': Konzepte des Diktaturvergleichs* (Paderborn-Munich: Ferdinand Schöningh, 1996), pp. 260–63.

13. This is only part of the argument of R. Steigmann-Gall, *The Holy Reich: Nazi Conceptions of Christianity, 1919–1945* (Cambridge: Cambridge University Press, 2003), which argues overly broadly the existence of a 'Christian Nazism'.

14. Hitler had earlier shown considerable interest in reading about religion (something not to be confused with Stalin's brief seminary education), and was acutely aware of the ideological indefinition of Nationalism on the level of formal philosophy. On his religious readings and speculations, which may have led him to belief in a sort of immanentist theism, revealed in and through himself, see T. W. Ryback, 'Hitler's Forgotten Library: The Man, His Books, and His Search for God', *The Atlantic Monthly* (May, 2003), 76–90.

15. See especially K. Vondung, *Magie und Manipulation. Ideologischer Kult und politische Religion des Nationalsozialismus* (Göttingen: Vandenhoeck & Ruprecht, 1971), as well as his *The Apocalypse in Germany* (Columbia and London: University of Missouri Press, 2000). The literature in this area is, of course, quite extensive.

16. D.-S. Suh, 'The *Juche* Idea and Political Religion in Korea' (unpublished conference paper).

17. H. S. Park, *North Korea. The Politics of Unconventional Wisdom* (Boulder-London: Lynne Riener, 2002).

18. On the Kim Il Sung cult, see D.-S. Suh, *Kim Il Sung: The North Korean Leader* (New York: Columbia, 1988).

19. See D. Apter, 'Political Religion in the New Nations', in C. Geertz. ed., *Old Societies and New States* (New York: Free Press, 1963), as well as Apter's *Ghana in Transition* (New York: Athenaeum, 1963); L. Binder, *The Ideological Revolution in the Middle East* (New York: John Wiley, 1964); and M. Halpern, *The Politics of Social Change in the Middle East and North Africa* (Princeton: Princeton University Press, 1963).

20. Smith, *Chosen Peoples*, 11–14.
21. I. Esquerra, *ETA pro nobis. El pecado original de la Iglesia vasca* (Barcelona: Planeta, 2000); J. Bastante, *Los curas de ETA. La Iglesia vasca entre la cruz y la ikurriña* (Madrid: La Esfera de los Libros, 2004); and N. Blázquez, *El nacional clericalismo vasco* (Madrid: Edibesa, 2004).
22. I. Sáez de la Fuente Aldama, *El Movimiento de Liberación Nacional Vasco, una religión de sustitución* (Bilbao: Instituto Diocesano de Teología y Pastoral, Desclé, 2002). In his *Nacional clericalismo vasco*, 12–13, Niceto Blázquez summarises this study as follows: 'Those who consider themselves the legitimate representatives of the "people" have the right to demand of the faithful that they kill in the name of the nationalist cause and, if necessary, become martyrs by immolating themselves like kamikazes. And not for reasons of faith in God but of faith in a sacred entity that transcends us and is worthy of any sacrifice. The God for whom the nationalist is to immolate himself is none other but "the people"'. Here there is no other God than the people as directed by the nationalist leaders.

    This study dissects the religious model of the Basque National Liberation Movement in doctrinal, ethical, symbolic, ritual and communitarian terms attempting to demonstrate how, by means of the transference of sacralisation, the nationalist left abandons the laic concept of politics typical of modern civil societies in favour of a new cultic object, the People, whose persistence is made visible through daily combat. Similarly, it points out how violence fuels a community of endogamy and endows it with a strong component of martyrdom on the principle that, before the altar of the Fatherland, any salvific sacrifice is acceptable: its vision of reality and its normative apparatus separate two categories of people divided by an uncrossable barrier between those in contact with the truth and the uninitiated who, having not received and internalised the revealed message or having renounced the faith, belong to the sphere of the profane and heretical. The call to the supposed primeval national unity or foundational myth pretends, in addition to justifying the recourse to violence, to develop mobilising liturgies on behalf of a singular Exodus to the Promised Land of a believing community led by the orthodoxy of a military group and its corresponding political arm.
23. Probably the best single exposition is P. E. Gottfried, *Multiculturalism and the Politics of Guilt: Toward a Secular Theocracy* (Columbia and London: University of Missouri Press, 2002).

3
The Missiological Roots of the Concept of 'Political Religion'[1]

Werner Ustorf

Many studies of political religion today reserve the term for the phenomenon of Europe's totalitarian regimes of the twentieth century. Part of the phenomenon, then, is secularisation; that is its setting in cultures that were previously Christian in character. More or less distinct from related conceptual approaches focussing upon on such phenomena as nationalism, totalitarianism or modern dictatorship, and in some tension with the tenets of the secularisation hypothesis, the paradigm of *political religion* is used better to illuminate what the other approaches have such difficulty in explaining: the unquestionable popular support for and devotion to political programmes that were intensely violent and plainly irrational. Political religion, as a concept, explains the force behind the psycho-social dispositions and political mechanisms of totalitarian rule as quasi-religious in character. In particular, it detects *mythologies* and *liturgies, sacred texts* and *doctrines, orthodoxies* and *heresies*, and *holy wars* and *inquisitions*. An even wider interpretation of this concept takes us beyond the limitations of twentieth-century Europe. Accordingly, political religion is a trans-historical and trans-religious or trans-cultural conceptual device to explore, in principle at least, *all* attempts to sacralise the political sphere. This raises much wider questions: do political religions require a secular context in which to develop? Are human beings essentially religious or do they have a propensity to choose disastrous political-religious options when traditional religions (or institutionalised secularism) are no longer attractive? My position is that the answer to these questions is bound up with fundamental assumptions about the nature of man and, therefore, that philosophical or theological considerations are part of the picture. This is unavoidable, and my point is precisely that the theological pedigree of the concept of political religion is fully legitimate.

A scholar of religious studies is purported to have said once – ironically, I suppose – that the purpose of religion was to prevent us from having even worse fantasies. Whether this statement is apocryphal, as seems likely, it may be asked, nevertheless: Is it *true*? Certainly, if political religions constitute these worst fantasies, then the statement does indeed make sense. Does this imply, therefore, that we had better stick with the less dangerous fantasy when organising political life? This need not necessarily be so, because there are unquestionably more options open to us. Indeed, we find ourselves in the very arena where world views collide and the debate about political religion itself takes place (see Note 1). I do not think it is a coincidence that the concept of *political religion*, developed in the 1930s, has been rediscovered in our own time.[2] The parameters of religious study tend to correspond to our changing perceptions of religion. I am not claiming that there are any direct historical parallels between now and the 1930s, but there is a certain familial resemblance to be observed in the way that intellectuals react to the unexpected return of religion. How much religion, and what kind of religion, can the West tolerate or, alternatively, does it require for its well-being? If communism and fascism, particularly in their worst incarnations, Stalinism and National Socialism, were indeed political *religions*, as the concept of political religion suggests, then we must also say that this is another major mutation in the interpretation of religion,[3] and that the secularisation hypothesis[4] and more generally, the secular bias of the Western academy[5] needs modifying. It is my conviction, and I am trying to make the case for it in this chapter, that the Western academy needs a more serious and, at the same time, a more relaxed attitude to religion. This is possible by introducing a theological distinction between the political, the religious and the divine.[6] I will do this by discussing the origin of the concept of *political religion* as it arose in the Christian experience of the 1930s. It is my contention that the primary context for this is to be found in the details of missionary practice and reflection. I shall therefore consider perspectives that have not yet been acknowledged as part of the debate. Finally, I shall endeavour to explain my conviction that *political religion* is a theological concept or, at least, one with a theological prehistory, and that its theological connotation, being neither outmoded nor exhausted, but rather provides a starting point for critical analysis. The counter-cultural discourse of theology, particularly that represented by the discussions on missiology that took place in the 1920s and 1930s as regards the relationship between Christianity and Western culture, produced two significant voices to whom I wish to return, namely Paul Schütz and Hans Ehrenberg.

In 1930, the Lutheran churchman and, later, Professor of Theology, Paul Schütz (1891–1985), published what he called a 'religious-political' account of his travels to the Near East two years earlier.[7] He undertook the journey, in 1928, as director of a smaller German mission society, with the intention of inspecting its performance there, including its relief work for the persecuted Armenian Christians, a task the mission had inherited from an American agency. His account would cost him, first, his directorship, and, once published, would render his name instantly controversial. Principally this was for four reasons: (1) he, the mission thinker, advised the missionary movement from the West to withdraw immediately from the Near East; (2) he described missionary activity as having been secularised and politicised; that is to say, that it received its real life force not from the spiritual, but from its participation in imperialistic projects; (3) he regarded Western Christianity as inwardly empty and incompatible with the genuineness of Islam; and (4) as a consequence of the foregoing, he advocated the liberation of Church and mission from their imprisonment in secularised and capitalist rationality.

Interesting as this frontal attack on the inherited missionary ideology may be, my concern is a different one. I want to show that, in the late 1920s, Paul Schütz formed his concept of *political religion*, above all, on the basis of his encounter with Islam. The initial experience happened in 1928, somewhere between Cairo and Teheran. Schütz's experience here is representative of a whole group of missionaries: Islam, or more precisely, a particular perception of Islam, became the provocation for Christian renewal. In the mission field, Schütz thought he had discovered how a new kind of Western creed had undermined Christianity's credibility, reducing missionary work to a mere supporting ideology. Missionary Christianity had become syncretistic, it was just a shell; inside were the powers from 'below', namely an imperialistic *Weltanschauung*. This new creed had translated the universal eschatology of Biblical Scripture into a political programme and had itself, as Schütz put it, now become 'messianic', making imperialism something sacred, democracy 'religious' and capitalism 'ethical'. This political religion, in Schütz's view, was not a pseudo-religion, but a real religion. However, it was not in the service of God the Creator, but rather in that of the created and finite.

Theologians like Paul Tillich had already helped with the preparation of this line of thought. In 1925, for example, Tillich presented capitalism as a religious civilisation that possessed demonic power and was based upon faith in a finite world and the self-sufficiency of human agency.[8] Another theologian, Karl Barth, in 1931, also spoke of a genuine, but demonic *religion*; namely the gathering forces of communism and fascism and, also, what he called 'Americanism'.[9] This form of critique did not come as a surprise to the missionary movement. When the new discipline of Missiology was established at the end of the nineteenth century, the question of whether Western civilisation could be a missionary partner was already a critical factor. In the 1920s, the answers given became increasingly negative. In 1928 the *International Missionary Council*, at its Jerusalem meeting, finally declared *secularism* to be the main problem facing Christian missions and, surprisingly, even contemplated cooperation between the Christian missions and other religions in order to withstand the further advance of what was coming to be increasingly regarded as yet another religion – namely modern secularity.[10] In other words, there was an established missiological discourse that subjected Western liberal culture to a radical theological critique.

The next meeting of the International Missionary Council in Madras in 1938, where the missiologist and historian of religions, Hendrik Kraemer, offered a remarkable analysis of political religion, can be seen as an attempt to cut off the missionary movement from this new religion.[11] The concept of *political religion* was, therefore, an integral part of this missiological debate in the 1930s. From there, it was absorbed by the churches, turning up, for example, in 1937 at the Oxford Conference (on church, community and state)[12] of the Life and Work branch of the ecumenical movement and, in the same year, in a memorandum issued by the Confessing Church in Württemberg.[13]

In 1932, in explicit continuation of the thoughts expressed in his travelogue, Schütz published a full study of what he then called *Secular Religion*.[14] The term, often used synonymously with *chiliasm* and *political religion*, also covers Nazism and communism – both seen as consequences of the collapse of a liberal occidental culture that, in turn, is understood to have been caused by the dissolution of *faith*, or by its mutation into *religion*. This is an important distinction. *Secular religion*, during the last two centuries, is for Schütz, the *religious* transgression of the eschatological boundary. Eschatology itself, however, is the critical knowledge of this boundary. Religion becomes secular or political when a fallen humankind, outraged about the existence of the boundary and determined to work towards its own salvation, claims Paradise, the Kingdom of God and the Resurrection on earth. Secular religion embraces falsity because it is unwilling to wake up to the 'true situation' and the 'depth of existence'; that is, to respect the otherness of God and the hiddenness of truth, and to accept our aphasia, our speechlessness in these matters. Instead, secular religion speaks unhesitatingly of God, truth, humanity and history, denying that these are purely self-generated images. Secular religion, therefore, is the dialectical amalgamation of *reality*, which is God's, and a *reflection* or *interpretation* of *reality* which is ours. This amalgamation is sinful because it removes the distance between the two. Ultimately, it makes God an attribute of man, and heaven a place on earth. Secular religion, in the end, is spiritual rebellion against God.

Theology is, in Schütz's view, as sinful as any other human activity; it cannot cross the boundary that separates it from God. Its search for God is only a pointer to what it is not. Theology, however, can help by alerting *faith* to this problem. The difference between faith and secular or even political religiosity is that faith becomes aware of the boundary. Because of the very 'otherness' of God, *faith* cannot regard Biblical Scripture or Church as a spiritual ultimate. Neither does faith produce instrumental knowledge; it takes us rather into a situation that Schütz calls 'abandonment without cover'. From here, there is no way to return to the positivism of images, or to holy activism. Negatively, however, there is the necessary job of unmasking the forces that are active in political religion. This is theology's prophetic role. However, how this non-religious *faith* was related to the Christian *religion*, its sacraments, liturgy and so on, was less than clear.

In 1935, Schütz generalised these ideas in a manuscript entitled *Political Religion: An Analysis of the Origin of Decline in History*.[15] In it, he radicalised his distinction between *faith* and *religion*, removing almost completely the difference between religion and political religion. He insisted that for all political purposes the gospel was 'completely useless', and claimed that genuine Christianity could be political only in a negative sense, that is, by refusing to acknowledge the divinity of Caesar. The political expression of this refusal was a passive one, operating through suffering, though in the sense of passion and martyrdom. *Political religion*, in contradistinction, was violent by nature and contained the recipe for its own destruction. Violence and conflict were the inevitable outcomes of its religious vision, which demanded the merger of God and man, of eternity and history. However, for Schütz, there is a much more general sense to it all: *political religion* is the driving force of history in general; it is the distinctive mark made by humanity in its rebellion against the loss of paradise, and against poverty, suffering and death; it is a quest for a full life now and for redemption in the hereafter, it is the will to power; and, finally, it is an expression of the *sicut deus*, of man becoming God in his own man-made religion. Its mode of believing is therefore not *faith*, rather it is an *obsession*. The parallels with Voegelin's approach are remarkable.[16]

But Schütz's answer to the question of where all this started is different. 'The founder of political religion is the Jewish nation', he argued apodictically (and with a clearly anti-Judaic tendency, even though the Nazis and not the Jews were his immediate target); the unitary cosmos of 'one nation – one state – one God' was invented in Old Israel (Voegelin thought, like Jan Assmann today, rather of Old Egypt).[17] The political messianism of the Jews as the chosen people is the archetype of man-made political religion and it holds, in Schütz's words, 'the God of heaven and earth in the narrow captivity of ethnic religion'.

Ever since, political religion has been found virtually everywhere: from the imperial state religion of the Roman Empire to the medieval Church, but also in the French Revolution and the immanentism of the twentieth-century's totalitarian movements. After Marx and Nietzsche – and at a time when technology and industrial production were advancing apace, and when nations had become masses, and persons individuals – Schütz argued that the inner emptiness of the masses, and their hunger for certainty did indeed provide political religions with particularly fertile ground. Schütz, like Voegelin although some years before him, could not see any other way to counteract political religions other than the way envisioned by *faith*. This meant that eternal life would be present within oneself. This response was not without its practical problems, for such faith could be neither created nor instrumentalised. Faith, in fact, would be defined by Schütz as 'God coming to man'.

The second voice I wish to draw attention to is that of Hans Ehrenberg (1883–1958). Ehrenberg's biography was remarkable. A Jewish convert to Christianity, he was also a professor of philosophy who had become a Lutheran pastor, and, at the time of the analysis, a German refugee in Britain campaigning for the Confessing Church. Equally remarkable is his take on the religious situation. In 1941 he published an analysis of National Socialism as a *religion* in the official journal of the *International Missionary Council*.[18] Like Paul Schütz, Ehrenberg saw a way out of the crisis through the recovery of the Christian vision. But, unlike Schütz, Ehrenberg assumed that this recovery would have to take place in a world that was, in principle, hostile to established religion. All scriptural religions were in crisis, not just Christianity. The *global* cultural development, in his view, was reaching a post-liberal and post-secular stage, characterised by a configuration of the following three elements: *modernisation*, the return of the *archaic* and *emancipation*. Briefly put, it means this: once the modernist and liberal project collapses, nations or politico-cultural systems make three specific efforts:

(1) to retain and increase the technological gains made by *modern* civilisation;
(2) to return to a religiously and culturally more authentic or *archaic* stage: for example, either to return society to its religious roots, or perhaps to a *pre-Christian, pre-Muslim, pre-Buddhist* or even *pre-pagan* situation, or even, where there is no such thing, to invent *new religions*, constructed along archaic or primal lines, that satisfy the emotional needs of 'primitive man';
(3) and directly related to point two, to complete the *emancipation* from established and older cultural and religious traditions and, by so doing, to arrive at a *post-Christian, post-Muslim* or *post-pagan* understanding.

Political religion, therefore, varies slightly from case to case on account of the cultural, political, religious and other historical factors to which it is reacting. We can observe that Ehrenberg, like other programmatic thinkers before and after him, postulates the existence of two different kinds of religion: one 'primitive' and responding to the archaic within us, the other 'higher', more reflective and requiring conscious and ethical decisions. Political religion, or better to say, its source of power, is squarely put in the primitive or archaic bracket, for it is from there that it gets its 'vital force'. Ehrenberg tests this view by applying it across several contexts. His theory holds that it is vitally important that Buddhism, Christianity and Islam, which he calls the 'higher' religions, have spiritually integrated older local religions, which he calls 'primitive'. Depending on circumstances, these older religions may resurface at any time, re-inventing themselves and, therefore, displaying simultaneously archaic as well as progressive, or pre- and post- features. Ehrenberg's full scenario is too complex to be discussed properly here. But I will select two cases, Japan and Germany, in order to show how his theory works:

Japan's emperor-worship is the earliest case of totalitarian modernity and Ehrenberg therefore calls it the 'forerunner' of political religions. When, in 1868, Japan dispensed with the aristocracy and feudalism, which for centuries had been supported by Buddhism, Shinto was resurrected as the religious expression of centralised totalitarianism. This was possible because this 'primitive' religion had survived Buddhism and maintained its 'primeval ties'. Totally different, however, was the situation in Germany. What he calls *Nazi religion* combines various elements of religious history, from animism to the monotheistic saviour traditions. It is a tempting religion, for Hitler's words remind the people 'of thoughts which they had met elsewhere and had once valued highly'. But, religiously, Nazism could not return to a pre-Christian past in the way that Japan could to pre-Buddhist Shinto. The reason is that Germany's religious past, analogous with Attatürk's Turkey, had been completely assimilated by Christianity. Nazism had to go for option three and invent its own religion; it is a form of post-Christianity or a kind of *anti-religion*, a *heresy* or *apostasy*, a religion of rebellion. Nazism, with all its fanaticism, totalitarianism, eschatology and *holy war* mentality was, for Ehrenberg, the new version of the Islamic threat, and that is why he speaks of *Nazi Islam* and of Hitler not as, say, a second Napoleon, but the ' "new Muhammad", the only prophet of God'. The name of this god is, as was to be expected, 'the prince of darkness'. Such language was also used by Schütz and Voegelin. In those interwar years, it was in fact an international theological idiom, a kind of *lingua franca* for a radically eschatological approach, perhaps best represented by the Russian existential philosopher Nicolai Berdyaev, who, from his political asylum in Paris, fought a spiritual battle against totalitarianism and the supremacy of society over personality.[19]

Let me recapitulate: I have tried to show that, from around 1930, the discipline of missiology, strongly influenced by the counter-cultural or eschatological trend in Western theology, produced an explicit and critical discourse on political religion. *Political religion* was a term used by mission theologians, and initially described what they saw as the counter-mission of secularism and imperialistic liberalism, and Christianity's captivity to it. The concept drew on the missionary experience outside the west, particularly that surrounding the Christian encounter with Islam. When Communism and Fascism threatened the life of the Church, the concept of political religion was extended to them. There were various attempts to conceptualise the term, but it would not be far off the mark to say that, generally, what we have are *theological theories of political religion*, capable of supporting historical or anthropological and still other layers of theory.

Two questions are still open and need to be answered: one, what did the missiological usage of the concept 'political religion' achieve in those years, and, two, what does it contribute to our understanding of religion in the twentieth century? In the first instance, it is clear that the ecumenical and missionary movements adopted this approach because they increasingly perceived Europe to be a post-Christian area, that is, as a missiological problem. Schütz's, Kraemer's and Ehrenberg's approaches provided Christianity with a diagnostic device capable of identifying the animating forces of the time with immense discernment. This is evident in all of these theological theories, including Voegelin's. It is also clear that they collectively suggested that any response to the crisis of the West must come out of *faith*. What the Christian faith would look like after the marriage of Church, State and capitalism had ended in a difficult divorce, and after the catastrophe of the political religions was, and remains, a difficult, and perhaps even an open question. It would not be an unfair generalisation to say that none of these approaches suggested a 'programme', or recipe for avoiding the regression to political religion. Instead, they introduced a fundamental or a prophetic distinction between God and World, or, in the words of Berdyaev, between the Christian idea of the Kingdom of God as an 'eschatological consciousness', and the 'idolizing of historical sanctities', whatever their names.[20] What they talked about was a deep and comprehensive approach to reality. Reality and realism – whether these topics were being addressed by Schütz, Kraemer and Ehrenberg, Tillich, Emil Brunner and Voegelin – relate to God. It is in the light of this reality that the contours of historical realities themselves become visible, including the falsity of political religions. What all these eminent thinkers were talking about was a profound, deeply personal encounter with a divine reality. This communion quite explicitly did not lead to certainty in matters of belief, nor did it remove any personal doubts.[21] The encounter was of a rather more disturbing nature, dismissing any dreams of making one's peace with the world and with God. In brief, the real achievement was the public and international dissemination of a critical theological distinction between God, religious order and political rule. It demolished what the adherents of political religions craved most: certainty.

Second, does this missiological discourse of the 1930s contribute to our understanding of religion in the twentieth century? It is a surprising fact that Barth, Schütz, Kraemer and Ehrenberg regarded political religions as real *religions*. The explanation I would venture in response is this: theology, and missiology in particular, had learned to share the Enlightenment's critique of religion and to accept the extended concept of religion employed by sociology and religious studies. But they kept a critical distance between themselves and the anthropocentrism that ruled in the humanities. Rather, what they advocated was a radical theological distinction which left – metaphorically speaking, on the one side, that is, the only side there could be – God or *reality*, and on the other the self-constructed human world. This world could be either *Heimat* or *nightmare*, including religion *and* political religion. In this perspective, there could be no *vera religio* – all religions pointed to something beyond themselves. It was possible to say, then, that the sacralisation of political rule was itself a religious process. Yet despite the fact that it had *replaced* an older religion, and that the one was very much different from the other, it was still not possible to say that the one was the real thing and the other the fake. For these theologians the *real* thing was 'God', and everything else, religious or not, was under critique.

Most of us would agree that a central part of the cultural knowledge we have acquired over the centuries is that the political order must not be sacralised. Political order can be achieved and changed pragmatically, as a result of the processes of consensus and negotiation. But the condition or, at least, the caveat for this is, as the critics of political religion in the 1930s have shown, that a *further* type of knowledge is available: that of the distinction between the penultimate and the ultimate. Such a distinction does not define, but rather points to what is real or ultimate, in my vocabulary: to God. However, theological language does not need to be privileged as long as other dictionaries, such as that of philosophy, address this distinction. It is my contention that such a further type of knowledge is conducive to the preservation of learning and memory, resistant to the regression into archaic illusions and, also, sufficiently critical and realistic as not to be too impressed by the *fascinosum* of salvation politics. It is vital that the distinction between the penultimate and the ultimate is remembered in Western society, particularly in the academy.

Notes

1. A bibliography of political religion as a concept and as an object of research is contained in Hans Maier and M. Schäfer (eds), *Totalitarismus und Politische Religionen: Konzepte des Diktaturvergleichs* (Paderborn: F. Schöningh, 2003) and Detlef Schmiechen-Ackermann, *Diktaturen im Vergleich* (Darmstadt: Wiss. Buchgesellschaft, 2002).
2. *Political religion* as a concept of academic inquiry stands in a longer theological tradition that begins with Jesus' teaching that we render unto Caesar *and* to God what is appropriately theirs (Mk 12: 13–17), and continues with Augustine's distinction between *civitas Dei* and *civitas terrena,* which Luther, during the Reformation, would confirm in opposition to the enthusiasts. Thomas Campanella's utopian *civitas solis* of 1623, however, is held together by the ideological glue of a *religio politica* – an early usage of the term. In 1793, the editor of the distinguished journal *Der Teutsche Merkur,* Christoph Martin Wieland, described the French Revolution as 'a new political religion': intolerant, violent, and missionary. See H. O. Seitschek, 'Frühe Verwendungen des Begriffs "Politische Religion": Campanella, Clasen, Wieland', in Maier (ed.), *Totalitarismus 3,* pp. 109–20. And in 1825, John Stuart Mill had used the term 'political religion' in a distinctly critical way in order to describe the attempts of 'rulers' to mislead their subjects by amalgamating the two spheres. Cp. the Westm. Review (April edn), p. 291, according to *The Compact Oxford*

English Dictionary 1379/32 2nd edn (London: BCA, 1993). This theological discourse continued also in the 1930s. The theological impossibility of having a *political theology* was shown by Erik Peterson, *Der Monotheismus als politisches Problem* (Leipzig, 1935). This study is discussed by Jan Assmann, *Herrschaft und Heil* (Frankfurt am Main: Fischer, 2002), 21 f.; and by Maier, *Totalitarismus* 3, p. 369. Peterson's thesis was that the doctrine of Trinity disabled the mutual relationship between other-worldly and this-worldly order, because Trinity could not be represented on the political level.

3. Another mutation is the term 'civil religion', which, since the 1960s (Robert N. Bellah), is used to describe sacralisation phenomena in democratic states ruled by a constitution; in America, for example, some presidencies from George Washington on have been analysed in terms of civil religion. See Richard V. Pierard and Robert D. Linder, *Civil Religion and the Presidency* (Grand Rapids: Academy Books, 1988). It is, however, important to note the conceptual difference here: civil religion, though it is like political religion not legitimated by institutionalised religion, does not make exclusivist claims – political religions do.

4. H. McLeod and W. Ustorf (eds), *The Decline of Christendom in Western Europe, 1750–2000* (Cambridge: CUP, 2003); in particular the Introduction by McLeod; also H. McLeod, *Secularisation in Western Europe 1848–1914* (London: Macmillan, 2000). It is a rather broad, but fair generalisation to say that secularisation (following Durkheim and Weber) is a teleological concept: sketching a future world that is free from the Church or religion in general.

5. The secular bias of the Western academy leaves little room for religion, it works on the basis of what Jeff Cox called 'the presumption of marginality'. Jeffrey Cox, *Imperial Fault Lines: Christianity and Colonial Power in India, 1818–1940* (Stanford CA: Stanford UP, 2002), p. 8. In Michael Ignatieff, *Blood & Belonging: Journeys into the New Nationalism* (London: Vintage, 1994), for example, the term religion is hardly mentioned at all. Already at an earlier stage Carlton Hayes used the term 'nationalism' to analyse the driving forces of his time. 'Integral nationalism' in particular is the term that describes what others called totalitarianism or political religion; see his *Essays on Nationalism* (New York: Macmillan, 1928) and *The Historical Evolution of Modern Nationalism* (New York: Macmillan, 1931).

6. I am aware that the discipline of philosophy is also fully able to make such distinctions. A philosophical treatment of our subject area is John E. Smith, *Quasi-Religion: Humanism, Marxism and Nationalism* (London: Macmillan, 1994). Smith occupied the Clark Chair of Philosophy at Yale until his retirement in 1991. His study points to the historical connection between what he calls 'the secular void' (8 f.) and the rise of quasi-religions. Being a philosopher, he is quite explicit in his assumptions about human nature: different from the historical religious traditions and the quasi-religions is 'the human religious need', p. 10. This need, and this is the crux, can be served in different ways. Smith distinguishes between 'religions proper' (traditional scriptural religions such as Judaism, Christianity, Islam, Buddhism and Hinduism – tribal or primal religions are not mentioned) and 'quasi-religions' by insisting upon the following observation: *proper* religions are responses to the sacred or the transcendent – and their respective Ultimate can be nothing finite; *quasi*-religions do also offer a supreme object, but their ultimate

is finite and conditioned (1 f., 7 f., pp. 121–23). They are *religions* because they perform some of the functions associated with 'proper' religions, but they are *quasi* only, because their ultimates are subject to corruption and idolatry. It is interesting that a philosopher uses terms taken from the Judeo-Christian tradition such as 'idolatry', 'idols', 'demonic distortions' and, on the other side, 'unmasking', 'prophetic criticism' or 'truly divine love, beauty and creativity' (pp. 121, 132, 134) in order to qualify this distinction even further. In fact, Smith is indebted to Paul Tillich, even in the choice of the term 'quasi-religions': see Paul Tillich, 'The Significance of the History of Religions for the Systematic Theologian', in J. C. Brauer (ed.), *The Future of Religions: Paul Tillich* (New York: Harper & Row, 1966), p. 90.

7. I have used *Zwischen Nil und Kaukasus. Ein Reisebericht zur religionspolitischen Lage im Orient*, 4th edn (Moers: Brendow, 1991), which also contains Schütz' introduction for the 3rd edn of 1953. For Schütz, see H.-W. Gensichen, *Biographical Dictionary of Christian Missions*, G. H. Anderson (ed.), (Grand Rapids: Eerdmans, 1998), p. 605; also Gensichen's apologetic 'Zur Orient- und Missionserfahrung von Paul Schütz', *Zeitschrift für Missionswissenschaft und Religionswissenschaft* 77 (1993), pp. 152–59. A critical biography still needs to be written. First steps are Rudolf Kremers, *Paul Schütz – Auf der Suche nach der Wirklichkeit* (Moers: Brendow, 1989), and shorter, but more critical pieces by Rainer Hering, 'Der Theologe Paul Schütz im "Dritten Reich"', *Mitteilungen des Oberhessischen Geschichtsvereins* 84 (1999), pp. 1–39, and his 'Das *Judentum bei Paul Schütz*', *Jahrbuch der Hessischen Kirchengeschichtlichen Vereinigung* 52 (2001), pp. 143–65. This important publication uses, among other primary materials, an unpublished manuscript by Schütz on political religion (see note 15).

8. Tillich in his *The Religious Situation* (New York: Meridian Books, 1960) and his *Die Sozialistische Entscheidung* (Potsdam: A. Protte, 1933). Tillich is discussed as one of the formative thinkers in the area of political religions in Maier, *Totalitarismus* 3, pp. 83 ff., 378.

9. Karl Barth, 'Fragen and das Christentum', *Zofinger Centralblatt* (December 1931); reprinted in idem, *Theologische Fragen und Antworten* 3 (Zürich: Theol. Verlag, 1957), pp. 93–99. I have been alerted to this by Kristian Hungar, emeritus professor in Heidelberg's theological faculty. Hungar is currently working on related issues, and I have used his unpublished 2004 paper on *Theologische Diagnose des Nationalsozialismus: Karl Barth*. See also W. Ustorf, 'German Missiology and Anti-Americanism', *Mission Studies* VI/1, 11 (1989), pp. 23–34.

10. Rufus M. Jones, 'Secular Civilization and the Christian Task', *Report of the Jerusalem Meeting of the International Missionary Council* 1 (London: OUP, 1928), pp. 284–338. See also the discussion in W. Ustorf, *Sailing on the Next Tide. Missions, Missiology, and the Third Reich* (Frankfurt am Main: P. Lang, 2000), 97 f.

11. Kraemer, *The Christian Message in a Non-Christian World* (London: Edinburgh House Press, 1938), p. 15. Kraemer says here:

> In their political and economic aspects they are gigantic efforts, inspired by universalist or nationalist ideas, to master the anarchy of our social and political world. Their particular characteristic, however, is that they

are primarily creeds, philosophies of life and religions of an extremely intolerant and absolutist type. They consequently develop mythologies, doctrinal systems, catechisms, 'churches', 'priests', 'prophets', 'saints', and 'mediators'. All the paraphernalia of a full-fledged religion are virtually present. They even make gods – for the race, the ideal communist society, and the State assume a distinctly God-like position. Absolute allegiance to these gods is demanded with religious fervour. Absolute devotion to their service is the ultimate standard of moral life, and releases in many individuals, as all ultimates do, marvellous manifestations of self-sacrifice, discipline and creativeness. These 'religions' impetuously claim dominion over life in all its ramifications. They intolerantly persecute other religions that do not subordinate their specific allegiance to the absolute one that is only due to their 'god'. Tillich justly remarks that the disintegrated masses, sensing the meaninglessness of life, hunger for 'new authorities and symbols'. The totalitarian systems satisfy this hunger, and millions of men gladly sacrifice their political, economic and spiritual autonomy. If we still need evidence that man, even de-religionised modern man, is a religious and metaphysical animal, here it is.

12. See my *Sailing on the Next Tide,* pp. 113–28, and my 'Kairos 1933 – Occidentosis, Christofascism, and Mission', U. van der Heyden and H. Stoecker (eds), *Mission und Macht. Europäische Missionsgesellschaften in politischen Spannungsfeldern in Afrika und Asien zwischen 1800 und 1945* (Stuttgart: Franz Steiner Verlag, 2005), pp. 621–32.
13. *Kirche oder Sekte* (April 1937). This anonymous text offers a concise description of National Socialism as a 'political religion' (religion 'in the full sense'). Nazi religion is presented as a 'state-church', different from and in no need of the 'pseudo-religion' of Hauer's neopaganism, engaged in a 'hidden religious war' against the Christian tradition and well described in its absolutist claims. Extracts in Klaus Behnken (ed.), *Deutschland-Berichte der Sozialdemokratischen Partei Deutschlands 1934–1940* (Salzhausen: P. Nettelbeck, Frankfurt am Main: Zweitausendeins, 1980), vol. 4, pp. 494–99. It is interesting that Michael Burleigh quotes this text without acknowledging that it was written by theologians, *The Third Reich: A New History* (London: Macmillan, 2000), 252 f.
14. *Säkulare Religion: Eine Studie über ihre Erscheinung in der Gegenwart und ihre Idee bei Schleiermacher und Blumhardt d.J.* (Tübingen: Mohr Siebeck, 1932), p. 224. The main part of the text was in fact his *Habilitation* (second doctorate) at the University of Giessen (1930).
15. *Die politische Religion: Eine Untersuchung über den Ursprung des Verfalls in der Geschichte.* This unpublished, type-written manuscript has 63 pages, a preface by Schütz (by hand, 1975) and two appendices: *Das hugenottische Leiden im deutschen Raum* (p. 14, hand-written) and *Der protestantische Mensch und der preußische Staatsgedanke* (p. 5, type-written). It is briefly discussed by Rainer Hering, 'Das Judentum bei Paul Schütz', 143 f.; but it has not been consulted by Schütz' biographer, Rudolf Kremers. The manuscript is available at *Staatsarchiv Hamburg, 622–1 Familie Paul Schütz, 248.* I am grateful to Prof. Hering for having made a photocopy available to me.
16. Eric Voegelin, *Die politischen Religionen,* Peter J. Opitz (ed.), 2nd edn (Munich: Fink, 1996). Voegelin offered a political theory from a Christian perspective,

though it must be said that the interwar years were awash with similar attempts to extend the religious terminology to phenomena outside the established religions. In fact Lucie Varga in 1937, Frederick A. Voigt in 1938, and, later, Raymond Aron also used the term. Voegelin was steadfast in his opinion that the modern mass movements of Communism and Fascism were religious in origin and both the result and symptom of the modern crisis of Western civilisation. The crisis consisted in the departure of this civilisation from its religious moorings, in the 'secularization of the mind' and, theologically, in the 'apostasy from God'. Overcoming the crisis, meant for Voegelin, working towards a 'religious renewal' or, as he later so succinctly put it, to move from 'the certainty of untruth' to the 'uncertain truth' of God. See Voegelin, *Der Gottesmord. Zur Genese und Gestalt der modernen politischen Gnosis,* Peter J. Opitz (ed.), (Munich: Fink, 1999), pp. 105–28. At the same time, however, he sketched the broad outlines of a more general theory of the relationship between the state and religion, from the Egyptian Pharaoh and 'Son of God', Tutankhamun, via certain thought patterns of late antiquity and the heretical movements of medieval Christianity, to Nazism. This theory suggested that the main problem of political religion was its misunderstanding of God's transcendence and the analogical nature of religious symbolic language. Its translation, as it were, into blueprints for immanent historical progress created a new type of religiosity: an inner-worldly or *political religion* that tried to put into the reality of this life what revelation had promised for the hereafter. Some critics felt that Voegelin simply blamed modern Western culture and the Enlightenment for Nazism and Communism. (See note 17).

17. The Egyptologist Jan Assmann of Heidelberg University objects to those interpretations of Voegelin's approach that conclude that the Enlightenment was ultimately responsible for Nazism and Communism. In fact, his approach is in some sense a restatement of Friedrich Schiller's enlightened position. See in particular, Assmann's attack on Voegelin in 'Der Sonderweg des christlichen Abendlandes', *Frankfurter Allgemeine Zeitung* (3 June 1994), p. 10; also *Moses the Egyptian: The Memory of Egypt in Western Monotheism* (Cambridge/Mass.: HUP, 1997); idem, *Herrschaft und Heil: Politische Theologie in Altägypten, Israel und Europa* (Frankfurt/M.: Fischer, 2002). See also the controversy between Assmann and Gerhard Kaiser in *Frankfurter Allgemeine Zeitung* of 2 November 2000 and 28 December 2000. Kaiser extended his critique in 'War der Exodus ein Sündenfall?', *Zeitschrift für Theologie und Kirche* 98 (2001), pp. 1–24. In *Herrschaft und Heil* Assmann argued (by reference to Voegelin's work and, more importantly, to Carl Schmitt's famous dictum of 1922 that 'all succinct terms of the modern theory of the state are secularised theological terms') that all succinct terms of theology 'are theologized political terms' (p. 20). Put more simply: 'what modernity moved from heaven down to earth, in a previous era had been lifted from earth up to heaven' (p. 12). This implies that neither the theological nor the secular are primordially given – they are both events of history. The sacralisation of the political, Assmann thinks had an Egyptian prelude; however, its memory survived in the 'mnemonic' figure of Moses. It led to the 'Mosaic distinction' (see *Moses the Egyptian,* 17 ff. and 24 ff.) namely a location of iconoclastic absoluteness from where other (usually polytheistic) traditions and religions could be condemned as idolatry, heathendom or superstition; a location from where it became

possible to engage in self-reflection and a determination of what is 'true'. This distinction between true and false, however, also introduced in all three Abrahamic religions a tremendous potential for violence, because the ability to differentiate between political enemies and enemies of the truth could be lost. Assmann's position is that the secularisation process was an event in history, just as the process of sacralisation had been. This necessarily forces the debate about *political religion* to paint its pictures on a canvass that is broader than any that would be required to accommodate a theory of apostasy. According to Assmann, any redefinition of the relationship between political rule and religious order must exhaust fully the historical space that the tension between the two processes of theologisation and of secularisation are opening up.

18. 'The Nazi Religion and the Christian Mission', *International Review of Missions* 30 (1941), pp. 363–73. I am also using his *Autobiography of a German Pastor* (London: SCM, 1943). For Ehrenberg see Ulrike Lange, 'Ehrenberg', *Metzler Lexikon Christlicher Denker,* M. Vinzent (ed.), (Stuttgart: Metzler, 2000), p. 224. Lange has also written a monograph about Ehrenberg's thought structures. See *Constancy and Change: Hans Ehrenberg's Three-Dimensional Methodology and the 'Jewish Question'* (1932–1954), (PhD thesis, University of Birmingham UK, 2004). The official biography is Günter Brakelmann, *Hans Ehrenberg.* Vol. 1: *Leben, Denken und Wirken, 1883–1932*; Vol. 2: *Widerstand, Verfolgung, Emigration, 1933–1939* (Waltrop: Spenner, 1997 and 1999).

19. See *The Destiny of Man* (London: G. Bles, 1937); and *Slavery and Freedom* (New York: Ch. Scribner's Sons, 1944). There is also a direct link between Schütz and Berdyaev because both (together with Fritz Lieb) edited the 1929–1934 journal *Orient und Occident.*

20. Berdyaev, *Slavery and Freedom,* p. 18. See also, though in an even more openly mystical language, P. Schütz, *Zwischen Nil und Kaukasus,* p. 262.

21. Berdyaev, *The Beginning & the End* (New York: Harper & Brothers, 1952), p. 155. He describes this encounter as a disruptive event, as an irruption into commonplace daily life. This communion would inevitably lead to a critique of the historical sanctities.

4
Is Castroism a Political Religion?

Eusebio Mujal-León and Eric Langenbacher

Introduction

For 47 years, from his entry into Havana in January 1959 until July 2006 when he suffered a serious illness and turned power over to his brother Raúl, Fidel Castro presided over a one-party, personalistic dictatorship in Cuba. Given the longevity of his rule, it would appear that a dense network of beliefs, rituals and ideology – in short, a political religion – developed to justify and support the regime. Indeed, there are many dimensions to Castroism that resemble a political religion, both theoretically and in comparison to other empirical cases. Examples include the symbolic iconography of the revolution, from major holidays like May Day and the anniversary of Castro's armed insurrection on 26 July 1953, to the veneration of revolutionary heroes, such as Che Guevera and, from another era, Jose Martí. Most important of all, of course, is the cult of personality that surrounds Castro himself. Communist ideology, itself one of the quintessential political religions, has provided one of the foundations for the legitimation of Castro's regime, just as it afforded Cuban leaders the blueprint for political structures and policy. But Castro has also relied on other ideas to legitimate his rule. He constantly used and reinforced Cuban nationalism, replete with a clearly defined enemy, the capitalist United States of America. The latter was a haven for the 'worms and parasites'[1] who fled the island after 1959. The Cuban regime also revealed messianic ambitions, trying to export its revolutionary model and post-colonial anti-Americanism throughout the developing world, and especially in Latin America.

Despite these affinities with the concept of a political religion, however, Castroism also demonstrates particular nuances. It has always been idiosyncratic, highly contradictory and extremely personalistic. Unlike

51

other revolutionary twentieth-century founders of political religions, Castro had neither a coherent plan at the outset, nor a developed doctrine (replete with iconic texts such as the *Communist Manifesto* or *Mein Kampf*), nor a comprehensive program beyond the overthrow of Fulgencio Batista, the destruction of the traditional élite and, most importantly, his installation as 'supreme leader.' 'History will absolve me!,'[2] Castro declared in the famous speech based on his trial after the failed 1953 attack on the Moncada barracks, a speech that constituted a fundamental indictment of the Batista regime, containing only vague programmatic references. Thus, at the outset far from a committed ideologue, Castro was a self-proclaimed man of action, relentless in his pursuit of power, exhibiting an extraordinary intuition for revolutionary agitation.[3]

Although there is some question as to what kinds of political views he held while conducting his guerilla campaign in the Sierra Maestra mountains before the seizure of power, he later claimed that in the 1950s he was a 'utopian Communist' and then an 'atypical Communist.' This implies that, despite his professed sympathies, he was not willing or ready to accept the discipline of the Communist party. In fact, Castro only formally embraced communism in April 1961, and, if at this point he threw himself (literally and unexpectedly) into the arms of the Soviet Union, this was because he needed a stronger ally to defend himself against the United States and the Cuban exiles who had settled there. Even so, as a copious scholarship amply demonstrates, his relationship with Marxist–Leninism and the Soviet Union was often strained. His policies were erratic and inconsistent, and the institutionalization of the party and regime relatively weak. Nevertheless, like other communist systems, the principal lines of authority have always been rigidly vertical and hierarchical. Castro may be *fidelista* to the core, but the instrument for the exercise of his power was the state.

Compounding the difficulties one faces in characterizing Castro's ideology are its changes and evolution over time. Indeed, we observe no fewer than three variants of Castroism, all of which roughly correspond to the various phases of his rule. First, there was the revolutionary variant that accompanied the seizure of and consolidation of power during the 1960s. The second was the more orthodox Communist version, sometimes referred to as 'bureaucratic socialism' that characterized the 1970s and mid-1980s, which also coincided with the regime's 'internationalist' interventions in places like Angola, Ethiopia and Nicaragua. The third variant coincided with the demise of the Soviet Union and its bloc. Since the end of the Cold War, erratic and frequently contradictory economic reforms combined with sharp nationalism, an even more intensive focus on Castro as person and leader, and a strident anti-Americanism. Castro was repeatedly able to update and reinvigorate this anti-Americanism, as in his responses to the Helms-Burton Act of 1996 and, especially, to the Elian Gonzalez incident in 2000. Elsewhere, one of the authors has characterized this phase as one of charismatic and truncated post-totalitarianism.[4]

This ideological heterogeneity and evolution over time complicate any analysis of Castroism. Yet, there are also more constant influences, a hard core, in all periods clearly showing that Castroism approximates a political religion. Statism, nationalism, anti-Americanism and, above all, his persona, have been the constant factors. To accommodate the Cuban case, we examine the theory and concept of a political religion and propose several modifications and refinements. Our central insight is that regimes or movements should be mapped on two continuous axes. One axis is a continuum with the ideal-typical and most completely realized political religions like German National Socialism on the one side, and 'mere' ideology on the other. The second axis ranges from traditional to non-traditional religion, and tries to capture the relationship between traditional religion or religious forms of legitimation with less orthodox forms. With this modified typology, we evaluate the degree to which Castroism approaches, but does not reach, a fully developed political religion. Alternately, we can examine how intervening factors – Castro's personality, Latin American geopolitical and cultural traditions, and world historical time (*Zeitgeist*) – have impeded full realization.

Theory and concepts

Though the term political religion has an honorable lineage, dating back to the philosophical ruminations of such authors as Eric Voegelin and Nikolai Burdiev, the concept has not gained widespread acceptance among most political and social scientists. There are three reasons for this lack of resonance. First, there is still a lingering disdain regarding cultural, ideational and historical phenomena among many political scientists. Too often, culture is considered a residual category where all unexplained factors end up. Alternately, culture is considered impossible to specify and immune to rigorous, quantitative analysis. Major conceptual and empirical advances in recent years, associated with authors like Ronald Inglehart, Russell Dalton, Thomas Rochon, Robert Putnam and Samuel Huntington, largely have silenced such skeptics. Second, the study of political religions has been closely tied to a handful of totalitarian ideologies, such as Nazi Germany, fascist Italy, Communism and, earlier, Jacobinism. It has been difficult to divorce the concept from the specificities of these cases of atypical transformative politics in order to show the more general validity, and applicability, to cases like Cuba. Perhaps the biggest obstacle has been definitional ambiguity, the challenge of differentiating the term not only from conventional religion and from other cognate phenomena such as civic religion, but also from better-known close conceptual substitutes, replete with their own literatures, such as 'ideology' or 'nationalism.' Nevertheless, the political religion term has witnessed a renaissance in recent years, resulting from, and contributing to, a useful though still nascent conceptual refinement.[5]

To begin with some definitions

> A political ideology is a set of ideas, beliefs, values and opinions, exhibiting a recurring pattern, that competes deliberately as well as unintentionally over providing plans of action for public policy making, in an attempt to justify, explain, contest or change the social and political arrangements and processes of a political community.[6]

Even this commonly used term is contentious, since authors employ it in both a neutral, descriptive sense and a more critical manner, where ideology connotes a distortion of reality and tendentious, self-serving propaganda. Yet ideology cannot accommodate or exhaust cases where the scope, ambition and expectations of the agents behind the set of beliefs are so great, with such exalted degrees of emotional intensity and extraordinary expectations of attitudinal compliance and conversion, and where the group or leaders in question have revolutionary, world-changing or cultural pretensions.

Religion represents precisely this kind of heightening of belief, and a qualitatively different attitudinal and behavioral phenomenon. There are multiple and competing definitions of religion, but several commonalities exist among them. Substantive definitions of religion stress belief in spiritual beings, experiential ones focus on a common experience of finding the infinite in the finite, and, most appropriately for the purposes of this chapter, structural – functional alternatives (in the spirit of Emile Durkheim) highlight the unifying function of a common moral community. Thus,

> a religion is a symbolic system (with associated beliefs and practices) which articulates the thought that there is a source of moral order

behind the world...there are important social and personal needs met...and its symbols have a typical content. They must purport to refer to transcendent realities which function as the ground of the natural order and the source or guarantors of morality.[7]

An alternative, and similarly useful, definition states that religions are 'control systems linking meaning and motivation...a sphere of activity where efforts are deliberately made to influence, manipulate and control people's thoughts, feelings and actions in accordance with various religious values.'[8] Central to any religion or religious phenomenon is the provision of meaning, motivation, control and, above all, legitimacy.

It is also essential to address the processes through which a religion is formed, institutionalized and continually reproduced – processes best deemed as sacralization. Emilio Gentile argues that sacralization occurs when: (1) the sanctity and primacy of a collective secular entity is consecrated; (2) such conceptions are incorporated into a code; (3) members are considered an elect community with a messianic function; and (4) a political liturgy and sacred history are formulated.[9] Even in the most postmodern and secularized environments, it would appear, there is some need for religion or an analogous phenomena that provides meaning or transcendence, while also, even minimally, helping with the needs for political legitimation (Voegelin, Billings and Scott, Marquand and Nettler),[10] and this suggests that the need for the religious impulse and processes of sacralization will not soon disappear. Indeed, as Max Weber acutely observed a century ago, there is a constant need for one of three types of legitimate authority. Under modern or modernizing circumstances, traditional authority wanes and is often incomplete, rational-legal authority (Weber's 'iron cage') lacks emotive bite. Charismatic forms of authority, of which religious phenomena are a perennial example, are perhaps even more common and needed today, as the examples of Hugo Chavez and Osama bin Laden attest.

If these religious needs and processes of sacralization may be accepted as givens, questions arise as to what elements are sacralized, and what accordingly are the results. There are three alternatives. The first focuses on the sacralization of political power, whereby traditional religion legitimizes power holders in a syncretistic manner, as for example with divine right monarchies, or Islamic theocratic states like Iran or Saudi Arabia. The second alternative is civic religion – an amalgamation and synthesis of traditional and newer secular phenomena – whose prominent examples include 'Americanism'[11] and the French *mission civilatrice*. Gentile classifies it thus:

> Civil religion is a form of sacralisation of politics that generally involves a secular entity, but at times is connected to a supernatural being conceived as a god; it is not linked to the ideology of any particular political movement, but acknowledges the full autonomy of the individual from the collective;…(it) appeals to spontaneous consensus…(and) exists side by side with traditional religions and various ideologies.[12]

As this definition suggests, authors often use this concept to differentiate between democratic and non-democratic versions of the sacralization process and results, but this point of differentiation does not map perfectly. For example, Francoism clearly contained a combination of secular and traditional religious tendencies as well as a partial acceptance of societal and political pluralism, yet this coincided in an undemocratic regime. Many forms of nationalism (pan-Slavism, pan-Germanism, political Islam, pan-Arabism) also contain analogous combinations (although certain forms cross over into the political religious category), yet they can be used to legitimize both democratic and non-democratic regimes. In our view, the pluralist or democratic dimension is less important than relationships with traditional religion, and it is useful to perceive these components as varying on a continuum.

Political religion may be defined as the

> sacralization of an ideology and integralist political movement that deifies the mythical secular entity; it does not accept coexistence with other ideologies and political movements…sanctifies violence… denies the autonomy of the individual and stresses the primacy of the community; it imposes a political cult and enforces obligatory observance of its commandments.[13]

The self is identified as an agent of Providence; there is a call to faith and a marked political eschatology.[14] New rituals, indoctrination, icons and symbols are crucial for the political religion. Hence, ambitious scope, radical or revolutionary ambitions and unquestioning belief and compliance are key dimensions. As Michael Burleigh points out, none of the other cognate phenomenon (such as nationalism) transformed citizens from passive spectators into active participants, and nor did they define good and evil and the un/making of humanity. In a real sense, they were underfreighted with ambition.[15] A reductionist, Manichean world of black and white/good and evil are characteristic of the worldview of political religions (and certain types of political regimes).

Thus, by definition, a political religion can exist only in an un-free, non-pluralist, often totalitarian political system, corresponding to Voegelin's notion of collective politics. Gentile observes that a totalitarian regime is accompanied by the militarization of the party, a concentration of power in a charismatic leader, all-encompassing capillary organizations that embrace collective indoctrination and an anthropological revolution – all of which employ coercion (sanctified, purifying violence), demagoguery and propagandistic pedagogy.[16] Juan Linz and Alfred Stepan also stress the key characteristics of constant mobilization, active persuasion and conversion (the new man).[17] A political religion claims an absolute monopoly on truth, belief and legitimacy. No dissent is allowed, and those who disagree are an enemy to be disqualified, expurgated and destroyed. There are no moral safeguards here, rather a moral imperative. In what is an essential difference with a civic religion, moreover, political religions (although all variations are inspired by and indebted to the forms and practices of conventional religion) envision themselves as direct competitors and replacements of traditional religions. There is no possibility or prospect for cooptation, cooperation or synthesis. Again, the relationship to traditional religion emerges as a central concern. Political religion also places intense focus on the charismatic leader, who becomes the quasi-religious father of the country. As Voegelin has observed, political religions differ from traditional forms by taking out most of the hierarchical mediation between God and the individual. Belief and dogma are generated, interpreted, transmitted and modified only through the supreme leader or, as Arthur Koestler put it in *Darkness at Noon*, by Number 1.

In an effort to move beyond some of these definitional ambiguities and to expand the conceptual range to a wider variety of cases,[18] we propose to move beyond the common tendency to present these conceptual categories as mutually exclusive. Our proposal is to envision two continuous axes that comprise a rudimentary typology.

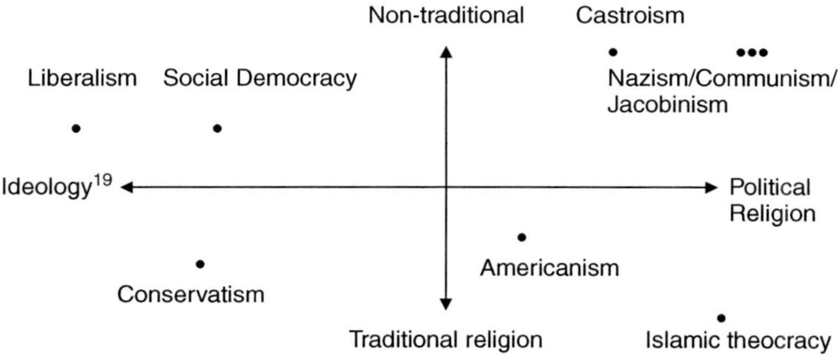

For us, the essential components of and/or conditions that facilitate a political religion include:

1. the existence of a non-democratic regime with little to no pluralism;
2. a regime that fuels intense nationalism;
3. a regime that clearly defines its enemy or enemies;
4. a single, monopolistic party – and capillary organizations for indoctrination;
5. a charismatic demagogic leader, the *Führerprinzip;*
6. a clear and well-developed doctrine – with revolutionary, world-changing (the 'new man'), cleansing and messianic ambitions;
7. well-developed symbols and iconography – with rituals and rallies to reinforce these;
8. the regime must also be an explicit competitor to traditional religious forms of legitimation.

It is also necessary briefly to review the common conditions of cases that have facilitated the emergence of political religions. In our view, a combination of two inter-related factors appears necessary. First, a modicum of modernity with the concomitant erosion of traditional authority is always present, yet these processes have not evolved enough to have completely destroyed the old power élite. This is the classic revolutionary situation. Moreover, as authors like Barrington Moore, Gregory Luebbert and Alexander Gerschenkron have long argued, the nature of the specific modernization process matters, particularly, whether development was more evolutionary (as in Britain and the United States) or more drastic (Germany and Russia). The latter cases are more prone to a revolutionary crisis and the salvation that political religions can provide. Second, countries that experienced political religions all had belated or incomplete nationhood: Germany, Italy, Japan, Russia, Slobodan Milosevic's Serbia. In Central and Eastern Europe this was largely due to the complicated ethnic settlement patterns in the old empires. Meanwhile in the other cases, expansionist drives were thwarted by the lack of a frontier or status quo, by the colonial powers (Germany, Japan) or the colonial powers' ruling and/or exit strategies that thwarted national realization (Vietnam, Korea). Each case went through an extraordinary identity crisis, spurred on by perceptions of an unfulfilled national destiny (thwarted by other powers or ethnicities). The interaction of these two factors, rapid but incomplete socio-economic modernization and unfulfilled national identity creates conditions under which religion or religious phenomena become especially important to provide needed meaning and to re-legitimate the system.

Founders of political religions exploit the unstable situation and tap the need for meaning, justice or resolution for which such societies yearn. Such leaders also take Weber's maxim to heart, namely that empirical reality is always a combination of real and ideal factors. Political religions, with their charismatic authority, do not just provide psychological comfort, but they are also a major means to impose absolute, coercive, but somehow legitimate, power. They help to create very real transformative and salvational regimes. To be clear, we are not proposing a causal explanation or prediction. For every successful attempt to create a political religion, there are many more that fail. Moreover, there is a big difference between the successful emergence of a political religion and its institutionalization into a sustainable doctrine or culture over time.

This conceptual discussion sets the frame-work for our analysis of Castroism. We now turn to a consideration of the central questions. Is Castroism a political religion? To what degree does Castroism correspond to, or deviate from, the components outlined above?

Preconditions and themes of Castroism

Just over a 100 years old as an independent nation, Cuba had a turbulent political history. Having won independence in 1902 (after Spain was defeated in the Spanish–American War), its sovereignty was still visibly truncated until the abrogation – in 1934 – of the so called Platt Amendment which had been inserted into the American Constitution and allowed the United States to intervene directly in Cuban affairs. The failure to consolidate democratic rule, rising authoritarianism, socio-economic tensions (especially between the urban hub of Havana and the rest of the country), an almost exclusive reliance on sugar as the core of the economy, extensive corruption, cronyism and rising political violence marked the first four decades of national life. Though a democratic constitution was implemented in 1940, the next 12 years did not signal the consolidation of democracy in Cuba. Rather, political chicanery and corruption dominated the political landscape, and along with the rise of organized political gangs, undermined the newly installed structures and contributed to its demise via a 1952 coup by the same General Fulgencio Batista who had been constitutional president between 1940 and 1944.

The 1952 coup cut short a presidential campaign in which it was almost universally anticipated that the victor would be the *Ortodoxo* party, whose political symbol was the broom, as opposed to the ruling *Autenticos*. Among the early and most virulent opponents of the Batista coup and regime was a young law graduate and abortive *Ortodoxo* candidate to Congress, Fidel Castro Ruz. Even from early on, Castro exhibited an extremely personalistic, yet inspirational, leadership style.[20] He eventually armed and led a small band of guerillas in a failed attack on the Moncada army barracks in Santiago on 26 July 1953 (from which derives the name of his political movement), and was then imprisoned for two years. After his release, he fled to Mexico where he raised funds, recruited more followers (including his brother Raúl and Ernesto (Che) Guevara) and returned to Cuba in 1956 on the ship named *Granma* (later the name of the state-run newspaper). Castro conducted a guerilla war in the Sierra Maestra mountains in the east of the country, against the largely inept Batista army, buttressed by urban guerilla groups and a pervasive and growing anti-Batista public opinion. By 1958, the official army was in disarray, general strikes began to paralyze the cities, university students led protests and, in March 1957, even assaulted the presidential palace and tried to assassinate Batista. Eventually the United States, long a pillar of the regime, began to withdraw its support. Batista fled on 1 January 1959, and Castro entered Havana on 8 January, marking the beginning of his rule.

The early years of the 'Revolution' (1959–1962) were full of turmoil and deep-seated changes: the nationalization of industry and agricultural holdings was swiftly followed by a massive exodus of the professional and middle classes, as well as many religious believers. Above all, relations became strained and outwardly hostile with the United States; amply exemplified by the failed Bay of Pigs Invasion in 1961 and the Cuban missile crisis in 1962. These events radicalized and entrenched Castro, the self-proclaimed national liberator of the first 'free territory in the Americas.' Indeed, the early and mid-1960s were a period of revolutionary euphoria, with the focus based on a radical transformation of society and the creation of a 'New Man.' Viewed on a more global scale, the 1960s were also a period when Castro and his closest associates, among them Che Guevara, came to see Cuba as a rival to the Soviet Union and China. This small group of Cuban revolutionaries increasingly regarded their island as a paragon, which had more to say and to teach the Third World (and especially Latin America) than either of the Communist giants. This stance created substantial friction with the Soviet leadership. Nonetheless, the

1967 death of Guevara in Bolivia while pursuing his *guerrillero* dream, growing economic problems and vulnerability and the need to assure himself of international support, all led Castro to reconcile Cuba with the Soviet Union. The 1970s saw a strategic convergence between Cuba and the USSR. Though it would be far too simplistic to view Castro as merely a pawn or surrogate for the Soviet Union during this period, it is nevertheless clear that he not only presided over Cuba's integration into the Communist economy and trade zone, but also committed Cuban troops to far-flung places where they served as a Soviet surrogate for intervention.

Change again set in during the mid- and late 1980s, first with a domestic process of ideological 'rectification' and institutional renewal, and then with the collapse of the Soviet Union, which provoked a deep economic and ideological crisis. Given that the Soviet Union subsidized the Cuban economy to the tune of 30–40% of its GDP by 1989, many thought the regime inevitably would collapse in the absence of such support. Surprisingly, Cuba and Castro weathered a difficult period of transition (the so-called 'special period'), during which the regime undertook some economic reforms (among them, the decision to allow the free circulation of dollars and the opening of farmers' markets). Such measures were only half-hearted and, in the case of the farmers' markets, Castro could not help but show his disdain and contempt for what he was convinced was a measure that re-introduced capitalism on the island. Not surprisingly, as soon as the economic situation improved slightly by the mid- to late 1990s, the regime tightened its controls over this and other 'free-market' sectors.

As we argued above, a regime must be totalitarian, or at least non-democratic with a totalitarian edge, for the political religion term to be applied appropriately. Institutionally, the Castro regime approximated this ideal type. It was a one-party state with the Communist Party of Cuba (PCC) the sole legal political organization. There was extensive state ownership (76% of all employment is with state entities), little independent civil society and no acceptance of pluralism. There were no free and fair elections, and there was little distinction between Party and state. Castro was omnipresent as President of the Republic, First Secretary of the Communist party, *comandante* and Commander-in-Chief of the Armed Forces, presiding over the Council of Ministers, the Council of State and the Politburo. His 40-year pattern of visiting factories and cooperatives, showed how much he relished micro-management of the economy while freely dispensing advice and instructions. As an otherwise sympathetic observer, the Polish journalist K. S. Karol put it in 1970:

> He has chosen a most demanding way of life for himself, rushing all over the country, explaining here, trying to keep up flagging spirits there, and preaching the virtues of disciplined action wherever he goes. But his achievements in the field are rather slim, especially compared with the tremendous effort he has put into them. The enthusiasm he kindles whenever he appears vanishes again soon after he leaves, and does not stand the test of the setbacks and hard realities of daily life. The discipline he tries to encourage is evanescent, and how, indeed, could it be otherwise in the absence of genuine discussions or any degree of real understanding? Worse still, many of his own interventions and decisions, made on the spur of the moment, show a great deal of confusion and everything but alleviate the most pressing problems. A single person cannot be an infallible expert in all fields of technical endeavor, cannot be competent on questions of cattle breeding and irrigation, on the best method of cutting sugar cane and on the advantages of coffee plantations in the *Cordon de la Habana*, not to mention a thousand other spheres calling for special knowledge of the soil and of the political realities... This is the point: the building of socialism cannot be the business of one man or of a single group of men, however well-intentioned.[21]

Castro always centralized control of the coercive apparatus of the state in his person, and never shared power in any meaningful way; neither with his brother, Raúl, first vice-president and defense minister, nor with Guevara. He ruthlessly eliminated any potential competitors, like the military hero Arnaldo Ochoa, executed in 1989. This constant, yet selective use of repression and violence is another hallmark of a totalitarian regime. In the Cuban case, the contours of an island rendered it easy to control who entered and left; that nearly 15% of the population went into exile helped consolidate the regime and decisively weakened any opposition; with nearly 15% of the population in exile (the capitalistic middle class; also meaning that the kinds of opponents to the regime that others like Pol Pot murdered, are abroad); a *Stasi*-like network of informants organized around the ubiquitous *Comités de Defensa de la Revolución* (CDRs); with some (heroic) dissidents but no opposition; and with a siege mentality fueled domestically and internationally – under these circumstances, control is possible with merely selective repression. A totalitarian regime is also one that endeavors to indoctrinate and mobilize the masses. Castro's success in this realm was unprecedented. The PCC has a membership of 770,000 (out of a total population of about 11 million), which, combined with its youth organizations, meant that one in six Cubans between the ages of 15 and 65 were members. Membership in the CDRs is over seven million, representing fully 85% of the population over the age of 14.[22] In 2005, approaching 78 years of age, a somewhat physically debilitated Castro continued to preside over mass rallies, including one on May Day in 2004, where more than one million people participated in Havana.

The Castro regime enjoys all of the institutional preconditions for a political religion. While, as we argued above, there has been a substantial evolution of the regime over the decades, with different phases and emphases, there remains a hard core of basic tenets that remains constant. It is to a consideration of these that we now turn, in order to ascertain the degree to which Castroism is a political religion.

The *Führerprinzip*

There needs to be more than the necessary institutional concentration of powers in the leader for a political religion to exist. The leader must be in full political and, just as importantly, ideational control. Not only must he express this role, but his followers and the masses must accept his status as the sole interpreter of the revolution, as more than a mere mortal, as someone endowed with a special vision, charisma. In other words, the leader must enjoy a unique role as an historical agent. A well-developed *Führerprinzip* also entails arbitrariness. The inspired, infallible leader, who is always right, can change his mind and policy, even flippantly. As Oliver Stone recounts, Castro points out that he tends to be self-critical, but 'not so much about being wrong, but about how we could have done things better, how we should improve.'[23] These aspects of political religious leadership have always characterized Castro and Castroism – already from his first political activities in the 1940s and 1950s.[24] Castro takes great pains to emphasize the honesty that characterizes his revolution, and it would appear, in fact, that there is little that embarrasses him. The one exception may well be his days as a university student, and the accusation that he was a participant in the political violence of the 1940s. As he recounted in 1955:

> (Gangsterism) germinated within the Auténtico Party and had its roots in the resentment and hate that Batista sowed during his eleven years of abuse and injustice (1933–1944). Those who saw the murder of their comrades wanted to avenge them, and a regime that was unable to establish justice allowed such vengeance. The blame cannot be placed on the young men who, moved by natural yearning and the legend of a heroic era, longed for a revolution that had not taken

place and at the time could not be started. Many of those victims of deceit, who died as gangsters, could very well be heroes today.[25]

Fidel Castro himself did not emphasize his quasi-divine status, preferring almost always to speak of the Revolution and revolutionaries, of which he, of course is their representative. A political-religious leader also must be a charismatic orator, an adept manipulator of the crowd, with bombastic, apocalyptic, ambitious, yet self-righteous rhetoric. The leader does not directly emphasize his importance, but rather merely conveys the strong impression that only he is capable of the sacrifice and duty of saving his country. He is the privileged messenger of providence. Typical of such sentiments was Castro's speech at his trial after the Moncada attack in 1953, and later published as *History Will Absolve Me*: 'As for myself, if I had to give up my rights or my honor to remain alive, I would prefer to die a thousand deaths…Condemn me, it does not matter. History will absolve me!'[26] Or, as he declared in 1953:

> (The) Revolution comes from the soul of the Cuban people. Its vanguard is a youth that wants a new Cuba, *a youth that has freed itself from all the faults, the mean ambitions, and the sins of the past* (authors' emphasis). The Revolution comes from new men with new methods, prepared with the patience, courage and decision of those who dedicate their lives to an ideal.[27]

Perhaps more importantly, it is in the writings of Castro's acolytes and followers that we see the lauding of the leader and his personal qualities, the pledging of their lives and eternal devotion; literally worshiping the paternalistic, all-knowing leader.[28] One such example occurred shortly before the trial and execution of General Arnaldo Ochoa. Ochoa, the former commander of Cuban forces in Angola, had been slated to take over the Western army in Cuba, but, instead, was arrested and eventually executed with several others on charges of corruption and drug smuggling; though it may have had more to with Castro's elimination of a potential rival. Accordingly, Raul Castro literally screamed at the prisoner: 'Listen, Fidel is our father…Look, if Fidel Castro had not been born, neither you nor I would be sitting here because he produced what Che (Guevara) called the social cataclysm. A true revolution was produced from this social cataclysm.'[29]

Guevara presents an equally revealing portrait with some of his references about Fidel Castro. Guevara accompanied Castro from the very beginning of the guerilla war in the Sierra Maestra, later becoming an influential figure in the new regime before going on to fight in other Latin American countries (dying in Bolivia in October 1967). He was also an 'organic intellectual' of the Revolution, authoritatively fleshing out ideas and substantiating the logic of Castroism, before eventually becoming an iconic cult figure both in Cuba and abroad. Who has not seen the photographs by Alberto Korda, or the sentimental and positive portrayal in the film *The Motorcycle Diaries*? And who has failed to see the posters and ubiquitous t-shirts of Che and not imagined we were seeing a twentieth-century version of Jesus Christ?

Despite his own magnetic force and personality, Guevara may be considered an acolyte of Fidel Castro, constantly and comprehensively subordinating himself to the man he once described as 'telluric force.' Hagiographical statements by Guevara about Castro abound. In 1961, Guevara asserted,

> He is a man of such great personality that in whatever movement in which he participates he should be the leader, and this he has done during the course of his career…He has the characteristics of a great conductor, a quality which when added to his personal qualities of audacity, strength, valor and his extraordinary desire to always express the will of the people, have taken him to the place of honor and sacrifice that he today occupies…But he has other important qualities, as in his capacity to assimilate knowledge and experience, to understand the entirety of a given situation, without losing sight of the details, his immense faith in the future and the breadth of his vision to foresee events and anticipate the facts, always seeing farther and better than his comrades.[30]

Guevara's September 1965 'Farewell Letter' continues the adulatory pattern:

> My only mistake of any gravity was not to have trusted more in you from the first moments in the Sierra Maestra and to have understood quickly enough your qualities as conductor and revolutionary. I lived magnificent days and, at your side, felt the pride of belonging to our people in the luminous and sad days of the crisis in the Caribbean (1962). Few times did there shine more brightly a statesman than in those days. I am proud, too, of having followed you without vacillation, with having identified with your manner of thinking and with having seen and appreciated the dangers and the principles…In the new fields of battle, I shall carry the faith you have inculcated in

me, the revolutionary spirit of my people, the feeling of fulfilling the most sacred of duties: to fight against imperialism wherever it may be...Thank you for your teachings and your example. I shall try to be faithful through the last consequences of my actions.[31]

Hardly a relic from the 'heroic' beginnings of the regime, the *Führerprinzip* remained alive and well in Cuba, exemplified by the pervasive slogan: 'With Fidel everything; against Fidel nothing.' The official Cuban government website noted that from the ranks of the younger generations in the 1950s 'a movement of a new type was born and at its head was Fidel Castro.' He also continues to seduce influential foreigners, a cast that over time has included Jean-Paul Sartre, Ernest Hemingway, Gabriel García Marquez and, most recently, Oliver Stone from the realm of arts and entertainment. The list also includes many influential politicians, especially in Latin America, most recently exemplified by Hugo Chavez.

The 'New Man' and the moral regeneration of Cuba

The next constant in Castroism reflects the pretension to transform not just the culture and behavior of Cubans, but their entire human make-up. True to revolutionary form, Castro has expressed this in a paternalistic fashion:

> It is not a man of the jungle that *we want* (emphasis added) to develop, a man of the jungle cannot be of any benefit to society. It is not that self-centered, savage mentality that can in any sense benefit human society. The more human society fights against those self-centered, savage, and anti-social attitudes, the closer it will come to embodying a way of life that is ideal and good for all...And the old society fostered exactly those sentiments, exactly those attitudes. And if today there are still many who have those attitudes...unquestionably it is because of that heritage...*We want* (emphasis added) the coming generations to receive the heritage of a very different attitude toward life, to receive the heritage of an education and a formation that is totally devoid of the sentiments appropriate to a man of the jungle.[32]

Moreover:

> *We cannot encourage or even permit selfish attitudes among men* (emphasis added) if we don't want man to be guided by the instinct

of selfishness…by the wolf instinct, the beast instinct…The concept of Socialism and Communism, the concept of a higher society, implies a man devoid of any of those feelings, a man who has overcome such instincts at any cost, placing above everything his sense of solidarity and brotherhood among men…If we fail because we believe in man's ability, in his ability to improve, then we shall fail, but we shall never renounce our faith in mankind.[33]

Rhetoric aside, Castro did, in fact, articulate a coherent plan to implement this 'anthropological revolution.' The regime would target youth, and the educational and political systems would be the means. In the speeches of Che Guevara, we find characterizations of youth as 'malleable clay,' combined with the assertion that 'the new generations will come free from original sin.'[34] In an October 1962 speech to the Communist Youth, Guevara insisted: '(You) young Communists…(will be) creators of the perfect society, human beings destined to live in a new world where all the obsolete, all the old, all that represents the society whose foundations have just been destroyed will have definitively disappeared.'[35]

Obviously this emphasis on youth and vigor was not an invention of Castro. Revolutionary movements the world over from the Young Turks to the Nazis, have always fetishized youth with the associated imagery of novelty, idealism and vigor (as well as an impetuousness that does not abjure violence), and contrasted this with the gerontocratic and corrupt status quo. Moreover, Cuban political culture has long worshipped the image and role of youth (recall the *Ortodoxo* appropriation of the broom) to a much greater degree than many other political cultures (perhaps in response to the merely semi-sovereign status that the country had long faced). In reality, youth, epitomized by the especially active university student milieu (as in many developing countries a small, centralized and élitist group concentrated in the capital), played a massive role in the country's political life; they were, for example, central to the fall of Batista. Therefore, even though Castro was no innovator in this regard, his and his regime's total success in harnessing and maintaining the image of youthful vigor (reinforced continually, most recently with the appropriation of Elián González), is a large part of his success over time.

The models for the 'New Man' were none other than the *guerrillero* and the *revolucionario* – committed, youthful and willing to fight and die. 'The guerilla' declared Che, 'foreshadows the man of the future.'[36]

In an almost perfect description of the totalitarian emphasis on constant mobilization, he then notes:

> The Revolutionary must struggle every day so that this love for living humanity is transformed into concrete acts, into acts that serve as an example for mobilization...the revolutionary consumes himself in this uninterrupted activity that had no other end than death, unless the construction of the new society is accomplished on a world scale.[37]

Castro never abandoned his rhetoric about the 'New Man' and the 'new society,' effectively always putting himself on the 'progressive' side of humanity and the Enlightenment.[38] Such efforts continue today, even as he has positioned himself as a leader of all anti-globalization forces. He has the solution. As he told Oliver Stone: 'Either the present problems (of the world) must be solved, or humanity will not survive the twenty-first century. I am inclined to believe rationality will win out in the end.'

Of course, there was another, less metaphysical and far more coercive side to creating the 'New Man.' As Guevara wrote in almost Pavlovian style: '(The) mass must be submitted to stimuli and pressures of certain intensity...the dictatorship (is) exercised not only over the defeated class, but also, individually over the victorious class.' The objective is, of course, to 'liberat(e) man from his alienation.'[39] It was also Che Guevara who observed as early as 1960 that 'every revolution, like it or not, inevitably has its share of Stalinism.'[40]

Accompanying this 'humanistic' effort to create a new and perfect man is the violent cleansing of the degeneration and filth characterizing the pre-revolutionary *ancién regime*. These themes of struggle against enemies within, and enemies without, have been a constant in Castroism, as with all political religions. Hitler expressed similar sentiments when he described 'Jews as vermin,' as well as socialists, the mentally handicapped, Jehova's Witnesses and homosexuals; all of whom needed to be purged from the German body politic for the real regeneration of the German nation to be possible. Similarly, there are numerous examples of the moral and moralistic tone Castro adopts with his respect to his friends and enemies. One of the most exemplary is his statement at the July 1989 session of the Council of State that upheld the conviction and death sentence of Ochoa, which also showed Castro's constant placement of himself in the deeper stream of Cuban history:

> Ochoa's level of corruption...and his moral degeneration are...the most shameful page in our history...Treason is to sell your country, and they sold the country. Treason is to put the nation in jeopardy,

and they placed the nation in serious jeopardy. Treason is to undermine the nation's morals and the revolution's prestige. They have been doing things that undermine the Revolution's morals and prestige... (They) morally destroyed the Ministry of the Interior... I think about those who fell in order to build a decent country, and not those who fell today, but those who fell 120 years ago. I think about those who fell at that time in order to create a republic where justice and law would prevail – a decent republic where there would not be corruption, impunity, dishonesty, embezzlement. They fell for an honorable, respectable country. They fell in two wars of independence, and they have fallen throughout this century. They are the ones I think about... the many valuables comrades who fell. I also think about the loved ones who lost them. I think of those who have died carrying out... honorable internationalist missions. It is on behalf of them, that we do not have any other alternative but to do what we are doing. It is on behalf of the ideals and of the fatherland that they loved, that we feel obligated to be severe.[41]

The moral tone of Castroism is not of recent vintage. From the very outset, the rationale for his opposition to the Batista regime, and the support Castro came to receive, was in reaction to the deep corruption of successive Batista (1940–1944), Ramon Grau (1944–1948) and Carlos Prio (1948–1952) administrations, as well as the pervasive de-legitimation suffered by nearly the entire traditional political class. The outflow of *batistianos* and the middle class after 1959 may be seen as part of the Castro purge, but his desire to cleanse Cuba was far more ambitious. In living up to the goal of creating a 'New Man,' Castro banned the gambling industry, tried to eliminate prostitution in Havana and persecuted homosexuals for decades, all in an attempt to cleanse the Cuban body politic.

Symbology

All true political religions attempt to recreate a symbology that can integrate and mobilize the masses, legitimize the new regime and facilitate the world-changing ambitions of the leader. Castro has been comprehensive in these efforts, in ways both large and small. Like the Jacobins with their new calendar, his regime re-named and designated the years. The year 2004 was the 'year of the 45th anniversary of the revolution'; 2003 was the 'year of the glorious anniversaries of Martí and Moncada'; 2002 was the 'year of the heroic prisoners of imperialism';

and 2001 was the 'year of the victorious revolution and the new millennium.' Castro created his stage, usually the Plaza of the Revolution in Havana, where he held mass rallies, akin to parades on Red Square or the Nazi Party rallies at Nuremberg. Like the devotional objects of Catholicism, pictures of Fidel and Che may be found in many homes and most public buildings.

A political religion must also have its pantheon of heroes, to be worshiped and called upon to legitimate the present, and preferably a list that includes traditional and more recent heroes (so as to situate the political religion into the stream of national history and to give it the patina of age). Among the most important are José Martí and Antonio Maceo from the pre-independence struggle, and Che Guevara. The 'canonization' of Guevara began even before the news of his death had been confirmed. Guevara, Castro declared in October 1967, was:

> ...a master, an artist of revolutionary war...(T)he artist may die, especially when one is an artist of such a dangerous art as the revolutionary struggle, but what will in no way die is the art to which he consecrated his life, to which he consecrated his intelligence...his death will serve in the long run as a seed from which will come many men who have decided to emulate him...Let us say to Che and with him to all the heroes who were in combat and fell with him. *Hasta la victoria siempre*! *Patria o Muerte*.[42]

Indeed, Guevara became the canonized icon of the revolution *par excellence*. The circumstances of his demise corresponded to a glorious, revolutionary death: 'Naturally all of us who know Che know that there is no way of capturing him alive, unless he is unconscious, unless he is completely immobilised by some wounds.'[43] When Castro employed the memory of Che, as when he clamped down on peasant markets and other forms of non-state sanctioned private activity. He often used the anniversary of Che's birth or death to make major speeches. When the Pope visited Cuba in January 1998, a massive poster of Che adorned a building on the plaza where the pope was conducting a mass. Religion confronted political religion.

Castro often showed uncommon political acumen and masterful understanding of the dynamics of political religions. Consider the evocative use as revolutionary icon of Elián González. In late 1999, the six-year-old boy, his mother and 10 others tried to escape from Cuba to the United States. Bad weather capsized the boat and all died except for Elián, who was picked up by the United States' Coast Guard. A protracted dispute arose over who would get custody and where he would stay, pitting distant relatives in Miami against the boy's father in Cuba. Eventually, the American Supreme Court ruled against the relatives and ordered the return of Gonzales to Cuba. From the outset, Castro seized the tragic case as a political gold mine. The regime built a museum in his home town of Cardenas, and Castro delivered major speeches on the boy's birthday, 5 December or, as it was now called, the anniversary of the 'War of Ideas.' Elián became more than a symbol; he was the instrument that an aging revolutionary used to reach out to the younger generation, and thus to give new impetus to a tired regime. Again, Castro showed his grasp of the practical pay-offs of capturing youthfulness.

Violence, death, the nation

All political religions glorify death and the nation, and all venerate the dead. This is perhaps the least distinctive aspect of Castroism, given the long tradition of the glorification of violence in Cuban history. The national anthem itself ends with the stanza, 'to die for the fatherland is to live.' Castro was himself a product of an environment and political culture that glorified 'political action,' and one that wrote poems of nationalist immolation. What is different about him is that he took these attitudes more seriously, and has acted on these principles for more than 40 years. Castro ended every speech with the phrase 'fatherland or death.' For him, what matters is not death, but how one dies. This is exactly where the worship of the guerilla mentality fits in, a constant from the early days of the revolution to the present.

The rhetoric of the maximalist, radical man of action (a kind of extreme political *machismo*) has permeated Castro's thoughts and policies. At the time of the invasion of Grenada in October 1983, he ordered the Cuban military commander 'not to surrender under any circumstances,' and when the officer later did so, in the face of overwhelming American troop superiority, Castro publicly cashiered him. Commenting on the breakdown of the Soviet system in 1989, he stated:

> The duty of communists is to fight under any circumstance, no matter how adverse the situation may be. The Paris commoners knew how to fight and die defending their ideas. The banners of the revolution and socialism are not handed over without a fight. Only cowards

and demoralized people surrender. Communists and revolutionaries do not surrender...We have never aspired to be recipients of the custody of the glorious banners and the principles the revolutionary movement has defended throughout its heroic and beautiful history. However, destiny assigns us the role of one day being among the last defenders of socialism; in a world in which the Yankee empire was able to make a reality of Hitler's dreams of dominating the world, we would know how to defend this bastion until the last drop of blood...They died fighting for true peace and security for all peoples; they died for the ideas of Cespedes and Maximo Gomez; they died for the ideas of Marti and Maceo; they died for the ideas of Marx, Engels and Lenin; they died for the ideas and the example spread to the world by the October Revolution; they died for socialism; they died for internationalism; they died for the dignified and revolutionary fatherland that is today's Cuba. We will be able to follow their example. Eternal glory to them! Socialism or death! Fatherland or death! We will win![44]

In the political rhetoric of Castroism there is a poignant life through death formulation accompanied by the constant focus on struggle, a trope that all political religions and dictators have emphasized.

As is evident from the various quotes we have reproduced in this chapter, the nation, patriotism, the fatherland and a strident nationalism emerge as a constant, much more so than references to Marxism–Leninism. This intensely nationalistic focus is another hallmark of many political religions. As the official government website states:

In short, all the efforts of the counterrevolution and of the imperialism against Cuba had been useless, because they have ignored something vital in our history: the Cuban people's capacity to resist, its intelligence and the capabilities of the revolutionary leadership. Moreover, they have ignored the justness of the struggle of our people for its independence.[45]

Enemies and competitors

Enemies and competitors are the final themes that we examine in our consideration of Castroism as a political religion. All political religions have a well-developed category list and image of their enemies, for whom the most detail is reserved, and against whom all of the cleansing, martial, violent and most memorable rhetoric is directed. Castro compares with all other political religious figureheads in this respect. There have been two main enemies Castroism has engaged over the past four decades. The first category includes the *gusanos y parasitos*, who compose the anti-Castro opposition in Miami, and who are variously referred to as thugs, counter-revolutionaries, Nazis and gangsters. The other enemy, perhaps more significant because opposition to it has projected Castro and Cuba on the world stage, has been the United States. The hyperbolic intensity of his attacks on the United States is unabated. The official history of Cuba on the governmental website speaks of 'US aggressions and imperialism' and the 'stern, cruel and illegal blockade.' Before the revolution, Castro did not appear to be particularly anti-American, but after his seizure of power and the Bay of Pigs débacle it became his public signature. The earliest Castro anti-American reference came in a 1957 letter which was not released until more than ten years later. Writing to his colleague Melba Hernandez, Castro declared:

> When I saw the rockets (supplied by the United States to Batista), I swore to myself that the North Americans were going to pay dearly for what they are doing. When this war is over, a much bigger and wider war will commence for me: the war that I am going to wage against them. I am aware that this is my true destiny.[46]

The rhetoric only became more radical and more constant over the years, where it served as a mainstay of the regime's propaganda.

Castroism and Catholicism

We turn now to an examination of the relationship between the political religion that Castro constructed over the decades and conventional religion, in this instance the Catholic Church. The pretensions of a movement to replace traditional religion, and its demonstrable success in doing so, are crucial to the determination of whether Castroism achieved a demonstrable political religious status. Castroism and Catholicism have been direct competitors. Moreover, religious institutions and the Catholic Church, in particular, have played an important role both as proto-opposition under diverse dictatorial regimes and, more generally, as key players in numerous transitions to democracy. This was the case in Italy during the 1940s, in Spain during the 1970s, in Nicaragua, El Salvador and the Philippines in the early to mid-1980s and in Eastern Europe from the late 1970s to the late 1980s. In addition to this role as national political force, the Church has also been a transnational agent and force. During the era of John Paul II, the Vatican vigorously presented itself as the exponent of a *terza via* between a vanquished 'state socialism' and a triumphant neo-liberalism. Thus, as the post-Castro era approaches, an analysis of the influence of the Church is crucial to understand how the transition will play out.

Castroism and Catholicism had their most direct face-off in January 1998 when John Paul II visited Cuba. Before examining the dynamics and importance of this confrontation, however, a few words about the Cuban Catholic Church and its relationship to the Revolution are in order. The Papal visit had been under negotiation for nearly a decade, and the Pope knew that the Church he would find in Cuba was far different from the one he had led in Poland. The Cuban Church had been weakly institutionalized and had already had a reduced social base during the colonial period. Far from being a repository of nationalist values as was the case with Poland or even Spain, it had been under the leadership of Spaniards (more specifically, Galician clergy) who had opposed national independence. Historically, the Church had also enjoyed very little penetration in the rural areas, where syncretic African religions (what may be loosely termed *Santeria*) continued to flourish. As Margaret Crahan has noted, Cuba in the 1950s had the lowest proportion of nominal Catholics in Latin America (72.5%), the lowest percentage of practicing Catholics (5–8%) and the highest percentage of non-members (19%).[47] The Cuban Church had also placed far less emphasis on pastoral work, concentrating resources in private education for the well-to-do, mainly in Havana and Santiago. Things did not change for the better with the Revolution. As relations between the Castro regime and the Church soured between 1960 and 1961, 70% of the 723 priests active in 1960 had fled by 1963, as did 90% of the 2225 members of religious orders.[48] Castro directly expelled other clergy for counter-revolutionary activities. The more devout were also disproportionately the most likely to flee. For example, a 1969 survey of Havana parishes, found that 50% of their members had left.

In the first years of the Revolution, the Castro regime embarked on a radical strategy of eliminating religious and Catholic Church influence. It closed all religious schools, expelled religious orders and placed strict controls on the numbers of priests, nuns and other devotees who could live and work in the country. Moreover, Castro eliminated religious holidays, actively worked on the young to adopt militant atheism and, in the late 1960s and 1970s, shipped priests to work camps, deliberately placing them with other 'social outcasts' like homosexuals. Alongside these measures are the well-documented efforts to challenge the primacy of the family (extensive volunteer work by the young aimed to keep the population 'mobilised,' while also breaking family controls and providing ample opportunities for unsupervised sexual activity), to make divorce easy and even to encourage the practice of abortion.

In parallel fashion, the regime also tried to weaken the Catholic Church by extending the hand of tolerance to SANTERÍA as well as to many smaller Protestant organizations (though not the Jehovah's Witnesses). Though SANTERÍA had an extensive presence in Cuban society, especially among poor blacks and in rural areas, it was also disorganized and lacked any institutional foundation from which it could challenge the regime or its political religion. The Protestant sects, for their part, were patently a minority. By favoring them and SANTERÍA, the regime could draw on their support or sympathy and disclaim any anti-religious bias in its anti-Catholic measures, even as it sought to build its militantly atheist 'New Man.'

The other aspect of the regime's strategy toward Catholicism was to support and actively collaborate with the advocates of liberation theology. This is not the place for an extended discussion of this phenomenon, but it should be noted that perhaps the central objection the Vatican has had to liberation theology has been less doctrinal (there has been and continues to be, after all, a powerful anti-capitalist strain in Catholic doctrine), than organizational. The touchstone of the dispute was over discipline. Operating as a transnational political religion, in any case, Castroism and its revolutionary allies in Latin America forged close links with this radicalized clergy, and viewed them as important allies in the struggle to weaken the traditional Church and its support for conservative or centrist political parties. This alliance strategy also connected to Castroism as a political religion. The support from, and identification with, 'progressive' clergy and laity helped legitimize both the Revolution and its secular-political religion. Furthermore, the struggle for social justice could serve as the bridge between one religion and the other. The now-famous Frey Betto interview with Castro amply demonstrates the mutual sympathy between *la iglesia de los pobres* and Castroism. In this climate, even the high-ranking Latin American figure, Cardinal Archbishop of Sao Paolo, Paulo Evaristo Arens, could send a 1989 note to the '*queridísimo* Fidel,' stating that 'the Christian faith discovered in the conquests of the Revolution the signs of the Kingdom of God.'[49]

Over several decades, the Cuban Catholic Church lost much ground to the competing political religion of Castroism. To the (selective) repression employed by the regime and the hemorrhaging of personnel were joined an intellectual failure to balance the competing demands of social justice and human rights. Few dared to openly oppose a militantly atheistic regime, while others assiduously tried to accommodate the Church and its doctrine to the new and victorious political religion. The Cuban Church began to emerge from its near catatonic state in the late 1970s, with the self-critical review begun under the *Encuentro Nacional Eclesial Cubano*. Over the next decade, the Church embraced nationalism through the appropriation of the nineteenth-century Cuban, Father Félix Varela, and began to focus on ways to expand its pastoral presence. Though some of its members embraced liberation theology, others looked to new winds of change in the world (especially the disintegration of the Soviet bloc) to adopt a more assertive position, even coming to call for a national reconciliation and to voice support for dissidents. Reeling from the disintegration of the Soviet Union, the regime had loosened some of its reins on Cuban society, and it was eager to reach a *modus vivendi* with the Church. Negotiations for a possible Papal visit began in the early 1990s, around the time the regime eliminated the term 'atheist' from the Constitution, also removing the bar on individuals of religious faith joining the Communist party.

The January 1998 Papal visit provides us with an extraordinary opportunity to take a snapshot of how the two religions stood in relation to the other at the turn of the century. The visit represented opportunity and risk for both sides. For Castroism, the visit would bring international legitimacy. At the same time, this would be first time in the history of the Revolution that Castro would cede public space, not just to someone else, but to someone who had brought Communism down in Poland and contributed decisively to its demise in the rest of the Soviet bloc. By allowing the visit, Castro was, in effect, saying his brand of 'political religion' was sufficiently strong enough to withstand any public challenge. In fact, he alluded to this in his welcoming remarks, when he declared: '(This is) an educated people to whom you can speak with all the liberty you wish, and with the security that this people possesses talent, a high political culture, deep convictions, absolute confidence in its ideas and all the awareness and respect in the world to listen to you.'[50]

If this constituted bravado, it was backed up by political intuition and tactical shrewdness. Castro was well aware of the weakness of the

Church in Cuba, and just in case some spontaneous display of support for the Pope would get out of hand, the government instructed its supporters not to shun, but rather to attend the ceremonies. If Castro understood the weakness of the Church, he may also have intuited the weakness of his own position; the reason why he needed the Pope publicly to recognize him and his religion. Castroism was dominant and hegemonic in Cuba, but it was also, in ideological and 'religious' terms, on its last legs. The regime had survived the collapse of the Soviet bloc, and it might even survive without Fidel. But it would not be the same. Castroism without Castro would not be a 'political religion.'

The Papal visit fits within a broader strategic scheme whose objective it was to make some political and economic concessions, while maintaining control. The Pope, for his part, had no desire or intention to challenge the hegemony of Castroism in Cuba, at least in and for the present. Yes, he wanted to lay the foundation for change, to plant the 'seed,' as it were. But John Paul II understood the weakness of the Church in contemporary Cuba. In what was a small but meaningful decision, Vatican aides and Cuban clergy distributed thousands of pamphlets with the Lord's Prayer and the Hail Mary to those who attended the masses of John Paul II. The Pope was also not interested in encouraging any potential de-stabilization of the situation. If John Paul II was an adversary of 'state socialism,' he was also an opponent of 'neo-liberalism' and consumer culture; or at least his emphases changed after 1989. His constant calls for national reconciliation and peaceful change reflected the desire for a managed transition, one within which the risk of violence would be minimized, the Church could recover lost ground, and 'neo-liberalism' could be kept from gaining too strong a foothold in Cuba.

An examination of the speeches the two men directed both at each other and to the national and international audiences that heard them allows us to gain a good sense of their respective positions. Thus, while Castro was critical of Church history (citing the decimation of indigenous people, the crimes of the Inquisition and pointing to how, as a boy, he had challenged the reactionary views of his Jesuit teachers), he also took great pains to show the affinities between the two 'religions,' freely employing religious terminology. Here are some direct and deeply revelatory quotes:

Like those Christians atrociously slandered in order to justify the crimes, we, similarly slandered, would prefer death one thousand times before renouncing our convictions. Just like the Church, the Revolution also has many martyrs.

We think like you on many important contemporary world issues and that is a source of great satisfaction to us…Our opinions differ, but we pay respectful homage to the deep conviction with which you defend your ideas.

Respect for believers and non-believers is a basic principle that we Cuban revolutionaries have inculcated in our compatriots. Those principles have been defined and are guaranteed by our Constitution and our laws. If difficulties have arisen at any time this has never been the fault of the Revolution.

There is no country better equipped to understand your felicitous idea, such as we understand it and so similar to what we preach, that the equitable distribution of wealth and solidarity among human beings and peoples must be globalised.

Cuba (is) like a new and one thousand times smaller David.

(When hearing the) calumnies against my country and my people, contrived by those who love no other God than money, I always recall the Christians of Ancient Rome, so atrociously calumnied.

A world without oppression or exploitation; without humiliation or contempt; without injustice or inequalities, where they could live with full moral and material dignity, in genuine liberty. That would be the most just world! Your ideas on evangelisation and ecumenism would not be in contradiction with such a world.[51]

Perhaps the most widely quoted phrase uttered by John Paul II during his visit to Cuba was his call for 'Cuba to open itself to the world and the world to open itself to Cuba.'[52] The Pope developed this idea in two directions. The first was critical of the American embargo of Cuba, while the second attacked the *ensimismamiento* (self-absorption) propounded by the regime. If criticism of the embargo was probably a pre-condition for the visit and undoubtedly pleased the regime, the notion of *apertura* challenged the very cosmology of Castroism as a political religion. As we noted above, this was the first time in nearly 40 years that anyone other than Castro had occupied public space, and presented a world-view critical of and different from the one espoused by his regime.

Though the Pope was unfailingly polite, he was also very direct in his comments and challenged castroism on a variety of grounds. One was methodological:

> The ideological and economic systems that followed one after the other over the past two centuries have frequently encouraged confrontation as a method…This profoundly conditioned their conception of man and their relations with others. Some of those systems have tried to reduce religion to the merely individual sphere, removing it from any influence or social relevance. In this sense, it is worth recalling that a modern State cannot make of atheism or of religion one of its political *ordenamientos*. The State (should be) far from any fanaticism or extreme secularism; it should promote a serene social climate and an adequate legislation that permits each person and each religion to live freely its faith, to express it in the spheres of public life, and to count with the sufficient space and means to bring their spiritual, moral, and civic riches to national life.[53]

Another related to the compatibility of social justice with freedom:

> For many political and economic systems prevailing today, the greatest challenge continues to be to be able to combine freedom with social justice, freedom with solidarity, so as not to relegate any one of these to an inferior plane. In this connection, the social doctrine of the Church aspires to illuminate and conciliate relations between the inalienable rights of every man and social needs, so that the person will attain his most profound aspirations and integral fulfillment.[54]

The Pope also spoke about fear, directing his message not only to individual Cubans but also to those who ran the state:

> Do not be afraid, open your families and schools to the values of the Gospel of Jesus Christ, which are never a danger for any social project.[55]

And he, then, took the occasion to distinguish between Catholicism and other religions, especially *santería*:

> There are some reductionist conceptions that try to place the Catholic Church at the same level as certain cultural manifestations of religiosity…(such as) the syncretic cults…(T)hough worthy of respect, these cannot be considered a religion proper but rather as a combination of traditions and beliefs.[56]

But it was with respect to the historic roots of Cuban nationalism, and the future of Cuban youth that John Paul II most clearly threw down the gauntlet. The Revolution, as conceived, articulated and defended by Fidel Castro, had been about the teaching of a certain Cuban history, with the ordering of events and martyrs and the claim that Fidel Castro was the possible heir and interpreter of the aspirations of the Cuban people. Speech after speech of Castro's is filled with references to José Martí and Antonio Maceo, all designed to demonstrate that the skein of history in which they played a role unfolded naturally into the leading role of Fidel. The Revolution had also been about youth and the future, about the claim that Castro and his colleagues were embarked on the noble task to create the 'New Man.' Excesses, it might be inferred, could be forgiven, given the greatness of the task.

John Paul II firmly and directly, if politely, challenged Castro on both issues. He sketched an alternative history of Cuba, one that placed a priest, not a man of war or someone who had died in battle, as the father of the both the nation and democracy. Félix Varela, John Paul II, noted:

> ...was the first one who spoke about independence in these lands. He also spoke of democracy, considering it the political project that was most harmonious with human nature and he also emphasised the demands that derive from it. Among these demands he underlined two...(The first was) that there be persons educated for liberty and for responsibility, with an ethical project forged within them...(The second) was...to dynamize the Rule of Law, essential guarantee of any human life together that can be considered democratic.[57]

The Pope then went on to link the ideas and values of Varela and Marti, thereby providing another reading of Cuban history:

> The torch that was lit by Father Varela was to illuminate the history of the Cuban people, and it was picked up shortly after his death by that relevant personality who is José Martí, writer, teacher in the broadest sense of the word, profoundly in favor of democracy and independence, patriot, loyal friend even with those who did not share his program. He was, above all, a man of light, coherent with his ethical values and animated by spirituality with eminently Christian roots. He is considered a continuator of the thought of Father Varela, whom he called 'the Cuban saint'.[58]

The Pope also quoted amply from Martí. Rather than the belligerent and anti-imperialist Martí of the Castro speeches, this Martí spoke about religion and love, and Pope used him to touch on the moral crisis in Cuba:

> José Martí's doctrine of love among all men has profoundly evangelical roots, thereby overcoming the false conflict between faith in God and love and service to the Motherland. Thus wrote this forefather 'Pure, disinterested, persecuted, martyred, poetic, and simple, the religion of the Nazarene seduced all honest men...Every people needs to be religious. This is so not only essentially, but it needs be so for its utility. An irreligious people will die, because nothing feeds virtue within'.[59]

The other important salvo that came from the Pope was directed at the theme of youth and the future. John Paul II again challenged the revolutionary cosmology, and pointed to the crisis of values in Cuba, and even took the closed-door policy of the regime to task for having undermined the values of youth:

> Many young people...(are) victims of cultural schemes devoid of (any) sense or of ideological schemes that do not offer high and precise moral values. This moral relativism generates egotism, division, marginalization, discrimination, fear and lack of confidence in others...(T)he shadow of the frightening present-day crisis of values that shakes the world also threatens the youth of this luminous Isle. A pernicious crisis of identity extends itself that leads youth to live without sentiments, with neither direction nor project for the future, asphyxiated by the immediate. Relativism, religious indifference and the absence of a moral dimension emerge, and there exists the temptation to surrender to the idols of consumer society, fascinated by their fleeting brightness. It goes so far that anything that comes from outside the country appears to dazzle.[60]

And as for the future, John Paul II declared:

> I am confident that in the future the Cubans will attain a civilization of justice and solidarity, of liberty and truth, a civilization of love and peace that, as Padre Varela said, 'would be the foundation of the great edifice of our happiness.'[61]

Conclusions

In this chapter, we have reviewed Castroism in terms of how well its ideas conform to the concept of a political religion. In a general sense, the term fits Castroism well. In the mid-20th century, Cuba experienced the kind of extraordinary crisis and a failure of its national mission that created fertile soil for charismatic leaders like Castro. Castro maintained his iron grip by virtue of a repressive political regime, and has explicitly tried to create a political religion. Many, if not most of the elements are there: the *Führerprinzip*, a pantheon of revolutionary icons, intense nationalism, efforts to rejuvenate and 'cleanse' the country, clearly defined enemies and so on. Castro has also explicitly competed with other legitimizing doctrines, most dramatically with the Catholic Church.

But as for Castro, his regime and Castroism as a political religion, what does the future hold for Cuba? Though the regime has gone through different phases, it always remained totalitarian in its ambition, if not, especially after the demise of the Soviet Union and because of the deep economic crisis this provoked, in terms of its capacity. There was at least one identifiable juncture (in the mid-1980s) when Fidel Castro directly, and personally, truncated what appeared to be a transition to a Soviet-style post-totalitarianism. Since the 1990s, important changes have begun to take place within Cuban society. The regime may still be capable of effective mobilization (see the Elián González phenomenon and even the recent 2004 May Day meeting attended by over a million people) and repression (witness the lengthy sentences meted out to 75 human rights activists and dissidents arrested in March 2003), but it is also evident that many of the 'emergency' measures the regime has implemented over the past 15 years in order to ensure its survival have diminished its quotient of power and led to the reintroduction of capitalism, albeit under the aegis of military managers.

The dollarization of the economy and the toleration of a certain space for private enterprise have visibly weakened the state's grip on society and led to significant social stratification. Today in Cuba there are two kinds of citizens, those with access to dollars and those without. The purchasing capacity of the former is dramatically greater than that of the latter. Along with stratification has come the resurgence of the 'old' social evils, not least of prostitution, which the regime had once upon a time claimed to have eliminated and erased. Today 15-year-old *jineteras* represent what is the 'pull' side of a phenomenon whose 'push' side is the 'sexual tourism' packages sold in Europe and elsewhere. There is also a change in leadership underway. In July 2006, an intestinal hemorrhage forced him to give up day-to-day running of the government, and his brother assumed the formal reins of power in February 2008. Alongside this succession, there is also a regime transition underway in Cuba. The new regime will be different in many ways from the previous one presided over by Fidel Castro, not the least in the likely decline in the intensity of 'political religion.'

Notes

1. These terms constantly appear in Castro's speeches. See 'Speech on the Second Anniversary of the Cuban Revolution,' 3 January 1961. Castro Speech Database:http://www1.lanic.utexas.edu/la/cb/cuba/castro.html.
2. Robert E. Quirk, *Fidel Castro* (New York: Norton, 1993), pp. 58–59.
3. He never directly commanded more than 3000 men, and this was only toward the end of the guerilla campaign.
4. Eusebio Mujal-León and Joshua Busby, 'Much Ado about Something? Regime Change in Cuba,' *Problems of Post-Communism* (2001).
5. Emilio Gentile, 'The Sacralisation of Politics: Definitions, Interpretations and Reflections on the Question of Secular Religion and Totalitarianism,' *Totalitarian Movements and Political Religions*, vol. 1, no. 1 (Summer 2000); Michael Burleigh, 'National Socialism as a Political Religion,' *Totalitarian Movements and Political Religions*, vol. 1, no. 2 (Autumn 2000); George Mosse, *The Fascist Revolution: Toward a General Theory of Fascism.* (New York: H. Fertig, 1999).
6. 'Ideology: Political Aspects,' *Encyclopedia of the Social Sciences* (2001).
7. 'Religion: Definition and Explanation,' *Encyclopedia of the Social Sciences* 2001.
8. Dwight B. Billings and Shaunna L. Scott, 'Religion and Political Legitimation,' *Annual Review of Sociology*, vol. 20 (1994), p. 174.
9. Gentile (2000), p. 22.
10. Eric Voegelin, *Die politische Religionen.* (Stockholm: Bermann-Fischer Verlag, 1939).
11. Sacvan Bercovitch, *The Rites of Assent: Transformations in the Symbolic Construction of America.* (New York: Routledge, 1993).
12. Gentile (2000), p. 24.
13. Ibid., p. 25.
14. Burleigh, p. 5.
15. Ibid., pp. 6–7.
16. Ibid., p. 20.
17. Juan Linz and Alfred Stepan, *Problems of Democratic Transition and Consolidation: Southern Europe, South America, and Post-Communist Europe.* (Baltimore: Johns Hopkins University Press, 1996).
18. One large problem with the political religion literature is that it developed from and for certain unequivocal cases such as Nazi Germany and Soviet Russia.

19. Movement from the left to right on the ideology axis denotes greater world-changing ambition, revolutionary fervor or radicalism. Movement away from the traditional religious pole represents more differentiation and competition on the part of the purveyors of the political religion.
20. See Quirk (1993).
21. K. S. Karol, *Guerrillas in Power; the Course of the Cuban Revolution*, translated from the French by Arnold Pomerans (New York: Hill & Wang, 1970), p. 459.
22. Economist Intelligence Unit, 'Country Profile 2003: Cuba' (London: Economist Intelligence Unit, 2003), pp. 9–10.
23. This quote was in conjunction with Stone's 2003 film *Comandante*. See http://www.kamera.co.uk/reviews_extra/commandante.php.
24. See Quirk (1993).
25. Ibid., p. 199.
26. Ibid., pp. 58–59.
27. Rolando Bonachea and Nelson Valdés, *Cuba in Revolution*. (Garden City: Anchor Books, 1972), p. 157.
28. Note again the parallel dynamics to the Nazis, especially as exemplified in Leni Riefenstahl's propaganda film *Triumph of the Will* – where Hitler never mentions himself, yet is literally worshipped by the masses. Hitler also always conveyed an impression that he only reluctantly took on the leadership of Germany – because there was no one else – always self-identifying as a simple artist. Similarly, before the fall of Batista, Castro never expressed a desire to lead the nation – rather stating that he wanted to return to the 'simple' life.
29. Julia Preston, 'The Ochoa Affair' in *The New York Review of Books*, p. 10.
30. Rolando Bonachea and Nelson Valdés, eds, *Che: Selected Works of Ernesto Guevara*. (Cambridge: MIT Press, 1969), p. 204.
31. Ibid., p. 35.
32. Speech on 13 March 1968 in Fagen, Richard R. *The Transformation of Political Culture in Cuba*. (Stanford: Stanford University Press, 1969), p. 13.
33. Speech on 28 September 1964 in ibid.
34. Bonachea and Valdés (1969), p. 195.
35. Ibid., p. 99.
36. Ibid., p. 184.
37. Ibid., p. 197.
38. His seductive appeal to leftists in many countries is perhaps not that much of a surprise. This is also one of the fundamental empirical differences between totalitarian political religions of the left versus of the right, and why Nazism is often considered worse than Communism.
39. Bonachea and Valdés (1969), p. 197.
40. Karol (1970), p. 47.
41. 'Castro Addresses State Council on Drug Trial,' 12 July 1989. Castro Speech Database, http://www1.lanic.utexas.edu/la/cb/cuba/castro.html.
42. Fidel Castro, *Che en la memoria de Fidel Castro* ed. David Deutschmann. (Melbourne and New York: Ocean Press, 1998), p. 85.
43. Ibid., p. 60.
44. 'Castro Honors Internationalists, Views Socialism,' 7 December 1989. Castro Speech Database, http://www1.lanic.utexas.edu/la/cb/cuba/castro.html.
45. http://www.cubagob.cu/ingles.

46. Bonachea and Valdés (1972), p. 179.
47. Margaret Crahan, 'Religion and Revolution: Cuba and Nicaragua.' Working Paper. (Washington, DC: The Wilson Center, Latin American Program, 1987), p. 4.
48. Ibid., pp. 258–59.
49. *Granma*, 6 January 1989.
50. Jorge María Bergoglio, ed. *Diálogos entre Juan Pablo II y Fidel Castro*. (Buenos Aires: Fundación Centro de Estudios Polítícos y Administrativos, 1998), p. 139.
51. Ibid., pp. 135–41.
52. Ibid., p. 66.
53. Homily in the Plaza de la Revolución, 25 January 1998 in ibid., pp. 110–11.
54. Ibid., p. 113.
55. Santa Clara, 22 January 1998 in ibid., p. 70.
56. Meeting with Cuban Bishops, 25 January 1998 in ibid., p. 118.
57. University of Havana, 23 January 1998 in ibid., pp. 89–90.
58. Ibid., p. 91.
59. Ibid., p. 114.
60. Ibid., p. 75.
61. Speech at the University of Havana, 23 January, 1998 in ibid., p. 92.

Part II
The Sacralization of Politics

5
Fascism as the Expression of a Spiritual Revolution in Italy

Robert Mallett

Emilio Gentile provides one of the most succinct contemporary 'definitions' of civil and political religion. Political religions, he stresses, 'reflect the manner in which political activity is perceived, experienced and represented through beliefs, myths, rituals and symbols that refer to a sacralised secular entity inspiring faith, devotion and togetherness among believers.'[1] If one accepts this conception of political religion in the twentieth century which, as Stanley Payne has argued, 'aimed at buttressing social solidarity and morality',[2] then the most critical element of it is the notion of 'sacredness'. It is the sacralised core of such political religious movements that provides them with their religious dimension. Therefore, case study analysis of specific regime models that are generally conceived of as working political religions – National Socialism in Germany, Stalinism in the Soviet Union, fascism in Italy to name but a few – must consider precisely what, if anything, gave this critical core element its 'sacredness'.

Any analysis of Italian fascism in political religious terms must begin with the premise that, as with Adolf Hitler and Josef Stalin, Benito Mussolini, the *Duce*, constituted the focus of attention for an entire political movement. The intrinsic system of beliefs and myths that, again in the words of Professor Gentile, 'define the meaning and ultimate purpose of social existence',[3] and set out the movement's perception of both good and evil, emanate from this central figure around whom the movement constructs a personality cult. Therefore, it is these beliefs and myths that make up the spiritual dimension of the entire movement. And it is the true 'spiritual' nature of Mussolini and *fascismo* that this chapter aims to assess and evaluate.

Mussolini and the fascist spiritual revolution

First and foremost Mussolini expressed fascist spirituality in patriotic, indeed highly nationalistic terms. During a key speech in Naples at the time of the March on Rome in October 1922, Mussolini, soon to be Prime Minister of an unstable and unruly Italy, declared that his young movement had already created its spiritual myth:

> The myth is a faith, a passion. It is not necessary for it to be a reality. It is a reality in the sense that it is a stimulus, is hope, is faith, is courage. Our myth is the nation, our myth is the greatness of the nation! And to this myth, this greatness, which we want to translate into a total reality, we subordinate everything else.[4]

But Mussolini's was a particular brand of nationalism invoked as a spiritual entity. Behind the carefully phrased rhetoric aimed at monopolising patriotic sentiments and winning over the largely Roman Catholic Italian people, lay notions of force, militarism and imperial expansion. During the same speech at Naples Mussolini also declared that 'A nation is great when it translates into reality the force of its spirit', a spirit which, for him and fascist ideologues like the futurist artist, Filippo Marinetti, was essentially martial. For Marinetti, the spirit of fascism was the only antidote 'to combat the parliamentary, bureaucratic, academic, and pessimist spirit' that prevailed in early 1920s Italy and beyond. In that sense he saw in Mussolini *Dux* the embodiment of those revolutionary spiritual virtues that would sweep away decades of decay: 'heroism, love of danger, violence rehabilitated as a decisive argument, the glorification of war, sole hygiene of the world'.[5]

Not surprisingly, such strident fascist spirituality clashed dramatically with the predominant religious orthodoxy of the time in Italy, the Roman Catholic Church. During the early phase of fascist rule – the period of coalition government between 1922 and 1926 – ardent fascists emphasised the need for all Italians to show total adherence to the new sacred credo of the *Duce*. As one commentator noted in 1925, 'who joins us either becomes ours in body and soul, in spirit and in the flesh, or they will be utterly eradicated'.[6] Plainly, those who did not demonstrate their full allegiance to the new fascist faith risked being regarded as enemies of the 'national religion'. The sacred inner core of the Church of Rome held the promise of spiritual salvation that would supposedly follow as a reward for individual pursuit of Catholic doctrine. Mussolini promised the Italian people a different form of spiritual rebirth, that was temporal rather than eternal. But this collective rebirth demanded and required widespread popular acceptance of the fascist faith. As Mussolini stressed to the Quinquennial Assembly of the regime in March 1929:

> Let us remember that Italy's energies are totally absorbed in the effort to create new institutions, a new type of civilisation which reconciles traditions with modernity, progress with faith, the machine with the spirit.

Only in this way, he argued using carefully chosen religious terminology, would Rome become the 'capital of a resurrected Italy'.[7] In that sense the *Duce*'s evocation of national greatness as the supreme spiritual value of the fascist faith proved a powerful, and binding axiom which, notwithstanding the frequently precarious nature of fascist–Catholic relations, proved difficult for any one individual to contest. If one believes Mussolinian disciples such as National Fascist Party Secretary Giovanni Giurati, this spiritual exaltation to fulfil the *Duce*'s prophecies of imminent national greatness appeared to work. By the end of 1930, 328,000 young men from all over Italy 'wearing their blackshirts and carrying the colours of Rome, affirmed in their oath the imperial will of fascism'.[8]

Two years later, in 1932, Mussolini's *Doctrine of Fascism* set out the new spiritual credo in unmistakably clear terms. Fascism was, he wrote, 'a religious concept' within which the individual was elevated to 'membership of a spiritual society'. But this society had one fundamental precept. 'The fascist state was', Mussolini continued, 'the will to power and empire. (...) In terms of fascist doctrine empire is not merely a territorial, military or mercantile expression, but, rather, it is spiritual and moral. We may think of building an empire, that is a nation which directly or indirectly guides other nations.'[9]

Expressing fascism's spiritual message: art and the media

Just as conventional religious forms like Roman Catholicism made use of artistic symbolism and the printed word to spread the central spiritual ethos of the faith, so, too, did fascism. Simonetta Falasca-Zamponi's 1997 study of Mussolini's aesthetic politics places considerable emphasis on the centrality of violence, war and ultra nationalism within the *Duce*'s use of metaphoric imagery.[10] But while her analysis is ostensibly useful in interpreting the meaning of fascist symbolism, it falls short of explaining this as, to all intents and purposes, religious symbolism with an explicit core meaning.

Let us look at a few examples. While scholars of fascism will be aware that there did not exist a truly fascist art form, there were artists who expressed the idea of a spiritual revolution in their work. This was certainly encouraged by leading figures of the regime like Giuseppe Bottai who urged all artists to promote the fascist faith. A central theme of the works that followed, for the large part propaganda art created by Modernists, was the idea of fascism as a spiritual revolution founded on nationalism and the idea of encouraging the evolution of the new, fascist man – *l'uomo fascista*. A good early example of this approach is in the poster by Paolo Garretto dating from 1932, and entitled simply *camicia nera* (Black shirt). The figure clearly represents the new fascist acolyte, rigid in form, with fist clenched around a pointed dagger. Most notable in this example is the emblem worn on the left side of the shirt, directly over the heart, which represents the Italian nation now being at one with the fascist lictor, the symbol of the revolution. Garretto suggests that the revolution in Italy had been an internal and spiritual one, carried forward by the legions of militarised fascists. The fact that the figure is headless illustrates the importance of the collective rather than the individual in achieving the goals of the revolution itself.

Xanti Schawinsky's poster commemorating the 1934 plebiscite illustrates the idea of both nationalism as being the true essence of the fascist spiritual renewal of Italy, and subsequently the 'divine' status of Mussolini, *Dux*. Simply entitled 'Si', the poster shows the allegedly overwhelming support for Mussolini as much as fascism right across Italy. In the poster Mussolini looks down at his people who, in effect, make up his physical body. The use of symbolism here is very powerful; Schawinsky evokes the idea of the collective being part of one spiritual community represented by the figure of the *Duce*. The work indicates that the collective have united for the good of Italy, fascism and the supreme leader, Mussolini, who, God-like, presides over and protects the nation.

Fascism's conception of nationalism was by no means a purely domestic idiom. The cover of an elementary school textbook by Carlo Vittorio Testi dating from 1938 shows that this new national revolution was exportable. In this instance the Italian nation is represented by the winged angel that has carried the lictor all the way to East Africa and holds it firmly in place over Ethiopia, conquered brutally by the regime between 1935 and 1936. Again the suggestion here is that the nation is one with the lictor, the symbol of the spiritual revolution. It is also

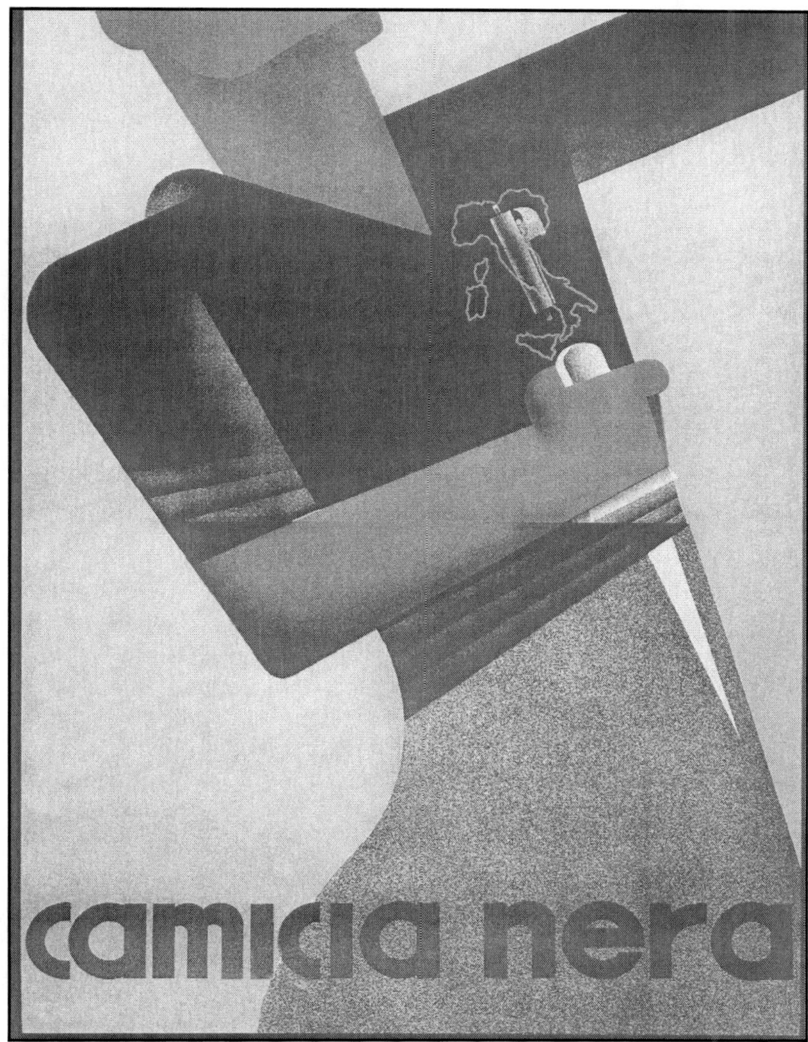

Figure 5.1 Camicia nera.

worth noting that the angelic figure faces defiantly towards the west, signifying the strength of Italy in facing down Anglo-French opposition to its war against Ethiopia.

That war and martial virtues were key central features of fascism's spiritual beliefs was never far from the surface. This anonymously painted

Figure 5.2 Mussolini's head and word 'SI'.

Figure 5.3   Image of Angel with the words 'L'Impero D'Italia' in red in original.

poster promoting the *Aero Club d'Italia* shows the three lictors, in this case representing the patriotic and dynamic spirits of the airmen Nobile, De Pinedo and de Bernardi, bearing the eternal flame of nationalism. Around the flame and the lictors, soaring high in the sky, are a flock of eagles signifying the next generation of aviators. The poster was entitled 'Young airmen inspired by the epic achievements of Nobile, De Pinedo and Bernardi must become fighters of the skies', and amply illustrates the spiritual virtues that the regime wished to instil among the young. A rather more direct approach to disseminating this theme is found in Guilio Cisari's 1935 poster that remembers the twentieth anniversary of Italy's entry into the Great War. The sword represents the fascist military, and its colour – black – is indicative both of fascism and of mourning for the war dead. The lictor is coloured red, the colour of blood, and symbolises the fascist martyrs who had died for the revolution. Both sword and lictor are enveloped in the national flag. One final example of strength being at the centre of the fascist idea can be found in Fortunato Depero's work *Acciaio* ('Steel') produced in 1934. Here Mussolini, as God, presides over legions of the faithful, the new fascist men. The idea being conveyed here is of Mussolini's powerful spirit leading a strong and renewed nation forward to a glittering future. Mussolini watches over his community while they protect and adore him.

Even a cursory examination of the newspaper media during the fascist era provides the researcher with further, quite striking, examples of fascism's promulgation of its sacred message to the world. In April 1921, at a point when the fascist movement was on the brink of becoming a mass party – the National Fascist Party (the *Partito Nazionale Fascista*) – the pro-fascist weekly, *I Vespri*, carried a front-page photograph of Mussolini under the headline '21 April – Rome's birthday and fascism's holy day'. The article presents the *Duce* of fascism in quasi divine terms. The author describes how Mussolini battles within his own troubled mind to create 'a national consciousness in Italy'. His very soul was, the author continued, 'the projection of the national spirit in its entirety'. In that sense Mussolini could, allegedly, foresee Italian greatness to come; he 'anticipated it, or better still, could divine it'. The article concluded with a prophesy of Mussolini's future role in national life:

And it was Mussolini who brought together these new, young energies in the form of the *fascio*; and fascism was and is the new life blood of Italy.[11]

Figure 5.4　Eagles hovering over flame.

Figure 5.5 Black sword shrouded by long Italian flag.

Two and a half years later, with Mussolini, as prime minister, heading a coalition government, the Italian pro-fascist press proudly proclaimed the 'consecration of the fascist revolution'. In a front-page article published on 27 October 1923 Mussolini's own paper, *Il Popolo d'Italia*, roundly

Figure 5.6   Mussolini's steel head and Roman number XI.

denounced the pre-fascist governments of Italy that had operated within the 'parliamentary abortion'. Now, Enrico Corradini stormed, a new political force governed Italy, a force that was 'warlike, aggressive, combatative and liberating'. This force, made up of ex-combatants from the Great War and led by Mussolini, was, Corradini concluded, more than a mere political party; it was a religious movement, with the 'cult

Figure 5.7   Il Popolo d'Italia.

of the unknown soldier' as its symbol. Fascism's objectives were simple: the cult of the unknown soldier represented the army of fascists, a 'new warlike militia', determined to reconquer Italy and ensure 'the greatness of the nation'. Fascism, he added, had been born in order that the sacrifice of the Italian soldier had not been in vain.[12]

Figure 5.8   Fiamma Nera.

As the *Ventennio* progressed, and the Mussolini-led coalition government transformed itself into a dictatorial regime over the period between 1924 and 1925, such ideas became enshrined by the press. On 26 March 1924, just a few months before the disgraceful murder

Figure 5.9   La Tribuna

of socialist deputy Giacomo Matteotti, the fascist daily, *Fiamma Nera*, declared that fascism could, now, begin the transformation of the Italian nation. 'We possess', Giuseppe Pizzarini announced:

> certain precise truths and realities that are at the very forefront of our spirit, and these are: the State which must be strong; the government which must defend the Nation from the attacks of destructive elements; class collaboration; respect for religion; the exaltation of all national energies. This doctrine is a doctrine of life, and not a doctrine of death.

What was important was that the future generations firmly adopted this doctrine as its law, as the very basis of fascist civilisation.[13]

The emphasis on youth carrying forward the core ideals of the revolution proved perennially popular. By 1927, with the regime now firmly established in Italy, newspapers like *La Tribuna* wrote of the new generations of fascists emerging from the youth groups – the *ballila* and the *avanguardisti* – organised by Renato Ricci and who, watched over by the great figure of Mussolini, were absorbed into the national revolution. It was vital, the paper noted, that the young understood the true greatness of the *Duce*, the epic nature of fascism's revolution and fully understood 'the doctrine of our faith'. Italy could now boast of 100,000 young fascists 'spiritually ready to join the Militia'.[14]

Certainly this ever expanding revolutionary idea had to find its expression in the domestic sphere. PNF secretary Augusto Turati, writing in the journal *Gerarchia* that same year – 1927 – noted that fascism's spiritual renewal of Italy was aimed at securing 'racial well being, the education of the young, the preparation of the militia' and 'the organisation and disciplining of the productive, cultural and sporting forces' of the nation.[15] But this great renewal, according to Maurizio Maraviglia of *La Tribuna*, found its ultimate expression in fascism's imperial policy. Under fascism's guidance Italian colonial policy was no longer a marginal or residual element of state activity. Now, the imperial idiom had become transformed into a 'real and vigorous national activity' that was a product of genuine impulses from within the 'Italian race'. This 'desire for expansion' held by the Italian people had become, in the hands of fascism, an objective of the state. Unlike pre-1922 Italian governments fascism did not discuss the merits or failings of the colonial idea, but, rather, considered 'colonial

Figure 5.10 *Il Popolo d'Italia.*

VENTUNO APRILE

Il Natale di Roma, giorno sacro al Fascismo

Compiono oggi 2675 anni dal nascimento sublime. Rossa di sangue fraterno in quell'alba prodigiosa del 21 aprile balzò Roma dal solco quadrato. Balzò e di là dove sorgeva il tempio di Saturno, dio seminatore, lanciò strade ai quattro venti per tutto l'orbe, le lanciò via per verdi campi e per deserti infuocati, tra selve profonde e sopra eterni ponti. E lungo le strade infinite corsero le bronzee legioni dei giovinetti in fiore erti sui cavalli scalpitanti. Il mondo fremeva e rimbombava sotto il piede di Roma terribile, che però subito mutava il volto sorridendo alle genti placate, e con quella mano stessa, che feriva e prostrava i nemici superbi, dettava le leggi e le arti della pace a rendere dolce e serena la vita.

Così Roma crebbe e signoreggiò. Vennero poi i barbari, invasero l'Urbe, la guastarono col ferro e col fuoco, ne pestarono le ceneri sacre. Ma a che prò? Roma eterna non muore. Se tutto ci fu tolto, se tutto perdemmo, armi e sostanze ed are e patria, non ci potè essere tolta la memoria, di ciò che fummo, rimasta scintilla capace di riaccendere presto o tardi il fuoco della grandezza antica. Spirito eterno, eterna forza è Roma, che sempre rinasce e sempre più alto celebra il suo trionfo.

Lo ha celebrato ieri portando nella grande guerra, con il peso decisivo delle sue armi, la forza invincibile dell'idea latina di diritto e di giustizia.

Lo celebra oggi in questa maravigliosa primavera rinnovatrice di tutti i più alti valori storici ed ideali della nostra stirpe contro il folle materialismo di dottrine e fazioni intese ad abbassare la gloria e il genio di Roma di fronte a straniere divinità false e bugiarde. Il trionfo di Roma è oggi in questo poderoso soffio di forza morale che si è suscitato e si è affermato per opera della forte e sana gioventù d'Italia e che nessuno può illudersi ormai più di soffocare e di spegnere.

Chi può negarlo? Siamo in un periodo aurorale. Ce lo dice in questi giorni tutto questo fermento di gioie e di lotte per vendicare, per glorificare tutto ciò che di più alto, di più puro, di più augusto è racchiuso nel santo nome d'Italia.

Il morfinoso torpore, iniettato nel paese da anime oblique, è vinto: le forze migliori di nostra gente sono oggi bendeste e veglianti.

Siamo al rosseggiare d'un'alba.

E perciò ci rinasce nell'anima l'antico rito di nostra gente in questo giorno sacro all'aurora della Patria: siamo spinti a consultare gli auspici.

A quale divinità ci volgiamo? A una sola, a colei che fu sempre presente: a Roma, forza eterna.

I fascisti d'Italia, che sotto l'egida dei tuoi simboli e del tuo spirito, o Dea madre, scesero alla nuova battaglia, ti salutano e gridano ai quattro maggiori punti del cielo il tuo nome immortale.

BENITO MUSSOLINI
FONDATORE E DUCE DEI FASCI

«... Ecco Mussolini con i suoi grandi vecchi di fede; ecco Mussolini con la sua parola tagliente. Mussolini si discute, si odia, si combatte, si ammira fino alla devozione, non si nega. Esiste. È un uomo che segna una linea del profilo italiano che combacia in gran parte col buon profilo italiano. Ha la razza buona, anzitutto di Romagna: ha il sangue buono, quello del popolo; ha il carattere buono, cioè la forza, la drittura, l'energia inflessibile...» e più avanti: «... Dicono che cede e sarà. Ma l'Italia soffre della tendenza ai compromessi a quella forma di cooperazione che cementava di scetticismo incontrarsi in un comune interesse, finisce per far credere che l'unica possibile collaborazione sia da noi la camorra».

Mussolini riassume nella tragedia della sua coscienza la faticosa formazione della coscienza nazionale in Italia, la sua anima è la proiezione dell'anima nazionale in tutta la sua interezza di aspetti e di trasformazioni, proiezione però che spesso riflette il futuro immediato verso il presente. Egli è quindi un anticipatore, o meglio un divinatore inconsapevole nei moti dell'anima sua.

Mussolini si sentì e fu socialista quando l'Italia, governata da politicanti attaccati al passato e pensierosi del solo presente e scente soltanto del presente proprio o della propria classe, aveva bisogno di una spinta verso l'avvenire e verso un ideale di giustizia sociale.

Mussolini lasciò per una ribellione divinatrice dell'anima il partito quando questo, esaurita la sua parte di forza evolutiva dell'animo nazionale, si accingeva con la speculazione politica del neutralismo, a scuotere il potere e a diventare da dinamico a statico, mentre l'evoluzione era ancora lontana dall'essere compiuta.

E si colse quindi alla formidabile ascesa... va il posto, cioè alla guerra doppiamente dinamica per noi, sia per se stessa, sia come prima prova e primo sforzo dell'Italia ripetuta da una aristocrazia di audaci.

Quando questa fu terminata, e la vita andava ripigliando il ritmo normale, Mussolini si sentì solo, scancero fra gli italiani che la guerra aveva solo stancati, una volgarità ai giovani ch'essa aveva capito nel suo vortice con l'anima ancora vergine e romantica, si giovanissimi che l'avevano capita e fatta con tutta l'anima loro (anche se non fatta materialmente) vide riflettere nei loro occhi il suo stesso disgusto del presente, e la sua stessa passione.

Un nuovo anima si era andato lentamente formando lungo la guerra, una quasi esclusivamente nei giovani ch'essa aveva trovato fanciulli e aveva loro dato vomini nuovi.

« Essi comprendevano che stavano ereditando tutto il patrimonio spirituale di una grande epoca; patrimonio che è al disopra di qualunque bene territoriale acquistato, di qualunque interesse di parte, di ogni arrivismo elettorale e di tutte le vecchie ideologie dei partiti italiani; patrimonio che dava loro i fremiti e gli spasimi della nuova creazione (P. F.)».

E Mussolini strinse in un fascio queste gioventù e nuove energie; e il fascismo fu ed è la nuova vita d'Italia.

Quando questa nuova vita sarà, il fascismo si confonderà nel tutto. I partiti continueranno allora a combattersi e ad integrarsi a vicenda segnando così il corso della storia; una nuova coscienza li guiderà, nuove forme e nuove maniere di sentire palpiteranno in essi, un'altra sarà la base di istituzioni, rapporti sociali da cui partirà la loro azione concreta.

Il fascismo ora si accinge ad attuare questa nuova base, rispondendo alla propria coscienza che è la nuova coscienza; e chiudendo così un periodo della storia d'Italia.

Mussolini vigila affinché sia ben chiuso.

Figure 5.11   I Vespri.

expansion as a struggle for living space'. It was this principal idea, stressed Maraviglia, that lay at the core of fascism's spiritual meaning: 'Colonisation means to conquer, to combat, to organise, to create and this is what fascism represents primordially and completely'.[16]

Of course, this entire nationalist revolutionary idiom found its greatest expression in 1940 when the fascist regime declared war on its Mediterranean antagonists, Great Britain and France. By this stage the fascist spiritual revolution had its own counterpart in that of the National Socialist regime that had run Germany since 1933. By August 1940 regime ideologues, writing in papers like *Il Popolo d'Italia*, spoke of the 'triumph of the fascist revolutions', and stressed that this great national renewal would not be limited to simply Italy or Germany, but Europe as a whole. Indeed, noted Mario Appelius, it was striking to behold how the entire European continent (80% of it) now accepted the impending Axis victory, the Axis revolution with great enthusiasm. This revolution, Appelius declared, would transform continental Europe. The 'Axis peace' would not be imposed by the jack boot, but it would be a peace based on the good sense of the divine genius (Hitler/Mussolini). In the glorious future to come the European economies would be united into one, harmonious whole; there would be no more class conflict; demagoguery would disappear from public life; money would be a means, and not an end; work and ingenuity would be the true driving forces in the new, Axis society. Hitler and Mussolini, with their great 'spiritual alliance', had brought all of this about. Their combined genius would truly unlock all of Europe's economic, political and spiritual potential. The article was entitled 'A swift glance at the Europe of tomorrow'.[17]

Conclusions

This chapter has attempted to define the nature of the spiritual revolution set in motion in Italy by Mussolini and fascist ideology. In that sense it has attempted to demonstrate how fascism functioned as a political religion, making use of official rhetoric, propaganda art and the newspaper media to illustrate its core sacred expression. What it has not had the time to do is illustrate the expression of fascist spirituality in other forms – architecture, newsreel, sport, literature, poetry, mass rituals and so on. Equally, what this paper has not been able to discuss is the extent to which this was accepted, or otherwise, by the Italian citizen living in Mussolini's times. All of these might be highly productive areas for future research into fascism and political religion.

George Mosse noted that the 'fascist aesthetic reflected fascism itself which (...) meant, at one and the same time, to uphold tradition and symbolize a revolutionary dynamic which was supposed to lead to a better future.' Fascism was, he added, 'based upon nationalism as a civic religion, and its aesthetic articulated this faith just as it did for the older established religions.'[18] At the very heart of this faith lay ideas of ultra nationalism, militarism and, ultimately, expansion overseas. This notion underpinned fascist ideology, and found its expression in many forms. As the final verse of the Hymn of the Young Fascists declares:

> Whatever will be, will be
> The Great Mother of Heroes will summon us
> For the Duce, the Fatherland, for the King!
> It is up to us! We will deliver
> Glory and Empire overseas!

Notes

1. E. Gentile, *Le religioni della politica*, Bari: Laterza, 2001, p. 206.
2. S. Payne, *The Problem of Political Religion*, unpublished essay, p. 1.
3. Gentile, *Religioni*, p. 206.
4. R. Griffin, 'Fascism's Myth: The Nation', Oxford: Oxford University Press, 1995, pp. 43–44.
5. Ibid., 'A Futurist Portrait of the New Prime Minister of Italy', pp. 45–46.
6. E. Gentile, *Il culto del Littorio*, Bari: Editori Laterza, 1998, p. 110.
7. Griffin, 'The Achievements of the Fascist Revolution', pp. 62–5.
8. Ibid., 'The Role of Youth Under Fascism', pp. 67–68.
9. B. Mussolini, *The Doctrine of Fascism*, Edizioni Larius, 1932, p. 2.
10. S. Falasca-Zamponi, *Fascist Spectacle: The Aesthetics of Power in Fascist Italy*, Berkley: University of California Press, 1997.
11. *I Vespri*, 21 April 1921.
12. *Il Popolo d'Italia*, 27 October 1923.
13. *Fiamma Nera*, 26 March 1924.
14. *La Tribuna*, 16 March 1927.
15. A. Turati, 'La rivoluzione in marcia', *Gerarchia*, October 1927.
16. *La Tribuna*, 19 March 1927.
17. *Il Popolo d'Italia*, 12 August 1940.
18. G. L. Mosse, 'Fascist Aesthetics and Society', in *The Fascist Revolution*, New York: Howard Fertig, 1999, p. 52.

6
What Insights Do We Gain from Interpreting National Socialism as a Political Religion?

Klaus Vondung

Over the last ten years, the concept of political religion has gained recognition as an instrument to capture certain characteristics of the totalitarian regimes of the twentieth century. Nonetheless, it is still under dispute. There is skepticism about the adequacy of the term, in particular with respect to the application of the term 'religion' to political and ideological phenomena. And there are historians and political scientists who doubt that the concept has any analytical value. In Germany, and with respect to National Socialism, these skeptics can be found, in particular, among the so-called 'structuralists' or 'functionalists', historians like Hans Mommsen or Martin Broszat, who attach greater importance to political structures and the mechanisms of power, than to individual persons or to ideological motivations and intentions.[1]

Before I start out to test the potentials of the concept of political religion with respect to National Socialism, a few general considerations are necessary, mainly in order to exclude one or the other possible meaning of political religion, or at least to clarify certain problems we encounter when interpreting National Socialism as a political religion. I must emphasise that these general considerations are undertaken in view of National Socialism and the historical situation of Germany. They do not pretend to be applicable to other political movements and regimes for which the concept of political religion has been used.

Stanley Payne opens his article on political religion with the statement: 'The usefulness of the concept of political religion (PR) in the modern world depends first of all on the definition of the term "religion"'.[2] This is certainly true. It is also true that we have no difficulties with interpreting National Socialism as a political religion if we employ Emile Durkheim's sociological definition of religion as, 'the organization of rites and rituals formed around a belief-system aimed at buttressing social solidarity and morality'.[3] We run into problems, however, if we consider the second definition to which Payne refers, namely the definition given by Rodney Stark, that 'religion consists of explanations based on supernatural assumptions and including statements about the nature of the supernatural and about ultimate meaning'.[4] Here we encounter a problem with the definition itself as well as a problem with its application to National Socialism. Leaving aside the discussion about Asian religions, there is still an uncertainty about the meaning of 'the supernatural'. If the supernatural is understood as transcendent, being fundamentally different and separate from the secular world, this definition would exclude all religions of cosmological societies as well as other ones, that are similar in structure and, at any rate, different from 'revelatory religions' like Judaism and Christianity. This point might be of relevance if one interprets National Socialism as a political religion. And we encounter a second problem with this definition. The common understanding is that if one speaks of 'religion' with respect to National Socialism, one does so in terms of a 'secular religion', which means that within the world-view of National Socialism, no matter how much certain features may resemble religious patterns, there is no belief in a transcendent divinity of genuine National Socialist character. But is this really true? The German political scientist Claus Bärsch, for instance, claims that both Hitler himself and other leading National Socialists like Alfred Rosenberg did believe in a transcendent power, and he maintains that such a belief is a condition for correctly employing the term political religion. Thus, in his view Marxism–Leninism is not a political religion because of its materialistic ideology.[5] I will return to this point in the course of my analysis.

A second consideration: apart from scholarly definitions of religion and their respective consequences for an epistemologically sound concept of political religion, we have to take into account the understanding of religion on the phenomenal level. This means that in Germany, in the first half of the twentieth century, the understanding of what a religion is was determined by Christianity. Despite a continued process of secularisation, Christianity was still the socially dominant paradigm for a religion. Next to Christianity, Judaism was present in consciousness to a certain degree, because of the existence of Jewish communities and also because of the Jewish heritage in Christianity itself. Finally, there was some knowledge about the pre-Christian Germanic religion, taken from sagas and other written sources as well as from archaeological excavations and some customs seemingly of Germanic origin. Although there were circles close to National Socialism who wanted to revitalise a 'Nordic' religion, or tried to turn the Christian belief into an Aryan confession by cleansing it from Jewish influences, these tendencies did not play a decisive role during the Third *Reich* and do not represent the core of what we may call the political religion of National Socialism. In *Mein Kampf* and on other occasions, Hitler warded off the 'backward-freaks' (*die Rückwärtse*) of the *völkisch* groups and in private conversations mocked Himmler's Germanic fancies.[6]

Again, at the time of National Socialism, Christianity was the major paradigm for the common understanding of what a religion meant in Europe, and this paradigm also influenced the original coinage of the concept of political religion as a kind of religion that was fundamentally different from, and hostile towards, Christianity. That it was also anti-Jewish, goes without saying. Nonetheless, the concept included the term religion. In consequence, National Socialism, being called a political religion, could appear, in the view of some critics, as a variant of the Christian religion, although a perverted one. Therefore these critics suggested as alternative terms either 'substitute religion' (*Ersatzreligion*) or 'substitute for religion' (*Religionsersatz*).[7] The former term would still designate a kind of religion, meant to replace the Christian one, the latter something different from religion, an ideology that only assumes the function of a religion. Both terms were obviously coined in order to express the derivative and mainly instrumental character of the National Socialist 'religion'. Whether this devaluation is adequate or, perhaps, whether the National Socialist political religion is in a way genuine and has an existential religious core, remains to be answered.

Talking about additional concepts and terms for possible connections between politics and religion, we can exclude theocracy and caesaropapism as means to describe the National Socialist case. Stanley Payne and Juan Linz have made this clear.[8] Among the reasons why these terms do not apply to the National Socialist combination of politics and religious elements, the main one is that in Western and Central Europe, in Byzantium and Russia, theocracy as well as caesaropapism were always connected with the Christian religion.

The situation is somewhat different if we talk about the politicisation of religion. Juan Linz has rightly stated that, 'the politicization of religion in the service of nationalism or nationalism in the service of religion is a central theme in nineteenth and twentieth century history and leads to phenomena that sometimes border on political religion'.[9] The same is true for the reverse development, the sacralisation of politics.[10] In Germany, we can observe, apart from the sacralisation of the nation and the *Reich*, in particular the sacralisation of the *Volk* and *Volksgeist*. Both developments, the politisation of religion and the sacralisation of politics, can be seen as prerequisites for the fully fledged and also institutionalised form of political religion that we find in Nazi Germany.

After these preliminary considerations, I will ask now whether there was an existential core to the National Socialist political religion, and what the concept of 'apocalypse' – again a concept of 'religious' origin – can contribute to the interpretation of National Socialism. I will leave out the area of organisation and cult, because it is the least controversial.[11] In this area, on a phenomenal and functional level, we do not need to go beyond Durkheim's definition of religion.

It is Eric Voegelin's particular merit that, in his book of 1938, he pointed out that National Socialism was not to be interpreted as a political religion simply because Nazis appropriated Christian linguistic symbols and ritual forms of the Christian church. The key reason why Voegelin understood National Socialism as a genuine religious phenomenon was that it had an existential core of a religious character, which means that at its root lay religious experiences that led to the manifestation of a new faith. In Voegelin's words:

> Wherever a reality discloses itself in the religious experience as sacred, it becomes the most real, a *realissimum*. This basic transformation from the natural to the divine results in a sacral and value-oriented recrystallization of reality around that aspect that has been recognized as being divine. Worlds of symbols, linguistic signs and concepts arrange themselves around the sacred center; they firm up as systems, become filled with the spirit of religious agitation and are fanatically defended as the 'right' order of being.[12]

Voegelin did not use the term 'sacralisation', but this is exactly what he described.

With respect to the *realissimum*, however, Voegelin made a basic distinction between 'trans-worldly religions' (*überweltliche Religionen*) such as Judaism and Christianity, and 'inner-worldly religions' (*innerweltliche Religionen*) 'that find the divine in the subcontents of the world'.[13] Given this distinction, it was possible to classify the religious elements manifest in National Socialism as being of the type of inner-worldly religions. The 'subcontents of the world', that the movement had elevated to the level of a *realissimum*, was the national community as a unit of common blood. Voegelin characterised the National Socialist national community as a 'particular ecclesia' (in contrast to the 'universal ecclesia' proclaimed in Christianity), and as a 'completely closed inner-worldly ecclesia' in which the community itself stood in place of God, 'as the source of legitimation of the collective person'.[14] Among the symbols used by National Socialism to represent the 'sacral substance' of the collective person or national community, Voegelin identified – alongside other terms drawn from the vocabulary of German Romanticism – that of the 'national spirit' or the 'spirit of the people' (*Volksgeist*). This spirit functioned as a *realissimum* lasting throughout the ages and becoming 'historical reality in individuals as members of their nation and in the works of such individuals'. The 'people in its plurality' becomes a national community 'through the political organization'. The organiser is the *Führer*; 'the spirit of the people becomes reality in him and the will of the people is formed in him'. As the spirit of the people is an inner-worldly sacral substance, namely one that is tied to the blood, 'the *Führer* becomes the speaker of the spirit of the people and the representative of the people because of his racial unity with the people'.[15]

I have outlined Voegelin's interpretation in some detail in order to illustrate how it incorporated a fundamental, anthropologically based definition of the term 'political religion'. For this understanding it is irrelevant that National Socialism did not have an elaborated and coherent ideology. What was important was the existential core and its unfolding into a particular set of articles of faith. Nonetheless, despite the appeal and plausibility of Voegelin's interpretation, it leaves some questions open, especially the question of whether the National Socialist political religion really was so radically inner-worldly, and had no concept of transcendence. Following this question, I must first comment on Voegelin's emphasis of the 'spirit of the people' (*Volksgeist*) as the sacral substance of the national community. In my judgement, it played a much less important role for most Nazis than Voegelin assumed. Obviously, for Hitler and other Nazis blood was the sacral substance and the centre of the National Socialist creed. This fact seems to confirm that the National Socialist political religion was indeed totally secular or inner-worldly. However, it is telling that Voegelin emphasised the 'spirit of the people', this symbol of Romantic origin that only some Nazi intellectuals used. He emphasised this symbol, I assume, because he sensed that in the National Socialist political religion the blood was charged with a spiritual quality. Indeed, this was the case.

This can be shown in Alfred Rosenberg's work even better than in *Mein Kampf* or in Hitler's speeches, because Rosenberg was more outspoken with respect to the 'nature' of the blood. Rosenberg had the reputation of being something approximating the 'chief ideologist' of the Nazi Party; he was editor-in-chief of the *Völkischer Beobachter* since 1921, in 1934 Hitler appointed him *Beauftragter des Führers für die Überwachung der gesamten geistigen und weltanschaulichen Schulung und Erziehung der NSDAP*. Although this pretentious title was not equalled by Rosenberg's position within the power structure of the Third Reich, and although there were ideological as well as political differences between Rosenberg and Hitler, he nonetheless provided with his book *Der Mythus des 20. Jahrhunderts*, published 1930, an authoritative ideological foundation of National Socialist race politics. The book was considered to be an official party publication; up to 1945 more than a million copies were printed.

Rosenberg's theory of race has nothing to do with the biological or anthropological doctrines of race and genetics of the twenties. Prominent theoreticians of race like Fritz Lenz and Walter Scheidt are not mentioned in *Der Mythus des 20. Jahrhunderts*. Hans Friedrich Karl Günther who, with his book *Rassenkunde des deutschen Volkes* of 1922 and many other publications, exercised a great influence on the National Socialist doctrine of race, is put aside in a footnote as 'not very important for the essential problem'.[16] Rosenberg's notions of race and blood primarily have a spiritual or cultural meaning. In his view, world history is determined by the fundamental difference between the 'Nordic' race and the anti-race of Judaism, and he discusses these differences as being rooted in cultural and ultimately religious differences. Consequently, he understands blood not as a biological substance, but calls it a 'myth',[17] that is, a spiritual entity, and he believes that it constitutes a 'soul of the race' (*Rassenseele*), – again a spiritual entity. 'Soul means race seen from inside, and, on the other hand, race is the exterior of the soul'.[18] Thus, when Rosenberg proclaims a 'religion of blood' (*Religion des Blutes*)[19] he certainly does not mean the veneration of biological matter.

Hitler did not use the term religion in connection with his world-view, or with the notions of 'race' and 'blood' in particular. However, the attitude of *Glaube* (belief, faith, sometimes even with the meaning 'creed') played a very important role in his thought and vocabulary. Hitler was convinced that without belief in the National Socialist world-view nothing could be achieved; he concluded that the general world-view must result in a definite 'political belief' (*politischer Glaube*).[20] Within this *Glaube*, in this case to be translated as 'creed', blood did assume a spiritual, if not holy, quality even in Hitler's thought, as the following declaration reveals, pronounced in a speech shortly before he seized power? 'Social rank passes away, classes change, human destinies are transformed, something remains and must remain with us: the people as such as the substance of flesh and blood'.[21] We can certainly rule out the possibility that Hitler had a sophisticated understanding of the theological or philosophical term 'substance'. However, the sense of the sentence quoted makes it clear that he did understand the meaning of 'substance' as something fundamental and primary, even as something absolute and divine, and that it was this which he sought to express.

But what about God? In *Mein Kampf* Hitler frequently speaks about God, the 'Almighty' and the 'Creator of the universe', and he expresses his conviction that he is acting in accordance with 'Divine Providence' and 'in line with the Almighty Creator'.[22] We can exclude that Hitler is speaking about the God of Christianity. Rosenberg contrasted his conception of God with Jahwe, who, in his view, is alien to men and hinders their self-realisation, whereas the Nordic man finds God in his own soul and realises himself by discovering the equivalence of his soul with God (*die Gottgleichheit der menschlichen Seele*).[23]

One cannot dismiss these statements as mere words or even propaganda. Must we therefore attribute to the National Socialist political religion the belief in a transcendent being, that manifests and realises itself in the soul of the Nordic man, equated with his blood? Let me tackle this question from a different angle. National Socialism claimed to dominate and control not only the political and social sphere, but all facets of life and, above all – and therefore we call it a political religion – it claimed to provide a meaning for personal existence, as well as for existence in society and history. In this respect the main competitor of National Socialism was Christianity. And one could not compete with the Christian religion by presenting a primitive, pantheistic or materialistic world-view.[24] Moreover, the authors of the National Socialist political religion were brought up as Christians and hence knew the paradigm only too well. Although they were no longer believing Christians, they longed, one may assume, on the emotional level for a meaning of existence that would transcend their individual lives. In the National Socialist political religion there is what one could call an 'aspiration to transcendence', a phenomenon that is typical for the age of secularisation and can be found in various forms. The Nobel Prize winner Heinrich Böll once ridiculed the non-Christian longing for a transcendent meaning as the belief in 'that higher being that we venerate' (*jenes höhere Wesen, das wir verehren*).[25]

I think that one has to agree with Voegelin that the political religion of National Socialism was, after all, an inner-worldly religion, despite its aspirations to transcendence. The concept of transcendence was void of spiritual meaning concerning the relationship between God and human beings, world and society. Ultimately, it boiled down to a hypostasis of the blood as a subcontent of the secular world.

The definition of National Socialism as a political religion given above – namely that National Socialism claimed to dominate and control not only the political and social sphere, but all facets of life and, above all, that it claimed to provide a meaning for personal existence as well as for existence in society and history – could also apply to the notion of 'totalitarianism'. The central characteristic of a totalitarian regime like the Third Reich is not so much the formal organisation and control of society that never can be absolutely 'total', but the endeavours to transform society, even the world, and to create a 'new man'. As Hannah Arendt put it: 'What totalitarian ideologies therefore aim at is not the transformation of the outside world or the revolutionising transmutation of society, but the transformation of human nature itself'.[26]

This aim has again been characterised in religious terms, for instance by Sigmund Neumann, as 'messianic',[27] or by Carl J. Friedrich as 'chiliastic'.[28] I prefer to use the term 'apocalyptic' for what is under discussion here. I understand the apocalyptic world-view of Hitler and other Nazis as the most poignant manifestation of the National Socialist political religion and, above all, as the only plausible explanation for the holocaust – if indeed an explanation in the sense of exposing motives and policy is possible at all. Time constraints do not permit us to show in any detail the structural parallels and symbolic equivalences of the National Socialist apocalypse with the religious apocalyptic tradition,[29] therefore I will confine myself to the most prominent characteristics.

In *Mein Kampf* and in many of his speeches, Hitler developed an apocalyptic image of the world, in which he himself undoubtedly believed. He viewed world history as being determined by the struggle between two universal forces, whose irreconcilability he chiefly expressed in the dualistic symbolism of 'light-darkness'. Subsequently, he believed the decisive battle to be close at hand, which would bring victory over the 'deadly enemy of all light'.[30] The 'power of evil' manifested itself for him in the Jews, the 'evil enemy of mankind',[31] onto whom he transferred the responsibility for all material deficits of the world, as well as other imaginary dangers and threats. Hitler viewed the well-being of the entire world as being dependent on Germany's victory in the final apocalyptic struggle:

> If our nation and our state becomes the victim of these bloodthirsty and avaricious Jewish tyrants of nations, the whole world will sink

into the tentacles of this polyp; if Germany liberates itself from its clutches, this danger greatest for all nations will have been eliminated for the entire world.[32]

Other leading Nazis presented the same apocalyptic world-view. Goebbels noted in his diary: 'The Jew is indeed the Antichrist of world history'.[33] Alfred Rosenberg also ascribed the role of the universal 'evil enemy' to 'World Jewry'; he assumed a 'worldwide conspiracy' between Jewish capitalism and Jewish bolshevism against the 'Nordic race of light'. Rosenberg fomented a fear of universal destruction by producing a terrifying vision of 'Jewish world revolution', and he prophesied an apocalyptic struggle, a 'decisive world war' (*ein entscheidender Weltkampf*).[34] The same view was propagated by less known Nazis, by literature and film.

My understanding of this apocalyptic world-view as the most poignant manifestation of the National Socialist political religion, and as an explanation of the holocaust marks the extreme point of disagreement between supporters and opponents of the concept of political religion. We do not have Hitler's direct order, let alone a written order, for the large-scale murder of the Jews, with the exception perhaps of one document concerning the deportation of the French Jews.[35] It is even more difficult to prove a linkage between Hitler's apocalyptic world-view, and the beliefs of Eichmann and other organisers of the Holocaust down to the perpetrators in the concentration camps. We will not get further than making the case plausible. But plausible it is, in my opinion, even to a high degree. The articles of faith of the National Socialist political religion were pronounced by Hitler himself and by other leading Nazis, visualised and enacted in numerous celebrations, and promulgated by 'believing intellectuals' of all sorts, from university professors to journalists and school teachers. Even if the 'believing intellectuals' were not necessarily identical with the perpetrators, even if the perpetrators were not themselves confident believers, the Nazi view of the world in its appearance as a political religion permeated the whole society, created a 'climate of opinion' and provided the guidelines for behaviour and action, and even for moral standards. And if one of the articles of faith said that the Jews were the 'evil enemy of mankind', and that the survival and well-being of all good people depended on the destruction of that 'power of evil', the implementation of this view was logical. Even for those who were not confident believers (and lacked other moral standards), this article provided at least a formal justification for their doings. In my opinion this explanation of the Holocaust is more plausible than Hans Mommsen's theorem of 'cumulative radicalization'.[36] There is no doubt, of course, that from the first measures of discrimination and persecution of Jews in 1933 up to the *Endlösung* there was a process of radicalisation, and that external factors played a critical role in the course this radicalisation took. But this process cannot explain its result, it cannot explain the decisive step from general anti-Semitism, even persecution, to organised mass-murder. I think one has to agree with Christopher Browning's view that, additional factors notwithstanding, the dynamics of radicalisation cannot be explained without Hitler's anti-Semitism and his determination to solve the 'Jewish question'.[37] That this 'solution' finally amounted to genocide becomes plausible as the perverse logic of the National Socialist political religion with its apocalyptic world-view.

Notes

1. See, for instance, Hans Mommsen, 'Nationalsozialismus als politische Religion', Hans Maier and Michael Schäfer (eds), *Totalitarismus und Politische Religionen: Konzepte des Diktaturvergleichs* 2 (Paderborn: Schöningh, 1997), pp. 173–81.

2. Stanley G. Payne, 'On the Heuristic Value of the Concept of Political Religion and its Application', *Totalitarian Movements and Political Religions*, 6:2 (September 2005), p. 163.

3. Ibid., referring to Durkheim's seminal study of 1912, *Les formes élémentaires de la vie religieuse*.

4. Rodney Stark, *For the Glory of God: How Monotheism Led to Reformation, Science, Witch-Hunts and the End of Slavery* (Princeton: Princeton University Press, 2003), pp. 4–5; cf. Payne (note 2).

5. Claus-Ekkehard Bärsch, *Die politische Religion des Nationalsozialismus: Die religiöse Dimension der NS-Ideologie in den Schriften von Dietrich Eckart, Joseph Goebbels, Alfred Rosenberg und Adolf Hitler* (Munich: Fink, 1998); id., 'The Religious Dimension in the Works of Dietrich Eckart, Joseph Goebbels, Alfred Rosenberg and Adolf Hitler', Glenn Hughes, Stephen A. McKnight and Geoffrey L. Price (eds), *Politics, Order and History: Essays on the Work of Eric Voegelin* (Sheffield: Sheffield Academic Press, 2001), pp. 104–24; id., 'Der Topos der Politischen Religion aus der Perspektive der Religionspolitologie', Michael Ley, Heinrich Neisser and Gilbert Weiss (eds), *Politische Religion? Politik, Religion und Anthropologie im Werk von Eric Voegelin* (Munich: Fink, 2003), pp. 176–97, esp. pp. 191, 196.

6. Adolf Hitler, *Mein Kampf*, 349th–351st edn (Munich: Eher, 1938), p. 396; id., Speech at Nuremberg, 5 November 1934, quoted from *Reichtagung in Nürnberg 1934* (Berlin, 1934).

7. Hans Buchheim, 'Despotie, Ersatzreligion, Religionsersatz', Hans Maier (ed.), *Totalitarismus und Politische Religionen: Konzepte des Diktaturvergleichs* (Paderborn: Schöningh, 1996), pp. 260–63.

8. (Note 1) and Juan J. Linz, 'Der religiöse Gebrauch der Politik und/oder der politische Gebrauch der Religion: Ersatzideologie gegen Ersatzreligion', Hans Maier (ed.), *Totalitarismus und Politische Religionen*, pp. 129–54.

9. Juan J. Linz, 'The Religious Use of Politics and/or the Political Use of Religion: Ersatz Ideology Versus Ersatz Religion', in *Totalitarianism and Political Religions: Concepts for the Comparison of Dictatorships*, ed. Hans Maier, trans. Jodi Bruhn (New York: Routledge, 2004), p. 112.

10. For the sacralization of politics, see Emilio Gentile, *The Sacralization of Politics in Fascist Italy* (Cambridge, MA: Harvard University Press, 1994).

11. I have dealt with this area in detail in my book *Magie und Manipulation: Ideologischer Kult und politische Religion des Nationalsozialismus* (Göttingen: Vandenhoeck & Ruprecht, 1971); also see my article 'National Socialism as a Political Religion: Potentials and Limits of a Political Concept', *Totalitarian Movements and Political Religions* 6/1 (June 2005), pp. 87–95.

12. Eric Voegelin, 'The Political Religions', Manfred Henningsen (ed.), *The Collected Works of Eric Voegelin* 5: *Modernity Without Restraint* (Columbia and London: University of Missouri Press, 2000), p. 32.

13. Ibid., pp. 32–33.

14. Ibid., pp. 59, 64.

15. Ibid., pp. 65–66.

16. Alfred Rosenberg, *Der Mythus des 20: Jahrhunderts. Eine Wertung der seelisch-geistigen Gestaltenkämpfe unserer Zeit*, 17th–20th edn (Munich: Hoheneichen, 1934), p. 86 (my translation).

17. Ibid., p. 216.

18. Ibid., p. 2 (my translation).

19. Ibid., p. 258.

20. Hitler, *Mein Kampf*, p. 471.

21. Speech by Hitler on 2 November 1932. Quoted from 'Das dichterische Wort im Werk Adolf Hitlers', *Wille und Macht*, 20 April 1938, n.p. (my translation).

22. Hitler, *Mein Kampf*, pp. 70, 146, 234, 314, 439 (my translation).

23. Rosenberg, *Der Mythus des 20: Jahrhunderts*, pp. 223, 246.

24. This would be in agreement with Hans Ehrenberg's view that Nazi religion could not fall back before Christianity. See Werner Ustorf's contribution in this book, p. 21.

25. Heinrich Böll, 'Doktor Murkes gesammeltes Schweigen', *Nicht nur zur Weihnachtszeit: Satiren* (Munich: Deutscher Taschenbuch Verlag, 1979), pp. 106–37.

26. Hannah Arendt, *The Origins of Totalitarianism* (New York: Harcourt Brace Jovanovich, 1958), p. 458.

27. Sigmund Neumann, *Permanent Revolution: The Total State in a World at War* 3 (New York: Harper, 1942), p. 229.

28. Carl J. Friedrich, 'The Unique Character of Totalitarian Society', *Totalitarianism* (Cambridge: Harvard University Press, 1953), p. 52.

29. See my book *The Apocalypse in Germany* (Columbia and London: University of Missouri Press, 2000).

30. Hitler, *Mein Kampf*, pp. 123, 216, 320, 421, 432, 724, 782, esp. pp. 346, 752.

31. Ibid., p. 724.

32. Ibid., p. 703 (my translation).

33. Helmut Heiber (ed.), *Das Tagebuch von Joseph Goebbels 1925–26*, 2nd edn (Stuttgart: Deutsche Verlags-Anstalt, 1960), p. 85.

34. Alfred Rosenberg, 'Der entscheidende Weltkampf'. Speech by the Reichsleiter Alfred Rosenberg to the party congress in Nuremberg in 1936, Munich, n.d., pp. 2, 4; id., *Der Mythus des 20. Jahrhunderts*, pp. 28, 590.

35. *Geheime Reichssache: Vermerk*, American National Archives, 10 December 1942. Facsimile in *Frankfurter Allgemeine Zeitung*, 24 January 2004, p. 33.

36. Hans Mommsen, 'Der Nationalsozialismus: Kumulative Radikalisierung und Selbstzerstörung des Regimes', *Meyers Enzyklopädisches Lexikon* 16 (Mannheim: Meyer, 1976), pp. 785–90. Meanwhile, there has been an approximation between the interpretations of 'intentionalists' and 'structuralists', see Hans Mommsen, 'Forschunhgskontroversen zum Nationalsozialismus', *Aus Politik und Zeitgeschichte* 57, Nr. 14–15 (2007), pp. 14–21.

37. Christopher R. Browning, *The Origins of the Final Solution: The Evolution of Nazi Jewish Policy, September 1939–March 1942* (Lincoln: University of Nebraska Press, and Jerusalem: Yad Vashem, 2004).

7
Marxism–Leninism as a Secular Religion*

Anatoly M. Khazanov

> … A new religion is coming to replace the old.
> That is why there are so many soldiers about
> > Feodor Dostoevsky, *The Devils. 1872.*
>
> There is now only void under the banner of Marxism from which men flee as if from a pest.
> > Ernest Gellner, *Homeland of the Unrevolution. 1994: 144.*

I would like to start with a few explanatory remarks. First, with regard to the nature of the Soviet state, I am on the side of those scholars, the 'cold war warriors,' as they are sometimes called by their revisionist opponents, who consider it totalitarian (Friedrich and Brzezinski, 1965; Laqueur, 1994; Malia, 1994; Pipes, 1995: 240ff.; Tormey, 1995; Linz and Stepan, 1996: 40ff.; Linz, 2000; on the history of debate, see Siegel, 1998). I have already argued my position in other works (Khazanov, 1995, 2004), and I do not see any reason to dwell on this question in this chapter. Suffice it to say that those who declared the totalitarian model to be politically incorrect and analytically wrong ignored the fact that the Soviet Union shared all three main characteristics of totalitarianism: ideology, organization (a single and mass party with a strict hierarchical structure), and terror (the arbitrary right to resort to any means of violence and compulsion), as pointed out already by Hannah Arendt (1966). Moreover, without denying (any) significant change that the country underwent after Stalin's death, I hold that it

---

*I would like to thank Alexander Dolinin, Patty Gray, and Dina Zisserman for their helpful comments on the earlier draft of this chapter.

remained essentially totalitarian, ideological, and repressive, until the *perestroika* period, when for a few years the late totalitarianism gave way to authoritarianism. One may agree with Michnik (1985: 7) that there is no such thing as non-totalitarian ruling communism; it either becomes totalitarian or it ceases to be communism.

Even without the large-scale terror that was characteristic only of specific periods of Soviet history, Soviet communism was markedly different from authoritarian capitalism not only in the degree of coercion, but also in the measure of ideological indoctrination, social control, and mass mobilization. Its main peculiarity was an almost complete monopoly which the party-state, and, in practical terms, the ruling elite strove to exercise not only over the political sphere, by also over the economic, societal, ideological, cultural, and all other spheres. A totalitarian society would be incomplete and, perhaps, impossible without an integral world-view, embracing all aspects of life. Totalitarianism always proclaims its ideological doctrine as both uniquely true and universally obligatory (Golomstock, 1990b: 21).

To the best of my knowledge, Raimond Aron (2001: 265) was the first who had already coined the term 'secular religion' in 1944. It was adopted by some other scholars (see, for example, Gellner, 1984: 123; Mosse, 1991: 2), and I am following suit. The word 'secular' seems to reflect specifics of Marxism–Leninism and some other totalitarian ideologies better than 'political' because it is more all-embracing and does not reduce the sacralized sphere to politics only (cf. Gentile, 2001; see also Payne, 2002). Besides, ideological legitimacy was more important to the totalitarian regimes than the political one, since it was ideology that to a large extent determined politics and put many constraints on actions of the Soviet leadership. As is noticed by Linz (2000: 70; see also Friedrich, 1969: 126), the totalitarian ideology goes beyond a particular program or definition of the boundaries of legitimate political action to provide, presumably, some ultimate meaning, sense of historical purpose, and interpretation of social reality.

For almost the entire twentieth century, intellectuals and scholars debated the origins of Russian/Soviet communism and its religious side, and this debate is resumed now in post-communist Russia. While some claimed that Marxism was a Western import to Russia alien to her indigenous tradition, others stated that it agreed with the distinctive character of the Russian historical process (Berdyaev, 1960: 107; Burbank, 1986).

The religious side of Russian/Soviet communism had both Western and native sources. Similarities between monotheistic religions, especially Christianity, and Marxism in general, and Marxism–Leninism in particular, were already noticed by a number of scholars (see, for example, Crossman, 1949; Jaspers, 1952; Tucker, 1961; MacIntyre, 1968; Bergman, 1990; Thrower, 1992; Yakovlev, 1993; Klinghoffer, 1996; and many others). Even classical Marxism had some religious characteristics. While rejecting the notions of God(s), the transcendental world, and the supernatural, that is the basic religious concepts, it adopted another notion, that of salvation, which first had been developed by the Axial Age religions, as well as the teleological perception of the purposeful historical process driven by forces external to man. In many respects, it smacked of deliberate imitation of Christianity. After all, the famous line from the communist anthem, the Internationale: 'We have been naught, we shall be all' resembles very much the Gospel's saying: 'many that are first shall be last and the last shall be first' (Matthew, 19:30). Later, the Soviets were literally repeating Paul's dictum that 'he who does not work, neither shall he eat.'

On Russian soil the religious characteristics of Marxism became much more conspicuous, and acquired many additional features. Although Linz (2000: 23) claims that the success of totalitarian movements was greater in secularized societies because religious ties resulted in some capacity to resist, in Russia, it was just the pseudo-religious character of communism that initially made it attractive to a great number of the intelligentsia and acceptable to the traditional mentality of the unsophisticated Christian believers. Several generations of the former were cherishing a special notion of *culpa* – a masochistic feeling of guilt before the suffering people whom they confused with masses. This happened in the essentially agrarian country, in which a negative attitude to Western capitalism was rather widespread, while ideals of collectivism, equalizing distribution, asceticism, and the like were still very much alive and attractive. Marxism as professed by the Bolsheviks fused Russian messianism and maximalism, an irrational belief in the specific Russian destiny (Duncan, 2000), with dreams of the Heavenly Kingdom on earth, which could be achieved through violence and compulsion almost immediately – if not tomorrow, then the day after tomorrow.

It was not accidental that the Bolshevik seizure of power was often perceived by its initial supporters, bedfellows, and sympathizers (including such great poets as Alexander Block, Sergei Esenin, and many other people) in Christian terms, as the Second Coming or Resurrection (Sinyavsky, 1990: p. 4ff.). In this regard, Russia also had had a long tradition, since many pre-Marxist revolutionaries in the country, even the atheists, had been inspired by the images of Jesus and early Christians (Bergman, 1990: 222ff.). This was not left unnoticed by some leading Bolsheviks. Thus, Anatoly Lunacharsky (1911: 159, quoted in Bergman, 1990: 231) compared the proletariat with Jesus Christ and stated that Gospel Christianity and Marxism are similar in that 'their ideals are partly congruent.' 'Scientific socialism is the most religious of all religions' – claimed Lunacharsky – 'and the true Socialist Democrat is the most deeply religious of all men' (1907: 23). His 'God-building' movement was severely criticized by Lenin but, later, Nikolai Bukharin admitted that communism in Russia was successfully placed on the fundament of the Christian idea.

For all these reasons, the militant atheism professed by the communists and their struggle against all religions in the country, which continued almost uninterrupted, although with varying intensity, until the *perestroika* period (see, for example, Powell, 1975; Thrower, 1983; Pospielovsky, 1987–1988; Luukkanen, 1994; Peris, 1998; Husband, 2000) needs explanation. First, atheism was a way of creating a religious vacuum, which then could be filled by Marxist–Leninist faith. Second, communism is a very jealous faith. The functional role of Marxism–Leninism as the official evangelical religion and, simultaneously, as the legitimizing ideology of the totalitarian state made it extremely intolerant to any and all rivals that might expose its falsity, or offer alternative world-views.

In a way, the very idea of the Higher Authority and transcendental world beyond human control is a direct challenge to the total ideology which strove to be absolutely monopolistic. It is not accidental that in the Lenin State Library – the main library of the country – catalogs excluded such unsavoury subjects as Immortality, Eternity, Transcendentalism, the Life Hereafter, the Afterworld and many others (Rogachevskii, 2002: 979). Remarkably, already in 1920, Felix Dzerzhinsky admitted that communism and religion are mutually exclusive, but that 'only the Cheka [the notorious political police] is capable of destroying religion' (Russkaia pravoslavnaia tserkov'... 1996: 146). For similar reasons, fascist movements and ideologies, as well as the Nazism, were anticlerical or had an uneasy cohabitation with the Church.

Be that as it may, in the Soviet Union the Marxist pseudo-science was converted into a pseudo-religious system. (Pipes, 2001: 159). It functioned in ways similar to real religions and in many details imitated them. To some actors the process might be almost spontaneous, and even subconscious, at least at first. But the logic of the emerging totalitarian state inevitably pushed in this direction, and the building blocks were already available. Initially, there was hardly a verifiable conspiracy to create a new religion, in which all Bolshevik leaders were involved. Often deliberate actions are carried out instinctively, intuitively, without really needing to spell it all out, but with key players understanding quite well what needs to be accomplished. This may be beguiling but not surprising, because, as Barrington Moore (1972: 168–69) aptly remarked, most revolutionaries, like most generals, 'march into the future facing resolutely backward.' In this chapter I can describe only the most conspicuous characteristics of Marxism–Leninism as a secular religion.

Theology and the notion of sacredness (the new sacred order)

The Marxist theology further developed by Soviet Marxism–Leninism was based on the Judeo-Christian eschatological model: The Garden of Eden – Original Sin and the Fall – Redemption – and the Second Coming. The alleged primitive communism was substituted for Eden, private property and the division of labor for the Fall, the proletarian revolution for the Redemption, and the future communist society for the Second Coming and return to Paradise. Salvation would be only collective, not individual, but the proletariat was perceived as the Chosen People and simultaneously acquired a soteriological function. It played a role of Saviour or Messiah.

Marxism–Leninism elaborated the original Marxist theology in several important respects. First, it introduced the notion of the Party and its elite – self-appointed leaders of the proletariat which, like the Roman popes, were infallible. Second, since the proletarian revolution had not resulted in the communist Paradise on Earth, the Soviet citizens were offered, instead, a sense of ultimate meaning. They were encouraged to make numerous and life-long sacrifices for the building of communism, and to be happy with that. That was the Marxist–Leninist substitution for a notion of salvation, and to be able to do this it had to borrow another religious concept, the notion of delayed reward.

Marxism–Leninism established its own sacred order and was constantly expanding and exploiting the notion of sacredness and its corresponding symbolic representations, which in classical Marxism had existed only in embryonic form. The Soviet Union itself was proclaimed the sacred communist space, the 'home country of all working people.' The building of socialism and of communism was a sacred cause; the World War II was a sacred war, although thousands of fallen soldiers have not received a proper burial to this very day (Tumarkin,

1994 and Weiner, 2001); service in the Soviet Army was a sacred duty. There were sacred historical events, sacred dates, sacred notions, sacred memories, sacred names, sacred graves, sacred places (like Red Square, which was never considered sacred in the pre-revolutionary times, but in the Soviet Union was proclaimed the center of the universe), sacred stones, sacred banners, and sacred songs. Even the Iron Curtain, that is the Soviet borders, was also proclaimed sacred.

Proselytism and messianism

These were inspired by more than pragmatic considerations, such as subversive activities against the capitalist countries, all of which were considered the Soviet adversaries, and/or justification of Soviet imperialism, although these factors should not be dismissed either. The messianic call of ideology stipulated that it was the holy mission of the Soviet Union, a kind of jihad, to spread communism by all means, either by persuasion or by force. Invasions into Hungary, Czechoslovakia, and even Afghanistan, as well as the Soviet Union's subversive activities in any other country, were characterized as the 'internationalist duty' of the communist state. In the last decades of Soviet history, this claim seemed so ridiculous and unpopular even to many Soviet citizens that it gave birth to a political joke: 'The USA is an aggressive country because it constantly intervenes in the internal affairs of the Soviet Union in Europe, Asia, Africa, and Latin America.' It was not accidental that the expansion of the Soviet empire was almost always accompanied by an imposition of communist rule upon conquered or subjugated countries. Likewise, the Soviet leadership to the very end of their country continued to provide financial and other support to the communist parties in capitalist and Third World countries, even in cases when practical benefits from this support were next to zero.

Deification of leaders

The vacant place of the world Savior was filled by the political authority, in the name of the Communist Party. The Party demanded that everything had to be rendered unto it: those things that are Caesar's and also those things that are God's. Thus, in the communist realm, there should not be the dichotomy of *regnum* and *sacerdotium*. This found a particular manifestation in the cult of the Ultimate Leader. The very word 'cult' implies religious worship, and this is just what it resembled in the Soviet Union. Linz (2000: 120) considers the Soviet (Stalinist) cult of personality as ideologically illegitimate. On the contrary, the cult of the Leader was an indispensable attribute of Marxist–Leninist secular religion, as well as of its other totalitarian counterparts. It was officially maintained even when it acquired grotesque and much-ridiculed forms as the cult of Brezhnev did.

The cult of Lenin, especially, bore many religious characteristics, including the notion of immortality beyond physical death (Tumarkin, 1983). Already in 1918, the Bolshevik poet Demian Bednyi in a poem, 'To the Leader,' called Lenin's writings 'the Holy Bible of Labor.' The same year, Grigory Zinoviev called Lenin's work *What Is to Be Done?* 'the Gospel,' and its author 'a leader of divine mercy' (Bergman, 1990: 243). Lenin's works had become the new Scriptures; his relic was venerated in a 'holy of holies,' the Mausoleum; the 'Lenin Corners' in public places were an overt appropriation of the icon corners which were a centuries-old Russian Orthodox tradition; important places in his life became sacred places of pilgrimage. Vladimir Mayakovsky's saying that Lenin is 'more alive than any living being' is but one of many thousands of absurd sayings and slogans of this sort.

The cult of God-like leaders, Lenin and, later, Stalin, was accompanied by the cult of communist saints and martyrs. The first ones were those communist dignitaries who were lucky to die in their own beds without having been accused of heresy or deviations from the Party line. The martyrs were revolutionaries killed by the enemies, or who sacrificed their health for the revolutionary cause. They were regarded with particular reverence. Their numerous biographies were not much different from hagiographies. Glorification of self-sacrifice and martyrdom is another characteristic which makes Marxism–Leninism related to world religions. When additional martyrs were in need, they were fabricated. This was a case with Pavlik Morozov, a boy who, allegedly inspired by communist ideals, had reported to the authorities on his *kulak* father and was killed for this by his reactionary relatives. A recent study has proven that the whole story was a fabrication (Druzhnikov, 1995).

The absolute truth, canon and holy scriptures

In the Soviet Union, the canon, a unitary body of dogmas, became the basis of ideological stability. Communist ideology in the country had acquired all of the characteristics of a closed system based on the sacred texts of Marx, to a lesser degree of Engels, and especially of Lenin and, during the dictator's rule, of Stalin. They were beyond any criticism but were constantly interpreted and re-interpreted in accordance with the

Party's policy at the moment. These sacred texts were supposed to provide a total world-view based on the Absolute Truth. The Soviet pseudo-clergy, numerous instructors, and 'scholars' of Marxism–Leninism served this goal and were zealous custodians of the official faith and its doctrinal purity. In addition, from 1938 to 1953 Soviet citizens were given catechism in the form of *The History of the Communist Party of the Soviet Union (Bolsheviks). Short Course*, especially its fourth chapter, 'On Dialectical and Historical Materialism.' It is hardly accidental that the main author of this catechism, Stalin, graduated from an Orthodox seminary.

The holistic pretensions of Marxism–Leninism explain its extreme dogmatism and intolerance to any doubt, to any alternative interpretations. The Soviet society, culture, every sphere of human life and behavior were never context-free. They were prescribed and ideologicized, and all deviations were considered as (sometimes not without a certain reason), at the least, a form of hidden dissent. The Party had a clear opinion on everything. From time to time its opinion on particular issues changed, but by the proper manipulation of quotations from the Marxist classics, its ideologists/priests were always able to easily prove that this change corresponded to the faith, and, thus, the faith remained intact.

Nothing was left to an individual's own discretion. It was the Party and its watchdogs and ideologists that had a monopoly on all decision-making regarding what was praiseworthy, what was acceptable, or, at least, tolerable, and what was incorrect and wrong. It was they who decided what people should think and in what they should believe, what they should be taught and study, what they should read, write, see in the theatres and cinemas, or watch on TV. Even in the late Soviet period, publications by Andrei Sakharov, Alexander Solzhenitsyn, and even George Orwell found during a search might mean a direct ticket to the Gulag. In all, Marxism–Leninism was a more demanding faith that any other religion in the twentieth century.

Since science and scholarship were subjected to ideology, there was a constant dread of free thinking. Marxism–Leninism was especially suspicious of new fields of science. At one time or another, genetics, cybernetics, computer science, comparative linguistics, sociology, some fields of physiology, psychology, astronomy, and geology were proclaimed 'pseudo-sciences.' The theory of relativity, labeled 'physical idealism,' was in danger too, and escaped this fate only because the physicists working on the nuclear program managed to persuade the Soviet rulers that this theory was indispensable for their work (Kostyrchenko, 2001: 601–09). Such an attitude toward science was accompanied by purely religious belief in miracles, including pseudo-scientific ones, which opened up great opportunities for all kinds of charlatans and scoundrels (Heller, 1988: 81ff.). Trofim Lysenko was only the most notorious of these.

Just like with other religions, the victory of Marxism–Leninism in the Soviet Union resulted in the creation of the specific language of the Party-State. It consisted of newspeak, a distinctive language culture, modes of writing, and a speech code with a lot of neologisms, acronyms, metaphors, catch phrases, clichés, and key words generously spiced with high Marxist rhetoric (Gorham, 2003: 9). This new language seemed almost esoteric to outsiders, but served well to segregate dedicated believers from non-believers, and initiates capable of reading between the lines from those who were not initiated (Thom, 1989; Smith, 1998; Brooks, 2000; Gorham, 2003).

Evil

In Marxism–Leninism, Evil played a much more important and conspicuous role than in any of the three monotheistic religions. In this regard, the former can rather be compared with Zoroastrianism, and especially with Manichaeism. In fact, the very concept of permanent class struggle implicitly contains a notion of Evil. Evil was indispensable because it presented the 'Other,' and it was the 'Other' that provided Marxism–Leninism with an important raison d'etre. Besides, Evil served a role of a scapegoat accountable for failures of the Soviet leadership. No wonder that in this secular religion Evil had acquired an eschatological dimension, since it was supposed to be defeated only with the final victory of communism. Until that time, Evil was ever-present and ubiquitous, although it had many incarnations.

Likewise, a struggle with Evil personified in numerous enemies justified the existence of repressive power. Evil was embodied in anthropomorphized devils. There were devils external and devils internal, and in alliance with each other they were constantly plotting against the Soviet Union. In the 1930s, Leon Trotsky served a role not much different from that of the Anti-Christ. But everybody who in deeds, words, or even in thoughts deviated from the Marxist–Leninist orthodoxy: open enemies, saboteurs, traitors, infidels, unbelievers, heretics, revisionists, and dissidents sided with Evil. Interestingly, as a rule, they did not benefit from their stand, because with the assistance of the believers, the loyal Soviet citizens, they were successfully exposed and persecuted by the secret police – the much more efficient and ruthless Soviet equivalent of the Inquisition. Just like the Inquisition, the Soviet punitive system paid great attention to the confession and repentance of heretics. The Inquisition, however, was concerned with the salvation of their souls, while to Soviet justice it meant a reconfirmation of its concept of Evil, as well as of the correctness of the Faith.

Heretics were especially dangerous; they might contaminate other people. Just like in Christianity, heretics were even more menacing and offensive than infidels. In principle, the latter might be converted, but the former claimed to follow genuine tradition and accused the leadership of deviation (Klinghoffer, 1996: 84). Czeslaw Milosz (1980: 214) summarized the attitude of the Marxist–Leninist orthodoxy toward heretics in the following words: 'The enemy, in a potential form, will always be there: the only friend will be the man who accepts the doctrine 100 per cent. If he accepts only 99 per cent, he will necessarily be considered a foe, for from the remaining 1 per cent a new church can arise.' But unbelievers did not deserve much mercy either. Nobody else but Stalin himself stated that, 'Not only is he who sabotages an enemy of the people. All those who doubt the correctness of the Party line are enemies as well. There are many of them in our midst, and we ought to eliminate them' (Vaiskopf, 2001:355–56).

In the high Stalinist period, the struggle with Evil acquired the character of mass hysteria. Despite many attempts, the Great Purge and its pseudo-religious frenzy can hardly be explained only in purely rational and instrumental terms. Rather, some parallels may be drawn with the witch-hunts in medieval Europe.

The believers and the new Soviet man

The Marxist–Leninist faith demanded that it should be believed in and professed, bluntly and unquestionably; but at the same time its attitude toward true believers was quite ambiguous. In this regard it was different from real religions. True believers might turn out to be unreliable and even dangerous, because many of them were activists; if and when they got disillusioned and disappointed, they tended to become apostates and heretics. Soviet history proved this time and again. Anyway, the number of true believers in the country was always much lower than it was sometimes assumed. The heroic image of Soviet citizens in the grip of enthusiasm inspired by the new faith was mainly the outcome of Soviet propaganda, which misled many Western sympathizers and even some professional scholars.

One should not confuse, as is often done, loyalty to the Soviet state, and even to its political regime, with a deep and sincere belief in Marxism–Leninism. Many communists, not only ambitious upstarts, promotees, and careerists, but even the nomenklatura members (perhaps, especially the latter), perceived the official creed as hardly much more than a loyalty test, a required norm of allegiance. The most fundamental tenet that they had learned from Leninism was the principles of hierarchy, discipline, and authority of those who had the right to 'know better.'

Actually, in the Christian, especially Catholic and Orthodox traditions, priests are also supposed to 'know better,' at least on ecclesiastical matters. Likewise, in the Jewish tradition, the authority of those, who know better, is also appreciated. It is said in the Mishnah (Avot, 1:6): 'Make yourself a *rav*,' that is find a teacher and respect his authority. In the Soviet case, however, one was not allowed to choose a *rav* voluntarily. Everybody who enjoyed more power should be accepted as a *rav*, who knew not only more, but also knew better.

The developments in contemporary Russia prove this point. The communist party there retains the loyalty of many its former members, in spite of the fact, or rather because of the fact, that it sloughed off its Marxist–Leninist ideology and phraseology in favor of xenophobic and populist nationalism. In the same fold, *Edinaiia Rossiia* (United Russia), the ruling party in Russia today, which consists mainly of ex-communists, combines the hierarchy, discipline, and authority in the absence of Marxist–Leninist ideology.

In the Soviet Union, few communists and lay people, even those who had to take compulsory courses on Marxism–Leninism at universities or graduated from special educational institutes, like the Institute of Marxism–Leninism, demonstrated sincere interest in, or serious knowledge of, Marx's and Lenin's actual writings. Few, if any, communists believed in their own Potemkin villages, an idealized representation of social reality. Already in the late 1920s intellectual debates on the meaning of socialism and communism were of no interest not only to rank-and-file communists, but even to the majority of the new ruling elite, as long as they held the reins of power and privilege (Brovkin, 1998: 46). Since the 1930s, there were no such debates at all. This became especially evident in the post-Stalin period, and was revealed in a popular joke: 'When a good communist is asked whether he ever deviated from the Party line, he replies: "Never. I was always deviating with the line itself." '

Ultimately, the communist rulers relied upon coercion, repression, and buying over much more than on preaching and persuasion. Intimidation, deception, and temptation went hand-in-hand. Marxism–Leninism inspired compliance, conformity, and ostentatious zealotry; but, much more than genuine religious feeling and enthusiasm, it demanded subservient obedience. This situation resulted in the spread of doublethink and doublespeak. Doublethink and doublespeak were more reliable than pure religiosity, because they did not give birth to dissent; they brought forth only fatalism and civic apathy, or cynicism and careerism. The capability to combine, sincerely and without guilt, absolutely incompatible beliefs and statements about one and the same subject, was one of the most permanent traits of the Soviet mentality (Kon, 1993: 406).

To the majority of the population in the secularized societies, ethical and moral choices are to a large extent disconnected from expectation of salvation or punishment in the afterworld. Things were different under Marxism–Leninism. Just like other religions, it established its own moral norms, which were very specific indeed. Young Marx (1842) declared, 'An end which requires unjustified means is no justifiable end.' His Russian followers were of a different opinion. In the Soviet Union, the ends justified the means. 'If a man does not want to build communism, his life is not indispensable,' threatened the 'liberal' communist leader Nikolai Bukharin. 'We have no morality applying to the whole mankind,' declared the Komsomol chief, A. Kosarev (*Pravda*, July 7, 1932), who a few years later would be eliminated by Stalin. 'If a "blood" relative turns out to be an enemy of the people, then he is no longer a relative but simply an enemy and there is no longer any reason to spare him,' sermonized the 'great humanist' Maxim Gorky (1958: 201). The kind of ideal man the Soviet rulers were dreaming of was revealed in the 1930s by the gifted poet Eduard Bagritsky (1958: 201), who at that time was greatly esteemed by the authorities:

> You look around – and see enemies everywhere;
> You hold out your hand – but there are no friends;
> But if He says: 'Lie!' – do lie!
> But if He says: 'Kill!' – do kill!

'He' in the poem referred to the century, or to history itself, but these were personified by the Party and its Holy leader.

It was the Soviet party-state, not the Soviet society that was totalitarian (Malia, 1994: 14). The Party decreed to the people their attitude not only toward socialism, capitalism, imperialism, Zionism, and the class struggle, but also toward artistic styles, beauty contests, rock music, new fashions, homosexuality, and birth control. Private life was suspicious. This explains the sexophobia and homophobia of the Stalin period and puritanical attitude toward sex of his successors. In the 1930s, Maxim Gorky stated: 'Destroy the homosexuals – fascism will disappear.' The nude almost completely disappeared from socialist realist art. Ungoverned emotional life and sexual behavior were considered only a little less dangerous than uncontrolled thought.

Nevertheless, 'the moral-political unity of the Party and the Soviet people' allegedly achieved in the Soviet Union was always a fiction. Two parallel and quite different moralities existed in the country. The first, official one, was promoted by the Party, the second was shared by many ordinary people, perhaps, even by the majority, and played a protective, contra-mobilizing and de-ideologizing role. Collaboration with the secret police and informing on other people was praised by the state as a patriotic duty, but was resented by the large society. *Stukachi* (snitches) were very much disliked and despised. Despite numerous anti-religious campaigns and constant propaganda, truly religious individuals evoked respect even of many atheists, as the people who had the courage to live in accordance with their convictions. The communist morality proclaimed that stealing from the state was a mortal sin. The parallel morality held that stealing from individuals was wrong, but it was much more tolerant to stealing from the state. Likewise, the general public was rather tolerant to drunkenness, pre- and extramarital sex, cheating on exams, hack-work, or money made on the side – the behavior that official ideology strongly condemned.

In 1976, Leonid Brezhnev declared in his report to the 25th Congress of the Communist Party that the New Soviet Man had already been created. He called this the 'most significant achievement of the last sixty years' (*Pravda*, February 25, 1976). However, the actual result was a very significant ideological disorientation of ordinary Soviet citizens.

While the majority could not be called true believers, neither were they non-believers, or even less atheists (i.e. the dissidents). With regard to the Marxist–Leninist faith they were rather ambivalent. Belief in the Ultimate Goal and discontent with the things that were going on, and, therefore, a partial disbelief in the Soviet propaganda coexisted within many people. To survive meant to justify. Complete and conscious rejection of Soviet reality was socially and psychologically dangerous, dysfunctional, and unbearable for the majority. In order to survive, to succeed, and even to retain a modicum of mental health, people wanted to believe, and in many cases actually did believe, if not in everyday realities, then in the truth of communist ideals and in the ultimate good of socialism. In this case, everything that was bad and wrong in the Soviet political, social, and economic order could be explained as temporary shortcomings and remediable deviations from the noble ideal. Thus, some people tried if not justify, then to rationalize the Great Terror, arguing that mistakes were inevitable in the course of historical events of such unprecedented scale: 'When the wood is chopped the chips flow.'

Socialism was not only a faith; it was also a source of identity (Kotkin, 1995: 360). The reality, if it were perceived to the very end, might be very painful and desperate, while the concept of wholeness offered by Marxism–Leninism might seem somewhat attractive. At any rate, it provided some justification for heavy sacrifices and, for the time being, a hope for a better future.

Salvation

In the Marxist–Leninist faith, salvation implied salvation of Man now and immediately and of the World only in the more or less distant future. Every day was the Day of Judgment. In other words, the creation of a new and higher specimen of Homo sapiens: Homo sovieticus, the New Soviet Man with a specific mindset, should precede the advent of communism. This Man was designed not in God's own image, but, to quote Stalin (*Pravda*, June 27, 1945), as a cog who keeps the great state machine in motion, that is as raw material in the pursuit of the State's goals. Contrary to the Christian tradition since the Renaissance rethinking, the value of the individual was reduced to nothing.

The most important qualities of this perfect man should be a total commitment to the building of communism, a selfless devotion to the Party and its leaders, and a willingness to subordinate one's own interests to the interests of society, that is those of the Soviet state and its ruling elite. This was a direct revision of classical Marxism, which claims that existence determines consciousness. The Soviet rulers wanted consciousness to determine existence. To be more precise, they wanted false existence in the true tradition of Zamiatin and Orwell to produce desirable human beings, who would believe in everything they were told to believe, would behave as they were prescribed to behave, and would do everything they were ordered to do. It is no wonder that in the late Soviet period dissent, and even discontent, not infrequently were considered mental illnesses. The faith of the Soviet leadership in the plasticity of human material was quite remarkable. This might explain the attraction of Lysenko's Lamarckian views for them. His claims that changes in external environment lead to internal changes in the organism, which could be handed down from generation to generation, seemed to open up the ways of reshaping man in the desired direction (Heller, 1988, 57).

Rituals and rites

Since the first days of the Bolshevik seizure of power, the Marxist–Leninist faith was constantly being reaffirmed by political holidays (except for New Year's Eve, all holidays in the Soviet Union were political), the carefully elaborated liturgy, quasi-religious celebrations, rituals and rites, iconic use of banners and portraits, and ceremonial systems for birth, marriage, and funerals. In Heller's (1988: 208) words: 'Soviet man is beset on all sides by rituals, like a wolf surrounded by hunters.' Mass participation in public rituals and ceremonial meetings as a proof of loyalty and commitment was practically obligatory, and it was almost impossible to avoid observation of at least some of them. In the course of time many celebrations, rites and rituals were changed or modified, and new ones were invented, but the tendency remained the same. Public rituals routinized and choreographed to minor details became an indispensable part of indoctrination. They became a tool in perpetuating the political status quo, hierarchy, discipline, and a way of inculcating the norms and values of the dominant ideology (Binns, 1979–1980; Lane, 1981: 15–19; Sartori, 1990; Petrone, 2000). The best examples of this practice were the May 1 and November 7 parades and mass demonstrations. Even immediately after the Chernobyl disaster in 1986 everyone, including the children, was out in the streets of the Ukraine and Byelorussia celebrating May Day.

Iconography

By the early 1930s, the Soviet rulers succeeded in imposing upon visual arts the political and ideological norm and context, which did not leave any room for the freedom of self-expression and experimentation. Just like in literature, socialist realism became the only permitted school. The new religion allocated to the fine arts only one role: to be an instrument of ideology and propaganda. Political intolerance corresponded to aesthetic intolerance, and ideological commitment had to be confirmed by a particular artistic style. Socialist realism was based on a system of prescribed forms, false and pathetic, and on a rigid aesthetic canon. The themes of ideologically laden painting were strictly regulated too. Countless portraits of the communist leaders, dignitaries, and heroes in paintings and monumental sculpture became icons for mass worship. Not infrequently, they were based on the Orthodox Christian iconographic tradition and were characterized by a solemn and frozen immobility that endowed the image with the qualities of an icon.

> The iconic symbol of the cross corresponds to the socialist device of the hammer and sickle; Lenin's hands can often be formally equated with God's; Stalin thrusting his arms invitingly towards the socialist viewer outside the picture might be compared to the figure of Jesus Christ sanctifying religious viewers in real space. Members of the Politbureau turn into archangels. (Holz, 1990: 77)

Likewise, numerous paintings of the so-called 'historical-revolutionary genre' used the compositional schemes of Christian iconography (Golomstock, 1990a: XVIII–XIX, XXII). Other canvases depicted idealized and mythologized events and glorified the Party and the New Soviet Man engaged in the way of life that allegedly existed, although everybody knew that that was a lie.

I will turn now to the fate of Marxism–Leninism as a secular religion. A remarkable characteristic of all pseudo-religions is that they are short-lived, especially in comparison with the real ones. This is not accidental indeed, and Marxism–Leninism was not an exception. Communism came to its ignominious end because it had failed to deliver all of its main initial promises: economic prosperity, social emancipation, and national liberation. But Marxism–Leninism as an inspiring faith had died long before the collapse of communism as a political and economic system, and the disintegration of the Soviet Union. Its inherent dogmatic weaknesses contributed to its failure as much as the Soviet realities.

Of these inherent weaknesses two are the most conspicuous. First, the Achilles' heel of all secular religions is that they promise that the Heavenly Kingdom on Earth was within historical striking distance. Just like in the monotheistic religions, in Marxism the finale was known beforehand. Eventually, this let it down. Marxism 'is a caricature and a bogus form of religion, since it presents its temporal eschatology as a scientific system, which religious mythologies do not purport to be' (Kolakowski, 1978: 526). Secularization of eschatology is a very dangerous endeavor, because in this case a promise of reward cannot be delayed indefinitely. Jews are still patiently waiting for the Messiah to come and to redeem this world, just like Christians are waiting for the Second Coming. But nobody was ready to wait for 2000 years for the advent of communist society, in which each would receive according to his needs. Marxism–Leninism ceased to be a utopia as soon as the Bolsheviks seized power in Russia. From that moment on the utopia had to fulfill its promise.

Lenin set an example when he promised that in ten years toilets in the communist paradise would be made of gold. His successors and their serving staff understood that they were racing against time; hence, their frenetic appeals and slogans which sounded like incantations: 'Tempos decide everything' (Stalin), 'Our god is speed' (Mayakovsky), 'Time, forward!' (Kataev), 'Fulfillment of the Five-Year Plan in Four Years (Party programs),' 'Acceleration' (Gorbachev). In 1947, a draft of the new program of the communist party claimed that communist society would be built in the country in the next 20 or 30 years. Remarkably, however, that the project was shelved and never published. Khrushchev's promise to deliver communism in 20 years, by 1981, was a desperate commitment in the same fold. But after so many unfulfilled previous promises, his words, 'The Party solemnly promises: This generation of the Soviet people will live under communism,' were immediately met with a widespread skepticism.

The introduction in the Brezhnev era of the new notion of 'actually existing socialism,' which allegedly would last for a long historical period, was an admission of failure. In practical terms, this meant that there would be no bright future. Soviet history had lost its meaning in the context of perceived human destiny. It entered the period which later, in Gorbachev's time, would be called the period of stagnation. The Marxist–Leninist faith ceased to be forward-looking. This development was accompanied by a growing understanding that in the Soviet Union, sinners were sent to hell already in this world and during their lifetime, but the sinless were left in chronic poverty and everlasting shortage, outside of paradise. Receding into the more and more distant future, the promise of communism became nothing more than a matter of subversive humor. The very word 'communism' was called a shortest political joke.

Actually, the failure was tacitly admitted much earlier. No later than in the 1930s, when Stalin proclaimed that 'living has gotten better, living has become jollier,' fiction once and for all substituted for ugly reality. The Soviet citizens were ordered to believe not only in the bright future but also in the happy present. The mighty machine of Soviet propaganda, including literature, cinema, and arts, was mobilized to assist them in this illusion. In 1934, the ideologist and party dignitary, Andrei Zhdanov, demanded that Soviet writers depicted Soviet life not as objective reality, but in its revolutionary development (*Pervyi vsesoiuznyi...*, 1934: 4). In other words, life should be depicted not as it actually was, but as it was dreamed of. Likewise, countless canvases of the socialist realist painters conveyed the illusion of mass enthusiasm, ecstasy, and exaltation of the

Soviet people engaged in joyful labor, sport, and merry feasts. Thus, the pretensions of Marxism–Leninism on scientific explanation of reality turned out to be false. It was nothing but a blind faith, moreover, a faith that concealed the real social order (Zinoviev, 1985: 45). A sad irony was the fact that it was doing just what other religions, labeled the 'opiate of the masses' by Marxists, were allegedly guilty of.

Still, for a long time Marxist–Leninist mythology was an indispensable part of the faith. Affirmed by all the state's might, including punitive measures, it did not have serious alternative competitors in mass consciousness. In the 1930s, a verse from the popular Soviet song claimed: 'I do not know any other country, where a man breathes so freely (as in the Soviet Union).' The Soviet rulers who isolated their country from the rest of the world did their best to help their people to remain ignorant. And those who knew were exterminated or jailed. This is why Stalin was so suspicious of his own victorious soldiers and other Soviet people who had had a chance to look at life in non-communist countries and, thus, became contaminated (Zubkova, 2000: 37ff.).

The second inherent weakness of Marxism–Leninism consisted of the contradiction between its universal claim and its national character par excellence. This became obvious as soon as the worldwide revolution was removed from the order of the day and was replaced by another goal: the building of socialism in one particular country. Simultaneously, the defence of the Soviet Union was proclaimed the main task of the workers all over the world. A change in terminology: Marxism–Leninism instead of Marxism only confirmed the new trend. The concept of the withering away of the state after the proletarian revolution was shelved once and forever. Since the 1930s, or even earlier, the official Soviet ideology began to supplement Marxist–Leninist faith with propagating loyalty to the Soviet state in the guise of patriotism. In the course of Soviet history, it increasingly smacked of Russian chauvinism.

In the post-war period, the Soviet military presence in Eastern Europe and the Brezhnev's doctrine were presented as assistance to, and cooperation with, the 'brotherly countries' of the Warsaw pact. Inside the Soviet Union, official ideology served to legitimize the ruling positions of ethnic Russians. The Russians were called the elder brother of all other Soviet peoples; the latter were relegated the role of 'junior brothers.' Only Russians were considered as deserving of the status 'the great people.' Historical figures of Russian history – princes, tsars, and generals who carried out the territorial expansion of Russia – were praised as progressive, and some were declared Russian national heroes. It turned out that never in her history Russia waged any aggressive war (Khazanov, 1995: 4ff.).

Victory in the World War II (the Great Patriotic War in the official lexicon) served as legitimation of the communist rule much better than the Bolshevik turnover in 1917. To a significant number of Russians, the War and the Victory justified the repressive, predatory, and hyper-centralized Soviet regime. The Victory had written off all disastrous blunders and incompetence of the Soviet leadership, avoidable losses and unnecessary suffering of the ruled, and unrepentant crimes of the rulers. It created a sense of national unity and extrapolated it into other periods of the Soviet history (Weiner, 2001; Gudkov, 2005). It is not accidental that the official master narrative of Putin's regime repeats and propagates mythologized and sacralized version of the War created in the Soviet period. In this case, the constructed past influences the present quite successfully, and in the time of vanishing canons on the national heritage battlefield, this one still holds the ground.

Just as Berdyaev (1960: 145) had predicted quite early: 'A communist revolution in a single country inevitably leads to a nationalist standpoint in political relations with other countries.' In the post-war period, the conflicts with Yugoslavia, China, Albania, and occasionally strained relations with some European communist parties confirmed that that 'internationalism' was but a fig-leaf for Soviet imperialism. The main achievement of the Party and its leaders was not the fulfillment of the original promises, but the creation of a superpower. Nowadays, the Russians are still debating whether the price they had to pay for this temporary success was too heavy and useless.

This situation could not last and did not last forever. Communism was rapidly approaching its own day of reckoning, although not in a way that had been predicted by its Founding Fathers. In the late Soviet period, Marxism–Leninism represented nothing more than an exhausted, ossified, and hollow ideology. It had to be supplemented by other indoctrinating ideologies, especially by nationalism and imperialism. Orthopraxy (ritualization of ideology) and ostentatious displays of loyalty substituted for Orthodoxy. An over-exploitation of the sacral resulted in its profanation. Despite the efforts of the Soviet rulers and ideologists, the regime lost the capacity for mass mobilization. Its revolutionary legitimacy was challenged on all grounds, including ideological. Thus, an attempt to re-animate the cult of Lenin undertaken in 1970 practically backfired. Its most noticeable outcome was a great number of jokes, which ridiculed both the Leader and its official cult. Except for empty emphasis on the public, Marxism–Leninism failed to offer appealing answers for the eternal questions of the meaning of life and death, and, thus, to penetrate into one's inner world.

During the last decades of the Soviet regime, a growing number of people were explaining their desire to become members of the Communist party by sheer career considerations. To acquire the reputation of an opportunist and conformist was better to them than to look as a fool who believes in official lies. Some Communist intelligentsia were on the mark when they privately joked that God gave a man three valuable qualities – brains, honesty, and Party membership, under condition that only two of them could be present in the same person.

True believers became extinct dinosaurs, while the numbers of non-believers and atheists (i.e. dissidents) were growing, as well as a number of those who preferred the capitalist hell to the socialist paradise. The New Soviet Man, infantile, intimidated, submissive, and devoid of initiative, nevertheless turned out to be far from being perfect and sinless. His low self-appraisal was revealed in the contemptuous word *sovok* (a dust-pan), a modal personality type whose characteristic traits were conformism, laziness, inefficiency, civic passivity, and moral irresponsibility. The satisfaction of his basic needs at a minimum level and an empty promise for improvements in the future was not enough for him anymore. He was as prone to consumerism as his capitalist counterparts. The only difference was that the consumerism of the former was for a very long time denied or suppressed.

A growing number of people practiced, as much as possible, a strategy of self-alienation from the Soviet society and its official values. The surveys carried out among Soviet workers and engineers in the 1970s, showed a distinct shift of personal interests away from the sphere of work and public affairs to private life and consumer activity (Kon, 1993: 397). An orientation toward self-discipline, meticulousness, and punctuality acquitted a negative connotation. All attempts to impose a kind of the communist variety of the Protestant work ethics – a higher job motivation and a stronger work discipline – undertaken by the Soviet rulers had failed completely. Andropov ordered special patrols to catch and to harass a significant number of people, who instead of being in their working places spent their time in cinemas, shops, or even public baths. However, the public opinion was not on his side and was revealed in a widespread joke: 'We pretend that we are working, and the state pretends that it is paying for our work.' Just like other similar attempts, that one did not work either.

In fact, by the early 1980s, one witnessed a complete failure of the Marxist–Leninist faith. It became unappealing even to many in the ruling elite. On the eve of the World War II, George Orwell posed a question, 'Is it just as possible to produce a breed of men who do not need liberty as to produce a breed of hornless cows?' Whatever direction the future development of Russia will take, the most encouraging moment in the Soviet experiment, perhaps the only one, is that in the long run it provided a negative answer to this question.

Actually, Marxism–Leninism has failed completely and in all its varieties not only as a secular religion but also as a scientific theory, perhaps, just because it tried to combine both. As a result, it might be attractive in principle, but it was always ugly in practice. It demonstrated a remarkable inability for drastic self-reformation. This is proven by the failure of the attempt at building 'socialism with a human face' (in Czechoslovakia in 1968 and in the Soviet Union during *perestroika*). Those former Marxist parties which transformed themselves into social democratic ones, like in Germany and many other West European countries, in the past, and nowadays in a growing number of post-communist countries of East Central Europe, had to throw Marxism overboard. In China, which turned to capitalist development, Marxism remains only a fig-leaf of the Communist Party's lust for power. Nowadays, the disintegration of the Soviet Union is perceived as the catastrophe by the former KGB officer and the Former Russian president Vladimir Putin and by the diehard Western communist Eric Hobsbawm (2005). Remarkably, however, that neither of them mourns the death of Marxism–Leninism, which is rather surprising in Hobsbawm's case.

Still, the reasons for the failure of Marxism–Leninism, and the lessons that may be drawn from this failure, seem to be less evident than one might expect. There are scholars who claim that 'socialism failed in this century because it mimicked capitalism too faithfully' (Buck-Morss, 2000: XV), although they do not trouble themselves with providing an explanation why the capitalist original turned out to be victorious. There are other scholars, even social scientists, who already have started to dream about new utopias (Kumar, 2001: 171ff.). So, without any hope to be listened to I would like to finish this chapter with a warning. It is well known that the road to hell is paved with good intentions. But the good intentions often start with wishful thinking. This is why one should beware of wishful thinking that strives for paradise on the Earth and, instead, results in another hell, the hell, which in Karl Popper's words (1962: 168), 'man alone prepares for his fellow men.'

References

Arendt, H. *The Origins of Totalitarianism* (New York: Harcourt, Brace & World, 1966 [first published in 1951]).

Aron, R. *The Opium of the Intellectuals* (New Brunswick and London: Transaction Publishers, 2001).

Bagritsky, E. *Stikhotvoreniia i poemy.* (Moscow-Leningrad: Sovetskii pisatel, 1964).

Berdyaev, N. *The Origin of Russian Communism* (Ann Arbor: The University of Michigan Press, 1960).

Bergman, J. 'The Image of Jesus in the Russian Revolutionary Movement. The Case of Russian Marxism,' *International Review of Social History*, XXXV (1990) 220–48.

Binns, Chr. A. P. 'The Changing Face of Power: Revolution and Accommodation in the Development of the Soviet Ceremonial System: Part I,' *Man*, vol. 14, no. 4 (December 1979) 585–606; Part II. *Man*, vol. 15, no. 1 (March 1980) 170–87.

Brooks, J. *Thank You, Comrade Stalin! Soviet Public Culture from Revolution to Cold War* (Princeton, N.J.: Princeton University Press, 2000).

Brovkin, V. *Russia after Lenin. Politics, Culture and Society, 1921–1929* (London and New York: Routledge, 1998).

Burbank, J. *Intelligentsia and Revolution. Russian Views of Bolshevism 1917–1922* (New York: Oxford University Press, 1986).

Buck-Morss, S. *Dreamworld and Catastrophe: The Passing of Mass Utopia in East and West* (Cambridge, Mass.: MIT Press, 2000).

Crossman, R. H. S. *The God That Failed* (New York: Harper, 1949).

Druzhnikov, Y. *Donoschik 001, ili voznesenie Pavlika Morozova* (Moscow: Moskovskii Rabochii, 1995).

Duncan, P. J. S. *Russian Messianism. Third Rome, Revolution, Communism and After* (London and New York: Routledge, 2000).

Friedrich, C. J. *Europe: An Emerging Nation?* (New York: Harper and Row, 1969).

Friedrich, C. J. and Brzezinski, Z. *Totalitarian Dictatorship and Autocracy*, 2nd edn (Cambridge, Mass.: Harvard University Press, 1965 [first published in 1956]).

Gellner, E. *Nations and Nationalism* (Cambridge: Cambridge University Press, 1984).

Gellner, E. 'Homeland of the Unrevolution,' *Daedalus*, vol. 22, no. 3 (1994) 141–53.

Gentile, E. *Le religioni della politica: Fra democrazie e totalitarismi* (Bari: Laterza, 2001).

Golomstock, I. 'Problems in the Study of Stalinist Culture,' in: Hans Günter (ed.), *The Culture of the Stalin Period* (New York: St. Martin's Press, 1990a), 110–31.

Golomstoch, I. *Totalitarian Art in the Soviet Union, the Third Reich, Fascist Italy, and the Peoples Republic of China* (New York: IconEditions, 1990b).

Gorham. M. S. *Speaking in Soviet Tongues. Language Culture and the Politics of Voice in Revolutionary Russia* (DeKalb: Northern Illinois University Press, 2003).

Gorky, M. *O detskoi literature* (Moscow: Goslitizdat, 1958).

Gudkov, L. 'Die Fesseln des Sieges Rußlands Identität aus der Erinnerung an den Krieg,' *Osteuropa*, 55 Jahrgang, Heft 4–6 (2005) 56–73.

Heller, M. *Cogs in the Soviet Wheel* (London: Collins Harvil, 1988).

Hobsbawm, E. 'The Last of the Utopian Projects' *The Guardian*, March 9, 2005.

Holz, W. 'Allegory and Iconography in Socialist Realist Painting,' in: Matthew Cullerie Brown and Brandon Taylor (eds). *Art of the Soviets. Painting, Sculpture, and Architecture in a One Party State, 1917–1992* (Manchester: Manchester University Press, 1990), 73–85.

Husband, W. B. *'Godless Communists.' Atheism and Society in Soviet Russia, 1917–1932* (De Kalb: Northern Illinois University Press, 2000).

Jaspers, K. *Reason and Anti-Reason in Our Time* (London: S.C.M., 1952).

Khazanov, A. M. *After the USSR. Ethnicity, Nationalism, and Politics in the Commonwealth of Independent States* (Madison: The University of Wisconsin Press, 1995).

Khazanov, A. M. 'What Went Wrong? Post-communist Transformations in Comparative Perspective,' in: Yitzhak Brudny, Jonathan Frankel, and Stefani Hoffman (eds), *Restructuring Post-Communist Russia* (Cambridge: Cambridge University Press, 2004).

Klinghoffer, A. J. *Red Apocalypse. The Religious Evolution of Soviet Communism* (Lanham, Maryland: University Press of America, 1996).

Kolakowski, L. *Main Currents of Marxism. Its Origin, Growth, and Dissolution. Vol. III. The Breakdown* (Oxford: Clarendon Press, 1978).

Kon, I. S. 'Identity Crisis and Postcommunist Psychology,' *Symbolic Interaction,* 16(4) (1993) 395–410.

Kostyrchenko, G. V. *Tainaia politika Stalina* (Moscow: Mezhdunarodnye otnosheniia, 2001).

Kotkin, S. *Magnetic Mountain. Stalinism as a Civilization* (Berkeley: University of California Press, 1995).

Kumar, K. *1989. Revolutionary Ideas and Ideals* (Minneapolis: University of Minnesota Press, 2001).

Lane, Chr. *The Rites of Rulers: Ritual in Industrial Society – The Soviet Case.* (Cambridge: Cambridge University Press, 1981).

Laqueur, W. *The Dream that Failed: Reflection on the Soviet Union* (Oxford: Oxford University Press, 1994).

Linz, J. J. *Totalitarian and Authoritarian Regimes* (Boulder, CO: Lynne Reinner, 2000).

Linz, J. J. and Stepan, A. *Problems of Democratic Transition and Consolidation* (Baltimore and London: The John Hopkins University Press, 1996).

Lunacharsky, A. V. 'Budushchee religii,' pt.1. *Obrazovanie,* N 10 (1907) 1–25.

Lunacharsky, A. V. *Religiia i Sotsialism,* vol. 2 (St. Petersburg, 1911).

Luukkanen, A. *The Party of Unbelief: The Religious Policy of the Bolshevik Party, 1917–1929* (Helsinki: Societas Historica Finlandiae, 1994).

MacIntyre, A. *Marxism and Christianity* (New York: Schocken, 1968).

Malia, M. *The Soviet Tragedy. A History of Socialism in Russia, 1917–1991* (New York: The Free Press, 1994).

Marx, K. 'Debatten über Preßfreiheit und Publikation der Landständischen Verhandlungen,' *Rheinische Zeitung,* Nr. 135, vol. 15, 1842.

Michnik, A. *Letters from Prison* (Berkeley: University of California Press, 1985).

Milosz, C. *The Captive Mind* (Harmondsworth: Penguin Books, 1980).

Moore, B., Jr. *Reflections: On the Courses of Human Misery* (London: The Penguin Press, 1972).

Mosse, G. L. *The Nationalization of the Masses. Political Symbolism and Mass Movements in Germany from the Napoleonic Wars through the Third Reich* (Ithaca and London: Cornell University Press, 1991 [first published in 1975]).

Payne, S. G. 'Emilio Gentile's Historical Analysis and Taxonomy of Political Religions,' *Totalitarian Movements and Political Religions,* vol. 3, no. 1 (2002) 122–30.

Rogachevskii, A. 'Homo Soveticus in the Library,' *Europe-Asia Studies,* vol. 54, no. 6 (2002) 975–88.

Peris, D. *Storming the Heavens: The Soviet League of the Militant Godless* (Ithaca, N.Y.: Cornell University Press, 1998).

Pervyi vsesoiuznyi s'ezd pisatelei. Stenograficheskii otchet (1934). (Reprint: Moscow: Sovetskii pisatel, 1994).

Petrone, K. *Life Has Become More Joyous, Comrades. Celebrations in the Time of Stalin* (Bloomington, IN: Indiana University Press, 2000).

Pipes, R. *Russia under the Bolshevik Regime* (New York: Vintage, 1995).

Pipes, R. *Communism. A History* (New York: The Modern Library, 2001).

Popper, K. R. *The Open Society and Its Enemies*, vol. I., 4th edn (London: Routledge and Kegan Paul, 1962).

Pospielovsky, D. V. *A History of Marxist-Leninist 'Scientific Atheism' and Soviet Anti-Religious Policies*, 3 vols (New York: St. Martin's Press, 1987–1988).

Powell, D. E., *Antireligious Propaganda in the Soviet Union: A Study of Mass Persuasion* (Cambridge, Mass.: MTI Press, 1975).

Russkaia pravoslavnaia tserkov' i kommunisticheskoe gosudarstvo, 1917–1941. Dokumenty i materially (Moscow, 1996)

Sartori, R. 'Stalinism and Carnival: Organisation and Aesthetics of Political Holydays,' in: Hans Günther (ed.), *The Culture of the Stalin Period* (New York: St. Martin's Press, 1990).

Siegel, A. (ed.), *The Totalitarian Paradigm After the End of Communism. Towards a Theoretical Reassessment* (Amsterdam – Atlanta, GA: Rodopi, 1998).

Sinyavsky, A. *Soviet Civilization. A Cultural History* (New York: Arcade Publishing, 1990).

Smith, M. G. *Language and Power in the Creation of the USSR* (Berlin: Mouton de Gruyter, 1998).

Thom, F. *Newspeak: The Language of Soviet Communism* (London: Claridge Press, 1989).

Thrower, J. *Marxist-Leninist 'Scientific Atheism' and the Study of Religion and Atheism in the USSR* (Berlin: Mouton, 1983).

Thrower, J. *Marxism-Leninism as the Civil Religion of Soviet Society. God's Commissar* (Lewinstone, NY: The Edwin Mellen Press, 1992).

Tormey, S. *Making Sense of Tyrany. Interpretations of Totalitarianism* (Manchester and New York: Manchester University Press, 1995).

Tucker, R. *Philosophy and Myth in the Thought of Karl Marx* (Cambridge: Cambridge University Press, 1961).

Tumarkin, N. *Lenin Lives! The Lenin Cult in Soviet Russia* (Cambridge, Mass.: Harvard University Press, 1983).

Tumarkin, N. *The Living and the Dead: The Rise and Fall of the Cult of the War* (New York: Basic Books, 1994).

Vaiskopf, M. *Pisatel' Stalin* (Moscow: Novoe Literaturnoe Obozrenie, 2001).

Weiner, A. *Making Sense of War. The Second World War and the Fate of the Bolshevik Revolution* (Princeton and Oxford: Princeton University Press, 2001).

Yakovlev, A. *The Fate of Marxism in Russia* (New Haven and London: Yale University Press, 1993).

Zinoviev, A. *The Reality of Communism* (London: Gollancz, 1985).

Zubkova, E. *Poslevoennoe sovetskoe obshchestvo: politika i povsednevnost.' 1945–1953* (Moscow: ROSSPEN, 2000).

8
Maoism in the Cultural Revolution: A Political Religion?

Rana Mitter

What is Maoism?

The cult of personality surrounding Mao Zedong peaked during the initial phase of the Great Proletarian Cultural Revolution (GPCR, 1966–1969). China's youth was mobilised behind the Chairman's call to 'bombard the headquarters', and eagerly took part in Mao's revolt against his own party. The role of the young Red Guards caught not only China but the world's attention. It seemed that they followed Mao not as a political leader, but rather as a god, 'the reddest of red suns in all our hearts'. This chapter will examine the case for interpreting this phenomenon in terms of 'political religion'. It will suggest that there is a strong case for arguing that the irrational and totalistic nature of the mass movement during the GPCR can be interpreted fruitfully as a secular theology. It urges caution, however, in using the term wholesale when considering the élite discourse which initiated the Cultural Revolution, and which did not seek actively to create a secular priesthood and religious community. It also suggests that the religious models most appropriate for comparison are not those of pre-modern China, but rather the European derived religious models which shaped Western political religions, and were well-known and understood by Mao and the Chinese Communist Party (CCP).

Mao has the distinction, along with Gandhi, of being one of the very small number of non-European political leaders to achieve brand-name status in the twentieth century. Mao has been used as an endorsement for a wide variety of movements, from the agricultural 'green revolution' in India, to the Khmer Rouge genocide in Cambodia, to the anti-establishment protests of Paris students in the 1960s. It is therefore important to make it clear just what Maoism is, before going on to discuss the viability of considering it as a political religion.

First, Maoism is, and must be, considered as a mode of Marxist thought. However, it was a Marxism shaped by a grassroots understanding of China's nature as an agricultural society which could not be changed by a Bolshevik-style, urban-based revolution.[1] The Mao who started to develop along these lines was not the paramount leader of later years. Although he was a founder member of the Party, and present at its first Congress in 1921, Mao's position waxed and waned, and in 1934–1935, he was effectively under house arrest. A crucial moment came in 1930, when Mao compiled a report on conditions in Xunwu county, in mountainous Jiangxi province, giving an immensely complex and sophisticated account of class divisions among the farmers and élites of the township.[2] From this period (actually a little earlier), Mao's phrase 'seek truth from facts' (later made famous by Deng Xiaoping) emerged. Throughout his career, even during moments of seemingly irrational ideological zeal, Mao continued to stress the importance of grassroots investigation and pragmatic application of theory rather than 'bookism' (*benbenzhuyi*) and practicality. Indeed, these values were still praised during the Cultural Revolution, though their meaning was now hopelessly perverted. In particular, the reality that China was a predominantly rural society with great poverty and inequality led to a concentration on rural revolution as the transformative approach favoured by the Party.

Additionally, Maoism can be seen as a strategic approach. Between the late 1920s, when the alliance with the Nationalists (Kuomintang) was abruptly ended, and victory in 1949, guerrilla techniques and strategic withdrawals became a necessary part of survival during the conflicts with the Nationalists, the Japanese, and then the Nationalists again during the Civil War. The corollary of guerrilla tactics was a need, enforced both by ideology and practicality, to become 'close to the people'.

These aspects of the Maoist project were the ones most in evidence during much of the Western academic debate on China through the 1970s, much of which looked at Mao's rise to power and rule post-1949 as a question of political science or development studies. These approaches, while immensely fruitful, also tended to stress positivistic and rational models as the most appropriate ones to analyse Mao's rule, and also to equate the governance of the PRC with Mao's personal rule.[3] This meant that the Cultural Revolution of the 1960s came as a seemingly inexplicable break from the CCP's trajectory up to that point. However, for those who cared to look at the less concrete and pragmatic aspects of Maoism, and at the importance of charismatic leadership to Mao's project, the Cultural Revolution seemed more like a logical, if by no means inevitable, end point. Yet these other aspects of the Maoist project have only more recently come under scrutiny in a concentrated way.[4]

Maoism, it is clear, became, from the 1930s onward, a project based very largely on charismatic leadership. Although the importance of the charismatic Maoist element within the wider framework of CCP governance varied, with high points including the Rectification Movement of 1941–1944, the Great Leap Forward of 1958–1962, and the Cultural Revolution, particularly in its earliest phase from 1966–1969, there was no stage at which charismatic Maoism was irrelevant after the consolidation of his position in the late 1930s. It is therefore the role of charismatic Maoism that will be explored below; it will be contrasted with pragmatic Maoism, and the interaction of the two will also be analysed. We will then go on to ask whether it is possible to classify it as a political religion, and how the term may be useful.

What, in essence, was charismatic Maoism? First of all, it was dependent on a cult of personality. Mao himself became the centre of ideological correctness and his work, codified as 'Marx-Leninist-Mao Zedong thought', positioned him in a line of succession to the canonical Marxist thinkers. Rather than having to boost his own image, Mao was supported by allies; in the 1940s, in Yan'an, his security chief Kang Sheng was instrumental, and during the 1950s and into the 1960s, Lin Biao and Chen Boda were responsible for propagating Mao's thought through the media and the army.

Charismatic Maoism was also dependent on the cultural currents which had shaped Mao himself during his early life, and which are clearly visible throughout his life. Well before he became a Marxist, Mao was shaped by the attacks on pre-modern Confucian norms which convulsed the political and intellectual climate of late Qing dynasty, and early Republican China. The 'New Culture' movement, closely related to the 'May Fourth Movement' of the 1910s and 1920s, became retrospectively canonised for being the birthplace of China's supposed vehicle of destiny, the CCP. Yet the other aspects of Western-derived thought, in particular a mystical romanticism based on the projection of the ego, also had a profound effect on many of the young thinkers of the era, Mao among them. The question must arise: Did the May Fourth era give rise to a political religion that would become known as Maoism? Emilio Gentile has argued that

> the totalitarian religions and, generally speaking, the totalitarian-
> isms of the twentieth century are not descendants of the sacralised

> politics of the French Revolution…they were new political religions
> that emerged from the Great War and the Russian Revolution, even
> if they contained pre-existing currents and had been influenced by
> earlier experiences of the sacralisation of politics…[5]

While stressing that charismatic Maoism, like Chinese communism
more widely, did owe a great deal to the French Revolution and the
Enlightenment, and also that it borrowed from pre-modern Chinese
political discourse, Gentile's point is as valid for Maoism as for the more
purely European political religions; the aftermath of the Great War, of
which China (with 100,000 Chinese workers on the Western Front in
Belgium) was indubitably a part, critically shaped all of its political path
for the twentieth century. 'Fascism and Nazism', Gentile argues, were
'the offspring of the war'; so was the May Fourth Movement. The fact
that Eurocentric history has generally not played up the term 'World War
I' to include Japan and China fully in the conflict's history, should not
conceal the fact that both societies' identities were profoundly changed
by their entry into that war.[6]

There is an important distinction that needs to be made early on,
however, and this is one where the typology of ideological difference
between conservatism and fascism, as has been discussed by George
Mosse and Stanley Payne, is relevant. Mosse and Payne differentiated
between conservatism, which was essentially reactionary and aspired to
a reversion from modernity, and fascism, which used a set of mental
maps associated with the right (blood, soil, honour, primordial values),
but which, as a political mode, embraced modern ideas of dynamism
and progress while condemning their bourgeois (i.e. democratic or
liberal) manifestations.

Similarly, the use of pre-modern vocabulary and forms for the
promotion of the Mao cult should not be confused with a return to
the old pre-modern world of the imperial system. It is important to
point out here that there are two potential traps that I will try to avoid
in the interpretation below. One is the idea that Mao in effect became
a new emperor, reverting to 'traditional' styles of leadership. This
interpretation was encouraged by Mao's own comparison of himself to
the first unifying emperor of China, Qin Shihuangdi, in the last years of
his life. This risks confusing form with substance. As will be seen below,
Mao's cult of personality, even when it drew on pre-modern forms,
was an essentially modern enterprise. It was based on an idea of the
individuated self, a rejection of Confucian values of 'moderation' and
'order', as well as respect for age, revered dynamism over stasis, and was

propagated through the media as an expression of collective, supposedly non-hierarchical mass values. It was profoundly different from, say, the brief attempt in 1915 by the Republican president Yuan Shikai to ascend the imperial throne and restore Confucianism as the official political doctrine, a genuinely conservative and reactionary move.

The other trap to avoid is what one might consider the reverse of the 'emperor' model; the idea that the Mao cult was purely and simply based on Soviet models, and Stalin's in particular: this view was more popular during the height of the Cold War, but is not unheard even now. Soviet models were indeed deeply important for shaping Mao's thought, and the dysfunctional, half-admiring, half-resentful relationship which Mao had with Stalin indicates quite how essential the *Vozhd*'s mode of thought was to Mao. But Mao's own experience makes a simple imitative model insufficient. The specifics of the May Fourth Movement, and Chinese cultural currents which were based in pre-modern norms but reshaped by modern practice, were also highly important.

Both of the models critically examined above are attempts to try and interpret charismatic Maoism purely as variants of pre-existing models, the pre-modern empire, and Soviet Bolshevism, and as such, suggest an unwillingness to admit that Maoism might not be an ersatz version of another model. Instead, it should be considered a dynamic hybrid in its own right, using the forms of pre-modern and modern identity, the assumptions of globalised modernity, and drawing on China's own experience, in particular during the May Fourth era of the early twentieth century (a period not paralleled either in early twentieth-century Russia or in pre-modern China), as well as on Mao's own individual personality.

Maoism as a political religion?

These notes of caution, however, are necessary before suggesting that despite caveats, we have identified the charismatic mode of Maoism as the one which might well be productively analysed as a political religion. The categories which have defined this term include: salvationist language, a penetration of the state into private life, ceremonies, and martyrs to the cause.[7] In considering the usefulness of this category in the context of Maoism, we need briefly to remind ourselves of the assumptions within the term itself.

The term 'political religion' has been most commonly used to define a European phenomenon, emerging with the separation of state and church and allowing religious and liturgical modes of behaviour to be transferred to essentially secular, and civil patterns of behaviour.

Ironically, in the nineteenth century, as religion became more secularised, safer, and sanitised, a space opened up for politics to become more irrational and shaped by romanticist ideas. The development of 'political religions' and the pseudo-religiosity of leadership cults in the major European dictatorships (Italy, Germany, the USSR) were based on their variation from an essentially Christological norm. The soteriological and individually transformative (palingenetic) nature of these entities necessarily derived from cultural norms shaped by Christianity, even when the ostensible forms of state ritual were strongly anti-religious (USSR), neo-pagan (Germany), or self-declaredly separate from the church (Italy). The nature of charismatic leadership under Mao was inevitably different because of China's predominantly non-Christian culture.

In some ways (and some ways only), Christian precedent provided a framework that was appropriate for projects of spiritual renewal such as fascism or Bolshevism. The central tenet of Christianity is that by accepting Jesus, sinners could be 'reborn'. This was different from the Confucian norms that had shaped statecraft in China for two millennia, although Confucianism had changed over that period as an epistemological mode, just as Christianity had. Confucian norms stressed stability and networks of hierarchy that would enable society to be both ordered and ethical. *Both* of the latter qualities were important, and rulers who provided order without ethics (as the Legalist school of Han Feizi was accused of doing by Confucians) were officially denigrated. Precedent and archaism, a harking back to the past, were mainstays of political culture. In a sense, the comparison between Confucianism and Christianity is an unfair one, since Confucianism was not a religion as such. Rather, it was an ethical and behavioural system, though it used its stress on hierarchy to stress the importance of piety towards one's parents, loyalty to one's ruler, worshipping ancestors, and so forth. Religious practice coexisted for the most part in pre-modern China, and therefore Taoism and Buddhism (the latter originally an alien import from India) were available to provide a more individualised and spiritual mode of religious practice: 'Amidist Buddhism' is one notable example of this tendency.

Imperial cults had existed for centuries, and powerful emperors certainly propagated their own images enthusiastically: the great Kangxi and Qianlong emperors of the high Qing are notable examples. Yet these cults were in significant measure different from the essentially modern cult of personality that Mao developed. However personally powerful the emperors had been, their power ultimately derived from the institution of emperor itself, with its fulcrum role between heaven and earth. The emperor's authority derived from his ability to embody the concepts of order and orthodoxy which the stable Confucian state demanded. Of course, religious practice did on many occasions go beyond the bounds of state-defined practice. Millenarian cults, in particular, depended on transcendent figures who advocated overthrow of the dynasty and government as they stood, such as Wang Lun's White Lotus Rebellion in the late eighteenth century and Hong Xiuquan's Taiping War in the late nineteenth.

These pre-modern precedents were not irrelevant to Mao and Maoism. But they were not the basis on which Mao's authority *primarily* depended, and it does a disservice to the modern project in China to dissociate Maoism too strongly from similar projects of renewal in the twentieth-century world. For a start, although his authority derived from his participation in the leadership of the CCP, it was not in his role as party chairman that his authority lay; indeed, during the Cultural Revolution, in organisational terms, his leadership of the party was balanced by Liu Shaoqi's installation as head of state, a means of dividing power after the disaster of the Great Leap Forward. Instead, the system of thought, Marx–Lenin–Mao Zedong thought, which he developed, reflected his own personal background and preferences, with which the party then came partly or fully into line. The historian Hans van de Ven has observed,

> Personality cults are common to many revolutionary...regimes and seem more modern than traditional. Can one imagine the Kangxi emperor holding mass peasant rallies? To understand the personality cult of Mao, would it not be more helpful to examine the political environments that produced Stalin, Hitler, and Nasser than to compare Mao with China's past emperors? Similarly, the reading and discussion of texts may have been features of dynastic China.... But again, the CCP shares its text-centeredness with other modern revolutions.[8]

The road to individuated salvation as expressed through Maoism seems both modern and Christological in its derivations.

The road to charismatic Maoism

One argument about Mao's leadership is that it moved from being ideologically grounded to being charismatic.[9] Although even at the height of his power, Mao's position of supremacy within the leadership was never as uncontested as was, say, Stalin's after the late 1920s, it is clear that Mao's status as first, and more, among equals, is fundamental to the formation of Chinese communism. The question of whether 'political religion' can be used as an interpretative tool for his political style is answered in part by returning to the early formative period in his thought.

Mao was a child of his time, the very late Qing dynasty and the early Republican era. When he was 18, the 1911 revolution overthrew the 2000-year-old imperial system, ushering in a period of Republican government marked by instability and militarism on the one hand, but a significant flowering of different models of political thought on the other. Politically weak governments allowed the spread of the innovative and often iconoclastic current of thought known as the 'May Fourth' or 'New Culture' period, dating approximately from the mid-1910s to the mid- to late 1920s. This period has become one of the most resonant cultural moments in twentieth-century Chinese history. The term 'May Fourth' comes from the student demonstrations in Beijing on 4 May 1919, protesting against the unjust treatment of China at the Paris Peace Conference; yet the 'May Fourth' or 'New Culture' period refers to a much wider sense of national crisis linked to cultural opportunity felt among many Chinese from the mid-1910s to the mid- to late 1920s. The idea of 'newness' shaped political discussion of the time, and was a rejection of the Confucian norm that age and precedent were preferable tools for dealing with crisis.

In fact, the whole of the late Qing and early Republican period was marked by a political culture where the 'new' and 'renewal' were an integral part of the discourse. The most prominent example of this was the development – by the late Qing political activist Liang Qichao – of the idea of the 'new citizen'. The 'new citizen' was contingent on the idea of a 'new people' [*xinmin*], and the definitions of the terms showed the debate between ideas of nationalism which were racially or civically defined.[10] From the mid-nineteenth century, Yan Fu and other thinkers brought powerful ideas of evolution and Social Darwinism to a troubled Chinese political class. Yet the May Fourth era took these ideas still further. In the interwar era, the internationalist climate, the rise of nationalism, and a new global obsession with youth and renewal helped to give wider context to China's attempt at intellectual and political regeneration.[11] 'The Chinese Enlightenment' or 'Chinese Renaissance', as it was later termed, was influenced by a variety of Western concepts both rational and romanticist, as well as influences from figures such as

Gandhi and Atatűrk, who both seemed to provide a non-European way forward against imperialism.[12]

What brought the May Fourth movement together, however disparate its elements, was the conviction that Confucian culture needed to be changed as China coped with modernity. For the most iconoclastic of that generation (such as Mao and the writer Lu Xun), this meant the complete destruction of the old Confucian norms, while the more moderate (such as the journalist Zou Taofen) argued for the adaptation of Confucian values in a hybrid modern form. A common thread among all of these, as well as the more conservative groups who lamented the arrival of the Republic and refused to accept modernity, was the conviction that the old ethical core of the Confucian value system had disappeared and that something new had to take its place.

For the moderates, who included Sun Yatsen, this ethical gap meant that they had to find a way of reconciling Confucian assumptions with modernity. For radicals such as Mao, however, the ending of the old world provided an exhilarating opportunity to re-cast ethics in a mould completely in opposition to the old norms; shaped by winds from Europe and the West, youth, violence, and dynamism became part of an anti-Confucian message of intoxicating potency. Mao became part of the group that would eventually seek a political solution in Marxism; among his fellow-founders of the CCP were Chen Duxiu, Li Dazhao, and Cai Hesen. But no May Fourth experience was felt in isolation: though Mao was a Marxist, he was also a romanticist, and that brush with the exhilaration of irrationality as part of modernity shaped his life from then on, all the way to the Cultural Revolution. Pragmatic Mao (and Maoism) and charismatic Mao (and Maoism) were not at war with each other. They were merely different facets of the May Fourth experience.

Mao was not the paramount leader of the party until the mid- to late 1930s, and it was the pragmatic Mao who manoeuvred past hostile political enemies and murderous internecine Party feuds before that time. The periods during which Mao's charismatic leadership seemed to have the greatest impact were, first of all, during the Rectification Movements of 1941–1944, while the Party's major base was in the Northwest of China, and then during the Great Proletarian Cultural Revolution, the most extreme period of which lasted from 1966 to 1969.

David Apter has suggestively analysed the Rectification period as one where the Party, and Mao in particular, used 'revealing' texts to create 'discourse communities' which had a 'transformational sense of their own difference, (that was) messianic'. Through a process of 'exegetical bonding', the Party was able to create 'symbolic capital' on which it could draw.[13] His interviews suggest that for CCP members of the time, 'Yan'an was the total and totalizing experience, the moral moment of the revolution and in their own lives'. The Cultural Revolution re-interpreted these experiences for a new generation that had known nothing but the People's Republic of China (PRC). It is here that we must look in detail at whether charismatic Maoism can be considered a political religion.

The cultural revolution: the élite discourse

In what respects did the Maoist cult of personality go beyond the rationalist, Enlightenment-derived discourse with which Chinese Communism had started, and draw instead on irrational and sacralised elements? Even while answering this question, it would be wrong to over-stress the differences between the supposed rationality of Enlightenment-derived communist modernity, and the irrationalism of the anti-Enlightenment fascist/primordialist one. The search for a new ethics and more general 'newness' in society which had been going on since the late Qing and into the May Fourth era was very much still on the agenda during the Cultural Revolution, and it was clear that a psychological, not just economic, change was at the centre of this search.

'The Great Proletarian Cultural Revolution now unfolding is a great revolution that touches people to their very souls', began the CCP Central Committee's 'Decision Concerning the Great Proletarian Cultural Revolution' (8 August 1966).[14] Just because the CC said this did not, of course, necessarily make it so. However, it turned out to be true; it was grassroots participation which made Maoist fervour as strong as it was during the Cultural Revolution. The establishment of ideologies in Germany and Italy which embraced the mystical and irrational, provided a state-sponsored framework in which irrationality could be given free rein. This was less feasible in Maoist China at the official level, where Mao, even at the height of his power, was no Führer, and where the state ideology needed simultaneously to balance its rationalist Enlightenment roots while embracing the charismatic romanticism of the Mao cult. We may therefore observe a phenomenon by which élite political declarations on the GPCR tried to hew to a relatively more rational discourse, whereas popular mass responses sacralised Mao Thought and took it beyond the range of the rational.

The original 'Decision' stresses that 'In the Great Proletarian Cultural Revolution, the only method is for the masses to liberate themselves, and any method of doing things on their behalf must not be used'.[15] The literal truth of this statement is not the issue here. As we know, attempts at genuine grassroots organisation such as the 1967 Shanghai Commune were quickly infiltrated by the Party leadership. However, it is notable that even during this most personalised of campaigns, the myth was maintained at élite discourse level that the masses' own will was the driving force of the movement. The force was not explicitly expressed as coming through a sacralised figure, a Duce or Führer. The initial document also permits the holding of different views, and the protection of minority opinions.[16]

At point 16 of the 'Decision', however, the role of Mao Zedong Thought is spelled out clearly. 'Mao Zedong's thought should be taken as the guide to action in the Cultural Revolution', it declares, and argues that Party committees 'at all levels'...

> must study over and over again Chairman Mao's writings on the Cultural Revolution and on the Party's method of leadership, such as *On New Democracy, Talks at the Yan'an Forum on Literature and Art, On the Correct Handling of Contradictions among the People*...and *Methods of Work of Party Committees*.

This technique of re-reading texts intensively brought back to mind the Rectification campaigns in Yan'an in the 1940s, when immersion in repeated text-reading was made the gateway for successful induction into the Party.

An important bridge between the more hesitant official discourse and the cultism of the mass response is the role of Lin Biao, minister of defence since the disgrace of Peng Dehuai in 1959. Lin used his position at the head of the People's Liberation Army to encourage a cult of Mao, starting in the PLA and moving outward within society. This enabled Mao to establish a base from which to oppose the elements in the Politburo, such as Liu Shaoqi, whom he felt were opposed to him, and had sought to downgrade his influence after the disaster of the Great Leap Forward.

The shift from pragmatic to charismatic explanations of Maoism is visible in an article, originally from *Red Flag* and reprinted in *Peking Review*, praising the Red Guards in September 1966. The language is simultaneously more orientated towards personalising the GPCR as Mao's own movement, and to describing its popular manifestations in terms of a natural, uncontrollable phenomenon, with metaphors of 'birth' and 'upbringing':

> The Red Guards are something new that has emerged in the tempest of the Great Proletarian Cultural Revolution...The Red Guards have been nurtured in their growth by Mao Zedong's thought...
>
> What our Red Guards love most of all is to read Chairman Mao's works and follow his teachings, and their love for Mao Zedong's thought is most ardent...
>
> Revolutionary dialectics tells us that the newborn forces are invincible, that they inevitably grow and develop in struggle, and in the end defeat the decaying forces. Therefore, we shall certainly sing the praises of the new, eulogize it, beat the drums to encourage it, bang the gongs to clear a way for it, and raise our hands high in welcome.[17]

This statement is an excellent example of how the pre-modern and modern elements that went to create the Mao cult came together. On the one hand, the repeated reading of texts, and the idea that entrance to salvation was through familiarity with a master-text, was one that would have been very familiar in various pre-modern contexts. In orthodox Chinese society, it was familiarity with the classics, and one's ability to carry out detailed literary criticism (*kaozheng*) and separate 'correct' from 'incorrect' interpretations which defined success in the old imperial bureaucracy. The term *kaozheng* was in fact used by inquisitors during the GPCR when reviewing the records of those accused of ideological crimes. The Confucian system had very clear ideas of what was heterodox and what was orthodox. In heterodox society, the emergence of millenarian cults (White Lotus, Taiping) was also in significant part based on texts. The Taiping state, which held sway in much of central China from the mid-1850s to 1864, used texts largely based on a rewriting of Old and New Testament material to create a framework for the new state (the Heavenly Kingdom of Great Peace) which it sought to establish.

Yet the source of legitimacy in the Maoist cult was different in a crucial regard from the pre-modern sources of legitimacy. Unlike either official imperial cults or millenarian rebellions, where the source of authority was external to the emperor or rebel religious leader himself, Mao's political legitimacy, particularly in the charismatic aspects boosted by Lin Biao, Kang Sheng, and Chen Boda, rested in Mao personally. Mao Zedong Thought was a self-legitimising project: Mao Thought was correct because it came from Mao. It did not self-legitimise so quite as unapologetically as Hitler or Mussolini's thought did, since, like the Stalinist cult of personality, it had to pay some lip-service to Enlightenment ideals of rationality. Yet its cult of man rather than higher authority was in effect a bow to the idea that man was the measure of all things, while encouraging a political style that seemed to demonstrate the opposite. Devotion was expressed in terms of 'love' of 'Mao Zedong Thought', implying something again beyond rationality.

The cultural assumptions are also very much grounded in the post-May Fourth, modern sensibility. Imperial cults were part of a strategy of control, as was Mao's cult. But the primary purpose of the imperial cult was to encourage order and stability, and like most of the dominant Confucian culture, it was dependent on harking back to a golden age and far-off practice. In contrast, the Cultural Revolution displayed a *reductio ad absurdum* of the most extreme radical anti-Confucian elements of the May Fourth era. Rejection of 'moderation' and condemnation of violence as a political tactic was at the centre of Mao's early Social Darwinist thinking for a post-Confucian China. The quote above betrays both Hegelian/Marxist and Social Darwinist assumptions by its emphasis on struggle, which had been such a powerful anti-Confucian model when first introduced into China by Yan Fu and others in the late Qing era, as well as metaphors of birth, evolution, and decay. It also follows the thread started in the very late Qing dynasty, and strongly developed during the May Fourth period by praising the new, rather than the old and venerable. This is a cult; but it is one based on modern, not pre-modern, assumptions.

The Mao cult was dependent on cheerleaders. Mao himself rarely praised his own role, and one even finds him making statements that ostensibly seem to play down the cult of personality. This seems disingenuous, however, when one sees how his advocates encouraged that cult. Even prime minister Zhou Enlai, who has in retrospect been portrayed as one of the voices of moderation within the leadership during the GPCR, wrote to a prominent group of Red Guards in September 1966: 'In the course of this Great Proletarian Cultural Revolution of ours there can only be one criterion of truth, and that is to measure everything against Mao Zedong Thought. Whatever accords with Mao Zedong Thought is right, while that which does not accord with Mao Zedong Thought is wrong'.[18]

Undoubtedly, the most important figure in this effort was Lin Biao. Lin's public speeches, an important part of the maintenance of the Mao cult during the GPCR, are more enthusiastic about the importance of

Mao Thought above all than the CC directives, yet still lack the absolute manic fervour of the Red Guards (considered below). In a speech at a mass rally on 18 August 1966 celebrating the Cultural Revolution, Lin declared that 'Chairman Mao is the most outstanding leader of contemporary times, the greatest talent of contemporary times'. He signs off with what would become an obligatory, 'Long live Chairman Mao! Long live! Long, long live!'[19]

Yet élite discourse, even as expressed by Lin Biao, still seems a step away from being a full-fledged political religion. The language is fawning and fulsome, but it is not yet sacralised. This is perhaps not surprising. It must be remembered that Mao himself did not expect the Cultural Revolution as we now know it – and including three years of near-anarchy – to emerge in the way that it did. He was thinking in terms of a much shorter campaign, perhaps several months, and it is unclear that he originally intended some of the most famous side effects such as the death by neglect of state president Liu Shaoqi. Lin Biao, Chen Boda, and Mao's other cheerleaders wished to make him into a leader above all others, but it seems unlikely that Lin saw himself in the role of a priest or evangelist (not least because the Christological tradition in which such a persona would have been formed was not part of his cultural assumptions in a way that it would have been for Europeans). Yet it is also undeniable that by the end of the most active phase of the GPCR, a movement had emerged that was theological rather than ideological in its appearance. To observe this phenomenon, one must turn to the mass movement, and in particular, the Red Guard movement.

The Red Guards

The most obvious and uncontrollable constituency to respond to Mao's calls to rebellion during the GPCR were the young who formed teams of 'Red Guards'. Since the 1920s, although youth sections remained important in the politics that emerged, particularly for the KMT and CCP, the autonomous role of youth was steadily suppressed within the straitjacket of politics shaped by national crisis. Mao's conscious decision to liberate the power of youth was based on a very modern sensibility, one shaped by the experience of May Fourth. Yet there was a crucial difference. May Fourth youth had experienced the post-Confucian intellectual atmosphere in a society that offered a multitude of choices. Like Weimar Germany, the precarious pluralism of the Republic reflected both weakness and opportunity. No one idea could dominate in politics or culture because there were too many competing forces: nascent Chinese nationalism, foreign imperialism, internal warlordism, and so forth. Post-1949 China was very different. It would be wrong to suggest that it was a successfully totalitarian society, in that we know that policies intended to change behaviour from within often failed to be reflected at the grassroots.[20] Yet it was a sealed and inward-looking society, that had little contact with the outside world, and little if any space for pluralist thought within the society itself. The generation who came of age in 1919, like Mao, had been exhilarated by the wealth of choices and arguments which they could make. The generation coming of age in 1966 were exhilarated, rather, by what purported to be scientific certainty being placed before them.

The glorification of the cult of Mao owed a great deal to twentieth-century cults, certainly in its fervour. The constant theme of interviews and memoirs by those who took part in the GPCR as young women and men was their genuine enthusiasm for the movement and Chairman Mao. This is reflected in the absolutism and devotion of the Red Guards. This reflects, ironically, the influence of the 'political religion' as understood in the West, an influence that was both soteriological and Christological. This should not be surprising. The Taiping had shown the power of the Christological model a century beforehand, and Christianity had been a powerful, if minority, political and cultural influence on China since the treaties signed with the imperial powers had allowed missionaries to proselytise in the hinterland. Furthermore, the organisational models most friendly to the spread of a political religion, Leninism and fascism, were well-known to Chinese activists who would become the core of the great political movements of the century.

One of the most notable phenomena of the Red Guard period was the use of Maoist language and norms as the vehicle for bonding and socialisation mechanisms of various types, something with which religious practice has always been associated. Just as religious practice appeals to a metaphysical source of authority to legitimate its socialisation, so Maoist practice among the Red Guards used 'Mao Zedong thought' and its variants as a declared good in its own right, and a good which served to justify and legitimate particular phenomena, and in doing so, reached a level of irrationality that went some way beyond what the élite discourse recommended.

These bonding mechanisms drew on modern and pre-modern practice. They included oaths, songs, confessions, as well as actions that involved struggle, endeavour, and pilgrimage. For example, in June

1966, Red Guards of the high school attached to Qinghua University declared in an oath of loyalty:

> We are Chairman Mao's Red Guard, and Chairman Mao is our highest leader. Here, facing our great leader Chairman Mao, facing our beloved party, facing the revolutionary peoples of all China and the whole world, we swear, with the revolutionary Red Guards' most flourishing and solemn oath: We shall preserve eternal faith in the proletariat! – eternal faith in Chairman Mao! – eternal faith in the proletarian revolutionary line represented by Chairman Mao!... We have unlimited trust in the people! We have the deepest hatred for our enemies! In life, we struggle for the party! In death, we give ourselves up for the benefit of the people!... With our blood and our lives, we swear to defend Chairman Mao! Chairman Mao, we have unlimited faith in you![21]

This expression of undying loyalty is typical of the modern mass movement that draws on the irrational. It does not owe much to the form, as opposed to the language, of pre-modern Chinese cults, nor, unlike the slightly cautious GPCR documents at the leadership level, does it try and anchor itself too much in the rationalist Enlightenment discourse which shaped most CCP discourse. Instead, it draws heavily on the mystical and irrational as a source of bonding. Oaths were always sworn by blood brotherhoods in pre-modern China, but by definition, these were part of a heterodox stratum of society that was at odds with the orthodox, state defined norms, even when they echoed them in part. The phenomenon of the public swearing of oaths, even if it was not consciously modelled on European fascist models, was part of a modern culture of political practice that had become globalised by the mid-twentieth century (Nazi oaths were part of initiation into exclusive parts of that movement, as in *SS-Mann, dein Ehre heisst Treue*). The emphasis on primordial elements (blood, life, death) also brings to mind the romanticist urge that had dominated the May Fourth movement, and which Mao had maintained throughout life in a way that Stalin did not. The repeated emphasis on the personal ('we...we'/ *women/women*) was also a legacy of the modern emphasis on the individuated self, heavily encouraged by the New Culture movement; the repeated use of the personal pronoun was very un-Confucian, despite the repeated references to 'loyalty' (*zhong*), which had been a core Confucian ethic. And of course, that loyalty was also modernised: the personalised fealty to Mao reflects the influence of the Stalin cult, and the importance of techniques of mass propaganda, media, and political socialisation to a state which was hermetically sealed from most outside influences.

The regenerative nature of Maoism, which owes something to the soteriological and neophiliac (and therefore non-Confucian) assumptions of the New Culture movement, as influenced by strains of Western modernism, is also evident in other Red Guard declarations. One such, now regarded perhaps as rather kitsch, was the demand from the Beijing Torch [*huoju*] high school that street names be given 'revolutionary' names as part of the process of renewal: thus 'Xuanwai Road' should become 'Wenge [Cultural Revolution] Road', 'Niu [Ox] Street' should become 'Tuanjie [Unity] Street', and 'Hufang street' should become 'Gongren [Worker] Street'.[22]

This romanticist, irrational devotion to Mao collided with a peculiarly modernist sensibility that violence and chaos were necessary transformative mechanisms for change in society. Again, a very clear link can be drawn with the May Fourth movement of the 1910s and 1920s, when the Leninist idea that evil could legitimately be done for the sake of a greater good became deeply attractive to the early Communists, for instance Cai Hesen. This is reflected in the repeated references by the Red Guards to 'rebellion' [*zaofan*], the legitimation of chaos and the overturning of social norms: 'Long live the spirit of revolutionary rebellion!', declared the students of the Torch high school.[23] It was China's anti-Confucian experience during the May Fourth movement that provided the most obvious precedent for this tendency, for after all, Confucianism made order a central part of its world-view. Yet the influences that shaped that 'rebellion' had come in significant part from the radical left and right in Europe. Futurists and Bolsheviks alike adored technology not just for its instrumental and material benefits, but because of the virility and power that it embodied, the ability to go beyond what had been previously possible. Both radical left and right also legitimated 'going beyond' what were perceived as bourgeois ethical norms of restraint, and embraced violence as a transformative mechanism, giving it a sacralised (though hardly Christian) value. A famous example of this was the young Red Guard Song Binbin, whose personal name means 'refined'. Her excellence in revolutionary destruction was noted by Mao, to whom she was presented, and at his suggestion, her inappropriate name was changed to 'Yaowu', meaning 'desiring violence'.[24]

Leninist ideas of 'terror' as a praiseworthy term were adopted by Red Guards enthusiastically, as with the 'Red Generation' group in Harbin, who put out a manifesto in September 1966:

We cry loudly: Long live Red Terror!

Today we will carry out Red Terror, and tomorrow we will carry out Red Terror. As long as there are things in existence which are not in accordance with Mao Zedong Thought, we must rebel and carry out Red Terror!

Chairman Mao said: 'Revolution is not a dinner party, it is not writing an essay.... Revolution is a violent movement; it is the violent overthrow of one class by another'.

Some people have seen our Red Terror [and said] 'It's too destructive'. What nonsense! The world [*tianxia*] is ours! The rivers and mountains are ours!... We oppose ox-demons and snake-spirits...

We are natural-born rebels, we are critics of the old world...

It is right to rebel! Rebel to the end!

Long live Red Terror![25]

Yet terror here, as in the French Revolution as well as the Bolshevik, became a sacralised term seemingly detached from the reality of physical attack, death, and destruction. The cautious directive of the Central Committee directives to avoid violence and allow dissenting views bore no resemblance to the use of 'Mao Zedong Thought' as a legitimation for acts of physical violence committed on grounds of dispute that were practically theological, depending on black-and-white understandings of 'right' and 'wrong'. Once again, the New Culture's inheritance of the idea of 'renewal', a new generation which rejected the failed past, also shaped the justification for 'red terror'. Furthermore, the use of a Mao quotation as a precept for particular behaviour emphasised the theological nature of Mao Zedong Thought.

The corollary of this was the characterisation of opponents as enemies, irredeemably evil, and beyond humanity. The more moderate note of 're-education', which marked at least some of the CCP's practice in the immediate post-1949 period, was abandoned for a language that suggested primal notions of good and evil taken from mythology: 'snake spirits', 'cow demons', 'ghosts' and 'devils' were all insults hurled at ideological enemies, literally dehumanising them.

Other modes of Red Guard behaviour also reflect a sacralised sensibility, although the object of veneration is Mao rather than any other-worldly entity. One such mode is the exercise of testing tasks. The 1934–1935 'Long March', of course, was the touchstone event of CCP mythology, not least because this extended retreat from the KMT forces had seen the rise to power of Mao as paramount leader, even though this position was not secure until the late 1930s. Since the embrace of physical vigour was yet another way in which the New Culture generation, including Mao, had rejected Confucian social norms, it was unsurprising that the Cultural Revolution generation were also keen to use it as a token of devotion, particularly when Mao himself used gestures such as swimming in the Yangtze to signal the start of a campaign of renewal. Physical vigour was used to highlight values of virility, youth, and strength. But it also had a reverse side: effort, and even pain and suffering were made to seem like necessary and worthy marks of experience to achieve entry to a politically enlightened state.

A Naval College 'Long March Red Guard team' decided to re-enact the march as, effectively, a pilgrimage, a mark of respect for the original event. The *People's Daily* reported the team's progress:

> From the first step of the Long March Red Guards' journey, difficulties appeared from start to finish...
>
> Rain soaked their clothes, sweat drenched their bodies, the journey consumed all of their strength.
>
> During that time, they clung to the 'Quotations from Chairman Mao,' reading as they walked, where it said: 'Be determined, don't be afraid of sacrifices. Remove all difficulties, and fight for victory.'
>
> After several days of walking, bloody blisters had appeared on their feet... every step that they took was painful...
>
> Mao Zedong Thought is their strength! What does rain matter, who cares about pain?[26]

The ultimate possible endpoint of the pilgrimage was, of course, direct contact with Mao himself, or at least a sighting of the 'reddest sun in our hearts'. The *People's Daily* reported the meeting of the Qinghua University Middle School Red Guards with Mao on 21 August 1966. The dialogue was hardly complex; as reported, the Red Guards told Mao 'Long live Chairman Mao; we want revolution, we want to rebel', to his face, while the Chairman reciprocated by saying 'I support you determinedly'.[27] Yet the legitimacy that could be claimed from a personal encounter with Mao was naturally immense. Even a distant sighting was worth a report and could lead to a transformative experience of 'rebirth'. Schoolteacher Bei Guancheng excitedly wrote home to colleagues in Shanghai in September 1966: 'Let me tell you the great news, greater than heaven...I saw our most most most most dearly beloved leader Chairman Mao!…I have decided to make today my birthday. Today I started a new life!!!'[28]

Penitence was also an important part of the sacralisation of Mao Thought. Dissent from Mao was no longer a matter of political view, but rather a sacrilege. This had effectively been the case during the 'Rectification Movements' as well, but the intervening period had seen a loosening of the stranglehold that Mao Thought had at the most radical period. Not so during the GPCR, however. Seven activists were presumably forced to offer a recantation of their political position in January 1967 to a rival Red Guard group. However, the way in which the recantation was phrased was as a 'Letter to Chairman Mao requesting punishment'. 'Respected Chairman Mao', it began, 'We request punishment from you. We were wrong, completely wrong'. Having then elucidated in detail on the errors of approach that they had made by coming to the capital to denounce a rival grouping, the writers say:

> We guarantee you the following:
>
> 1. Determinedly to read Your [my translation uses capitalization of 'Your' as the respectful *nin* rather than normal *ni* is used for 'you'] books, hear Your words, and act according to Your directions, becoming Your good students…
>
> 2. We were completely wrong to come to the capital with our accusation, and will receive the criticism of the Scarlet Red Guards.
>
> Long live the reddest of red suns in our hearts, Chairman Mao! Long live! Long, long live![29]

The language echoes religious practice very strongly. It casts the writers as supplicants or students to a higher body, addressed with a pronoun that indicates superiority, and whose edicts must be obeyed without question. The use of *nin*, the respectful pronoun meaning 'you' is particularly notable; the Cultural Revolution was supposedly a period of egalitarianism, yet Mao is addressed with a pronoun which had fallen out of general use because of its 'bourgeois' and hierarchical overtones. Finally, the role of Mao as icon in this letter is worth reiterating. There must be some doubt as to whether Mao himself would ever have seen such a letter. The aim was to underscore ideologically a victory of one 'red' group over another, which had probably been won by force. The appearance in black and white of a 'confession' couched in terms of sin against the driving force of the GPCR, gave the winning group a moral legitimacy that mere violence could not on its own supply. (In Chinese history, there is a long tradition of 'official histories' which record defeated leaders humbly asking for punishment for the sin of having rebelled against the legitimate ruler. Ironically, although Cultural Revolution confessions seem to be in this tradition, the petitioners here are effectively demanding punishment for *not* having 'rebelled' – though that rebellion was defined purely in the narrow sense of the Cultural Revolution.)

Finally, one other recourse to primordial sources of legitimacy must be mentioned: the kitsch, implicitly gendered division between male and female that defined 'duty'. In July 1967, the soldier Wu Kejiang wrote a poem supposedly to dismiss the fears of an overprotective mother. 'Fearing that I might be killed by "white bandits" at the school', Wu wrote, 'my mama pulled me back. I said –

> Let me go, mama!
> Don't be afraid for your child,
> Our allies in struggle are everywhere,
> What good are the 'white bandits' sword and shield?

The poem continues over four verses, noting the in the last stanza:

> Goodbye mama!
> Our highest commander Mao Zedong orders us to set out...
> Until we have obtained thorough victory in the Great
>   Cultural Revolution,
> I swear...never to return home![30]

Conclusion: clinging to reason

Because charismatic Maoism was rarely dominant and part of a precarious balance, it does not have the all-encompassing nature that the 'classic' political religions seem to have managed. Perhaps the nearest thing to a fully sacralised Maoist political religion was not in China itself, but the heavily Maoist influenced Khmer Rouge regime in Cambodia. Yet on the other hand, the totalistic and sacralised nature of the discourse used by the Red Guards is undeniably theological in nature. Mao *was* a god to the Red Guards – to dispute this seems to be quibbling to find a rationality that is simply not there.

There is, however, something that makes one still a little uneasy about using the 'political religion' model for the whole of the phenomenon of charismatic Maoism, even though it provides so many points of reference. In the last resort, the fascist systems, particularly in Germany and Italy, and the related ultra-nationalist project in early Shoowa

Japan, used modernity to transcend reason, and did so explicitly. Whether it was the romantic strain in German nationalist thought, or the influence of Zen and Nichiren, which delighted in paradox, on the Japanese, there was a powerful intellectual assumption that reason needed to be put in its place. Famously, in the midst of the war, the Kyoto School held a conference on 'overcoming modernity'. No Chinese political movement which achieved significance, whether Kuomintang, Communist, or collaborationist, rejected modernity in that way.

Even at its most utterly irrational (the Cultural Revolution in particular), the cult of Maoism stuck to a language that claimed its legitimacy came from rationality, even when it patently did not. It could not openly portray itself as a religion and irrational phenomenon – Lin Biao would not have acknowledged himself as a high priest. Many aspects of charismatic Maoism do bear a resemblance to religious practice which has a secular, rather than spiritual object of veneration. But much of the religious practice to which they bear resemblance is Judeo-Christian (because of the May Fourth influence), rather than pre-modern Chinese political practice. Therefore, the political religion argument is more of a discussion about different varieties of modernity and their entry into China, than about the revival of pre-modern cults. The Chinese case is relevant to the wider discussion over whether political religion is as valid an interpretation of Communist as of fascist regimes, not as an example of supposed Chinese 'uniqueness'. In terms of the Mao cult, we have a modern cult with Chinese characteristics. But it is the similarity rather than the difference with Western personality cults that we need to keep in mind. Returning to the 'brand name' leaders with whom we began, it is Gandhi, not Mao, who is the harder figure to categorise from a Western perspective.

Notes

1. As ever, brief summaries of this sort do scant justice to the highly complex and sophisticated debates that have been conducted on the origins of the Chinese Communist revolution and the nature of Mao's contribution to the rural revolution.
2. Mao Zedong, Roger R. Thompson (trans.), *Report from Xunwu*.
3. Among the most sophisticated analyses are the various volumes by Stuart Schram and Frederick Teiwes.
4. See, for example, Frederick Teiwes with Warren Sun, 'From a Leninist to a Charismatic Party: The CCP's Changing Leadership, 1937–1945', Tony Saich and Hans van de Ven (eds), *New Perspectives on the Chinese Communist Revolution* (Armonk, 1995).

5. Emilio Gentile, R. Mallett (trans.), 'The Sacralisation of Politics: Definitions, Interpretations and Reflections on the Question of Secular Religion and Totalitarianism', *Totalitarian Movements and Political Religions* 1/1 (Summer 2000), p. 39.
6. For innovative work on the impact of the Great War in East Asia, see Frederick Dickinson, *War and National Reinvention: Japan in the Great War, 1914–1919* (Cambridge, MA, 1999) and Xu Guoqi, *China and the Great War: China's Pursuit of a New National Identity and Internationalization* (Cambridge, 2005).
7. Gentile (Note 5), p. 25.
8. Hans van de Ven, 'Introduction', Saich and Van de Ven, *New Perspectives*, p. xx.
9. See, for example, David Apter, 'Discourse as Power: Yan'an and the Chinese Revolution', in Saich and Van de Ven (Note 8).
10. Joan Judge, *Print and Politics: 'Shibao' and the Culture of Reform in Late Qing China* (Stanford, 1996).
11. There is a wealth of scholarship on the May Fourth movement, including key works such as Chow (1960) and Schwarcz (1986). An attempt to bring together some of these threads of interpretation about the Movement and its legacy is Rana Mitter, *A Bitter Revolution: China's Struggle with the Modern World* (Oxford, 2004).
12. See Mitter (Note 11), pp. 129–33.
13. Apter (Note 9), p. 195.
14. CCP Central Committee, 'Decision Concerning the Great Proletarian Cultural Revolution', in Michael Schoenhals, *China's Cultural Revolution, 1966–69: Not a Dinner Party*, p. 33.
15. Ibid., p. 36.
16. Ibid., p. 37.
17. Red Flag, 'In Praise of the Red Guards' (Note 14), p. 45.
18. Zhou Enlai, 'Mao Zedong Thought is the Sole Criterion of Truth' (Note 14), p. 27.
19. Lin Biao, CCR 3/14 (1966). See also 3/18 (1966); 3/21 (1966).
20. The new wave of studies from post-1949 archives show how local level society often changed less than the centralised state claimed. See, for example, Neil Diamant, *Revolutionizing the Family* (2000).
21. 'Zhesi baowei wuchanjieji zhuanzheng', Song Yianyi et al. (ed.), *Chinese Cultural Revolution Database* 6/38 (1966).
22. 'Ba weida de Mao Zedong sixiang de huoju gaogao juqi' (Note 21), 6/15 (1966).
23. Ibid.
24. 'Wo gei Mao zhuxi daishangle hong xiuzhang' (Note 21), 6/39 (1966).
25. 'XXX – hongse kongbu wansui' (Note 21), 6/98 (1966).
26. 'Women de duiwu xiang taiyang' (Note 21), 6/125 (1966).
27. 'Mao zhuxi jianle women "Hong weibing"' (Note 21), 6/38.
28. Bei Guancheng, 'I saw Chairman Mao!!!' in Schoenhals, *China's Cultural Revolution*, pp.148–49.
29. 'Shanghai ergang jiu ge zhi weiduiyuan xiede...' (Note 21), 6/18 (1967).
30. Wu Kejiang, 'Fangkai wo, mama!' (Note 21), 6/67 (1967).

Part III
The Politicization of Religion

9
An Islamist Turkish Party's Journey to Democracy and Modernity

Kemal H. Karpat

On 3 November 2002 Turkey and the world witnessed a peaceful civil, political, social and cultural revolution, which they did not expect and in some cases, did not desire. The name of the party responsible reflects its hybrid traditional–modern nature along with its search for authenticity and contemporaneity. The *Adalet ve Kalkinma Partisi* (AKP – Justice and Development Party) takes the first word of its name from the Arabic *adalat*; while the second word, coined recently, is 'pure' Turkish deriving from the verb *kalkmak* (to rise). The original pure Turkish term for development that has replaced the old Arabic *inkishaf* was *gelişmek*.

The AKP was established on 14 August 2001 under the leadership of Recep Tayyip Erdoğan and some of his friends, including Abdullah Gül. Erdoğan, at the time, was in jail for having recited some patriotic verses written by a prominent nationalist intellectual during the War of Liberation in the early 1920s, urging the Turks to resist foreign invasion. Then, about ten days after the party's establishment was announced, Erdoğan was indicted for a speech he had delivered in 1994, in which he had declared that one 'cannot be a Muslim and a secularist'.

Observers of the Turkish political scene were quick to say Erdoğan's indictment was intended to prevent him from establishing a new Islamic party that would undermine Turkey's secular order. More subtle students of Turkish politics, however, interpreted the government's action as an astute move designed to keep all the Islamists in the one existing religious party. The *Refah Partisi* (RP – Welfare Party) already was viewed by the public as promoting an Islamist regime, and as long as the party continued to carry the labels 'Islamist', 'reactionary', 'anti-Kemalist' and so on, the ruling élite could easily indict any of its members, especially those with popular appeal, on charges of Islamist activity, dooming them to political failure. The self-proclaimed secularists and Kemalists, who not only often interpreted Atatürk's ideas to suit their ideological stands, but also had wielded power since 1923, stood ready to resort to almost any action in order to 'save the modernist regime' and in the process retain their own privileges.

Yet paradoxically, as often is the case in Turkey, this undemocratic attitude of the ruling élite was tempered by a readiness to accept the verdict of the electorate. Like their Ottoman predecessors, the leaders of the Republican Turkey combined in an uneasy way the fierce autocratic nature of the state, which they embraced while in power, with the individuals' mellow, humane and egalitarian yearnings they displayed in private life. Although the materialism and power embodied in the state seemed to dominate, they did not supersede the individual spirituality, quiet and contentment preached by the far right. The victory of the AKP in 2002, and its policies since assuming government power, can be better understood if presented in an historical framework that could place certain developments in their proper historical, and cultural-political perspective.

Turkey has had a variety of 'Islamic' parties since a multiparty democracy was established in 1945/1946. Of these parties, the *Milli Nizam* (MN – National Order), established by Necmeddin Erbakan, an engineering professor with some teaching experience in Germany, was the most important. Although closed for being anti-secularist, the MN re-emerged as the *Milli Selamet Partisi* (MSP – National Salvation Party) in 1973, only to be closed repeatedly after the military intervention of 1980 and under different names thereafter. The party's durability and survival were based on a rather secularist ideology known as the *Milli Görüş* (National View), which had been formulated by Erbakan as early as 1967 and found followers among the youth. This ideology envisioned first the creation of a political front or organisation that rested on a national-religious (Turkish-Islamic) identity, and regarded development based on technology as a fundamental goal. Its actual driving force was a nationalism that had absorbed certain features of the faith, while discarding some of the ethnic vocabulary of the secular nationalists. The ideology also advocated rapprochement with the Arab countries and displayed a rather ambiguous attitude towards the West, Turkish modernism and secularism. Erbakan himself pursued a pragmatic and opportunistic policy, and it would prove disastrous in the end despite his constant allusions to Islam and its virtues. He returned from exile, at the request of the military who had ousted him, to establish an Islamic party in order to draw the youth away from the leftist ideologies rising in good part as a reaction to the military rule. Consequently, the old party, that is the MSP, re-emerged once more in 1983 under the name of the Refah Party. The rather odd rapprochement between Erbakan, the main spokesman for a political Islam, and the military, the chief promoters of secularism, inevitably raised doubts about Erbakan's ideological commitment to Islam and the military's adherence to secularism.

It should be mentioned that the Refah Party, despite its name changes, remained under the leadership of Erbakan and his associates, some of whom were truly dedicated to a political Islam and regime change. As the party received limited popular support and a share of the vote that ranged between just 7 and 11 per cent until the 1990s, the party came more under the influence of its younger members. These sincere Muslims shared the ideas of the *Milli Görüş* and were deeply impressed by Khomeini's revolution in Iran, but the same young, somewhat radical members of the party had been brought up in the increasingly liberal, free and democratic atmosphere prevailing in Turkish cities since the 1950s. Despite their ideological orientation, they shared to a good extent the lifestyle and modes of thinking of the rest of society. Islamists in thought and practicing Muslims, they lived a modernist, secularist life without seeing contradiction between them. Instead they believed that Islam, if divorced from the economic and cultural factors and simple human needs of society, had little chance of attracting the popular vote.

Behind the young Islamists' realistic appraisal of the Turkish electorate was a fundamental social and cultural development affecting Turkish society in its entirety. In the mid-1950s Turkey had experienced a village-to-city migration that raised the proportion of the urban population from roughly 20 per cent in the 1950s to over 50 per cent in the 1990s. The chief reasons for the migration, as this writer has explained in a published work,[1] were poverty and a lack of educational facilities in the villages. Education in the Turkish context provided an avenue for upward social mobility and an opportunity for 'enlightenment', a word pregnant with profound political, social and ideological connotations. Although the original migrants were happy to live in docility amid even the most modest amenities of an urban environment, their children reacted – sometimes violently – against their social, economic and cultural marginalisation, especially when educated.

Turkish society is basically egalitarian. The lack of a blood aristocracy in the Ottoman state in accordance with Islam's tenets has imbued society with a profound sense of equality, while meritocracy practiced by the early Ottoman rulers (and lately among the financiers and industrialists) has created an élite relying on political power or money. Because secular education generally awakens the political consciousness of one's social situation and helps define the culprit for one's real or imaginary suffering, the educated children of the *gecekondu* (migrant shanty towns) evaluated their social status not with the eyes of their contended parents, but with those of the established urban population that saw them as marginal semi-peasants.

The democracy of Turkey, although still incomplete, provided an excellent avenue for this marginalised group to air its discontent and seize the levers of power. The village migrants and their descendants considered themselves good Muslims by the standards of rural Turkey. In the city they preserved and even strengthened their attachment to Islam both as a means of psychological and cultural self-defence and as a yardstick for censuring the 'moral decay', 'selfishness' and 'materialism' of the urban areas. The old inhabitants of the city, who held the reins of power and wealth, defined the Turks' identity by selected secular criteria, and Necmeddin Erbakan, the leader of the Refah Party, was bound to his own narrow and largely formal understanding of Islam. Neither realised that the rising younger generation demanded a much more dynamic, worldly and militant Islam that would not merely make the Turks more pious, but would advance them economically and technologically while also making them more respectful of morality, ethics and spirituality. They were thus rebelling against a positivist secularism that regarded religion as a form of backwardness. As a result, the individuals who took an active role in the Refah Party formed three main groups: the old-time Islamists clustered around Erbakan, the younger descendants of village migrants and the politically motivated intellectuals of various shades, including some secular-minded modernists who hoped that Islam as a faith would somehow dampen the corruption, materialism and hedonism often bound under the label of modernity.

Recep Tayyip Erdoğan best personifies the new type populist Islamist leadership that arose in late twentieth-century Turkey. Born in 1954, in the Kasımpaşa district of Istanbul to an immigrant family from the Black Sea region, he was educated first in a religious high school and then graduated from the School of Economics and Trade of Marmara University. At the age of 16, he had embraced the views of the *Milli Görüş* and by 1975 was the head of the youth organisation of the MSP on the European side of Istanbul. Then, in 1984, he became the head of the Beyoğlu branch (Pera, the modern district) of the Refah Party, and on 27 March 1994 was elected mayor of Istanbul, a position of extraordinary prestige and power.

Following closely the political events in Turkey, I was fascinated by Erdoğan's rapid rise and especially by his failure to fulfil the 'Islamic' promises he had made during the election to build a mosque in Taksim, the heart of modern Istanbul, and close the bars. In the belief that he was acting simply out of consideration for the public wish that opposed this Islamisation from above, I focused on Erdoğan's basic democratic spirit, rather than on his undemocratic militant statements. When I asked Mayor Erdoğan for an interview, after several refusals (some of his aides seemed to question my affiliation with an American institution) he agreed to see me thanks to the intervention of a prominent journalist friend whom he cultivated. Thus, much of what follows is based on my glimpses from this interview and from other social encounters with Erdoğan as well as on the memoirs and writings of his friends and associates such as Mehmet Metiner. Erdoğan's former consultant, Metiner is intimately familiar with the Islamic movements in Turkey, some of which he led and like many other militants of the left and the right who converted to democracy, provides excellent insights into the ideological transformation of Turkey.

Beginning in the 1990s, the Refah Party, under pressure from its lower and younger cadres, adopted a more practical platform to address the economic, cultural and educational needs voiced by the electorate. Although the party had promised implicitly to 'replace the faithless state' with a more religious order, it now began to pay closer attention to bread-and-butter issues and attracted new middle-of-the-road voters. Indeed having made the slogan *adil düzen* (just order) its motto it attracted many voters of all ideological shades, and in the elections of 1995 won 21 per cent of the popular vote to become the major party. After the major 'secularist' parties failed to form a government, the RP entered into a coalition with the *Doğru Yol Partisi* (DYP – True Path Party) then headed by Tansu Çiller, who shortly before had declared total opposition to the RP. Necmeddin Erbakan established his government early in 1996, dismissing the parliamentary inquiry of corruption against Çiller as the price for her joining the coalition, before he travelled to Muslim countries in order to form a Muslim Union, appointed radical Islamists to positions of power such as the Justice Ministry and sought to bring committed Islamists into the government. He also supported the small businesses in Anatolia, nicknaming them *Anadolu Kaplanlari* (Anatolian Tigers), a clear nationalist rebuff to the old dominant cosmopolitan financial-industrial circles clustered in Istanbul and Izmir. This was part of the populist appeal of the party, which, important as is, cannot be discussed further.

The activities of Erbakan's Islamic government, particularly his haphazard utopianism and his humiliation by petty Arab rulers who gave him 'lessons in democracy,' antagonized both the secularist sector and many of the party's own members. The result was the military's memorandum of 28 February 1997, that led to Erbakan's resignation and his slow descent into obscurity.

This military semi-coup of 1997, in contrast to the three previous interventions, received only mild criticism not only because the target was 'Islamic', but also because Erbakan's 'Islamic' policies threatened the very existence of Turkey. What these political events of 1995–1997 in Turkey show is that a substantial number of Turks, regardless of their religious affiliations and personal feelings, finally understood that the civil and public spheres had their own autonomous existence, and that the state, acting as a body above the society, could actually play the role of an arbiter defending both the public sphere and the individual's freedom of faith and thought. Many Turks realised that Islam is not a state but a religion, and that secularism is the granting of rights to all religions rather than their denial. As some of the new thinkers of Islam, modernity and democracy expressed it, the events of 1995–1997 showed that political Islam was as bad as political secularism. In addition, the existence of Turks as 'Turks' in their own national state had created both a new political identity, and a certain harmony and reconciliation between Turkishness and Islam. A survey conducted by *Milliyet*, a major national newspaper, on 2 February 1994 indicated that 69 per cent of the respondents identified themselves as Turks, 21 per cent as Muslim Turks and only 4 per cent as Muslims.

The events of 1995–1997 and the resulting change of thought and attitude that drew the line between faith and politics finally brought into the open a long-standing conflict within the Refah Party. Closed by the military, it re-emerged as *Fazilet* (Virtue) and ultimately on 20 July 2001 as *Saadet* (Felicity). The party's convention of 2000 failed to elect as chairman the candidate of the young reformed Islamists, Abdullah Gül (currently – September 2005 – Foreign Minister) short a mere 122 votes, but chose party chairman Recai Kutan, a rather colourless politician who acted as the proxy of Erbakan, whom a court had banned from politics for five years. Although Erdoğan did not openly participate in all these events (as mentioned before, he was in jail for various anti-secularist utterances), he actually directed the opposition to the old leaders of the Refah Party from the beginning. As expected, the rebellion resulted in the establishment of the AKP on 14 August 2001, a fact already mentioned. The result of the elections held only 14 months later completely surprised everybody. The AKP openly or implicitly accepted democracy, modernity, constitutionalism, Kemalism, republicanism and secularism as principles of state, and declared all to be compatible with Islam, which they regarded both as part of the society's values and beliefs and as a matter of individual choice. The party's Islamist opponents in the Saadet Party (SP) under Erbakan's covert guidance accused the AKP of having betrayed Islamic ideals, calling it a party of opportunist novices unworthy of public trust. The elections put all these claims to the test.

The AKP won 34 per cent of the popular vote and, due to the electoral system of Turkey, initially about 370 of the 550 seats in the National Assembly. Erbakan's SP, which claimed to represent the true Islamic constituency of Turkey, won a mere 2.5 per cent of the popular vote. The other major political parties that had ruled Turkey for the past decades received less than 10 per cent of the required popular vote, and were unable to send any deputies to the National Assembly (despite minor changes in party representation in the Assembly, the AKP maintained its overwhelming majority). The opposition Republican People's Party won about 19 per cent of the votes, and secured some 160 seats in the Assembly.

The AKP has been in power for almost three years without encountering any major crisis. True, the 'turban' continues to be a contentious issue viewed by secularists as a blatant Islamist defiance of Kemalism, yet it is considered by the Islamists and many other Turks to be a matter of freedom and personal choice in attire. Women wearing it are not allowed to enter official buildings, including schools, and the AKP government's attempt to lift the ban was met with an outcry. So, too, were other 'Islamic' attempts to placate the radicals in the party, such as lifting limitations on the graduates of religious schools wishing to enter the universities, the redefinition of adultery to the woman's detriment and so on. Yet, these are minor issues, despite the outcry of the so-called secularists, many posing as Kemalists, who complain that religious reaction is on the rise.

The AKP government has ended the economic crisis (although some credit goes to its predecessor) and has enlarged democratic freedoms to a degree unknown in the past. For instance, it has given the Kurds and other minorities freedom to use their own languages in publishing newspapers and books, and on television. In addition, the National Security Council, dominated by the military, has been placed under civilian control. Some of these measures clearly were intended to qualify Turkey for membership of the European Union, but that membership (and together with it, globalisation and multinational, cultural and religious dialogues) was a supreme goal of the AKP government. The AKP sought to improve relations with the Arab world and in a rather awkward sign of solidarity, criticised Israel's policy towards the Palestinians, and hurt Turkey's extensive and lucrative relations with Israel.

The three-year rule of the AKP government including all such positive and negative aspects can be studied in greater depth, but that is not the purpose of this essay. Here, the essential fact to keep in mind is that since its inception as a Republic in 1923 Turkey has been divided into two groups, the rulers and the ruled. Only the structure of the ruling group has changed while its leadership (the military, most of academia and the judiciary, etc.) has remained more or less constant, despite the existence of political parties and regular elections. In other words, there is all the formal and visible outfit of democracy but not its spirit. For its part, the ruling group has justified its constant hold on power as an absolute necessity to implement modernisation, Kemalism, secularism and progress which only they could understand, implement and maintain properly against the tide of religious reaction of the masses.

Yet ironically, it has been the underdog remainder of society, the ruled that has supplied the ruling élites with fresh blood. Indeed, many military men, high officials in the security organisations, have very modest origins. The ruling group has considered the ruled incapable of joining contemporary civilisation, or of participating in self-government because of their immersion into religion, that is, Islam. Although Turkey as a whole has made extraordinary progress in every field of endeavour, maintaining this split of the society into progressivist-modernists on the one hand and obscurantist, religion-bound masses on the other, has provided the rulers with the pretext to intervene and topple elected governments. Certainly, Erbakan's erratic 11-month government reinforced this situation.

The ruler–ruled split in Turkish society, which defies the basic spirit of democracy, can be healed only by a movement from below. People from the people, acting for the people must maintain their identity, culture and values while sincerely embracing democracy, modernity, progress and respect for other cultures and religions. And this is exactly what was achieved in the elections of 2002, when the population took the opportunity to bring to power a government that respected the country's Islamic identity, culture and values while providing it with modernity, economic development and real democracy. Usually, political parties devise a platform of ideas, projects and programmes to inspire and attract the voters, but in the Turkish elections of 2002 the electorate voted overwhelmingly in favour of the AKP, simply because it was able to articulate best the majority's wish to bring together faith and modernity and open the way to a real democracy. Moreover, this was an internal process, free of foreign pressure or interference and both

Europe and the United States, which were deeply upset with the result of elections in Turkey, eventually accepted it.

Thus, as a truly popular movement led by simple citizens and backed by a large segment of the Turks, the AKP gained control of the government. Its leaders, including Prime Minister Erdoğan are pious, practicing Muslims as much as they are (or claim to be) modernist, republican, democratic and secular. In the ultimate analysis, what happened in Turkey, that is the reconciliation of democracy and modernity with Islam, the coexistence of spirituality and materialism, resulted from a dialectical process, a constant interaction between various groups, ideologies and sheer individual ambition and vision. It can easily occur elsewhere in other Islamic lands. I sincerely hope that first the Turks and then the rest of the world understand in depth and appreciate the marriage of modernity and Islam in Turkey.

Post scriptum

The above essay was written in 2005 – since then the antagonism of the 'real' (skin-deep) government towards the popularly elected AK government has escalated into a constitutional crisis. The army opposed the election of Abdulah Gul as President – after the tenure of Ahmet Sezer, a 'secularist' and friend of the military, ended. The Costitutional Court imposed on the National Assembly an arbitrary quorum while the military issued a rather obscure warning to the government. Subsequently, new elections were held in July 2007 that gave the AK party 47 per cent of the vote and brought Abdulah Gul to the Presidency at Cankaya (Turkish White House) along with his turbaned wife. This was considered not only a victory of the 'reactionary' islamists but also an immediate danger to the regime. Consequently, in March 2008 the Prosecutor of the Republic filed a complaint with the Constitutional Court and asked for the closure of the AK party and the banning from politics of some 70 members including Premier Erdogan. Named the 'law-legal-coup', the case is being tried in the Constitutional Court as at the time of this writing.

Note

1. K. H. Karpat, *The Gecekondu: Rural Migration and Urbanization* (Cambridge: Cambridge University Press, 1976).

10
Hindutva as a Political Religion: An Historical Perspective

Robert E. Frykenberg

This essay attempts to show how – from an analytical or from an historical perspective – Hindutva is a melding of Hindu fascism and Hindu fundamentalism. Claims that it is a profoundly religious and profoundly, even aggressively, political form of militant nationalism are clear. From earliest glimmerings of its inception, its agents have combined ambiguity with confrontation, compromise, and contradiction as tactical devices for achieving long range corporatist designs for gaining paramount power and imposing a totalistic agenda upon all of India. This agenda of 'Hindutva' or 'Ram Rajiya' ('Rama's Realm') aims to forge 'One Nation (in One State), One Culture, One Religion, and One Language.' In Lord Rama's name, a single 'Hindu Nation' for the whole Indian Continent must be ruled by the precepts of *Arya Dharm,* or *Sanātana Dharma.*[1] *Sanskriti* icons, norms, and symbols, invoking cosmic and eternal verities of Vedic Law, must be reflected in principles on which this Nation must stand. Under this regime, a changeless social structure of the Four Colour Categories (*Chatur Varnya*), as manifest in *varnāshramadharma,* both reflected the proper place of each birth (*jāt*) or caste (*jāti*) in its rightful rank and status – its strata of purity or impurity. Birth and Earth, Genomes in Sacred Blood and Molecules of Sacred Soil, determined everyone's place and rank within an all-encompassing and cosmic 'World Order' (*Vishwa Dharma*).

Justifications for this ideology were and still are, of course, complex and convoluted. Much rests not just upon what events are selected and taken as facts, what evidence is taken as valid, or what meanings have been drawn from interpretations of those facts, but upon what meanings have been attached to the concepts being used. Basic clarifications are in order. What Hindutva is, or is not – as a cultural movement, a religious movement, or a political (nationalist) movement (or movements) – depends, quite obviously, on how the concepts 'Hindu' or 'Hinduism' are used. Many contested discourses, often heavily theoretical disquisitions, cloak dogma under the guise of theory. They start by assuming that 'we all know' what such concepts mean. But not bothering to define concepts leads, all too often, down a spiraling staircase into confusion, if not obfuscation. Clarity may perhaps be increased by tracing these concepts within appropriate historical contexts, before turning more specifically to the growth of Hindutva ideology during the past century and its evolution as a political religion.

Constructions of modern Hindu institutions

'Hindu' is a modern term, hardly two centuries old.[2] Originally used to describe anything 'native' to India, it encompassed Christians and Muslims, 'Tribals' (*Adivāsi* people), and 'Untouchables' (*Āvarna* people). Subsequently, the term evolved and was increasingly applied mainly to religious phenomena within the Indian subcontinent. Thereafter, from being as an English term, its norms were increasingly determined by heavy 'Hindu' ('Native') input, mainly Brahmanical or high-born, in virtually every phase of its manifold constructions.

The concept, needless to say, has also been molded by events. These events, as processes, gradually reified and ultimately 'communalized' the concept and its manifold meanings.[3] What occurred was neither simple nor straightforward. The events that brought about 'reconstructions' of the concept have been multilayered, multiplex, and highly complex, with sometimes complementary and sometimes contradictory overtones. However viewed, these events also transformed the concept, adding new meanings without shedding older ones. Initially a utilitarian instrument for achieving and describing inclusion – hallowing all that existed within the confines of the subcontinent – the same term has increasingly, during the past century, become an instrument for exclusion – for repudiating all that does not conform to specific norms of *sacred birth* and *sacred earth*. Today, the term is used to exclude Muslims and Christians while, at the same time, it is also used as a device for incorporating, *by definition*, all Buddhist, Sikh, Tribal, and Untouchable communities (even though, for the most part, such communities themselves have vehemently resented being so defined). Many communities contest such inclusion, seeing it as yet another form of 'Hindu' colonialism and domination that will continue to perpetuate the ritual pollution, social apartheid, and thraldom that they have suffered for untold centuries. They see such co-opting, such 'inclusion-by-definition,' as a rhetorical device for perpetuating communal imprisonment and marginalization. 'Hinduism' as a concept, in short, is a bone of contention – a weapon used ceaselessly in increasingly uncivil wars of words.

An intermingling of historical processes, or sequences of events, can be identified as lying behind or beneath constructions of the term 'Hindu' as we now know it. While undoubtedly more might be mentioned, at least three or four – or two sets of two – constructions have contributed to the politics of Hindutva. All hark back to the East India Company's Raj and to the establishment of the Indian Empire. All have a hybrid, or hyphenated, character – a mixed and multiple parentage that is at once both European and Indian. But, as already indicated, beneath all else, always muddying the water, lies the initial meaning: – of 'Hindu' as applying to or meaning anything and everything 'Native' to 'India' (or 'Hindustan'). So seen in their origins, two Indo-British concepts – 'Hindu' and 'India' – are twins.

These processes of modern construction began, first of all, with policies of Warren Hastings. India's first Governor-General (1773–1785) gave personal encouragement and official support to that vast enterprise known as 'Orientalism.' Out of this enterprise came some of the earliest constructions of this concept.[4] Hosts of scholars, *both* European and Native Indian, became avidly engaged in this venture of discovery – a project of uncovering, describing, surveying, preserving, and studying the entire corpus of artifacts which constituted the cultural heritage of India's ancient civilization. Only considerably later, after Napoleon's conquest of Egypt, was the term also applied to other civilizations of Asia and the Near East. 'Orientalism,' as a by-product of the Enlightenment, soon gained world-wide recognition and academic respectability. Chairs of 'Indology' and Sanskrit became established at major universities around the world. 'Hindoo' then became a generic label for describing all manifestations of life, whether social, ritual, or cultural, within India. While it was mainly applied to 'high' cultural and religious traditions, as defined by Brahmans within the Sanskritic (and Vedic) literatures, it also came more loosely to include any and all forms of ritual and social practices, institutions, and values 'native' to India.[5]

But behind all that was 'Hindu,' in the sense of the high traditions being uncovered by Orientalists (i.e. Indologists), stood the influence of twice-born (*dvija*) scholars. Most of these were servants of the Company or local gentry from high-born families related to Company officals. All, from the very beginning, had long been connected, in one way or another, with the rise of the Indian Empire. Champions and defenders of all things 'Native' (i.e. 'Hindu' or 'Indian'), these persons came, at least initially, from that class of indigenous notables which best understood the cultural and social foundations of political power. No class was more intimately involved in the pursuit of Indology than they. Having already long served as official *dubashis, munshis,* and *vakils,* it was they who played a vital role as teachers and translators for each new generation of European servants of the Company. As diplomatic agents, go-betweens, and interpreters between the Company and various levels of Indian rulership, from highest of lordly princes (Mughals and Maharajas) down to petty village zamindars, they played a pivotal part in the construction both of Empire and of modern 'Hinduism.' This Warren Hastings well understood.

Not surprisingly, therefore, it was also from the ranks of Indians themselves, mainly Brahmans, that many if not most advances in Orientalist and Indological understanding came. In concert with Indologists and Sanskritists around the world, Indian scholars ceaselessly unearthed and translated, interpreted, and published fresh findings. In fields of ancient history, philosophy, and religion, the 'wonder that was India' was constantly being rediscovered.[6] (This process of 'unearthing' India's antiquity is still going on, despite its having been so hotly contested by disciples of Edward Said.[7]) Epitomized by Max Müller's *The Sacred Books of the East,* a huge series of 50 volumes that began to emerge between 1879 and 1910,[8] over a century after Warren Hastings had first launched such efforts, Orientalism came to fruition in the work of such scholarly giants as R.C. Majumdar, K.A. Nilakantha Sastri, and Sarvepalli Radhakrishnan. These scholars symbolized hosts of nameless predecessors whose transcriptions and translations provided a vast corpus of intellectual and philosophical substance for a newly reifying high religion called 'Hinduism.' More than that, since political logic called for eclectic and syncretistic impulses necessary for continuing processes of imperial (and national) integration, this Orientalist Hinduism emphasized and hallowed doctrines of restraint and tolerance. After being unveiled by Swami Vivekananda before the Parliament of World Religions at Chicago in 1893, this newly discovered 'Hinduism' achieved legitimation and recognition among theologically liberal thinkers in the West as a full-fledged 'World Religion.'[9]

The second process was no less significant. This arose out of legislation decreeing that, henceforth, imperial governments in India would take direct responsibility for the care, maintenance, and support of all *pukka* Native ('Hindoo') religious and charitable institutions. The imperial State made itself the guardian of all endowments, temples, places of pilgrimage, sectarian academies (*mutths*), ceremonies, and festivals. Bengal Regulation X of 1810 and Madras Regulation XVII of 1817, for example, brought scores of thousands of proper temples, pilgrimage centers, and monastic institutions (*mutths*), great and small, under official protection, management, and tax exemption. By this means, and almost unbeknownst to Britain, the Indian Empire became, for all practical purposes, a *de facto* 'Hindu' Raj. This officially (if 'silently') sponsored policy of 'Hinduization' (or 'nationalization') of all cultural and religious institutions in India, while later heavily assailed by opponents and subsequently modified (by legislation in 1863 and 1926), never ended and, in many respects, still continues to be in force.[10]

Officials administered temple endowments (*devasthanams*, &c); they made temple repairs or renovations, and oversaw rituals (through the agency of *dharmakartas*, *pujaris*, and *stanikars*); they bestowed homage and worship (*puja*), and also official recognition and titles (such as *rasika* or *sampradayika*) on each deity; and they, Europeans and Indians alike, made personal donations to deities or contributed munificently to ostentatious observances. Ceremonies conducted within temples under the direct or indirect supervision of the state thereby silently, if not formally, legitimized the Hindu cosmic order (*dharma*). In the South, neither the largest and oldest temples of Kanchipuram, Madurai, Srirangam, and Tirupati nor the smallest and meanest of fledgling shrines springing up beside dusty thorough fares escaped close attention. Colonial officials not only controlled temple revenues and expenditures, but watched over ritual practices. Soldiers of the empire, including Christians, Muslims, and Sikhs, stood on parade and saluted local deities, attended blood sacrifices, and marched in processions (*yatras*), remaining prominently visible at all great religious festivals (often in defiance of private consciences). Civil officials collected tolls from pilgrims and taxes at fairs and festivals, and commandeered huge drafts of involuntary labour from hundreds of thousands for the pulling of enormous temple cars (*ratha*-s), turning their heads when someone, propitiously, 'happened' to be crushed beneath the huge wheels of Lord Jagganatha.[11] Even temple dancing, music, and prostitution, involving hundreds of thousands of *devadasis*, came under the eye of government. All these activities came, at least in some measure, within the rubric of this second or 'official' kind of Hinduism.

The third and fourth processes were reactive and critical of the first two. One, initiated and supported by Europeans (Westerners) and Indians alike, was progressively reformist, while the other (as is shown below) was radically romantic and militantly reactionary, revivalist, and totalistic. Beginning well before the Company's Raj gained full paramountcy over the subcontinent, there were those in India, both European and Native, who denigrated what they saw as inhuman practices, and protested against human sacrifice, infanticide, and widow burning. One branch of protests came out of the modern missionary movement, generated by the Evangelical Christian awakenings in the West. Officially forbidden entry into British India, this group cautiously joined Indian Christians in protesting against what were seen as intolerant and oppressive treatment by local officials of the East India Company. Before Parliament forced the Company to admit missionaries into its territories, even as the term 'Hindu' was beginning to appear in writings of Company servants, there were some such servants who wanted to bring about 'social reforms.' Charles Grant and John Shore (aka Lord Teignmouth), converts to Evangelicalism who had risen to high positions within the Government of India, argued that admission of Christian missionaries into Company domains would help to bring about a moral transformation in India. Claudius Buchanan, Company chaplain and Vice-Provost of Fort William College, whose *Christian Researches in Asia* (1811, in later editions) was highly critical of 'Hindoo' institutions, did the same. But, among the chief architects of 'Hindooism' as a vast monolithic system of religion, possibly no single person did more than David Ward. In his four-volume *Account of the Writings, Religion, and Manners of the Hindoos, Including Translations from Their Principal Works*, first published at Serampore in 1811, appearing in its third edition in 1817–1820, not long before his death, this (British) Baptist missionary 'constructed' or 'invented' something that had never before existed.[12] Responding to this work, Raja Ram Mohan Roy and other progressive notables among the Calcutta gentry (*bhadralok*) joined officials and missionaries in a campaign to eradicate decadent 'Hindoo' customs and institutions, especially female infanticide and widow burning. Roy, in reacting to Orientalist scholarship and negative views of 'Hindooism' strove to redefine high religious traditions of India in grand, Brahmanical, and monistic, if not monotheistic, terms, doing so through organizing a progressive reform society known as Brahmo Samāj (1828). Such was his influence that he is still credited with being 'the father of modern India.'[13]

But it is important to recall, in this regard, that prior to the 1790s, Christians already had a long history in India, largely characterized by accommodation to India's cultural, social, and religious institutions. Indeed, for many centuries, Thomas (Syrian Orthodox) Christians of Kerala had flourished as integral parts of local, indigenous cultures.

Indigenous or 'Hindu' forms of Christianity had been deeply rooted in the Indian soil long before critical attitudes among some missionaries from the West gained currency. Moreover, some among the most gifted earlier generations of missionaries from Europe, both Catholic and Protestant, had made acculturating contributions to indigenous (Hindoo) cultures, customs, and institutions, doing so in comprehensive and positive terms.[14] Later, leaders among indigenous movements of newly converted communities in South India – whether in Tarangambadi, Thanjāvur, Tirunelvēli, or Thiruvanthapuram (Travancore) – had petitioned Parliament for protection from persecution, doing so as 'Hindu' or 'Native' Christian subjects of the Company.

For the most part, attacks against support for the official 'Hindu Establishment' within the Company-ruled Indian Empire came to nothing. In one case, when several hundred European (Christian) officials, outraged by what they saw as government participation in 'heathen' practices and rituals, signed a formal protest, their mutinous 'conspiracy' brought immediate and swift retribution. The Anglican Bishop of Madras (Daniel Corrie) was sharply reprimanded, and many others, including the commanding general in Madras (Peregrine Maitland), were forced to resign. Thereafter, efforts by dissidents who returned to London to organize the 'Anti-Idolatry Connexion League' and who launched a pamphlet campaign against the Company's evil 'Hindu' empire, largely came to naught. After many years of lobbying for 'religious neutrality,' such concessions as were made, in legislations of 1863 and 1926, turned out in the end to be more cosmetic than real.

But it was the fourth movement that reconstructed and redefined the concept 'Hindu' much more radically. Responding to and building upon the three movements just described, and growing in tandem with them, this movement was the true progenitor of modern Hindutva. Extremely conservative, but also romantic, reactionary, and revivalist in character, it was defensive, chauvinistic, and xenophobic, especially in response to Western influences and especially as manifested in negative attitudes of some foreign missionaries and officials toward India's ancient 'Hindu' cultures. This movement arose despite the fact that some European (British) officials propitiated local deities and made endowments to local temples and that some missionaries, such as theological liberals and Unitarians, enthusiastically embraced 'Hindu' ideas and philosophies. What really most disturbed traditionalists in India were radical conversion movements, especially those among the lowest, most untouchable castes and tribes. Conversion threatened social structure (*varnāshramadharma*='colour-ranking-order'), based as it was upon conceptions of ritual purity (free of pollution) and sacred blood and earth.

Increasingly aggressive, especially in forms manifest after the 1920s, the most extreme of this collection of movements, now known as the *Sangh Parivar* (i.e. roughly: 'Family of Societies' or 'Kindred Societies') ultimately exhibited what may now be seen as fascist and fundamentalist features that are the theme of this essay. Responding to what were interpreted as invidious attacks against indigenous institutions and against the purity of sacred birth and sacred earth, some high-born elites, especially Brahmans of Maharashtra and regions of the north, resorted to various forms of resistance, both overt and covert. Activist, agitative, and aggressive, and organized in defense of the 'old order' (*sanāthana dharm*), local and regional leaders formed voluntary associations. They initiated and organized petition drives (*arzi-s*), launched public protests (*hartals*) and formed violent forms of unrest (riots, insurrections, &c). In doing so, they demonstrated, and discovered, latent strengths hitherto never fully realized, enabling them to mobilize resources of political power within traditionally dominant social elites. In so doing, they embarked upon programs of constructing, defining, and then demonstrating a new kind of 'Hindu' consciousness. This was a new kind of self-conscious 'Hinduism' such as had never before existed. Those who did these things came from reactionary elements among the very same classes of notables and some of the very same families that, in earlier generations, had served the Raj, either directly, as officials, or as providers of financial and professional services that were essential sinews of the Empire. They reacted against any and all efforts to tamper with social customs or to undermine traditions, especially in matters pertaining to family practices and rituals. These were 'Hindus' in a new sense. They sharply defined and increasingly emphasized salient features of the world that they themselves had helped to build – a system that they now wished to preserve and reify. What they now saw endangered and threatened were sacred elements of their own birthright and their own native land.

These nativistic and much more militant kinds of 'Hindu' reaction became, simultaneously, avowedly both 'political' and 'religious.' Borrowing methods from those very missionary societies which they viewed as most threatening, they mobilized as many supporters as possible. They took concerted actions *against* anything and everything which disturbed local sensibilities or local traditions, especially *against* government collusion in actions which might smack of interference in indigenous ceremonies, customs, institutions, or rituals. Long-established customs and traditions which had long held sway within each high-caste or 'twice-born' birth group (*jāti*), each domestic or sectarian community, especially those which had held sway within elite families and local domains – domains too sacred and sensitive to be 'touched,' and thereby 'polluted' by outsiders – were precisely what they felt needed to be defended.

The first glimmers of this kind of catalytic reaction can be seen as early as 1799, when dominant elites in Tirunelvēli Country, aided by local warlords, tried to put a stop to a massive movement of conversion to Christianity that was taking place within the lowly Shanar (later known as Nadar) community. After whole villages had turned Christian, converting village temples into prayer-school halls, such violators of the old order were stripped and driven into the jungle to die. One consequence of this persecution among surviving refugees was the establishment of separate 'villages of refuge' for Christians. These defensive enclaves, in due time, prospered, and, midst further pogroms, they multiplied. Among further movements of violent 'Hindu' reaction against mass conversions in Tirunelvēli Country that organized during the 1820s, 1830s, and 1840s, were the Vibuthi Sangam (Sacred Ashes Society) in Tirunelvēli, the Chatur Veda Siddhanta Sabha (or Salay Street Society) of Madras, and branches of the Dharma Sabha from Bengal. Later, in Western and Northern India, other movements arose, such as the Arya Samaj (1875) of Swami Dayanand Saraswati and the Nagari Pracharini Sabha (1893), led by Shyam Sundar Das, Ram Narayan Mishra, and Shiv Kumar Singh.[15] The latter sought to replace Urdu with Hindi, and Perso-Arabic with Deva Nagari script, in all places of 'public' discourse, government offices, and courts of law. All of these nineteenth-century movements, in turn, set precedents for the rise of ever more militant movements and anti-cow-killing campaigns in Bengal, Maharashtra, and Punjab, events that were fueled by the extremist rhetoric of Bankimchandra Chattopadhyay, the ideas of Swami Vivekananda (Narendranath Datta), the symbols of Bal Gangadhar Tilak, and the mystic spirituality of Shri Aurobindo (Ghose).

Thus it was that modern 'Hinduism' – or, to be more precise, belief in an all-embracing and monolithic 'Hindu community' – came into being. This kind of 'Hindu consciousness,' as commonly defined today, is really a relatively recent development. It became necessary, in Romila Thapar's view, 'when there was competition for political and economic resources between various groups in a colonial situation' and 'a need to change from a segmental identity to a community which cut across caste, sect and religion.'[16] What emerged out of the socio-cultural, socio-economic, socio-political, and socio-religious reform movements that grew up during the nineteenth century was a growing sense of community which, in turn, became increasingly self-conscious about its fears and ever more aggressively militant about its aspirations. Leaders of this 'imagined' community then laid claim to being sole representatives of India's 'majority.' Seeing India's 'sacred destiny' as its legitimate legacy and its sole possession, 'Hindus' demanded total submission from all other communities in India. Thus, both 'Hinduism' as a 'Hindu community' and 'India' as a Nation-State developed as parallel and simultaneous by-products of modern constructions that had begun to form under the Raj. While the mobilizing of new systems of loyalty had initially been used for constructing support for the Imperial State and while these same processes soon also served to buttress post-imperial constructions of the National (or Nation) State, an entity ostensibly 'secular' (as defined in Indian terms), such processes did not stop there. Both, in turn, threatened many of those contractual substructures of obligation which had initially served to construct and undergird the socio-political constitution of modern India.

Out of all of these earlier, pre-Hindutva forms of Hindu reaction to the West, and especially to Western Christianity, came ever more militant Hindu ideologies and organizations. None of them were explicitly 'Hindutva' (at least in the later use of that term). Yet these movements led directly to the founding of the Hindu Mahasabha by Vinayak Damodar Savarkar in 1916 and the Rashtriya Swayamsevak Sangh (RSS) by Kesnav Baliram Hedgewar in 1925. Successors of Hedgewar, from Madhav Sadashiv Golwalkar in 1940 onward, formed subsidiary agencies of the RSS, such as the Bharatiya Jana Sangh in 1951, the Vishwa Hindu Parishad (VHP) in 1964, the Bharatiya Janatha Party (BJP) in 1980, that headed the Government of India from 1998 to 2004, and the ever more violent Bajrang Dal youth movement of the 1990s. All of these new movements were inspired and led by Maratha Brahmans, especially by Chitpavans of Maharashtra centered in Nagpur and Pune. At the same time, a parallel Non-Brahman party, the Shiv Sena (Shiva's Army) led by Bal Thackeray, also began to come to prominence in the 1960s. In the late 1980s, this blatantly anti-Muslim and violent movement took control of Mumbai (Bombay), and then, with the BJP, of Maharashtra State. In 1984, all Hindutva organizations joined together and formed the *Dharma Samsad* – or 'General Dharmic Council.' This overarching consortium aimed for the establishment of the Righteous Realm, Reign, and Rule of Ram Rajiya. Together, all of such allied organizations began to call themselves the *Sangh Parivar* (or the 'Family of Societies'). Together, they constitute the very heart of Hindutva, Hindu Fundamentalism, and/or Hindu Nationalism.

Genesis of Hindu nationalism and 'Hindutva'

Before probing more deeply into what 'Hindutva' itself really means, what it represents, what resources, strategies, and tactics it deployed, and how its agenda been pursued, especially as designed and orchestrated by the RSS into a pseudo- or proto-fascist and fundamentalist form of political religion, two further important preconditions need to be identified, however briefly: (1) the All-India Census; and (2) processes bringing about ever more increasingly representative government. These, together, hastened self-conscious movements of social mobilization leading, on one hand, to communalism and, on the other, to nationalism.

The first censuses were local. Begun in the 1820s, they culminated in the All-India Census of 1871. Continuing every decade thereafter, this instrument publicly defined and standardized communal, occupational, social, and religious concepts and categories for all societies in India. Since it was administered by local cadres of the civil service, most of whom were themselves Brahmans, it codified and ossified the caste stratified social system (*varnāshramadharma*) in such a way that virtually all who were not Christians, Jews, or Muslims, were defined, by default, as 'Hindus.' Since pollution-free, twice-born (*dvija*) castes – Brahmans, Kshatriyas, and Vaishiyas – made up hardly more than 15 percent of the population (or 5 percent in each category), since Ṣudra caste communities throughout the subcontinent came to hardly more than 35–40 percent of the population, since polluting, 'untouchable,' or non-caste (*āvarna*) and aboriginal (*adivāsi*) or tribal peoples came to some 20 percent of the population, and since Muslims, Christians, and Jews came to another 20–25 percent of the total population of the empire, census figures revealed, for all to see, that the 'pure,' 'twice-born,' or 'Aryan' castes, were a minority whose hitherto dominant position could become precarious. Census categories and concepts, for this reason, were manipulated in such a way as to show that, by defining hitherto excluded untouchables and tribals as 'Hindus' and by excluding hitherto included communities of culturally respectable Indian Christians and Muslims, one could construct an immutable and permanent 'Hindu majority community.' From 1871 onward, acts of 'inclusion' or 'exclusion' from the 'Hindu fold' by definition became powerful catalysts for change.

The second process resulted from raising the unthinkable specter of a possible future subjection among the high-born. The evolution of con-stitutional institutions promising democratically elected representative self-government, first in local councils and then, progressively, to higher levels made clear this possibility. By the 1870s and 1880s, Indians were already beginning to gain seats in Parliament, in Executive, and Legislative Councils, and on the benches of various High Courts. The time was coming, Sir Sayyed Ahmad Khan pointed out, when 'representative Indians' who were predominantly 'caste Hindus' would rule the land and when most of these could be militantly anti-Muslim. Census figures and democratic elections, taken together, could spell trouble. Thus, both Hindu elites and Muslim elites, could sense the possibility of future conflict. What punctuated such concerns was a newly rising incidence of Hindu–Muslim riots.

The first openly fundamentalistic Hindu agency, responding to these new processes, was the 'Hindu Sabha.' This Punjabi association, 'ardent and watchful in the interests of the Hindu community,' was formed in 1907. The All-India Hindu Mahasabha, reacting to the formation of the All India Muslim League, came into being in 1915, as an adjunct (or caucus) of the Indian National Congress (which allowed dual memberships).[17] By the 1920, alarmed by the Lucknow Pact (1916) in which the INC made concessions on 'separate electorates,' by the *jihads* of the Khilafat movement, and by Mappilla massacres of Hindu landlords in Malabar, the Hindu Mahasabha became increasingly militant. When Gandhi called off his non-violent *satyāgraha* (or campaign of non-cooperation) after the mob massacre of 22 police at Chauri Chaura in early 1922, Hindu disenchantment increased. In 1923, at Benares (aka Varanasi), Pandit Madan Mohan Malaviya called for 'means to arrest the deterioration and decline of Hindus and to effect an improvement of the Hindus as a community.' He encouraged Hindus to model *kshatriya* valor by forming academies (*akharas*) for training in martial skills. Lala Lajpat Rai declared that Gandhi's tactics only weakened Hindu solidarity and engendered a 'slave mentality.' Directing its actions more and more against the Muslim community, the Hindu Mahasabha did little to discourage the Hindu–Muslim riots that kept mounting in scale, intensity, and violence throughout the 1920s.

Perhaps no single person was more influential, or symptomatic of rising Hindu militancy, than Vinayak Damodar Savarkar. It was he who re-discovered and re-invented the term 'Hindutva' or 'Hinduness.' Savarkar was a Chitpavan Brahman of Maharashtra who, after going to England to study law at Grey's Inn, had engaged in revolutionary activities and written a book about the 1857 Mutiny or Rebellion of North India entitled *The Indian War of Independence* (London: 1909). Arrested in 1910 after being implicated in the assassination of a British official, he had been transported for life to the Andaman Islands. There he had remained for ten years before serving 17 more years in Indian prisons. It was while incarcerated in Ratnagiri Prison (1922) that he penned his most famous work. *Hindutva: Who Is a Hindu?* (first published in 1923 but not appearing in English until 1942 and still in print), which became the Hindutva bible. By the time of his release in 1937, Savarkar had acquired a near cult-like status as a *rishi* among his devoted followers.

In comprehensive terms, Hindutva became the name for the most militantly chauvinistic and nativistic form of genomic and geocentric nationalism that had ever existed in India. Centered in sacred cultures and countries, peoples and places, the doctrine defined essentials of an extremely militant form of 'cultural' nationalism and remained a fundamentalistic fount of inspiration. Savarkar proclaimed that Hindus, who were the original people of the land and that this people, formed out of the intermingling of Aryan blood and culture, should forever remain a single nation (*rashtra*). Whatever a person's community or caste, culture or language, region or sect, a Hindu was one whose blood aroused feelings of strong devotion to common ethnic ties, rooted in sacred 'birth' and 'earth,' to all that is India (*Hindusthan*). The 'fundamentals' of '*Hindutva*,' in short, were already imprinted within genetic codes of sacred blood and sacred soil and, indeed, of cosmic sacred sound from whence all being and knowledge (*veda*) came. Any person was Hindu so long as he could feel the pulse of Hindutva's timeless 'antiquity' and 'unity' (*sanghatan*). It was this heritage, this 'inner text' that bound India's peoples to their divine fatherland (*pitrubhu*) and their divine country (*punyabhu*). This 'holy land' was watered by all-encompassing eternal rivers (Indus, Ganga, and Brahmaputra, Yamuna, Saraswati, Narmada, etc.) that flowed from their common 'Home of Snows' (Himalayas) down to the three eternal and sacred seas that met and mingled at Kanyakumari. Here, indeed, within a special kind of fundamentalism in its classic form[18] was the ideology of a political religion *par excellence*.

The Rashtriya Swayamsevak Sangh, or 'RSS,' was founded in 1925 by Dr Kesnav Baliram Hedgewar, another Maharashtrian (Chitpavan) Brahman. Hedgewar was deeply disturbed by the lack of overarching Hindu institutions or Hindu solidarity within India. In his view, linguistic, regional, and social fragmentation had opened the country to Muslim and European subjugation. Disillusioned and frustrated by the tactics of non-violent non-cooperation (*ahimsa* and *satyagraha*) underlying Gandhi's campaigns, he decided to devote his life to restoring the 'essential unity' (*sanghatan*) of Hindutva.[19] This could only be done by bringing about deeper cultural, psychological, and religious changes within the entire country. A carefully and deeply planted movement of totalistic transformation within the entire society would require radical commitment involving a profound, if not radical, transformation of outlook within each person.[20] He decided to build a 'brotherhood' of 'national volunteers.' This had to be made up of totally dedicated individuals, true believers who could transcend personal agendas and petty or narrow-minded rivalries. A carefully built cadre of totally transformed and committed persons would serve as the foundation for slowly building a totally new kind organization, something truly national and revolutionary. Only by thoroughly awakening a new self-consciousness through rigorous self-discipline and a new sense of community of 'Hindus' could this be accomplished. To achieve this, Hedgewar elaborated upon a suggestion from Sister Nevedita:[21] 'Congregate and pray together for fifteen minutes every day, and Hindu society will become an invincible society.'[22]

To that end, 12–15-year-old schoolboys and college youths, idealistic lads not yet corrupted by worldly concerns or preoccupied with domestic duties, were recruited – but only after carefully scrutinizing their capacity for total, unquestioning loyalty, and obedience. Each coterie of utterly dedicated followers was then trained in martial exercises and rigorously indoctrinated. Bound to each other by exceptionally strong emotional and political ties, each peer group, as its members grew up together, retained its own special collection of shared memories that would last a lifetime.

The first *sevaks* came from a fencing academy or gymnasium (*akhara*) in Nagpur. All were Brahmans of Maharashtra who nursed historical traditions of having long been conspicuous as warriors and rulers. On a vacant lot in Nagpur – where Hedgewar Bhavan, the RSS headquarters, now stands – Hedgewar himself personally supervised prayers, physical training, martial drills, and intellectual exercises. These activities accompanied the telling and retelling of stories about exploits of great Hindu heroes, such as Shivaji, Rana Pratab, or Nana Sahib. Personal ties were deepened by means of outings, picnics, and sporting events. Such events gave each person an élan, a sense of self-importance and proud independence, insomuch that each member of the group felt superior and, at the same time, prepared to do anything on command, at the beck and call of his supreme commander.

Thus, in early 1926, the first *shakha* (brigade or regimented 'branch') came into being. Other *shakhas* soon followed, each composed of especially 'enlightened' *swayamsevaks* ('dedicated-servants' or 'volunteers'). Within a very short time, the number of *akharas*, martial arts academies known for *kshatriya* ideals, jumped from 230 to 570.[23] Each new *shakha* was disciplined by daily 'character-building' exercises. These were designed to be physically, mentally, and spiritually rigorous. Paramilitary drills with weapons (brass-bound quarter-staffs, swords, daggers, and spears) reflected warrior (*kshatriya*) ideals and norms, mandating instant readiness for 'action' or 'service' (*seva*). Indoctrinations were accompanied by oaths, prayers, and salutes. Only a select few of the very best and most dedicated would be judged fit for 'life oaths.' Rituals of fealty before the Guruji or Supreme Sangh Guide (*Sar-Sanghchalak*), the Saffron-colored Banner (*Bhagva Dwaj*),[24] and to the Maruti Deva (aka Hanuman) and other deities, as well as to Shivaji's guru Ramdas Swami, were performed whenever *shakhas* took part in forced marches, forest camps, weekly discussions, or special events.

Formally inaugurated during Dasara (September) 1925, on the annual festival for celebrating Rama's victory over Ravana, the name Rashtriya Swayam Sevak was publicly proclaimed at the Ram Navami of 1926. At that event, uniformed volunteers of the first *shakha*, in knee-length khaki shorts, white shirts, black hats, and quarter-staffs (*lathis*) marched, sang verses from Ram Das, poured drinking water for thirsty pilgrims, and drove away corrupt pandarams and sadhus. But the public reputation of the RSS did not become fixed until 1927, after the first training camp for *swayamsevaks* and after the outbreak of communal rioting in Nagpur. Circulating 'news' that Muslims were planning an attack, 16 RSS squads moved into 'respectable' neighborhoods to provide 'protection.' When not a single Hindu locality was attacked, Hindutva's reputation for valor was established. The Hindu Mahasabha then invited uniformed RSS brigades to its Bombay session. Thereafter, numbers of *swayamsevak* recruits multiplied and *shakha* brigades proliferated. Between 1931 and 1939, the number of *shakhas* grew from 60 to 500, with 60,000 active members (roughly half Marathi-speakers). After 1929, an elaborate hierarchy of RSS leaders and officials began to emerge. These came by promoting elite *swayamsevaks,* ranked by year, to squad leaders (*gatanayaks*), ordinary and superior instructors (*gata-* and *mukhya shikshaks*), secretaries (*karyavahs*), celibate staff commanders (*pracharaks* of different ranks: local, regional, national), and directors (*sanghchalaks*: city/district and regional). All were under the ultimate authority of the RSS's Supreme Guide (*Sar-Sanghchalak).*

Despite all its political activism and regimentation, the RSS scrupulously avoided involvement in provincial or national politics. Indeed, outcries of consternation, criticism, and disappointment over avoidance of involvement in electoral politics did not disappear until after Independence. Savarkar, after his release from prison in 1937, expressed his disgust over this 'purely cultural' agenda and predicted that the RSS would never amount to much. Anna Sohani resigned after uniformed RSS squads were ordered to avoid provocatively marching in front of mosques on Fridays so as not to insight violence, especially when Muslim paramilitary groups, such as the Khaksars, were being violently provocative, as also Akali Dal Sikh forces. After one RSS General Secretary, G.M. Huddar, was reprimanded for resorting to armed robbery so as to fund violence, an action that landed him in prison, he drifted away from the RSS. Even privately initiated political actions by known RSS members were repudiated. When the RSS refused to join the Hindu Mahasabha in agitations against the Nizam's Dominions of Hyderabad in 1938–1939, once warm relations between the Mahasabha and the RSS cooled. When the RSS avoided anti-British actions during the World War II, refusing to militarize Hindus or to undermine the loyalty within the Indian Army, links with the Hindu Mahasabha deteriorated still further.

Hedgewar died in 1940. His place was taken over by Madhav Sadashiv Golwalkar. The new Supreme Leader (*Sar-Sanghchalak*) was an ascetic ex-teacher and *sunnyasi*. While even less interested in open political involvement, he was blunt and forthright. Instead, he developed a systematic ideology for the RSS. *We, or Our Nationhood Defined* (1938), an abridgement of G.D. ['Babarao'] Savarkar's *Rashtra Mimansa*, explained the essence of Hindutva ideology:

> The non-Hindu peoples in Hindustan must either adopt the Hindu culture and language, must learn to respect and hold in reverence Hindu religion, must entertain no idea but glorification of the Hindu race and culture: i.e., they must not only give up their attitude of intolerance and ungratefulness towards this land and its age-old traditions, but must also cultivate a positive attitude of love and devotion...In a word, they must cease to be foreigners, or must stay in this country wholly subordinated to the Hindu nation, claiming nothing, deserving no privileges, far less any preferential treatment, not even citizen's rights.[25]

Mobilization of political confrontation

After Independence in 1947, the RSS saw an enormous expansion in numbers of new *swayamsevaks* and a proliferation of disciplined and drilled *shakhas*. This occurred despite Gandhi's assassination

(January 30, 1948) by Nathuram Vinayak Godse,[26] a former *sevak* and despite being outlawed. Some 20,000 RSS members were jailed. After their release, Golwalkar strove to improve the public image of the RSS by sending volunteers to aid thousands of refugees from the Partition and from the wars with Pakistan (1950, 1965, & 1971) and China (1962). He also assigned RSS workers to help Vinobha Bhave in his Gandhian program of persuading landlords to donate land to the landless. Even so, when, in 1975–1977, just before and during the Emergency it joined the resistance against Indira Gandhi's government, the RSS was again outlawed. Yet, by 1989, after riding a wave of Hindu revivalism (*Hindu jagaram*) that it had helped to generate, the RSS could claim that it commanded over 1.8 million disciplined and trained *sewaks*, drilling in over 25,000 *shakhas* and 18,800 urban and rural centers. By then, the Hindutva movement was ready to move up to the next stage of cultural, social, and political expansion – bringing it national attention.

Despite being frustrated by what they saw as their Supreme Leader's failure to involve them more directly in the political process, which they felt might have prevented the Partition, RSS rank and file never forgave the Congress for its complicity in the destruction of Greater India's political unity. This resentment continued to smolder even after the ban imposed after Gandhi's assassination was lifted on July 11, 1949. After their release from prison, several RSS *pracharaks* – Eknath Ranade, Vasant Rao Oke [Oak], M.D. [Balasahib] Deores, Deen Dayal Upadhyaya and others – talked Syma Prasad Mookerjee into forming a new party. Dr Mookerjee, former president of the Hindu Mahasabha, had also become increasingly frustrated with Nehru and Patel. He resigned from the Union Cabinet in April 1950 in protest against the Indo-Pakistan Delhi Agreement. In May 1951, he joined a segment of RSS leaders to form the Bharatiya Jan Sangh (BJS) and to become its President.[27]

Thus, even as the RSS discretely stayed out of open politics, and continued its campaign to convert more and more people to cause of Hindutva, its new party engaged in political combat. The Jan Sangh soon aroused public attention. Not only was Mookerjee popular, but cadres of disciplined, efficient and experienced organizations drawn from the Arya Samaj and Hindu Mahasabha soon achieved quick results. The Jan Sangh became a Hindutva composite, with Arya Samaj, Hindu Mahasabha, and Ram Rajya Parishad branches grafted onto its RSS trunk. Mookerjee hoped to generate an appeal broad enough to displace the Congress. These hopes were dashed three years later when Mookerjee suddenly died (in Kashmir: May 1953).

For the next two decades the Jan Sangh followed a narrowly focused agenda. Efforts to impose the Hindi language upon all of India, while popular in the north, provoked regional alienation. The party's exclusive and restrictive doctrines, 'inspired by an activist version of Hindu nationalism and, indirectly, by the values of Brahmanism rather than the quietist values of popular Hinduism,'[28] failed to appeal to a wider constituency. In 1971, despite softening its Hindutva voice and joining a 'grand alliance,' it was not successful. Indira Gandhi, having just won the Bangladesh War, seemed invincible. With tactical brilliance, she co-opted opposition appeals on behalf of the poor with her slogan of *garibi hatao* ('abolish poverty') and adroitly used vast powers of patronage within the Congress apparatus. But, eventually, Congress arrogance, corruption, and scandals accomplished what her opposition had never been able to do. In 1974, Hindutva cadres of the Jan Sangh, backed by the RSS and VHP, joined Jaya Prakash Narayan's new 'total revolution.' Electoral success in Gujarat and a U.P. High Court decision invalidating Indira's seat in Parliament, together with JP's appeal for the military to stop obeying 'illegal orders,' precipitated an ultimate showdown. Indira responded by declaring a 'State of Emergency,' thereby authorizing the government's crackdown on all opposition parties, placing 'subversive elements' under 'preventive detention,' and imposing censorship.[29]

*

The Emergency of 1975–1977 came as a boon for Hindutva forces. Underground RSS *pracharaks* and *swayamsevaks* rapidly gained strength and prepared for what would soon follow. In the elections that Indira later called to validate her legitimacy, India saw its first non-Congress government. The Janatha government, led by Moraji Desai, a former Congressman who was also long-time Hindutva sympathizer, contained three Jan Sangh members: Atal Behari Vajpayee (External Affairs), Lal Krishnan Advani (Information and Broadcasting), and Brij Lal Varma (Industry). But the coalition was too fragile and faction-ridden to survive. Since all Jan Sangh leaders were RSS *pracharak*s and since the RSS had vastly increased its membership and gained public respect during the Emergency, Hindutva (RSS) influence and 'divided loyalty' within the Janata Party became an issue. The dual membership controversy undoubtedly contributed to the Janata's disastrous electoral defeat in January 1980. The Janata, blaming the Jan Sangh for its defeat, then outlawed dual membership, thereby driving the Jan Sangh and its allies into forming a new party. Some 3500 delegates who met on April 5, 1980 named this party the 'Bharatiya Janata Party' (BJP).

Formation of the BJP marked the next major advance for Hindutva's Sangh Parivar in India. As a subsidiary of the RSS, it could henceforth draw upon all the mobilizing disciplines of RSS cadres, utilizing skills that had been honed for over 50 years. At the same time, a curiously ironic reversal of roles occurred. As the new Indira government became embroiled in communalist and separatist troubles in Assam, Kashmir, and Punjab, the BJP portrayed itself as representing the true essence of Hindutva's India. Indira countered by playing her own 'Hindu card' – inviting her jet-setting sadhu to give 'spiritual guidance,' going on pilgrimages to sacred rivers, shrines, and temples, and extolling 'Hindu hegemony' in Hindi heartland, conjuring anti-Muslim fears in Kashmir, and ignoring Sikh pleas against being counted as Hindus. Her efforts did nothing to weaken Hindutva aspirations.

And then, in October 1981, when Indira released Sant Jarnail Singh Bhindranwale, the militant leader of the Damdami Taksal, she unwittingly courted her own destruction. Bhindranwale's forces took control of the Golden Temple in Amritsar (July 1982), and killings escalated. When Sikh *swayamsevaks* of the RSS entered Punjab and tried to convince Khalistani militants that the RSS considered Sikhs to belong within the 'Hindu community,' the Sant countered by gruesomely displaying disemboweled cow carcasses within Hindu temples.[30] What followed next did little for the structural stability of India. Operation Blue Star; violation of the Akal Takht in the Golden Temple; destruction of Bhindranwale (5 June 1984); assassination of Indira Gandhi by her Sikh bodyguards (31 October); and subsequent slaughter of over 3000 Delhi Sikhs during the 'night of long knives' that followed did little to assuage anxiety.[31] Elections that followed further 'communalized' and fractured national unity. Rajiv Gandhi's landslide victory, undoubtedly due to a sympathy vote, owed much to his co-opting of BJP issues and encroaching upon BJP constituencies, efforts by which he blatantly exploited the 'competitive communalism' of 'vote banks.'[32]

**

The BJP defeat of 1984, coming so soon after the Amritsar bloodbath and Indira assassination, marked another turning point for Hindutva. Sikhs were by no means the only, nor even the most important, community whose hostile relations with Hindutva India were seen as important. For this reason, by the mid-1980s, as other communities began to raise serious challenges, Hindu Revivalism (*Hindutva Jagaran*) became *the* single most pervasive presence in Indian politics.

Yet, Hindutva strategies entailed inherent contradictions – between reality and rhetoric, inclusive claims and exclusive demands.[33]On one hand, they went to greater and greater lengths, often by extra-constitutional or violent means (pogroms, riots, &c), to exclude and marginalize communities that had long been legally incorporated within society and within the body politic. Hindutva forces turned a special and new animus against Muslims and Christians. On the other hand, agencies within the Sangh Parivar determined that, henceforth, all-out efforts should be made to expand 'Hindu' constituencies, by reaching out, co-opting, and incorporating hitherto excluded and marginalized communities – especially the *adivāsi* (aboriginal or 'tribal') and *āvarna* (outcaste, non-caste, 'colourless' or 'untouchable') communities. Lal Krishnan Advani, as BJP president, pushed this aggressive Hindutva agenda to unprecedented lengths. This strategy called for closer coordination between all agencies within the 'Hindutva' Sangh Parivar. Mobilization of a full-scale country-wide *Hindutva Jagaran* (Hindu Revivalism) followed; and this brought the Vishwa Hindu Parishad (or VHP) into the center of the political stage.

Among organizations which took this contradiction of exclusion and inclusion to its farthest limit, none was more persistent in seeking to create a permanent Hindutva Religious Establishment for all of India than the Vishwa Hindu Parishad. Founded by Golwalkar in 1964, it was another affiliated junior 'relative' of the RSS 'family.' Led by some of the most aggressive and select RSS *pracharaks*, its shock troops were dedicated to molding together a unified Hindu society by whatever means necessary. It worked mainly through its own educational and missionary channels, striving to eradicate all traces of 'foreign' ideologies, influences, and institutions from the land and to thwart all separatist movements in the country. At the same time, it courted or sought to 'convert,' by means of *shuddi* ceremonies, all hitherto outcaste, marginalized, or polluted peoples who, previously being seen as 'non-Hindu,' had been denied drinking water or entry into temples. Prior to 1980, the main activities of the VHP had been among 'backward,' 'tribal' and 'untouchable' peoples. In order to counter and reverse Christian missionary achievements, its most dedicated *sevaks* had set up schools, clinics, and temples. Its goal was to block and reverse Non-Hindutva (Christian, Muslim, Dalit, and other) influences that were poisoning India's ancient and pure culture.

What first brought the VHP into the limelight was an incident in 1981–1982. This event concentrated 'Hindutva' minds all over India. What took place occurred within the Tamil village of Meenakshipuram. It was here that some 1500 *dalits*,[34] despairing of ever escaping from centuries of abject thraldom under 'clean caste' overlords, decided to turn to Islam. Their bold and desperate action, widely publicized by the media, was furiously debated. If all of India's tribals and untouchables, amounting to between 200 and 300 million people, were ever to turn Muslim or/and Christian, the damage to Hindutva Dharm could be incalculable. VHP proponents raised the alarm of 'Hinduism in Danger!' Unless such conversions were immediately stopped, Hindus might become 'a minority in their own country.' 'Meenakshipuram' became a symbol for catalyzing Hindutva solidarity. A nationwide *Ekamata Yajna* or 'Sacrifice for One Mother' (Unity) was launched. Processions (*yatras*) in support of reconversion (*shuddi*) took place. One long *yajna*, lasting a month, according to the VHP, involved 60 million people and covered 85,000 kilometers. Water from the sacred Ganga, mingled with waters from other sacred rivers, was sold along the way. No danger clearly could be worse than for Dalits to begin collaborating with Muslims.

But, if the Meenakshipuram conversions exposed Hindutva protagonists to dangers of Dalit mobilization, events no less portentous took place in the north. This crisis among Muslims was over the explosive case of Shah Bano. The conflict had started in 1978 when, after Ahmed Shah divorced his wife of 44 years, and gave back her 3000 rupee dowry (*mehr*) as required by Muslim Law (*Shariat*), Shah Bano, instigated by her sons, sued him for alimony. When courts first awarded her 25 and then 180 rupees per mensem, Ahmed Shah appealed, and the case eventually ascended all the way to the Supreme Court of India. At issue was a conflict between substantive and procedural law. Under the legal system constructed during the 1780s, indigenous substance and alien procedure had been grafted together. Each community's own (civic and domestic) customs had been allowed to prevail so long as 'civic peace' was not endangered or the State security undermined. But procedures for determining 'facts,' whether Civil or Criminal, were to conform to principles of English Law. There were occasions of intrusion into the substance of any community's domestic law, with precedents going back two centuries, that applied, for example, to various forms of 'communal' or 'domestic' violence. Widow burning, female infanticide, human sacrifice, and ritual murder had long ago been defined as 'criminal' offenses. The Supreme Court of India decided that an ex-husband should provide support for a former wife who had no other means and raised

Shah Bano's award to 500 rupees. But the Chief Justice (Chandrachud) also pronounced an opinion that the Court's ruling adhered to the *Quran,* as well as the *Shariat,* more faithfully than prior rulings made by Muslim clerics (*ulema*). He also suggested that the time had come for all communities in India, irrespective of community customs, to conform to a common code. By saying this, his opinion went beyond previous rulings.

Many Muslims in India were outraged. Even those who wanted to see advances in the rights of Muslim women were incensed. If agencies of the State were now going break precedent by interfering in domestic governance of various communities, something which neither the Mughals nor the British had dared to do, then the 'contract' between each community and the State might be undermined, and the entire 'contractual' structure of the body politic, and the constitutional nature of India as 'secular state,' might be jeopardized. As it was, any further attempt to impose a uniform 'law of the land' and call into question the accumulated wisdom of a community's highest religious authorities, including Arif Khan, the then Home Minister, was bound to endanger the alliance between Muslims, who held over a quarter of the seats in the Lok Sabha, and the Congress-led government. Meanwhile, at the very same time, VHP rhetoric about eradicating all mosques and erecting temples in their place grew louder. After violence broke out in Ayodhya (see below), Hindu–Muslim riots also erupted in Old Delhi, Kashmir, and Gujarat; and anxieties within Muslim community increased. Late in March 1986, a huge rally of a half million Muslims gathered at the New Delhi Boat Club to voice woes and demand government protection of 'Muslim rights.'

Prime Minister Rajiv Gandhi, faced with possible loss of Muslim support, introduced the Muslim Women (Protection of Rights on Divorce) Bill. But his action raised another storm of opposition from Hindutva proponents. The very essentials of public order and political stability in India seemed to be at stake. Public discourse was wide ranging. The radical feminist, Madhu Kishwar, editor of *Manushi,* declared that concern over Muslim women by upper class Hindus merely reflected their condescension and contempt for Muslims. Muslims joined together to resist what they saw as Hindu bigotry and 'colonialism.' Ironically, the bill that was finally passed (May 6, 1987), actually incorporated the substance of *Shariyat* provisions: a Muslim woman would have no right of support from her ex-husband and could receive support only from her own family and relatives or from the local *waqf* (charitable endowments) board. At any event, by that time, Shah Bano had long since withdrawn her claim: no individual had a right to overrule the consensus (*uma*) of the community.[35]

Countdown to the climacteric of Ayodhya

All the while, storm clouds had been gathering over what was to be the single most momentous confrontation of all, a climacteric from which there would be no return. Hindutva forces alleged that the 'sacred soil' of 'Lord Rama's birthplace' in Ayodhya had been violated and needed to be liberated. A more popular or sensitive symbol could hardly have been selected. The Babri Masjid, built by Emperor Babur in 1528, had been a place in continual contention since 1853. At that time, Muslim mujahhids, trying to oust Bairagis from the Hanumangarhi Mandir (a temple given them by Mansoor Ali, the Nawab of Awadh), had suffered a ferocious attack. During the Great Rebellion of 1857, the Mahant of the Hanumangarhi, had entered the Babri Masjid compound and raised a worship platform (*chabutra*). Muslim *maulvis* had then petitioned for removal of the platform. Authorities had erected a fence in 1859, so as to keep Hindu and Muslim activists separated. Attempts by the Mahant to construct a pukka temple on the site had continued, with sporadic incidents occurring in almost every decade. These had culminated on the night of December 22–23, 1949 when an image of Rama was installed in the mosque. After riots, the government had locked the premises. One month later, when the dispute over erecting a 'Ramjanmabhumi Mandir' within the Babri Masjid had come before him, the District Collector/Magistrate had declared the property was a mosque and not a temple. This ruling had then been reversed by the Civil Judge in 1951, and again in 1955. The Allahabad High Court allowed the Rama image to remain because, in the words of Justice Deoki Nandan Agarwal, 'the continued existence of such mosque-like structure is galling to the Hindu psyche and a matter of National shame.'[36] Pleas by officials of the Muslim *waqf* board for removal of the idols had failed. And the gates remained locked.

In April 1984, a Religious Council (Dharma Sansad) in the Vidyan Bhavan, New Delhi, issued a national call to action. Lord Rama was still 'behind bars' and his abode needed to be purified and the offending mosque removed. A gigantic campaign – the 'Sri Ramajanmabhumi Mukti Yajna' – was launched. Six months later, an enormous 'chariot-cavalcade' (*rath-yatra*) – actually a motorcade of lorries carrying images and posters of 'Lord Rama Behind Bars' and tens of thousands of dedicated *kar sevaks* (service givers) armed with swords and tridents (*trishuls*) left Bihar and slowly progressed toward Ayodhya. Just as the *yatra* was reaching Ayodhya, actions suddenly halted. The Prime Minister of India, Indira Gandhi, was assassinated. The campaign had to be called off. Two years later, in 1986, matters again came to a head: a court judge's (*munsif's*) refusal to lift restrictions on performing Hindu puja within the mosque was countermanded by a higher court; and the Faizabad District Judge ordered not only that the gates to the mosque be unlocked but that Muslims be forbidden to enter the mosque for prayers (*namaz*). Hindutva forces, led by L.K. Advani, continued to turn up the pressure.

In the forefront of this fray were the interlinked forces of the BJP, the VHP, and the RSS, along with their affiliated youth brigade, the Bajrang Dal. The Shiv Sena, a non-Brahman Hindutva party not affiliated to the RSS, confined its activities to Mumbai, and Maharashtra. Each element of the Sangh Parivar, at this point, had its own part to play in the concerted bid to take control of the entire country in the name of 'Hindutva.' L.K. Advani, becoming BJP president in 1986, organized a 'grass-roots' effort to generate a massive Hindu backlash against the escalating violence in Punjab and Kashmir, from whence surviving Hindu refugees were fleeing for their lives. In the general elections of 1989 and 1991, as violence mounted, the Babri Masjid–Ramjanma-bhumi conflict and the 'multi-dimensional challenge of Mandalism' aiming to provide affirmative action for backward communities, loomed larger and larger.

During these electoral contests, the 'communal card' was played more blatantly than ever. The BJP symbol in 1989 was the 'Ram-Shila.' Sacred 'Ram-bricks' (*ramshilas*) by the millions were sent to cities, towns, and villages all over India, each inscribed with Hindutva words indicating that it was for the Ram Janmasthan Mandir (Temple of Ram's Birth Place) that was being constructed. Blueprints for this huge temple – 270 feet long, 126 feet broad, and 132 feet high, with 34,000 feet of floor space and costing 55 crores (550 million rupees) – showed that its inner 'sanctum sanctorum' (*garbhagraha*) for the image of Ram would be located exactly where the mosque stood. A huge Shila Puja began on September 30. On November 9–10, after a ceremonial brick consecration (*shilanyas*), foundations for the temple's plinth were dug.

But the very next day construction again had to be halted when a General Election was called for November 22–26. The National Front, formed with tacit BJP approval, was a fragile blending of extreme left and extreme right wing parties. It could not survive without BJP support. V.P. (Vishvanath Pratap) Singh, leader of newly formed Janata Dal, became Prime Minister. But the BJP, with 86 out of 545 seats (up from two in 1984, the third largest party in the coalition), played a pivotal role. It adroitly remained just 'outside' the government, enjoying power without being held responsible for government decisions.

It was only a matter of time before a rupture brought down this government. This happened ten months later. Singh, attempting to build an independent political base out of all the alienated, backward, excluded, and untouchable communities, appointed the Mandal Commission. On August 9, 1990, he announced a plan to implement Mandal Commission recommendations, reserving 27 percent of all government positions for 'Other Backward Castes' (OBCs: Untouchables, &c). L.K. Advani faced a major dilemma: If he opposed Mandal, he would lose votes among the rural and backward poor; but if he supported Mandal, he would lose support of the urban and upwardly mobile (some of whose youth were immolating themselves in protest against the Mandal law). The solution was to resort to Hindutva's most trusty weapon: violence.

Demolition of the Babri Masjid and construction of the Rama Mandir, as announced, was to take place on October 30, 1990. Another giant *Rath Yatra*, with huge processions from all over the 'Hindi Heartland,' organized rallies. Thirty-six organizations hoisted saffron flags and sent squadrons of volunteers (*kar sevaks*) to march on Ayodhya. But again, just as the 'grand progress' of Hindutva forces approached, the U.P. Government, led by Mulayam Singh Yadav (an OBC), ordered state security forces into block their way. Thousands were injured, and many killed. On the day of the takeover by *kar sevaks*, 'tens of thousands' broke through police barricades, swept into the compound, and planted flags on top of the mosque dome. Lathi charges, rubber bullets, and tear gas then drove the militants away. An estimated 200,000 *kar sevaks* were taken into custody, including BJP legislators and leading Hindutva figures. *India Today* (November 15, 1990) reported: 'a crisis of near unmanageable dimensions, the dreadful fall-out of which will effect not just the leadership of the country by the very well-being and stability of the nation.'

Singh's stand on the 'masjid–mandir' issue brought his immediate downfall after Advani was arrested (October 23) and the BJP withdrew its support. Congress (I) leaders then offered to support a breakaway group of 60 MPs who, renaming themselves the Janatha Dal(S), crossed the aisle to join the 211 Congress(I) MPs. Their leader, a rustic named Chandra Shekar, was asked to form a new government. But when his shaky coalition also failed to muster a vote of confidence, Chandra Shekar also resigned. On March 7, 1991, Parliament was dissolved and another General Election was called.

Hindutva forces felt that, at long last, their time had come. Again, posters showing 'Lord Ram Behind Bars' symbolized the BJP campaign. A half million supporters gathered in New Delhi on April 4 and voiced their demands in the name of Hindutva and Ram Mandir. Again, processions of jeeps, cars, and lorries moved across the land, carrying thousands of people waving banners and posters, and dispensing sacred river water. At the same time, the BJP called for 'Ram, Bread, and Justice!' and offered large numbers of seats to 'OBC' and 'Harijan' candidates. Beyond the 'cow belt' of the Hindi Heartland, the BJP went into the deep south, contesting parliamentary seats and seeking support. Playing up polls showing that voters were fed up with the rampant corruption, petty squabbles, and total absence of principles in government, BJP billboards proclaimed: 'You have tested everyone else. Give us a chance!!' Since the recent violence in Ayodhya had frightened the whole country, the BJP toned down its 'masjid–mandir' rhetoric. But, its sister organization, the VHP, did just the opposite. The unifying role of 'Hindu Nationalism' was declared to be far superior to the 'bogus' or 'pseudo-secularist' currying of favor among the 'so-called minorities' and the coddling of Muslims, as exemplified in the recent Muslim Women's Bill. Again Hindutva forces were confident.

What dashed Hindutva prospects, once gain, was an assassination, this time of Rajiv Gandhi. He was campaigning in south India when a woman representing Tamil militants from Sri Lanka blew herself up while bending to touch his feet. Once more, as in the post-Emergency poll, voters across the land gave no single party a clear majority (Congress, 225 seats; BJP, 115; and Janata Dal, 55; &c.) This time, the Congress 'Old Guard,' led by P.V. Narasimha Rao, cobbled another coalition government. With BJP's power in the Hindi Heartland and Gujarat having expanded by 33 more seats than in 1989, Hindutva forces were confident that their day was coming. More than that, the BJP gained control of four more state governments (Uttar Pradesh, Madhya Pradesh, Himachal Pradesh, and Rajasthan). Clearly, disciplined cadres of saffron forces had put the BJP in a much stronger position. Yet when, in November, VHP and Bajrang Dal militants stormed the Babri Masjid and tried to demolish it, their efforts again failed. More than 300 were arrested. The U.P. State Government under BJP Chief Minister Kalyan Singh also dragged its feet; and the local court order forbade turning over the three acres of disputed land or starting new construction thereon.

In January 1992, the campaign again began to gain momentum. Pressures for construction of the Ram Temple (*mandir*) mounted. By October, thousands of VHP sadhus, sants, and pandarams were able to stage a grand replay of their previous assault. This time the sending of Rama's 'bricks for worship' (*shīla puja*) started with a nationwide worship of Rama's sandals (*paduka puja*) and donations to pay for building the mandir. To counter 'Ayodhya fatigue' and flagging Ramjanmabhumi fervor, the VHP called 6000 sadhus and sants together for another Dharma Sansad ('Religious Assembly'), and issued an ultimatum to the Government of India. When this expired, it announced that voluntary construction (*kar seva*) would begin on December 6. Para-military troops were dispatched to the site ostensibly to prevent anyone from attacking the Babri Masjid. On the morning of December 6, a throng of over 200,000 *kar sevaks* arrived at the site. In the early afternoon, well-drilled groups of *kar sevaks* began to systematically demolish the mosque. The small numbers of police who had been posted at the mosque by the BJP state government stood aside. Top BJP and RSS leaders who had come in the morning departed for Delhi, leaving local VHP and BJP leaders in charge. As slogans of encouragement were chanted and shouted, demolition continued. Some journalists and photographers were beaten and their equipment smashed. By evening, destruction had been completed and the mosque no longer existed. The date of December 6, 1992 is indelibly etched upon the minds of the peoples of India, may perhaps never to be forgotten. The event shook the whole of India as no other in the previous half century.[37]

Aftermath of Ayodhya

Repercussions of December 6, 1992, have continued ever since. The BJP government of U.P. resigned that very afternoon. As *kar sevaks* quickly disbursed, the whole country went into shock. The Prime Minister of India, P.V. Narasimha Rao, never erased the stain of having done nothing to stop the carnage. An Aruvelu Niyoji Brahman Telugu scholar from Karimnagar (Andhra Pradesh) who had faithfully served Indira and Rajiv, his inaction spoke more loudly than anything he could say. Hindutva engineered pogroms, euphemistically labelled 'riots,' soon broke out across the land. Nothing could match the terrible killings in Bombay during January and February of 1993. How many tens of thousands died, mainly poor and weak Muslims (children, women, infirm, or older people) living in shanty-towns (*basti*-s) will never be known. Police stood aside, or found themselves unable to cope. Journalists and photographers from around the world recorded gory details. Hindutva forces, brimming with confidence, multiplied. Visibility achieved by *rath yatra* brought an enormous increase in membership. Regiments of disciplined *shakhas*, drilling in khaki shorts, white shirts, black caps, and shouldered staffs (*lathī-s*), became a ubiquitous presence in many cities, towns, and villages. A BJP White Paper, justifying the Babri-Masjid destruction and the carnage that followed, proclaimed that Hindutva forces would go to almost any lengths to achieve Ram Rashtriya.

Even so, when repeated efforts failed to bring an absolute majority, the BJP learned to work within weak coalitions. Caught between its own fundamentalism, on one hand, and demands of its wobbly allies, on the other, it had to compromise. What resulted was neither a 'coalition government' nor an 'alliance government,' but a mixture of both. Only after the 1999 election was the BJP leader, Atal Vajpayee, able to form a government and take control of such key portfolios in the Government of India as the Home, Finance, Foreign Affairs, and Education ministries. More significantly, the 1999 poll left a splintered Opposition which, bereft of any binding ideology or public reputation, was too weak to block the fulfillment of Hindutva ambitions.

During the five years that followed, Hindutva forces were able to intimidate and strike terror among those whom they considered to be the foes of India. Despite constraints of the National Democratic Alliance (NDA), a totalistic, majoritarian, and authoritarian agenda of Ram Rashtriya was vigorously proclaimed. Under the euphemistic slogan of 'saffronization,' plans for the building of the Ram Mandir were frequently published, without regard for voices of opposition from so-called 'minorities.' 'Saffronization' became a blanket concept for covering many forms of internal colonialism. Inclusivistic policies of the Hindutva project, under a wide array of programs, strove to thoroughly 'Hinduize' or bring 'into the Hindu fold,' by whatever means including force if necessary, as many peoples as possible. All knowledge, whether academic or practical, was also to be completely saffronized and made to conform with Hindutva ideology. Historians, for example, were obliged to conform to this agenda, whether in research or in the content of state-controlled textbooks. Since all truth was and would always be Hindutva Truth, all history had to be Hindutva History and all science became Hindutva Science. One authority declared that when protoplasm first squirmed from the slime and became a living organism, the first intelligible sound ever uttered in the universe had been '*om.*' Regardless of what senior historians, such as Romila Thapar,[38] wrote, Hindutva historians insisted that evidence showed that all life, especially that life-form called mankind (*manusha*), had originated in the Indo-Gangetic Plain. By such logic, since Aryans had originated in India, Aryan civilization and Indus civilization were the same.[39] No policy more clearly exemplified Hindutva determination more than attempts to incorporate all hitherto marginalized peoples, whether polluting outcaste and untouchable peoples (*āvarna jāti-s*) or ancient, aboriginal tribes (*adivāsi jāti-s*), thereby forcing them into the perpetual submission and thralldom from which, as self-defined *dalits*, they had tried for so long to extricate themselves.

Any or all peoples within the subcontinent seen as being utterly incapable of saffronization, were demonized and, wherever possible, attacked. Hindutva rhetoric called for the destruction or extirpation of 'alien' elements. Foremost among such peoples were some 170 million Muslims and some rapidly increasing 70–90 million Christians. These peoples were, in fact, as 'Hindu' or 'Native' in their origins as anyone else. But, their successes in helping low caste and tribal peoples to escape from thraldom by means of conversion, made them into a mortal danger to Hindutva. Small wonder that laws against conversion and religious freedom were passed in several BJP-ruled or dominated states. One has but to observe what has been done to Muslims and Christians during the past decade to see that, in one way or another, those refusing to submit to Hindutva would suffer.

This campaign became evident in Gujarat during February 2002. Some 10,000 Muslims – mostly poor families, with women, children, infirm, and elderly folks – were done to death in one of the worst pogroms of recent times. That this whole event was planned seems clear. The pogrom began with a carefully engineered provocation. On a station platform at Godhra, a Muslim girl was captured and dragged onto a train full of *kar sevaks* returning from Ayodhya. When local Muslims then retaliated by burning the train and causing many deaths, hundreds of lorries, full of pre-prepared bottled gasoline bombs, were unleashed against Muslim houses in the city of Ahmedabad in order to teach Muslims a lesson about Hindutva. As a consequence, many thousands of Muslims – men, women, children, and elderly as well as prominent citizens – were burned alive.[40] The Gujarat incident, along with Ayodhya and Bombay incidents, have been burned into the memories of Muslims, just as the night of long knives after Indira was assassinated has been burned into the minds of Sikhs. What happened in Gujarat was merely another in a long line of Hindutva events stretching back over a century, punctuated by the holocaust of Hindu-Muslim killings that took place in 1947.

If poorer Muslims fared badly, Christians also had to pay a price of not conforming to Hindutva.[41] Thousands of incidents occurred during these decades, most of them involving church burnings, killings of nuns and priests, pogroms against tribal (*adivasi*) Christians, and discrimination against lowest-caste Christians. Documented brutal incidents have been so many that they cannot be listed here. Suffice it to say that the plight of Christians and Muslims under Hindutva regimes, where Hindutva forces were not even in total control of state machinery, looked bleak. Counted as aliens and foreigners, they would have stood to be excluded from the benefits and privileges of citizenship had the overly confident BJP-led Government of India not fallen in the spring election of 2004.

Conclusion

How then does Hindutva, as seen from a historical perspective, measure up as a political religion and as a fascist and/or fundamentalist faith? Deep and strong religious commitments of any sort, whether theistic or non-theistic, have the potential of being transformatively totalizing. If strongly enough held, any 'political religion' can become totalistic, if not totalitarian in some measure. This is particularly so within cultures and societies where a 'wall of separation' between religious and secular impulses and institutions has not been deliberately constructed. In modern times, this tendency has become more pronounced, for the most part, the further eastward from the Atlantic one moves. The sole possible exception, sans Hindutva, has been the Indian Empire, and the Republic of India which succeeded it. Indeed, India could not have existed as a single political entity had it not been built upon foundations of accommodation, pluralism, and toleration between hundreds of competing and ritually distinct communities and constituencies.

Hindutva, in its steady and transforming mobilization of cultural and social consciousness during the past 80 years, has worked at laying foundations for an altogether different India. These, from the very beginning, have been ideologically fundamentalist and instrumentally proto-fascist: Fascist means employed to achieve fundamentalist ends. Indeed, except for failure to achieve totalitarian control, there is not one of the elements in Stanley Payne's 'Typological Description of Fascism' that cannot be found within the Hindutva movement. Hindutva's slogan of 'One Nation! One Culture! One Religion! One Language!!' sounds not so different from the Nazi slogan of 'Ein Volk! Ein Reich! Ein Fuehrer!' Italian Fascism, German Nazism (National Socialism), and Hindutva were born at virtually the same time in the 1920s. Marching fascist or swastika (*svastika*) banners, black or brown shirts and khaki shorts, saffron flags, black hats, and tridents, with clenched fist salutes, and even romantic invocations to Aryan and Nordic gods of racial solidarity, seem eerily to share symbols taken from some common source. Thus, when Savarkar extolled Adolf Hitler's models of 'cultural nationalism,' he was outdone by Golwalkar:

> German national pride has now become the topic of the day. To keep up the purity of the nation and its culture, Germany shocked the world by her purging the country of the semitic races – the Jews. National pride at its highest has been manifested here. Germany has shown how well-nigh impossible it is for races and cultures, having differences going to the root, to be assimilated into one united whole, a good lesson for us in Hindustan to learn and profit by.[42]

> From this standpoint…the non-Hindu people in Hindustan must either adopt the Hindu culture and language, must learn to respect and revere Hindu religion, must entertain no idea but the glorification of the Hindu nation. They must not only give up their attitude of intolerance and ingratitude toward this land and its age-long traditions, but must also cultivate the positive attitude of love and devotion instead; in one word, they must cease to be foreigners or may in the country wholly subordinated to the Hindu nation, claiming nothing, deserving no privileges, far less preferential treatment, not even a citizen's rights.[43]

Perhaps the great difference between Hindutva and classical European models of Fascism, especially in Italy and Germany, but less clearly evident in such cases as Spain and Soviet Russia, has to do with speed, timing, and ultimate success. Fascism in Italy and Germany was totally achieved, and then totally spent, to the point of self-destruction, by 1945. In contrast, Hindutva grew gradually, biding its time, getting stronger and stronger over 80 years and, to date, has yet to fully achieve totalitarian power. Not until totalitarianism, in each case, was achieved, so that Mussolini and Hitler had each fully taken control of the state apparatus, did they become totally fascist. If so, perhaps we have yet to see what the leaders of Hindutva will do if and when they finally gain an absolute majority and total control of the Government of India. In an India founded on a pluralistic empire that retains a structure of federal states and highly segmented and complex plural cultures, totalitarian control would be extremely difficult to achieve. Yet, given Hindutva's history of violence and resorts to extra-constitutional action, whether in mobilizing mass agitations or fomenting riots, totalitarianism seems an altogether possible, if improbable, attainment. While Mahatma Gandhi perfected the technologies of mobilizing extra-constitutional, ostensibly non-violent, protest campaigns from 1919 onward, there is not one of these that did not end in violence. He was murdered when he was seen as having betrayed Hindutva by trying to make concessions of the Muslim community.[44] A thread of continuity in fascist methods can be traced back to the beginnings of Hindutva.

Finally, when seen from a historical perspective, taking the long view, it is possible to notice that processes of 'traditionalization' – starting with Indological Orientalism and the 'Hindu Raj' at the end of the eighteenth century – began 'by assuming the hegemony of Brahmanical text over Indian society, incorporating that hegemony into the law-making process.'[45] The language of this 'reconstituted tradition' has provided the instruments used by subsequent rulers, colonial and national alike. These have served, repeatedly, to revaluate and 'reform' cultural, social, and political structures. The same process, taken over and raised to the next level by Hindutva forces, gradually enabled them to develop and refine an ideology designed to assure Brahmanical hegemony within Ram Rajiya.

It is this same process, encompassing the whole Hindutva agenda, that since its very beginnings has been slowly and carefully reshaping the entire public consciousness so as to make it conform to the Hindutva ideology. To be sure, circumstances of events that brought Hindutva to prominence have been riddled with complexities and contradictions. These can be seen in events that led from *Rath-Yatras* to Ayodhya, Bombay riots, and Gujarat pogroms. Throughout, the forces of Hindutva managed events to their advantage, skillfully deploying resources and turning strategies or tactics, in different places or different points of time, so as to occupy spaces left vacant by less active, less attentive, less ruthless or less visionary opponents. All along the way, in pursuit of its overall vision of Hindu Rashtriya (or Ram Rajiya), in the process of taking over more and more of the central squares of Indian politics, Hindutva has employed a double-edged, Janus-faced, and apparently contradictory strategy that runs along parallel tracks. On one track, borrowing from the tactics first perfected by Gandhi during the 1920s, it has created a 'parallel nation' or 'parallel state' apparatus that uses its own vocabulary. On the other track, it has striven to capture more and more institutions within civil society (e.g. communications, education, entertainment, media, etc.) so as to assert its widening hegemony. Despite major shifts in tactics, central directors of the Hindutva agenda have managed to hold together apparently divergent voices, at least sufficiently to meet each challenge.

Any summary of the rise of Hindutva reveals central features that, despite tactical shifts, have remained consistent. First, as Savarkar declared over 80 years ago, Hindutva is both a history and a geography. It posits a political 'culture' as a foundational 'political religion' on which all structures must rest. The entire economy, polity, and society of Hindu Rashtriya must conform to principles of Hindu civilization. Next, both geography and history compel Hindutva to build and preserve the Hindu community and Hindu identity by means of a kind of majoritarianism that is totalistic. Third, Hindutva requires a strong and totalistic Hindu Nation that alone can defend Hindu culture and civilization from all enemies, both internal and external, an all-powerful totalitarian leadership that can efficiently direct a highly centralized governing machinery, and a completely pliant, servile, and submissive society. Also, fourth, Hindutva's vision calls for a political rhetoric that, while couched in devoutly religious and traditional language, can reinterpret Hindu civilization so that it can be thoroughly modernist, if not contemporary. And finally, any sufficiently Hindu community, Hindu culture, and Hindu identity entails conformity within a totalistic process of social amalgamation and/or homogenization. To achieve this calls for 'corrections' of past distortions and misinterpretations of history and of reality. Misrepresentations of Hindutva's cultural verities in history and geography demand the marginalization and suppression, if not the obliteration, of all those elements or communities that pollute the culture.

The logic of these five features, or principles, have enabled forces of Hindutva to pursue a very long-term and systematic scheme for capturing and then filling every kind of institution of society with the Hindutva ethos. Manifold examples of this within the last few decades are contained within this essay. Steady Hindutva penetration into all levels of the media, education, ecology, research, including industry and commerce at all levels, has been such that it is still steadily transforming common understandings of reality in the minds of more and more people. The hijacking or infiltration of institutions is, by now, a very old and unending process, and one that is still accelerating. The aim at every level has been to achieve a total cultural and ideological hegemony that, in the end, will lead steadily toward a totalistic political hegemony. What has yet to be seen is what agencies run by the Sangh Parivar, specifically the RSS-created BJP and VHP, would do if absolute control were achieved at the Center.[46]

Notes

1. *Sanātana Dharma*: meaning 'Old' 'Ancient Order/System' implying also 'Eternal Order' and/or 'Universal Order, or Rightness,' with its rightly structured categories or colors (*varnas*). This term, which came into vogue in the nineteenth century before the concept of 'Hinduism' became more pervasive, was pushed by two kinds of champions: Pandit Guru Sahib (as in *Sanātanadharmamārttanda*) via Manu's *Dharmasastra*; and Annie Besant's work for Central Hindu College at Varanasi. Her work, *Sanatana Dharma: An Advanced Text-Book on Hindu Religion and Ethics* (Benares: Central Hindu College, 1903, 1904, 1910, &c), placing special stress on the *Gita*, is still in print.
2. John Stratton Hawley, 'Naming Hinduism,' *The Wilson Quarterly*, XV: 3 (Summer 1991), pp. 30–34, highlights this problem.
3. How this occurred is nowhere more acutely shown than in Wilfred Cantwell Smith, *The Meaning and End of Religion: A New Approach to the Religious Traditions of Mankind* (New York: Macmillan, 1963).
4. This process of exploration, like the Lewis and Clark expedition, sought to uncover a whole continent.
5. Romila Thapar, writing about pre-modern India, points out the mistake of assuming some sort of 'inclusive Hinduism' existed when 'the reality perhaps lay in looking at it as a cluster of distinctive sects and cults, observing common civilizational symbols, but with belief and ritual ranging from atheism to animism and a variety of religious organizations identifying themselves by location, language, and caste' (1989: 229). No sense of community bound the population together. Small communities, birth groups, and religious sects – now explained in Brahmanism, Shramanism, Shaktism, Puranic Shaivism and Vaishnavism, Bhaktism, &c – separated 'high' or textual cultures from innumerable local, 'low' or popular religious cultures: a 'mosaic of distinct cults, deities, sects and ideas' adjusting and distancing themselves from each other. What bound communities to each other, if at all, were manufactured structures of Statecraft. These, while often positive and supportive of local religious and sectarian institutions, had to remain 'impartial,' 'neutral,' or 'secular.' In this logic, Kautiliya's ideas find much in common with ideas of Machiavelli and Hobbes.
6. A. L. Basham, *The Wonder That Was India* (London: Sidgwick & Jackson, 1954, 1956, &c), pp. xxi, 568, reflects this view.
7. A superbly thorough and incisive dismissal of Edward Said's *Orientalism* (New York: Pantheon Books, 1978) is found in Robert Irwin, *For Lust of Knowing: The Orientalists and Their Enemies* (London: Allen Lane, The Penguin Press, 2006), aka *Dangerous Knowledge* (New York: Overlook, 2006), as reviewed in the *TLS* (May 19, 2006), p. 6 and *Wall Street Journal* (November 4–5, 2006), P. 10. It is high time for this 'unfairly maligned honourable pursuit' to be restored to its former respectability.
8. *The Sacred books of the East* (Oxford, Clarendon Press, 1879–1910), 50 v., translated by various Oriental [Indian] scholars and edited by Friedrich Max Müller.
9. Eric J. Ziolkowski, 'Heavenly Visions and Worldly Intentions: Chicago's Columbian Exposition and World's Parliament of Religions (1893),' *Journal*

of American Culture, 13: 4 (1990), 11–12, documents this 'discovery.' For proceedings of that event, see John Henry Barrows, *The World's Parliament of Religions…of 1893* (Chicago: Parliament Publishing, 1893), in two volumes.

10. Franklin A. Presler, *Religion under Bureaucracy: Policy and Administration of Hindu Temples in South India* (Cambridge: Cambridge University Press, 1987), explores later ramifications of this policy.

11. The very term 'juggernaut,' coming from Jagannath, Lord of the Universe and avatar of Vishnu, entered the English vocabulary, denotes any relentlessly destroying vehicle, force, or object of devotion, whereby devotees sometimes immolated themselves beneath giant wheels of the deity's Great Car at Puri.

12. Geoffrey O. Oddie, Geoffrey O., 'Constructing Hinduism: The Impact of the Protestant Missionary Movement on Hindu Self-Understanding,' *Christians and Missionaries in India: Cross-Cultural Communication since 1500* (Grand Rapids & London: Curzon and RoutledgeCurzon, 2003), pp. 155–182. Edited by Robert Eric Frykenberg. Also see Oddie's *Imagined Hinduism* (New Delhi; Thousand Oaks, Calif.: Sage Publications, 2006), which develops this theme further.

13. Bruce Carlisle Robertson, *Raja Rammohan Ray: The Father of Modern India* (Delhi: Oxford University Press, 1995) is the best comprehensive and penetrating study to have emerged so far. Both Roy's Brahmo Samaj (Brahma Society) and Prārthana Samaj (Prayer Society: 1868) of Mahadev Govind Ranade are excluded from discussion within this essay, since neither were militantly nativist precursors of Hindutva.

14. Two examples exemplify this perspective:

.   (1) Abbe J. A. Dubois, *Description of the Character, Manners, and Customs of the People of India; and of Their Institutions, Religious and Civil* (London: 1817; Madras 1872), from French MSS purchased in 1808 by East India Company. As *Hindu Manners, Customs and Ceremonies* (Oxford: Clarendon Press, 1953 [3rd. edn], *c.* 1906), translated again and edited with notes, corrections, and biography by Henry K. Beauchamp; with a prefatory note by F. Max Müller, it remains a classic. The late Sylvia Murr has shown that this work was plagiarized from the much earlier 1776–1777 work of the Jesuit Gaston-Laurent Cœrdoux entitled *Mœus et Coutemes des Indiens.* cf.: Sylvia Murr, 'Nicolas Jacques Desvaulx (1745–1823) veritable auteur de Moeurs, institutions et cérémonies des peuples de l'Inde, de l'abbé Dubois?' *Purusartha*, III (Paris: 1977) 245–67; and Will Sweetman, *Mapping Hinduism: 'Hinduism' and the Study of Indian Religions, 1600–1776* (Halle: Verlag der Franckeshe Stiftungen za Halle, 2003), 125–153.

  (2) Copies of Bartholomäus Ziegenbalg's MSS, *Genealogie der malabarischen Götter* sent to Copenhagen, Halle and London in 1713 reveals an open appreciation for South Indian institutions and learning. Daniel Jeyaraj's English translation of his German scholarship on this work, entitled *Genealogy of the South Indian Deities* (London: Routledge, 2005), is a translation of his Halle.

15. Kenneth W. Jones, *Arya Dharm: Hindu Consciousness in 19th-Century Punjab* (Berkeley: University of California Press, 1976); Christopher R. King, *One*

Language, Two Scripts: The Hindi Movement in Nineteenth Century North India (Bombay: Oxford University Press, 1994).

16. Romila Thapar, 'Imagined Religious Communities? Ancient History and the Modern Search for Hindu Identity,' *Modern Asian Studies* (1989), 23: 2, 229. Professor Thapar also coined the concept of 'Syndicated Moksha' or 'Syndicated Hinduism.'

17. For those who, all along, felt that the Hindu Mahasabha was not 'orthodox' enough or who felt offended by the reformist appeals of the Arya Samaj, there was the Sanathana Dharm Sabha; or, later on, the Ram Rajiya Parishad (RRP).

18. Here defined as a *radical* and *militant* reaction to certain elements of change and perceived threats (from an alien, hostile, modernist, secularistic world) which are seen to be inherently contradictory to 'The Truth' (of a world view) as found in a literal or strict interpretation of an inerrant body of scriptural text, imprinted in genomes and cosmic sounds of Brahma (stemming from the *Rig Veda*, as conveyed from the mouths of sages or prophets). See Andersen & Damlé: p. 76.

19. G.S. Hingle, *Hindutva Reawakened* (New Delhi: Vikas, 1999) is the latest work on his life.

20. For the anatomy of conversion: Robert Eric Frykenberg 'On the Study of Conversion Movements: A Review Articles and a Research Note,' *The Indian Economic and Social History Review*, **XVII**, 1 (January–March, 1980), 121–38; article (1988) in Bjorkman (ed.); or Introduction to *Accounting for Fundamentalisms* (vol. 3).

21. Alias Miss Margaret Elizabeth Noble, *Web of Indian Live* (New York, 1916), an Irish nationalist and feminist, she was one of Swami Vivekananda's noteworthy disciples.

22. From an interview with G. S. Sudarshan, General Secretary of the RSS, given to Tapan Basu et al., authors of *Khaki Shorts and Saffron Flags* (1993), pp. 16, 54.

23. Walter K. Anderson and Shridhar D. Damlé, *The Brotherhood in Saffron: The Rashtriya Swayam Sevak* (Boulder, CO: Westview Press, 1987), p. 35.

24. Allegedly belonging to Ram, and used by Shivaji, these symbols gave the entire movement a strongly Maharashtrian appearance.

25. Mahadev Sadashiv Golwakar, *WE, or Our Nationhood Defined* (Nagpur: Bharat Prakashan, 1939 [1947 edition]), pp. 55–56.

26. Godse felt that Gandhi had insulted the Hindu Nation, weakened it by advocating *ahimsa*, and, by his fasts, had catered to Muslim fanatics. Andersen & Damlé: 51 (from 1969 interview with Gopal Godse by Damlé).

27. Myron Weiner, *Party-Politics in India: The Development of the Multi-Party System* (Princeton: 1957), pp. 190–94.

28. Bruce D. Graham, *Hindu Nationalism and Indian Politics: The Origin and Development of the Bharatiya Jana Sangh* (Cambridge: CUP, 1990), p. 256.

29. Robert Eric Frykenberg, 'The Last Emergency of the Raj,' *Indira Gandhi's India: A Political System Reappraised* (Madison WI: UW Press, 1976). Edited by Henry C. Hart, pp. 37–66, shows that virtually all the machinery perfected under the Raj, and perfected during the Gandhi-led 'Quit India' Movement of 1942, was still in place. Indeed, even some of the staff were the same.

30. Mark Tully and Satish Jacob, *Amritsar: Mrs. Gandhi's Last Battle* (London: Cape, 1985), p. 150.

31. Atul Kohli, *Democracy and Discontent: India's Growing Crisis of Government* (Cambridge: CUP, 1990), p. 4.
32. Ashgar Ali Engineer, 'Lok Sabha Elections and Communalism in Politics,' *Economic and Political Weekly [EPW]* (July 6–13, 1991); idem, 'The Causes of Communal Riots in the Post-Partition Period,' *Communal Riots in Post Partition India* (Hyderabad: Sangam Books, 1984), pp. 33–41, idem. 'Old Delhi in the Grip of Communal Frenzy,' *EPW* (June 27, 1987).
33. Paul R. Brass, *The Politics of India since Independence* (Cambridge: CUP, 1990), pp. 16–17. [*New Cambridge History of India* series, vol. 4: no. 1.]
34. The term, ironically from Sanskrit, meaning 'crushed' or 'oppressed,' is the only self-describing label that non-caste or outcaste untouchable peoples are seem to accept. Gandhi's term for them, *Harijan* (or 'Children of Hari' or Krishna) sticks in their throats. See J. C. B. Webster, *Religion and Dalit Liberation: An Examination of Perspectives* (New Delhi: Manohar, 1999).
35. Ainslie T. Embree, *Utopias in Conflict: Religion and Nationalism in Modern India* (Berkeley: UC Press, 1990), pp. 92–110.
36. A. G. Noorani, 'Legal Aspects of the Issue,' *The Anatomy of A Confrontation: The Babri-Masjid-Ramjanmabhumi Issue* (New Delhi: Penguin Books India, 1990, 1991), pp. 58–98. Edited by Sarvepalli Gopal.
37. Thomas Blom Hansen, *The Saffron Wave: Democracy and Hindu Nationalism in Modern India* (Princeton, N.J.: Princeton University Press, c. 1999), pp. 181–85.
38. Romila Thapar's book, *Somanatha: The Many Voices of History* (New Delhi: Viking, 2004), confronts Hindutva interpretations of history. She is far from alone. Almost all of the historical profession has joined her in combating Hindutva impositions.
39. Jwala Prasad Singhal, *The Sphinx Speaks: Or, the Story of the Prehistoric Nations* (New Delhi: Sadgyan Sadan, 1963), Chapter 1. 'The Tethys Sea in the Rig Veda' and Chapter 2. 'Geological Account – Lemuria Continent,' pp. 1–28.
40. What happened, as detailed in hundreds of media reports, both printed and electronic, was well summarized in papers delivered by Cedric Prakash, Teesta Setalvad, Kamal Chenoy, Sumit Ganguly, and Sunil Khilnani at Center for Ethics and Public Policy on June 10, 2002. 'Hindu Nationalism vs. Islamic Jihad: Religious Militancy in South Asia,' *Center Conversations* (Washington: EPPC, February 2003), Occasional Paper, Number 17, pp. 1–13.
41. Shushil J. Aaron, *Christianity and Political Conflict in India: The Case of Gujarat* (Colombo: Regional Centre for Strategic Studies, June 2002), no. 23., pp. 1–91. Hundreds of reports have been published.
42. M. S. Golwalkar, *WE, or Our Nationhood Defined* (Nagpur: Bharat Prakashan, 1939), p. 27.
43. Ibid., p. 52. Also found in Tapan Basu (et al.), *Khaki Shorts, Saffron Flags* (Hyderabad: Longmans, 1993), p. 26.
44. A. G. Noorani, 'Gandhi's Murder,' *Savarkar and Hindutva: The Godse Connection* (New Delhi: Left Word, 2002), pp. 95–139, convincingly shows that the murder was very carefully organized and orchestrated this event, cleverly remained in the shadows and, as much as possible, hid tracks that might lead to him. This work is dedicated 'to the victims of the Pogrom of Gujarat 2002, and to the media, print and electronic, which did India proud.'
45. Vakulabharnam Rajagopal, 'The Rhetorical Strategy of an Autobiography: Reading Satyavati's *Atmacaritamu*' (Madison: University of Wisconsin,

unpublished paper, *c.* 2003), pp. 13–14. I am deeply indebted to Rajagopal for sharing this paper.
46. Rajarama Tolpady, 'The Dynamics of Hindutva Politics: Case for Dakshina Kannada,' *The Retrieved Acre: Nature and Culture in the World of Tuluva* (Mangalagangothri: Prasaranga, Mangalore University, 2003). Edited by B. Surendra Rao and K. Chinnappa Gowda, pp. 164–80.

Bibliographical References and Sources

Ahmad, Aijaz, *Lineages of the Present: Ideology and Politics of Contemporary South Asia* (London, New York: Verso, 2000), pp. xvi, 366. Bibliography [325–49], Index.

Almond, Gabriel A., Appleby, R., Scott and Sivan, Emmanuel, *Strong Religion: The Rise of Fundamentalism Around the World* (Chicago & London: University of Chicago Press, 2003), p. 281, Index.

Anand, Vidya Sagar (1939–), *Savarkar: A Study in the Evolution of Indian Nationalism* (London: Cecil & Amelia Woolf, 1967), p. 95, plate, port. Bibliography [88–95].

Anand, Subhash (1943–), *Hindutva: A Christian Response* (Indore: Satprakashan Sanchar Kendra, 2001), pp. xii, 140. Notes, References.

Andersen, Walter K., Damlé, Shridhar D., *The Brotherhood in Saffron: The Rashtriya Swayam Sevak Sangh and Hindu Revivalism* (Boulder: Westview Press, 1987, *c.* 1986), pp. xiii, 317.

Banerjee, Sikata, *Warriors in Politics: Hindu Nationalism, Violence, and the Shiv Sena in India* (Boulder, Colo.: Westview Press, 2000), pp. xvi, 207. Bibliographical references (pp. 195–99) and index. Basu, Tapan [et al.], *Khaki Short and Saffron Flags* (Hyderabad: Orient Longman, 1993), pp. xii, 116 [Tracts for the Times: series: 1].

Bhambhri, Chandra Prakash, *Hindutva: A Challenge to Multi-Cultural Democracy* (Delhi: Shipra Publications, 2003), pp. viii, 200. Bibliographical references.

Bhatt, Chetan, *Hindu Nationalism: Origins, Ideologies and Modern Myths* (Oxford, New York: Berg, 2001), pp. viii, 231. Bibliography [213–25], Index.

Biardeau, Madeleine, *Hinduism: The Anthropology of a Civilization* (Delhi: Oxford University Press, 1989, 1991], pp. vi, 189. Notes, Glossary. [Original Edition in French, *L.' Hindouisme: Anthropologie d' une Civilization* (Paris: Flammarion, 1981)]

Brass, Paul R., *The Production of Hindu-Muslim Violence in Contemporary India* (Seattle: University of Washington Press, *c.* 2003), pp. xix, 476, ill., maps.

Chatterjee, Abhas, *The Concept of Hindu Nation* (New Delhi: Voice of India, 1995), p. 69.

Chitkara, M. G. (1932–), *Hindutva Parivar* (New Delhi: A. P. H. Pub. Corp., 2003), pp. xx, 259. Bibliographical references [248–253] and index.

Curran, J. A. (Jean Alonzo), *Militant Hinduism in Indian Politics: A Study of the R.S.S* (New Delhi: All India Quami Ekta Sammelan, [1951], 1979), pp. xv, 104. Bibliography [103–04]. Edited by N. Damodaran Nayar; Introduction, Raj Narain. Introduction in English and Hindi.

Deshpande, B. V. et al., *Dr. Hedgewar, The Epoch-Maker: A Biography* (Bangalore: Sahitya Sindhu: Sole Distributors, Rashtrotthana Sahitya, 1981), pp. v, 212, [2] of plates: ill. [Compiled by B. V. Deshpande and S. R. Ramaswamy; edited by H. V. Seshadri.]

Dubois, J. A. (Abbé Jean Antoine, 1765–1848), *Hindu Manners, Customs and Ceremonies* (Oxford: Clarendon Press, 1953 [3rd. edn], *c.* 1906), pp. xxxiv, 741, port. [Trans. again from author's French ms. and edited with notes, corrections and biography by Henry K. Beauchamp; with a prefatory note by the Right Hon. F. Max Müller and a portrait. Originally purchased by the East India Company in 1808, brought to London, translated, and published (London: 1817; Madras 1872, as *Description of the Character, Manners, and Customs of the People of India; and of Their Institutions, Religious and Civil.* This is now known to have been plagiarized.

Eckert, Julia M., *The Charisma of Direct Action: Power, Politics, and the Shiv Sena* (New Delhi, New York: Oxford University Press, 2003), p. 307. Bibliographical References [282–95].

Elst, Koenraad (1959–), *The Saffron Swastika: The Notion of 'Hindu Fascism'* (New Delhi: Voice of India, 2001). 2 vols, pp. x, 1070.

Embree, Ainslie T., *Utopias in Conflict: Religion and Nationalism in Modern India* (Berkeley, &c: University of California Press, 1990), pp. xiv, 144. Index.

Felice, Renzo de, *Fascism: An Informal Introduction to Its Theory and Practice* (New Brunswick, NJ: Transaction Books, 1977 [Italian edn, 1975], p. 128, Notes. Interview with Michael Ledeen.

Fernandes, Walter (1939–), *The Role of Christians in National Integration* (New Delhi: Indian Social Institute, 1988), p. 45. [Ideas for action series: 4; Revision of a paper presented at the general body meeting of the Catholic Bishops' Conference of India at Kottayam in April 1988.] Bibliography [42–45].

Frykenberg, Robert Eric, 'The Concept of "Majority" as a Devilish Force in the Politics of Modern India,' *Journal of Commonwealth and Comparative Politics*, **XXV** 3 (November, 1987), 267–74.

Frykenberg, Robert Eric, 'Constructions of Hinduism at the Nexus of History and Religion,' *Journal of Interdisciplinary History*, **XXIII** 3 (Winter 1993), 523–550.

Frykenberg, Robert Eric, 'Hindu Fundamentalism and the Structural Stability of India,' *Fundamentalisms and the State: Remaking Polities, Economies, and Militance* (Chicago: University of Chicago Press, 1993), pp. 233–55. *The Fundamentalism Project: Volume III.* Edited by Martin Marty and R. Scott Appleby.

Frykenberg, Robert Eric, 'The Emergence of Modern "Hinduism" as a Concept and as an Institution: A Reappraisal with Special Reference to South India,' *Hinduism Reconsidered* (Heidelberg: South Asia Institute, 1989), pp. 1–29. Edited by Gunther Sontheimer and Hermann Kulke. Republished, expanded (New Delhi: Manohar Books, 1997), pp. 82–107.

Golwalkar, M. S. [Madhav Sadashiv], *Bunch of Thoughts* (Bangalore, Vikrama Prakashan; sole distributors: Rashtrotthana Sahitya, 1966), pp. xxxiv, 437.

Golwalkar, M. S. [Madhav Sadashiv], *We or Our Nationhood Defined* (Nagpur, Bharat Prakashan, 1939 [1st edn], 1944 [2nd edn, p. 73], 1945 [3rd edn], 1949 [4th edn]), pp. xxi, 5, 77.

Gopal, Sarvepalli (ed.), *Anatomy of a Confrontation: The Babri Masjid-Ram Janmabhumi Issue* (New Delhi, Oxford, New York: Viking [Penguin]), p. 240, Index.

Gottfried, Paul Edward, *Multiculturalism and the Politics of Guilt* (Columbia and London: University of Missouri Press, 2002), pp. x, 158.

Graham, Bruce Desmond, *Hindu Nationalism and Indian Politics: The Origins and Development of the Bharatiya Jana Sangh* (Cambridge [England]; New York: Cambridge University Press, 1990), pp. xii, 283, ill., maps.

Griffin, Roger (ed.), *Fascism* (Oxford & New York: Oxford University Press, 1995), pp. xvii, 410. Bibliography [393–99], Index. [Oxford Readers: Series]

Griffin, Roger and Feldman, Matthew, *Fascism: Critical Concepts in Political Science* (London: New York: Routledge, 2004), 5 vols Bibliographies, Indexes. [1 vol. *The Nature of Fascism*—2 vol. *The Social Dynamics of Fascism*—3 vol. *Fascism and Culture*—4 vol. *The 'Fascist Epoch'*—5 vol.]. *Post-war Fascisms.*

Gupta, Dipankar, *Nativism in a Metropolis: The Shiv Sena in Bombay* (New Delhi: Manohar, pp. xv, 227, maps. Bibliography [206–20], Index. [Revision of Ph D Dissertation (Jawaharlal Nehru University, 1977)].

Hansen, Thomas Blom (1958–), *The Saffron Wave: Democracy and Hindu Nationalism in Modern India* (Princeton, N.J.: Princeton University Press, *c.* 1999), pp. vi, 293. Bibliography [273–88], Index.

Hellman, Eva, *Political Hinduism: The Challenge of the Visva Hindu Parishad* (Uppsala: Uppsala University Doctoral Dissertation, 1993), p. 222, Bibliography [203–22].

Hingle, G. S., *Hindutva Reawakened* (New Delhi: Vikas Pub. House: Distributors, UBS Publishers' Distributors, 1999), pp. xix, 221.

Innaiah, N. (1937–), *Saffron Star over Andhra Pradesh: Genesis, Growth, and Critical Analysis of Telugu Desam Party* (Hyderabad: N. Innaiah: Distributors, Book Links Corp., 1984), p. 168. Bibliography [153–68].

Jaffrelot, Christophe, *The Hindu Nationalist Movement and Indian Politics: 1925 to the 1990s: Strategies of Identity-Building, Implantation and Mobilisation (with Special Reference to Central India)* (London: Hurst, 1996), pp. xiii, 592, ill., maps [Original title: *Nationalistes Hindoues*].

Jhangiani, Motilal A., *Jana Sangh and Swatantra: A Profile of the Rightist Parties in India* (Bombay: Manaktalas, 1967), pp. xiv, 223. Bibliography [207–17], Index.

Jones, Kenneth W., *Arya Dharm: Hindu Consciousness in 19th-Century Punjab* (Berkeley: University of California Press, 1976), pp. xvii, 343. Appendices, Bibliographical Note, Index.

Juergensmeyer, Mark, *The New Cold War? Religious Nationalism Confronts the State* (Berkeley, London, &c: University of California Press, 1994), pp. xiv, 292. Bibliography [249–76], Index.

Keer, Dhananjay. *Savarkar and His Times* (Bombay A. V. Keer 1950), pp. vi, 421.

King, Christopher R., *One Language, Two Scripts: The Hindi Movement in Nineteenth Century North India* (Bombay, &c: Oxford University Press, 1994), pp. xi, 232. Glossary, Bibliography, Index.

Lipner, Julius I., 'On Hinduism: Re-modelling the Banyan Tree,' (Cambridge: Faculty of Divinity, University of Cambridge, unpublished paper, 2000) n.d. [*c.* 200].

Lobo, Lancy, *Globalisation, Hindu Nationalism, and Christians in India* (Jaipur: Rawat Publications, 2002), p. 240. Bibliographical references [232–36] and index. [Variant Title: Globalization, Hindu Nationalism, and Christians in India].

Louis, Prakash, *The Emerging Hindutva Force: The Ascent of Hindu Nationalism* New Delhi: Indian Social Institute, *c.* 2000), pp. x, 308. Bibliography [278–84]. [Variant Title: *Hindutva Force*; Summary on Hinduism and State with Special Reference to the Activities of Rashtriya Swayam Sevak Sangh, Fundamentalist Political Party from India].

Ludden, David (ed.), *Making India Hindu: Religion, Community, and the Politics of Democracy in India* (Delhi: Oxford University Press, 1996). [Variant Title: *Contesting the Nation: Religion, Community, and the Politics of Democracy in India* (Philadelphia: University of Pennsylvania Press, *c.* 1996), pp. ix, 346.

Madan, T. N., *Modern Myths, Locked Minds: Secularism and Fundamentalism in India* (Delhi, New York: Oxford University Press, 1997), pp. xv, 323. Bibliography [285–306], Index.

Mallet, Robert, *Mussolini and the Origins of the Second World War, 1933–1940* (London & New York: Palgrave [Macmillan branch of St. Martin's Press], 2003), pp. ix, 266.

Malik, Yogendra K. and Singh, V. B., *Hindu Nationalists in India: The Rise of the Bharatiya Janata Party* (Boulder: Westview Press, 1994), pp. x, 262, ill., maps, Bibliography [243–53], Index.

Mandal, D., *Ayodhya: Archaeology after Demolition – A Critique of the 'New' and 'Fresh' Discoveries* (Hyderabad: Orient Longman, 1993), pp. xiii, 69. [Series: Tracts for the Times/5].

Marshall, P. J. (ed.), *The British Discovery of Hinduism in the Eighteenth Century* (Cambridge: Cambridge University Press, 1970), pp. x, 310. Index.

Mathew, C. V., *The Saffron Mission: A Historical Analysis of Modern Hindu Missionary Ideologies and Practices* (Delhi: Indian Society for Promoting Christian Knowledge, 1999), pp. xvi, 317. Bibliography [305–17].

Misra, R. S., Dr., *Hinduism and Secularism: A Critical Study* (Delhi: Motilal Banarsidass Publishers, 1996), p. 200.

Mujahid, Abdul Malik, *Conversion to Islam: Untouchables' Strategy for Protest in India* (Chambersburg: Amina Books, 1989), pp. vii, 159. Bibliography [143–49], Index. [Foreword by Lloyd I Rudolph and Susanne Hoeber Rudolph].

Noorani, A. G., *Savarkar and Hindutva: The Godse Connection* (New Delhi: LeftWord, 2002), p. 169.

Oddie, Geoffrey O., 'Constructing "Hinduism": The Impact of the Protestant Missionary Movement on Hindu Self-Understanding,' *Christians and Missionaries in India: Cross-cultural Communication since 1500* (Grand Rapids & London: Curzon and RoutledgeCurzon, 2003), pp. 155–82.

Pandy, Gyanendra (ed.), *Hindus and Others: The Question of Identity in India Today* (New Delhi: Viking [Penguin India], 1993), pp. ix, 313. Index.

Panikkar, K. N., *An Agenda for Cultural Action and Other Essays* (New Delhi: Three Essays Press, 2002), pp. xxi, 103. Bibliographical references [Readings (Three Essays Press)].

Panikkar, K. N., *Before the Night Falls: Forebodings of Fascism in India* (Bangalore: Books for Change, 2002), pp. xvii, 146. Bibliography, Index.

Pattanaik, D. D. (1951–), *Hindu Nationalism in India* (New Delhi: Deep & Deep Publications, *c.* 1998), 1 vol., p. 178. Bibliographical references [164–74], Indexes. [Foreword by M. M. Sankhdher] [1 vol. Conceptual Foundation; 2 vol. Modern Trends; 3 vol. Ideological Corollaries; 4 vol. Non-Conventional School]. [Dedicated to Professor Rajendra Singh – Mananiya Raju Bhatya – Sarsanghprachalak, Rashtriya Swayam Sevak Sangh].

Payne, Stanley G., *Fascism: Comparison and Definition* (Madison: University of Wisconsin Press, 1980), pp. viii, 234. Bibliographical Note, Index.

Payne, Stanley G., *A History of Fascism, 1914–1945* (Madison: University of Wisconsin Press, 1995), pp. xiv, 613. Bibliography [533–77], Index, Illus., Tables. [Introduction. Fascism: A Working Definition]. [cf. *Fascism: Comparison and Definition* (Madison: UWPress, 1980), pp. vii, 234. Bibliographical Note, Index].

Payne, Stanley G., 'The Problem of Political Religion' (Madison: UW, unpublished paper, *c.* 2003), p. 11.

Puri, Balraj, *Kashmir: Towards Insurgency* (Hyderabad: Orient Longman, 1993), pp. viii, 107. Chronology, Bibliography [105–7].

Rajshekar Shetty, V. T., *Hinduism, Fascism, and Gandhiism: A Guide to Every Intelligent Indian* (Bangalore, India: Dalit Sahitya Akademy, 1985), p. 86. Bibliography, Index.

Ram, P. R., *Fascism of Sangh Parivar* (Mumbai: EKTA, 1999 [2nd edn], p. 96. Bibliography.

Savarkar, Vinayak Damodar (1883–1966), *Hindutva; Who Is a Hindu?* (Bombay, Veer Savarkar Prakashan, 1923 [5th Edn, 1969]), pp. xiv, 141.

Savarkar, Vinayak Damodar (1883–1966), *An Echo from Andamans: Letters written by Savarkar to his Brother, Dr. Savarkar, Pleader* (Nagpur: Vishvanath Vinayak Kelkar, [1928?]), [2], p. 126.

Savarkar, Vinayak Damodar (1883–1966), *Hindutva* (New Delhi: Central Hindu Yuvak Sabha, 1938), pp. [8], 184; [2] leaves of plates [*Vinayakrao Damodar Savarkar*].

Savarkar, Vinayak Damodar (1883–1966), *Hindu-Pad-Padashahi, or, A Review of the Hindu Empire of Maharashtra* (Madras: B.G. Paul & Co., 1925], 1971), pp. xvii, 296.

Savarkar, Vinayak Damodar (1883–1966), *Hindu Rashtra Darshan: A Collection of the Presidential Speeches delivered from the Hindu Mahasabha Platform* (Bombay: Khare, 1949), p. 309, [5] leaves of plates (1 fold): ill.

Savarkar, Vinayak Damodar (1883–1966), *Historic Statements [by] V. D. Savarkar* (Bombay [G. P. Parchure]; sole selling agents: Popular Prakashan [1967]), pp. 4, 244. [Edited by S. S. Savarkar [and] G. M. Joshi].

Savarkar, Vinayak Damodar, *The Indian War of Independence of 1857. By an Indian Nationalist* ([London: 1909]), p. 451.

Savarkar, Vinayak Damodar (1883–1966), *My Transportation for Life* (Bombay: [1949] Veer Savarkar Prakashan, 1984, 2nd edn), p. 572. [Original title: *Majhī janmathepa;* translation by V. N. Naik].

Sharma, Jyotirmaya, *Hindutva: Exploring the Ideas of Hindu Nationalism* (New Delhi: Penguin/Viking, 2003), p. 205.

Shukla, I. K., *Hindutva: An Autopsy of Fascism as a Theoterrorist Cult and Other Essays* (Delhi: Media House, 2003), p. 176.

Shyam Chand, *Saffron Fascism* (Delhi: Hemkunt Publishers, 2002), pp. x, 178, ills. Bibliographical references [176–78]

Singhal, Jwala Prasad, *The Sphinx Speaks: Or, The Story of the Prehistoric Nations* (New Delhi: Sadgyan Sadan, 1963), pp. viii, xii, 163. Index, Map of 'Saptasindhu in Rigveda.'

Smith, Wilfred Cantwell, *The Meaning and End of Religion; a New Approach to the Religious Traditions of Mankind* (New York, Macmillan, 1963), p. 340.

Sontheimer, Günther-Dietz and Kulke Hermann (eds), *Hinduism Reconsidered* (New Delhi: Manohar Publishers & Distributors, 1997, Second Edition, revised [1989]), pp. vi, 359.

Suntharalingam, R. *Indian Nationalism: An Historical Analysis* New Delhi: Vikas Pub. House, *c.* 1983), pp. viii, 471. Bibliography, Index.

Upadhyaya, [Shri] Deendayal, *Presidential Address* (Delhi: Navchetan Press, [1967?]), p. 26.

Upadhyaya, Deendayal, *Integral Humanism* (Delhi: Deendayal Research Institute, 1991).

Vaidya, Prem, *Savarkar, A Lifelong Crusader* (New Delhi: New Age International (P) Ltd., *c.* 1996), pp. viii, 124, ill. bibliographical references, Index. [Biography of Vinayak Damodar Savarkar, 1883–1966, Nationalist and Indian Freedom Fighter.]

Van der Veer, Peter, *Religious Nationalism: Hindus and Muslims in India* (Berkeley & London: University of California Press, 1994), pp. xvi, 245. Bibliography [223–35], Index.

Young, Richard Fox, *Resistant Hinduism: Sanskrit Sources on Anti-Christian Apologetics in Early Nineteenth Century India* (Delhi, Leiden, Vienna: E. J. Brill, 1981), p. 200. Appendix, Bibliography, Index [177–200]. [De Nobili Research Library, Indological Institute, University of Vienna].

Zavos, John, *The Emergence of Hindu Nationalism in India* (Delhi, Oxford: Oxford University Press, 2000), pp. viii, 245. Bibliographical references [228–39], Index.

11
The United States: Messianism, Apocalypticism, and Political Religion

Chip Berlet

> I believe…that an unbridled passion for the total elimination of this or that evil can be as dangerous as any of the delusions of our time.
>
> —Richard Hofstadter[1]

Can a nation of civilized religions and civil religion produce political religions? Why should the United States be an exception? Beyond the marginal totalitarian groups that we easily identify as political religions, however, is a larger question of how an American sense of messianic destiny continuously pushes social and political movements toward political religion, in ways that periodically gain mass support and influence public policy.

The tendency toward political religion in the United States is fed by the apocalyptic and messianic tradition brought to our shores by certain forms of Protestantism and the legacy of a civil religion that incorporates a messianic vision of national historic destiny. This makes it difficult to separate a national identity from a national ideology. Richard Hofstadter once quipped, 'In earlier days, after all, it had been our fate as a nation not to have ideologies but to be one.'[2] Alas, it is too soon to consign this tendency to 'earlier days.'

American exceptionalism was conceptualized by Alexis de Tocqueville, and it helped produce what Gunnar Myrdal labeled the 'American Creed,' later clarified by Robert N. Bellah who explained that, 'there actually exists alongside of and rather clearly differentiated from the churches an elaborate and well-institutionalized civil religion in America.'[3] This creed extols individualism, limited government, religious belief, patriotism, the constitutional republic, and a 'free market.'

The salience of civil religion in public and political life varies over time, surfing historic currents and waving with the flag. During America's bicentennial celebrations, John M. Mulder, a theologian, observed that:

> The Bicentennial and civil religion pose once again a perpetual dilemma for the church. Sermons can be preached against the identification of religion with politics, of the church blessing the state, of 'piety along the Potomac.' Such sermons would help to check the possibilities of a 'revivified' civil religion.[4]

Check but not checkmate. Consider the present situation. For some in America, it is time to return to the good old days, even if those days never really existed except as a mythical reconstructed rear-view projection. For others, it is time to stop the slide of America into the steamy swamp of decaying morality and stinking sin. For a significant number of political leaders, it is time to look forward to America as the benevolent hegemonic superpower. Moreover, all of these visionaries see time as running out.

In America, syncretic religions and sectarian political movements breed like guppies. Within the contemporary political right are those that fear creeping corporatism, by which they mean the growth of the social welfare state, government regulations, and taxes. Further to the right, there is fear of government political repression and a New World Order, especially within the Christian Right, where many see it as a fulfillment of biblical prophecy signaling the apocalyptic End Times. Many on the political left share a fear of repression, but for them corporatism is chiefly the threat of globalized business conglomerates. Nevertheless, they also fear the potential for theocracy posed by the Christian Right. The terror attacks on September 11, 2001 – and the government's response to them – accelerated the energy of these movements.

At some point, sectarian political and social movements cross over a line into political religions.[5] Where do we draw the line? In the United States, this question is made more complicated by a history in which syncretic religions have repeatedly played a role in producing sectarian political and social movements. Unlike many European countries, there is neither a *de jure* nor a *de facto* central established religion in the United States, and no legacy of a divinely ordained monarchy. There is, however, a strong civil religion. Teasing out political religion will require some precision and careful terminology.

This chapter will look at political religion in the United States as a way to explore how movement leaders can construct political religion in any setting. I begin by unpeeling the fruitful analytical model of political religion, pulling out the juicy component sections, and exploring how they relate to totalitarianism and fascism. Then I explore the relationships among totalitarianism, fascism, and religion to examine the role of apocalypticism. To illustrate the less obvious forms of political religion in the United States, I start with the most obvious totalitarian movements, with a special look at the charismatic totalitarian political religions led by the Reverend Sun Myung Moon, Minister Louis Farrakhan, and Lyndon H. LaRouche, Jr., along with a brief mention of the extreme right and extreme left. How the American dream is built upon notions of a transcendent messianic mission to save the world narrows the focus. Examples of how some groups wrap a political religion around militant forms of apocalyptic Christianity include a look at Christian Identity, Christian Reconstructionism, and the Christian Right. Finally, we arrive at the Bush Administration and the strange coalition between the Christian Right and the neoconservatives, which some authors have described as the merger of 'apocalyptic religion and American empire' or simply 'messianic militarism.'[6]

Components

There are important psychological aspects to the way that leaders and followers engage in a synergistic relationship in political religions.[7] Many sociologists, however, do not think that people who join social movements are psychologically dysfunctional or irrational. They see people with a grievance who mobilize resources, exploit political opportunities, develop their own culture, and create frames, stories, and slogans in ways that are both strategic and instrumental.[8] Several scholars have found this to be true as well for most participants in extreme right movements.[9]

A 'frame' in sociology is simply a specific point of view or perspective created by movement leaders to illustrate a power struggle in terms that are both accessible, and highly resonant in the target audience.[10] Master frames are broad perspectives that undergird an entire movement.[11] Here I use the term 'metaframe' to describe a broad frame that is so pervasive in a culture that many different movements can use it, despite ideological differences. In sociological jargon, a narrative is a story told within a movement. It has a plot, heroes and villains, and an instructive text or subtext. A narrative helps bind movement recruits closer to the movement, and demonstrates which ideas and actions are valued and which are condemned.[12]

I have written a number of studies that look at the sociological aspects of right-wing political religions, and especially the specific components involved.[13] Some of these components are essential to the formation of a political religion; the addition of other components make a political religion totalitarian. Tweak it one way and it gives us Hitler, tweak it another way and it gives us Stalin.

Political religion

In a political religion, a secular entity is sacralized.[14] If this entity is merely venerated, it is not a political religion. What is the problem if people worship a sacred cabbage? If the sacralised entity is something that people need to defend through political action, then we have a political religion. Roger Griffin writes of the 'palingenetic' call for the heroic rebirth of the nation after a period of decay and decline.[15] This involves the perception that time is running out for good to triumph over evil. This apocalyptic and dualistic vision interpolates heroic warriors for the cosmological battle. Using a 'chrono-ethological' approach, Griffin points to the elements of 'mystic purification and immortality' embraced by those who sacralize a particular entity that needs defense.[16] It is the apocalyptic dream of perfection that creates the nightmare of totalitarian movements and political religions.[17]

Aggression and violence occurs when a palingenetic apocalyptic movement becomes politically active and demands, in a totalitarian way, that the sacred entity is 'an absolute principle of collective existence, considers it the main source of values for individual and mass behaviour, and exalts it as the supreme ethical precept of public life.'[18] This divides the society into those that defend the sacred entity, and those from whom the sacred entity needs to be defended.

Disassembling this set of claims reveals the components:

Palingenesis is an *ideological goal* for a political religion. Griffin uses the term palingenesis to describe fascism as a movement.[19] The concept of palingenesis is behind the ideological goal shared by all political religions: the establishment of a nation or other entity rebuilt by the sanctified through a purifying catharsis that removes the slag of decadence and dissent just as steel is forged in a fiery cauldron. Add a timetable to palingenesis and you invoke apocalypticism.

Apocalypticism is a *metaframe* that involves the sense of expectation that dramatic events are about to unfold during which good must confront evil in a confrontation that will change the world forever, and reveal hidden truths.[20] Apocalyptic movements believe that time is running out. The term millenarianism describes movements that are apocalyptic, with millennialism referring to such movements built around a theme involving a 1000-year span (or some other lengthy period).[21] Robert J. Lifton observes that 'historically the apocalyptic imagination has usually been nonviolent in nature,' but it can also generate horrific violence.[22] An apocalyptic leader may take on the mantle of the messiah. In all political religions, leaders portray the sacred entity as threatened by malevolent forces. This creates dualism.

Dualism is a *metaframe* through which people see the world divided into the forces of good and evil. Manichaeism gave dualism a boost into Christianity. Richard Hostadter noted that the 'fundamentalist mind...is essentially Manichean.'[23] Anthony and Robbins coined the term 'exemplary dualism,' to describe a hyperbolic form of dualism in which 'contemporary sociopolitical or socioreligious forces are transmogrified into absolute contrast categories embodying moral, eschatological, and cosmic polarities upon which hinge the millennial destiny of humankind.'[24] They find this in 'totalist' religious and ideological movements 'with highly dualistic worldviews,' and 'an absolutist apocalyptic outlook' where members cast a 'projection of negativity and rejected elements of self onto ideologically designated scapegoats.'[25]

Scapegoating is a *process* by which a person or group of people are wrongfully stereotyped as sharing negative traits and are singled out for blame for causing societal problems, while the primary source of the problem (if it is real rather than imaginary) is overlooked or absolved of blame. It is easier to get people to scapegoat if the target is demonized.[26]

Demonization is a *process* through which people target individuals or groups as the embodiment of evil.[27] This involves a sequence of denigration, dehumanization, and demonization, which results in generating hatred of the objectified target.[28] One way to do this is to claim that the demonized scapegoat is plotting against the public good.[29] This often involves demagogic appeals. With demagoguery, followers must see the movement leader as charismatic, or the performance is easily interpreted as buffoonery. Demagoguery has been used historically not only by populists to denounce corrupt élites, but also by government officials to justify political repression – in both instances based on fears of conspiracies by real and imaginary subversive elements.[30]

Conspiracism is a *narrative*. In this context, a conspiracy theory is a narrative form of scapegoating. Conspiracist thinking exists around the world, and in some circumstances can move easily from the margins to the mainstream, as has happened repeatedly in the United States.[31]

Totalitarianism

To shift political religion into its mode as totalitarianism requires a few more components, which I will simply list:[32]

- Authoritarianism.
- Assertion of dominance.
- Hierarchical organization.
- Single party or movement.
- Political repression.
- Intrusion into private life.
- Manipulative propaganda.

Not all forms of totalitarianism are fascist, and so we collect one more set of components.

Fascism

While there is much contention over definitions of fascism, some basic elements of fascism as a movement repeatedly turn up in major studies. In addition to the components listed above, these include ultra-nationalism, right-wing populism, trans-class coalitions, integralism, organic leadership, anti-liberalism, anti-left militancy, militarism, a glorification of violence, and a revolutionary plan to topple the existing regime.[33] We can see how the elements for political religion and totalitarianism end up in definitions of fascism by looking at the one proposed by Griffin:

> [F]ascism is best defined as a revolutionary form of nationalism, one that sets out to be a political, social and ethical revolution, welding the 'people' into a dynamic national community under new elites infused with new heroic values. The core myth which inspires this project is that only a populist, trans-class movement of purifying, cathartic national rebirth (palingenesis) can stem the tide of decadence[34]

The Framework

Political religion assembles its components in linked sets: it pursues apocalyptic palingenesis using the processes of dualistic demonization, and conspiracist scapegoating. Not all examples of political religion are totalitarian, but all totalitarian movements have sacralized some entity and are thus political religions. Fascism is a form of totalitarian political religion, and on most maps drops anchor on the extreme right of the political spectrum. If we can demonstrate a relationship between the most militant form of fascism – Nazism – and connect it to both apocalypticism and religion, it will prove a stronger framework for the sections that follow.

Fascism, religion, and apocalypticism

How to sort out civil religion, religion, fundamentalism, and fascism has attracted much recent scholarly attention.[35] The specific intersection of fascism with religion causes heavy intellectual traffic and no few collisions. Griffin's definition of fascism (above) seems like it could be compatible with religion, yet Griffin argues that when the two forms collide, the religious aspect is syncretic or even 'counterfeit.'[36] Gentile sees fascism as a form of political religion, but by this he does not imply that fascism is a religion, but that the sacralization of politics is an aspect of totalitarianism whereby the state, the party, or some other entity in political life is raised to a cosmological level of significance, as in a religion.[37] On the other hand, Roger Eatwell is critical of 'much of liberal historiography's demonisation of fascism as an un-intellectual creed' and suggests that when discussing fascism and religion one must admit, 'all modern ideologies exhibit dimensions of religions.'[38] Stanley G. Payne listed as interwar fascist movements several groups that incorporated a strong religious element, including the Hungarian Arrow Cross, the Romanian Iron Guard, and the Croatian Ustasa.[39] I have argued elsewhere that we can see an 'Escher–like picture in which the "sacralisation of politics" leads up the down staircase to groups that build a theological dimension into a totalitarian political ideology that is palingenetic.'[40]

A number of scholars argue that Hitler's Nazism was highly influenced by apocalyptic millennialism or millenarianism.[41] Tom Gibbons, citing the work of Cohn and Weber, concludes that in fascism:

> we may see both Marxist 'scientific socialism' and German National Socialism as secularized forms of pre-Christian Zoroastrian apocalyptic tradition, filtered through Judaeo-Christian scripture, with a top-dressing of Victorian pseudo-science.[42]

Redles writes about the Nazis, but sees a wider 'apocalypse complex' that is 'a collection of symbols that generates a sense of order to replace the perception of chaos.' We can see the 'archetypal nature' of this complex in its historic continuity; and all subsequent apocalyptic visions are 'explained and elaborated by pre-existing millennial traditions.'[43] Richard Steigmann-Gall agrees that 'for "totalitarian" regimes in general, the use of physical space and prophetic language was indeed often consciously derived from religious sources,' yet he deprecates the idea of political religion, saying 'At the end of the day the most recent works on political religion and totalitarianism theory offer little new beyond Voegelin's earlier theories.'[44] According to Steigmann-Gall, Hitler and the Nazis eventually crafted an ideology that was complementary to highly racialized versions of Protestantism in Germany. He is naming a forest without seeing the trees. It is precisely the elements of apocalyptic palingenesis, dualistic demonization, and conspiracist scapegoating – shared by certain historic manifestations of Christianity – that creates the complementary aspects. The leaders of German Nazism imbibed these in their youth with their communion wine and later spat them out as refurbished tropes in the face of those Christian leaders who objected to their millennial Reich.

Thus Nazism was connected to Christianity, not because Nazism was a Christian movement, but because Christianity wrote the most popular apocalyptic script in Western culture. All political religions, and indeed all totalitarian movements, utilize the millenarian call for heroic transformation and rebirth, alongside the scapegoating and conspiracism generated by apocalyptic dualism. Demagogues utilize this constellation of frames, processes, and narratives to sacralize a secular entity and create a political religion. At the very least, the concept of political religion has to find some way to incorporate not only the clerical fascist movements of the interwar period, but also contemporary totalitarian and neofascist movements built around pre-existing and syncretic religious doctrines.

All neofascist movements in the United States are forms of political religion (the sacralization of politics), but not all are examples of a politicized religion. Those that are a form of an existing religion can be part of a broad category of theocratic fascist movements (including movements that create marginal syncretic and hybridized forms of a religion); or the narrower subcategory of clerical fascist movements that integrally involve the clergy of a significant institutionalized religion.[45]

Totalitarian groups in the United States

Political religion is only one element found in totalitarianism, but if we start by reviewing obvious totalitarian movements in the United States, it is easier to see how political religion works as we move closer to the political center.

Charismatic totalistic groups

In all small totalitarian groups led by a charismatic leader, the collective assembled around the feet of the master is sacralized as an entity that has a mythic destiny and heroic mission. This is similar to Voegelin's description of how National Socialism constructed 'the people' as an entity.[46] There are hundreds of totalist groups in the United States, as there are multiple totalist groups in many countries.[47] Three totalist groups play a role on the wider political scene in the United States: the networks run by the Reverend Sun Myung Moon, Minister Louis Farrakhan, and Lyndon H. LaRouche, Jr. All these groups are built around a charismatic demagogue.[48]

The Moon network

The Reverend Sun Myung Moon runs an international network of religious, political, and commercial organizations that spans the world, and has established a strong presence in the United States. Moon originally was based in Korea, but he has helped Japanese multinationals by serving as their intermediary across Asia, and has assisted right-wing politicians in the United States by supporting ultra-conservative foreign and domestic policies.[49] Run largely as a totalitarian religious group (some say 'cult'), the organization was for many years built around Moon's Unification Church movement, but now frequently operates as the Family Federation for World Peace and Unification.[50]

Frederick Clarkson writes that the Moon network is a 'theocrat movement' that is 'propelled by the politics of demons,' and represents a form of 'mainstream fascism.'[51] Russ Bellant calls Moon 'a theocratic authoritarian who considers himself the Son of God and the new Messiah.'[52] Nonetheless, Moon is a major player in US politics. Moon controls a daily newspaper in the nation's capital, the *Washington Times*. According to a 2004 column in the *Washington Post*, the Unification Church 'has bankrolled huge losses at the Times, which several sources estimated have totaled more than $1 billion over the past 22 years. The paper's losses are running about $20 million annually.'[53] The network run by Moon has close ties to the Bush Administration, and has access to and support from a number of US elected officials.[54]

Moon, the Unification Church, and assorted related front groups have a longstanding relationship with the Christian Right and other conservative political activists. This relationship was originally forged around the issue of anticommunism.[55] For example, Moon's network directly participated with Christian Right groups in the World Anti-Communist League. At one point, media attention forced the League to evict from membership a number of openly fascistic groups.[56] The Moon network has also been involved in domestic social issues, and in the 1980s, Moon funded a coalition called Conservatives Against Liberal Legislation.[57] 'In 1984 and 1985,' after Moon was convicted of tax fraud and related charges, and briefly imprisoned, 'Moon's followers spent millions of dollars courting Christian ministers to support Moon as a "victim" of government prosecution.'[58]

The 'infusion of Moon money into the Christian Right' created embarrassment for Tim LaHaye when press reports noted that LaHaye's American Coalition for Traditional Values was made up of the same Christian Right leaders who joined the Coalition for Religious Freedom, set up and funded by Moon's Unification Church. LaHaye and others then tried to distance themselves from charges that they were accepting 'Moonie' funds.[59] Some conservative Christian evangelicals have protested against the funding and networking of Christian Right groups by Moon.[60]

The Farrakhan network

The Nation of Islam (NOI) led by Minister Louis Farrakhan is a syncretic offshoot of a form of Islam in the United States. Master W. Fard Muhammad originally synthesized the theology behind the NOI in the early 1930s, and his first disciple, Honorable Elijah Muhammad, founded the NOI as a major religious Black Nationalist movement.[61] Farrakhan remained loyal to Elijah Muhammad after Malcolm X criticized the founder in 1964 and left to form a new group; however, Farrakhan said that despite their differences, he still considered Malcolm X a mentor. Members of the NOI assassinated Malcolm X during the dispute.[62] Today Farrakhan is widely respected in the Black community for the way in which he speaks out against white supremacy, and the services provided by various NOI agencies in poor Black neighbourhoods. The Nation of Islam displays all the main features of a theocratic political religion, and it plays a significant role in Black electoral politics in the United States. It also has leaders and activists who work in a coalition with the Lyndon LaRouche network to spread conspiracy theories about Jewish power.[63]

The LaRouche network

Journalists and scholars often dismiss the international network run by Lyndon H. LaRouche, Jr., as a lunatic cult. Nevertheless, the LaRouchites also run a sophisticated worldwide intelligence gathering and propaganda operation that briefly had close ties to the Reagan Administration, with members invited to provide intelligence briefings to staff of the National Security Council and the CIA.[64] The LaRouche network began as 'an offshoot of the radical student movement that metamorphosed into a fascist organization in the early 1970s.'[65] Union officials have used LaRouche intelligence operatives in campaigns against reform candidates in labor unions including the Teamsters, United Auto Workers, and United Mineworkers of America.[66] The LaRouchites started rumors about the mental health of 1988 Democratic presidential candidate Michael Dukakis that spawned major national news stories and damaged his candidacy.[67]

In their original edition of *Dope, Inc.: Britain's Opium War against the U.S.* the LaRouchites claimed that the British royal family (including the Queen) controlled global drug running. They also cited the antisemitic hoax document, the *Protocols of the Elders of Zion* (and defended its authenticity), and included a chart showing the alleged role of the Rothschild banking family in the global conspiracy, along with mentions on more than 20 pages of text.[68] Subsequent editions dropped the mention of the Protocols, and the LaRouchites thereafter developed a more coded form of antisemitic conspiracy theories implicating in an evil plot the British Monarchy, Jewish families such as the Rothschilds, the B'nai B'rith, Henry Kissinger, The Bush family, and vice president Dick Cheney. Their widely distributed pamphlets on the US neoconservative movement resurrect the rhetoric of the medieval blood libel by titling the series 'The Children of Satan.'[69] The LaRouchites supply conspiracist claims and analysis to government and corporate contacts around the globe, and are considered legitimate sources in a number of media outlets in the Middle East. They actively recruit on campus.[70]

Sectarian totalitarian groups

On the political Left and Right there are a number of sectarian political groups in the United States that often have charismatic leaders, but pursue a totalitarian dream rooted in the more traditional forms crafted within fascism and communism.

On the extreme Left, several communist cadre organizations qualify as political religions.[71] These include the Revolutionary Communist Party, Workers World Party, and Spartacist League, all of which extend the political influence of their small memberships by actively working in broader left coalitions against US militarism, government repression, and neo-Nazis, as well as supporting some labor struggles.

On the extreme Right, there are numerous fascist, neo-Nazi, and white supremacist groups with enough substance and ideological coherence to be political religions. Among the more notable are the National Alliance, Creativity Movement, and the National Socialist Movement.[72] A larger though more diffuse movement is Christian Identity, a fusion of Protestant millennialism and Nazi race theory, which is discussed in detail later in the chapter.

Hyperbolic paradigms

When scholars look at political religion they often set aside groups the public and the media label 'cults' or 'the lunatic fringe.' Surely, these labels would have fit the early stages of the Hitler movement. Robert J. Lifton called groups built around a totalitarian system 'totalist' groups.[73] He argues that for members of such groups, 'existence comes to depend upon creed (I believe, therefore I am), upon submission (I obey, therefore I am) and beyond these, upon a sense of total merger with the ideological movement.' Lifton specifically links this to an apocalyptic worldview.[74] By studying totalist groups, we can see in an exaggerated and hyperbolic form the same recruitment and retention mechanisms, and the same use of apocalyptic frames and conspiracist narratives, that we study in those movements more commonly identified as forms of political religion. How far outside the political mainstream are these mechanisms, frames, narratives, and processes in the United States?

American dreams

In the land of rugged individualism, the pioneer spirit evolved from the spiritual vision and mission of the Pilgrims and Puritans who brought Calvinist baggage on their ships from Europe.[75] This version of Calvinist Protantism was highly apocalyptic.[76] In England, the Calvinist Puritans had developed an 'apocalyptic tradition [that] envisioned the ultimate sacralization of England as God's chosen nation.'[77] The Calvinism that came to the new colonies was also elitist, with a rigid hierarchy of leadership and belief. Max Weber argued in *The Protestant Ethic and the*

Spirit of Capitalism that Calvinism grew in a symbiotic relationship with the rise of capitalist economies with their emphasis on individualism.[78] Early 'Calvinists justified their accumulation of wealth, even at the expense of others, on the grounds that they were somehow destined to prosper. It is no surprise that such notions still find resonance within the Christian Right,' writes Sara Diamond.[79]

Protestantism in the colonies, and later the United States, divided and morphed through Calvinism, the revolt of revivalist evangelicalism, and the counter-revolt of fundamentalism. Over many decades the Protestant evangelical movement spread across the country with a message that rejected many of the tenets of Elitist Calvinism in favor of a more participatory and democratic theological vision.[80] The attention to social conditions by the Unitarians and Quakers overlapped with the Second Great Awakening, which ran from the 1790s to the 1840s. Theologically, there was 'a vigorous emphasis on "sanctification," often called "perfectionism"'.[81] Sin was seen as tied to selfishness. Good Christians should strive to behave in a way that benefited the public good. This in turn would transform and purify the society as a whole in anticipation of the coming Apocalypse. America was seen as a Christian Nation that would fulfill Biblical prophecy. Evangelical Protestants, explains Martin:

> …were so convinced their efforts could ring in the millennium, a literal thousand years of peace and prosperity that would culminate in the glorious second advent of Christ, that they threw themselves into fervent campaigns to eradicate war, drunkenness, slavery, subjugation of women, poverty, prostitution, Sabbath-breaking, dueling, profanity, card-playing, and other impediments to a perfect society.[82]

Some of the aspects of this evangelical revival were institutionalized into existing Protestant churches such as the Presbyterians, Baptists, and Methodists; and these denominations grew even as they remained separate from the evangelicals. Meanwhile, the Anglicans, Quakers, and Congregationalists who directly opposed the evangelicals began to fade in importance.[83] By the late 1800s, most major Protestant denominations (called 'Mainline' denominations) had found some accommodation with the discoveries of science and secular civic arrangements such as separation of church and state favored by Enlightenment values.[84] There was also a 'growing interest by churches in social service, often called the Social Gospel, [which] undercut evangelicalism's traditional emphasis on personal salvation.'[85]

Postmillenialism

During this period, most Protestants in the United States understood the timetable of the apocalyptic End Times prophesied in the Bible (especially the book of Revelation) in a specific way called 'postmillennialism.' This meant that they believed that Jesus Christ would return only after Christians had converted enough people to establish a Godly Christian society purified and prepared for his triumphant arrival. This is why the Protestants who sought the abolition of slavery in the mid-1800s would sing the Battle Hymn of the Republic, in which they proclaimed 'Mine eyes have seen the glory of the coming of the Lord.'[86] As Michael Northcott explains, 'American postmillennial apocalyptic involves the claim that the American Republic, and in particular the free market combined with a form of marketized democracy, is the first appearance in history of a redeemed human society, a true godly Kingdom.'[87]

When the fundamentalist movement emerged after World War I, it was a backlash movement that denounced mainline Protestant denominations for their truce with the Enlightenment, science, and evolution. Early fundamentalists tended to be socially conservative, although within many fundamentalist churches there was still an emphasis on an individual's right to read the Bible and think about religion independently. While abandoning the idea of predestination, the fundamentalists restored other aspects of early Calvinism and at least implicitly re-invoked the idea that success and wealth were signs of Godliness. If that is so, then God must not favor people who slip through the social safety net. In this view, the poor need to try extra hard to rise above their failure, and conversely, government social program actually weaken the moral fiber of the individual and thus the nation.[88] Because in Calvinism people are seen as being born in sin, and constantly struggling against their own evil ways, there is a tendency to rely on punishment, shame, and discipline to change behavior – with children, in communities, and for national policy.[89]

Premillennialism

Most fundamentalists today also embrace a form of apocalyptic belief that burgeoned in the late 1800s called 'premillennial dispensationalism,' in which Jesus Christ returns at the beginning of a thousand years of godly rule – a millennium.[90] Evangelical and fundamentalist premillennialists scan the Bible for 'signs of the times,' by which they mean signs of what they think are the approaching End Times prophesied in the Bible's book of Revelation. This means the Bible has to be read as a literal script of past, present, and future events; and it increases the urge to convert people to a 'born again' form of Christianity, and thus save souls before time literally runs out.[91] These ideas became central to several groups of Protestants, today represented by denominations such as the Southern Baptists and the Assemblies of God.[92] Premillennialists concerned with the End Times also framed the burgeoning US government apparatus, the spread of Soviet and Chinese communism, and the United Nations as part of the End Times/Antichrist system.[93]

It is a common error to think that premillennialists eschew political activism and simply wait for Jesus to return and restore Godly rule. Some do, some don't. This is even true among those premillennialists who believe that just before Christ's second coming, God will sweep them up in a safe embrace called the Rapture, while the tribulations on earth are followed by Gods angry flushing away into Hell of sinners, agents of the Antichrist, false prophets, recalcitrant non-Christians, lackadaisical Christians, and (one assumes) most academics. This is the plotline of the popular *Left Behind* series of novels that have sold over 70 million copies worldwide.

How can this possibly affect politics in the United States? Consider the following:

> A TIME/CNN poll finds that more than one-third of Americans say they are paying more attention now to how the news might relate to the end of the world, and have talked about what the Bible has to say on the subject. Fully 59% say they believe the events in Revelation are going to come true, and nearly one-quarter think the Bible predicted the Sept. 11 attack.[94]

Some treat this cynically. Bumper stickers proclaim, 'In Case of Rapture, Can I Have Your Car?' For others it is pop culture. In one episode of the TV series *Buffy the Vampire Slayer*, Buffy heads out the door holding up her cell phone, and tells her friends, 'If the Apocalypse comes, beep me.'[95]

Contemporary christian apocalypticism

Several Christian sociopolitical movements in the Unites States have pushed the importance of a transcendent relationship with God onto the back burner in order to carry on flame wars with secular society. By starting with the most syncretic and militant forms and working toward the political center, we can see how they draw from the same components from which all political religions are built.

Christian Identity

Christian Identity is a highly syncretic form of Protestantism that traces the roots of Christianity back through biblical genealogy to claim that a lost tribe of Israel settled the British Isles and then migrated to America – the prophesied Promised Land. Thus, white Christians in the New World are heirs to God's covenant with Israel. Identity grew out of British Israelism, a theology from the mid-1800s that made similar claims.[96] In the United States, many adherents of Christian Identity adopt a version that highlights white Aryan biological supremacy, which they extend to a form of racialized anti-Semitism in which Jews are wrongly characterized as a 'race.'[97] Christian Identity has no national institutionalized church hierarchy. Practitioners generally meet in homes or small churches, and a few have formed small isolated compounds in anticipation of a coming apocalyptic race war. For many years, its most significant institution was the Aryan Nations compound in rural Idaho, now dismantled.[98]

The premillennialist theology of Christian Identity sees 'all of history as a Manichaean struggle between white, divine, Anglo-Saxon Christians, and Satanic Jews.'[99] Christian Identity believers have carried out a number of acts of violence in the United States including shootings and murders. For Christian Identity the premillennial apocalypse brings a race war in which white Christians will seize the country, then debate whether they will expel or expunge Jews and Blacks.[100] Christian Identity, however, rejects the concept of the Rapture, thus believers expect to stand and fight their End Times race war during the Tribulations prophesied in the Bible's book of Revelation.[101] Identity believers see Jews as agents of the Satanic Antichrist who tries to build a one-world government or New World Order in the End Times. Another intra-Identity debate is whether Jews are the children of Cain, the Biblical bad brother seedline, or are literally the children of Satan through the conjugal union of Eve and the devilish trickster in the Garden of Eden.[102]

Christian Reconstructionism

Christian Reconstructionism is a theology than envisions a theocratic form of government called a theonomy. It believes that as more Christians adopt this belief and successfully convert the majority of Americans, that the country will realize that the US Constitution and Bill of Rights are merely codicils to Old Testament biblical law. Then

Godly men will rule, while adulterers, homosexuals, and recalcitrant children will face the death penalty for repeated offenses. Because they believe this is God's will, they scoff at criticism that what they plan is a revolutionary overthrow of the existing system of government.[103]

Bruce Barron explains that, 'unlike the Christian Right, Reconstructionism is not simply or primarily a political movement; it is first and foremost an educational movement fearlessly proclaiming an ideology of total world transformation.'[104] Over the past 20 years, the leading proponents of dominion theology have included Rousas John (R. J.) Rushdoony, Gary North, Greg Bahnsen, David Chilton, Gary DeMar, and Andrew Sandlin. The Chalcedon Foundation seeks to spread the idea of Christian Reconstructionism among evangelicals.[105] William Martin notes, 'Because it is so genuinely radical, most leaders of the Religious Right are careful to distance themselves from' Christian Reconstructionism.[106] Yet Martin and other scholars have shown that a number of Christian Right leaders have read and been influenced by Christian Reconstructionist ideas. Sara Diamond argues, 'the primary importance of the [Christian Reconstructionist] ideology is its role as a catalyst for what is loosely called "dominion theology,"' which is the 'concept that Christians are Biblically mandated to "occupy" all secular institutions.' According to Diamond, this has become 'the *central unifying ideology* for the Christian Right.'[107]

The late R. J. Rushdoony, founder of Christian Reconstructionism, was a postmillennialist, and thus believed that after Godly Christians ruled in righteousness for a thousand years (or thereabouts), Jesus would return in triumph. Since most Christian evangelicals in the United States are premillennialists, the influence of Christian Reconstructionism in shaping dominionism in the Christian Right is remarkable. Karen Armstrong detects a whiff of potential fascism in Christian Reconstructionism because it is 'totalitarian…[t]here is no room for any other view or policy, no democratic tolerance for rival parties, no individual freedom.'[108] Matthew N. Lyons and I call Christian Reconstructionism a 'new form of clerical fascist politics.'[109]

The Christian Right

Paul S. Boyer observes that religious views in the United States have 'always had an enormous, if indirect and underrecognized, role [in] shaping public policy.'[110] There has always been a Christian Right in the United States, but its access to power varies widely over time. Starting in the late 1970s, the latest incarnation of the Christian Right was part of the New Right revolt of ultra-conservatives, corporate conservatives, libertarians, and others who swept Ronald Reagan into office as President.[111] The Christian Right is composed primarily of politically conservative Protestants mobilized into a social movement around what they call 'traditional' moral and family values. Conservative political strategists have linked this religious social movement to a political movement that seeks political power through elections and legislation.

Different polling questions produce different results, so there are somewhere between 45 and 100 million 'born again' or evangelical Christians in the United States. In the 2000 presidential election, 32 percent of the votes George W. Bush received came from church-going white evangelicals; and 14 percent of all voters identified themselves as part of the Christian Right.[112] The Christian Right and their allies in the Republican Party have used fear, demonization, and scapegoating as part of a strategy of 'mobilizing resentment.'[113] John C. Danforth, who is both an Episcopal priest and a former US Senator from Missouri, puts this in a framework that reveals the issue clearly.

> Republicans have transformed our party into the political arm of conservative Christians…The problem is not with people or churches that are politically active. It is with a party that has gone so far in adopting a sectarian agenda that it has become the political extension of a religious movement.[114]

Frances FitzGerald traced the role of Christian millennialism in shaping the policies of the Reagan Administration.[115] While the Cold War was hot, 'the primary foreign policy concern of the Christian right and its precursors was the anticommunist struggle,' notes Duane Oldfield.[116] After the collapse of communism in Europe, the Christian Right continued to press for conservative social issues, but shifted much of its international focus to defending the state of Israel. There was a special interest in the prophetic role of the Temple Mount in Jerusalem as the location that Jews must control in order for Jesus to return in his Second Coming.[117] According to Andrea Smith, the evangelical political discourse of the Christian Right represents a very narrow and specific reading of Biblical text that emphasizes an aggressive and masculinist model.[118] Paul Boyer argues there is not enough attention paid to the 'shadowy but vital way that belief in biblical prophecy is helping mold grassroots attitudes toward current US foreign policy,' especially in the Middle East.[119]

Christian Zionism

This interest in Israel among conservative evangelicals, and a broader unilateralist and aggressive stance on foreign policy, is 'rooted in [their] reading of biblical prophecy...from the 1970s, when Hal Lindsey's *The Late Great Planet Earth* was the decade's best-selling non-fiction book to the current success of Tim LaHaye and Jerry Jenkins's *Left Behind* series,' argues Oldfield.[120] This has led to a political pressure bloc of conservative evangelicals called 'Christian Zionism.' For over a decade, Christian Zionists have sent millions of dollars annually to support projects in Israel ranging from settlements, to relocation of immigrants, to planting vines. Many Christian Zionists are premillennialists who believe they are living in the prophetic End Times, culminating in the apocalyptic battle of Armageddon. Some further suspect that this involves a war between godly Christians and evil Muslims. This idea has had increasing resonance among Christian evangelicals since the terror attacks of September 11, 2001.[121]

Christian Zionism, and apocalyptic expectation in general, has been spurred on in the United States by the *Left Behind* series of 12 novels, of which 70 million copies have been sold.[122] Published between 1995 and 2004, the *Left Behind* series has not ended, but spawned both a children's and young adult series, and several other offshoots.[123] The *Left Behind* series is set in the End Times, after the Rapture, in the period of Tribulations during which those flawed Christians 'left behind' may still secure a place in heaven through militant action against the forces of evil, represented by the Antichrist (the head of the European Union), and other agents of Satan. Who is the Antichrist in this plotline? 'Nicolae Carpathia, the man who turned the United Nations into a one-world government with himself as dictator,' explains Gershom Gorenberg, who has blasted the series for its open 'contempt for Judaism.'[124] Gorenberg also objects to the series because:

> They promote conspiracy theories; they demonize proponents of arms control, ecumenicalism, abortion rights and everyone else disliked by the Christian right; and they justify assassination as a political tool. Their anti-Jewishness is exceeded by their anti-Catholicism. Most basically, they reject the very idea of open, democratic debate. In the world of *Left Behind*, there exists a single truth, based on a purportedly literal reading of Scripture; anyone who disagrees with that truth is deceived or evil.[125]

Different peas, same pod

I am not trying to suggest that Christian Identity, Christian Reconstructionism, and the Christian Right are peas in a pod, but I am arguing that all these peas come from the same historic theological pod, and are cooked in the cauldron of apocalyptic dualism. They all are palingenetic, demonize their opponents, and engage in conspiracist scapegoating. In the broader landscape, though, what is most important is to see how a wide range of political ideology and political activism in the United States draws from both the premillennial and postmillennial theological viewpoints, even when the activists deny (or are unaware of) these historic legacies. Mona Harrington calls the outcome of this 'the myth of deliverance from evil' in American politics.[126]

Bush, God, neoconservatives, and apocalypse

President George W. Bush sees himself as carrying out a divine mission, especially in the arena of foreign policy[127] During his second inaugural address, Bush used carefully chosen language that would be recognized by Christian evangelicals as referring to Biblical verses.[128] Michael Northcott, a specialist in theology and politics at the University of Edinburgh has written a ringing indictment, *An Angel Directs the Storm: Apocalyptic Religion & American Empire*, in which he argues that 'Bush uses…apocalyptic language to advance an imperial vision of American power and in so doing he taps into a core feature of American evangelicalism.'[129] Looking back through US history, Northcott ties this American exceptionalism, and notes the 'sacred narrative of America's origins is nowhere more clearly revealed than in the hallowing of America's wars':

> …in the twentieth century with the Nazis, the Communists, and now the Muslims. This hallowing reflects the apocalyptic and millenarian beliefs of the Puritans who first migrated to America and it has become a dominant feature of the modern American evangelical and fundamentalist imaginary.[130]

Anatole Lieven echoes this analysis, and points out that the legacy of 'nationalism and the "American Creed" on which it is based,' produces the current 'rhetoric of spreading democracy and freedom' which has roots in 'a central feature of the messianic tradition in American civic nationalism.'[131]

Matthew Rothschild of the Progressive magazine coined the phrase 'Messianic Militarism' to describe the Bush foreign policy initiatives.[132] In his column, Rothschild interviewed Lee Quinby, one of the leading scholars of apocalypticism. According to Quinby, 'what I hear is a holy trinity of militarism, masculinism, and messianic zeal':

> It does follow the logic of apocalyptic thought, which has a religious base but is now secularized in the militaristic mode. Apocalyptic thought always has an element of instilling helplessness and promising victory in the face of that powerlessness. In this instance, Bush plays up the vulnerability we feel because of terrorism or Saddam Hussein and then accentuates the military as the assurance that our helplessness will be transformed.[133]

Neoconservatives: secular American apocalyptic

The radical left of the 1970s shocked a number of liberals. Open experimentation with sex and drugs to the anarchic beat of rock and roll pushed them to the edge. Indifference to (or an open alliance with) communists in coalitions protesting against the war in Vietnam sent these hawkish liberals right over the edge into conservatism.[134] Thus, these newly minted conservative became known as the 'neoconservatives.'

> Neoconservatives, including many Jewish and Catholic intellectuals rooted in Cold War liberalism, clustered around publications such as *Public Interest* and *Commentary* and organizations such as the Committee on the Present Danger. They emphasized foreign policy, where they advocated aggressive anticommunism, US global dominance, and international alliances. Although they attacked feminism, gay rights, and multiculturalism, 'neocons' often placed less emphasis on social policy issues, and many of them opposed school prayer or a ban on abortion.[135]

Neoconservatives became the dominant intellectual tendency shaping US foreign policy in the Bush presidential administration.[136] Some critics have slipped into anti-semitic stereotyping, or soared into conspiracy theories about the neoconservatives.[137] Nonetheless, there is plenty of sensible and careful analysis of neoconservatism. The neoconservatives spent many years honing their ideology in relative obscurity, at least in the sense of public awareness of them playing a role on the political scene.[138] One criticism of neoconservatives is that they see themselves as Machiavellian élites defending democracy from the rabble; which some attribute to the influence of University of Chicago philosopher Leo Strauss.[139] One major way the neoconservatives formulated their foreign policy agenda was through the Project for a New American Century.[140]

According to Stefan A. Halper and Jonathan Clarke, neoconservatives 'unite around three common themes':

A belief deriving from religious conviction that the human condition is defined as a choice between good and evil and that the true measure of political character is to be found in the willingness by the former (themselves) to confront the latter;

An assertion that the fundamental determinant of the relationship between states rests on military power and the willingness to use it;

A primary focus on the Middle East and global Islam as the principal theater for American overseas interests.[141]

While neoconservatives claim they are exercising a legitimate role as the sole superpower at the dawn of the twenty-first century, critics suggest they are using military force to protect an aging empire from decline.[142] Sheldon S. Wolin goes further and charges 'Like previous forms of totalitarianism, the Bush administration boasts a reckless unilateralism.'[143] There are other factors at work. When Samuel Huntington warns of a 'clash of civilizations,' some see xenophobia, nativism, racism, and chauvinism. Amitai Etzioni wrote he would avoid those words, but then scolded Huntington as a 'systematic and articulate advocate of nationalism, militaristic regimes, and an earlier America in which there was one homogenous creed and little tolerance for pluralism.'[144]

Strange brew

There is a synergy between the neoconservatives and the Christian Right in both foreign policy and some domestic policies. George Monbiot looks at how both the Bush administration and the neoconservatives have constructed United States' economic policy, and sees the return of Calvinist Puritanism via the conservative evangelicals. He writes, 'the enrichment of the élite and impoverishment of the lower classes requires a justifying ideology,' and that in America 'this ideology has to be a religious one.' Monbiot argues this is more about Puritanism than fascism, and states, 'we must look not to the 1930s, but to the 1630s.'[145]

Hugh Urban was separately studying the neoconservatives and the fictional *Left Behind* series of novels popular among Christian evangelicals when he noticed an eerie reverberating echo involving foreign policy. Urban saw a 'fit or affinity between the evangelical vision of the New Millennium and the Neoconservative ideal of a New American Century.' He wrote that if we updated Weber's classic book, we 'might call this affinity "the Evangelical Ethic and the Spirit of Neo-Imperialism." '[146] According to Urban, evangelicals and neoconservatives are not engaged in some 'conspiratorial plot,' but the two sectors of the US political right:

> have enough similar interests to find common ground in the Prodigal Son, George W. As a relatively empty, unformed 'floating signifier,' Bush serves as the key link in this elective affinity, the point at which the otherwise conflicting interests of the Neocons and the evangelicals come together in a disturbingly powerful way.[147]

Pollster James Zogby agrees. 'Although the neo-conservatives are secular (and oftentimes quite liberal in their social outlook) and the religious right is theologically based, these two currents share a number of ideas.'[148] According to Zogby:

- both currents are Manicheistic, i.e., they see the world in absolute black and white, good and evil;
- both currents define the forces of good as being led by the U.S. and Israel and see the forces of evil (once defined as the Soviet Union and now see as 'the axis of evil' states supporting terror) as including Arabs and Islam;
- both currents are confrontational and uncompromising. They believe that there can be no accommodation made with those representing evil. Both, therefore, seek confrontation and conflict, not a resolution of tensions through negotiations; and
- both currents are absolutist, since their ideology will allow only for total victory.[149]

Northcott carries forward this line of argument when he claims that the neoconservatives have a 'conception of political economy [that] is as apocalyptic as more openly religious forms of millennialism.' This is true because it 'sets up an ideology of human redemption which its advocates believe they are charged to follow regardless of the destruction and violence it may entail.'[150]

The F Word

When critics of the Christian Right, neoconservatism, or the Bush administration invoke the word 'fascism,' they generally use the term as an epithet and use simplistic and erroneous definitions of the term itself.[151] Many critics create laundry lists of what could be found in Germany under Hitler and what can be seen in the United States under Bush, and declare this as proof.[152] It is, however, a logical fallacy to argue that since the Bush administration and fascism share common elements they are therefore identical. The Internet palpitates with histrionic denunciations of Bush as a fascist.

Some writers have more cautiously suggested that by looking at scholarly definitions, we may better decide what is excess and what is echo.[153] One of the most cited recent attempts at a definition comes from Robert O. Paxton:

> A form of political behavior marked by obsessive preoccupation with community decline, humiliation or victimhood and by compensatory cults of unity, energy and purity, in which a mass-based party of committed nationalist militants, working in uneasy but effective collaboration with traditional elites, abandons democratic liberties and pursues with redemptive violence and without ethical or legal restraints goals of internal cleansing and external expansion.[154]

Using this definition, we can certainly see similarities, but it is still difficult to argue that the Bush administration, the Christian Right, or the neoconservatives are accurately described as a full-blown example of fascism; nor are they fully totalitarian. Nevertheless, do they approximate a political religion? Christian Reconstructionism, for example, *is* a theocratic political religion. Since it already plays a role in the Christian Right, it is fair to speculate on the possibility that some dramatic events could shift the bulk of the Christian Right over the line into being a full-fledged theocratic political religion. Given the messianic, apocalyptic, and dualistic themes within the Christian Right, speculation about the future is valid. The same is true when considering the potential for a more secular movement of apocalyptic aggression that the neoconservatives might spark. Another major terrorist attack on United States soil could fuse together a political religion of messianic ultrapatriotism. George W. Bush is playing with fire in a world littered with matchbooks. As Normon Solomon argues, 'we should not gloss over the reality that the Bush team has neared some elements of fascism in its day-to-day operations.'[155] Of these elements, apocalypticism deserves more attention.

Playing the apocalypse card

> Historically, US messianism has always been at war with US pragmatism. In the end pragmatism has usually won.....My fear is that as in Vietnam, the return to pragmatism may come only after the United States has inflicted a whole series of disasters on itself and the world.
>
> —Anatole Lieven[156]

The neoconservatives in the United States are heirs of the apocalyptic postmillennial paradigm that motivated the Puritans to establish the New Jerusalem, the City on the Hill, the Redeemer Nation.[157] That neoconservatives pursue this millenarian apocalypse in an apparently secular manner does not negate the roots of this dream of perfection and redemption in Puritan and Pilgrim Calvinism as filtered through the historic modifications applied by American Christian evangelicalism. The premillennial dispensationalists of the Christian Right draw on the same millenarian legacies woven into the American psyche, while revising the timetable for the apocalypse.

The apocalyptic violence of the terrorist attacks on 9/11 was a shock to the United States, but it has become all too common in other countries, especially in the Middle East. According to Robert Jay Lifton, 'apocalyptic terrorists can connect with mainstream emotions,' in societies where there exist 'religious, ideological, and political bridges' into the mainstream. Fear and anger are simultaneously reflected and generated, and 'thereby influence a society's rhetoric and policies.'[158] This has happened in both Israel and the United States. Retribution is on the agenda.

Among some premillennialists with a militant worldview, 'apocalyptic violence can be accepted, even welcomed, as a means of cosmic purification,' as Lifton recently noted.[159] Is this part of the justification for the US invasion of Afghanistan and Iraq in the war on terrorism? According to Lifton:

> one must ask whether fundamentalists within the Bush administra-
> tion, who *are* engaging in violence, do not at some psychological

level envision the war on terrorism as a vehicle for their own salvation, for a new American regeneration through violence, for not only destroying evil worldwide but cleansing ourselves of our own sins and revitalizing our spiritual energies through our predominant military power.[160]

Conclusions

In studying the United States, we have seen how civil can intersect with politicized religion and produce political religions. Political religion is a necessary component in constructing a totalitarian movement or regime, and it can come from secular or religious sources or a blend. If a political religion ever gains a mass base in the United States, it is unlikely that a Moon, Farrakhan, or LaRouche will lead it. Yet the elements used by these obvious totalist demagogues to attract and discipline their members are not alien to the United States. This is a country with a messianic sense of destiny, millenarian energy, millennialist scripts, and apocalyptic timetables. Political religions do not just pop up fully formed like a shell-shocked anti-Aphrodite borne of foaming waves of resentment. Demagogues use dualism to incubate political religion. As the demonization increases, the palingenetic aspect becomes more apocalyptic. They draw from pre-existing apocalyptic frames and conspiracist narratives to identify scapegoats that will seem plausible as enemies of the people.

In the post-Cold War, palingenetic transformation of the United States, we might rise as a superpower phoenix from the ashes of the conflicts we have caused. Whether or not this might happen is unpredictable; so is the possibility that in our future there could be a large-scale mass movement accurately labeled a political religion.

Acknowledgments

Thanks to Stanley G. Payne for setting the stage, and Roger Griffin, Robert Mallett, and the folks at *Totalitarian Movements and Political Religions* for inviting me to the table. My research would not be possible without the support of Political Research Associates where I have worked for over 20 years.

My interest in apocalypticism has been assisted by conversations with and encouragement from my colleagues at the Center for Millennial Studies, especially Richard A. Landes, Brenda E. Brasher, Michael Barkun, Stephen D. O'Leary, Lee Quinby, Andrew Gow, and David Redles.

Much of my work in this area involved joint work with Matthew N. Lyons with whom I co-authored *Right Wing Populism in America* from which I expropriated (with permission) ideas and text.

Notes

1. R. Hofstadter, *Anti–Intellectualism in American Life*, New York: Alfred A. Knopf, 1963, p. 23.
2. Hofstadter, above, cited and discussed in S. Huntington, 'The Erosion of American National Interests,' *Foreign Affairs*, 1997, vol. 76, no. 5, p. 29; and H. Kohn, *American Nationalism: An Interpretative Essay*, New York: Macmillan, 1957, p. 13.
3. A. de Tocqueville, as cited by S. M. Lipset, *American Exceptionalism: A Double–Edged Sword*; New York: W. W. Norton & Company, 1997, p. 18; G. Myrdal, *An American Dilemma: The Negro Problem and Modern Democracy*, New York: Harper & Brothers, 1944; R. N. Bellah, 'Civil Religion in America,' *Daedalus*, 1967, vol. 96, no. 1, pp. 1–21; reprinted in *Daedalus* vol. 134, no. 4, 2005 (Fall), pp. 40–56.
4. J. Mulder, 'The Bicentennial Book Band,' *Theology Today*, 1975, vol. 32, no. 3, http://theologytoday.ptsem.edu/oct1975/v32–3-tabletalk1.htm (accessed 12 January 2006).
5. How this happened in Germany is covered in M. Burleigh, *The Third Reich: A New History*, New York: Hill & Wang, 2000.
6. M. Northcott, *An Angel Directs The Storm: Apocalyptic Religion & American Empire*. London: I. B. Tauris, 2004; for 'messianic militarism,' M. Rothschild, 'Bush's Messiah Complex,' the *Progressive*, February 2003, http://progressive.org/node/1344 (accessed 17 February 2006).
7. R. J. Lifton, *Thought Reform and the Psychology of Totalism*, reprint, Chapel Hill: University of North Carolina Press [1961] 1989; R. Altemeyer, *The Authoritarian Specter*, Cambridge, MA: Harvard University Press, 1996; L. Noël, *Intolerance, A General Survey*, trans. A. Bennett, Montreal: McGill-Queen's University Press, 1994; E. Young-Bruehl, *The Anatomy of Prejudices*, Cambridge, MA: Harvard University Press, 1996. For an excellent overview, see E. R. Harrington, 'The Social Psychology of Hatred,' *Journal of Hate Studies*, 2003/04, vol. 3, no. 1, http://guweb2.gonzaga.edu/againsthate/journal3/GHS110.pdf (accessed 12 January 2006).
8. D. McAdam, J. D. McCarthy, and M. N. Zald (eds), *Comparative Perspectives on Social Movements: Political Opportunities, Mobilizing Structures, and Cultural Framings*, Cambridge, UK: Cambridge University Press, 1996.
9. J. A. Aho, *The Politics of Righteousness: Idaho Christian Patriotism*, Seattle: University of Washington Press, 1990; B. A. Dobratz, and S. L. Shanks-Meile, *'White Power, White Pride!' The White Separatist Movement in the United States*, New York: Twayne Publishers, 1997; K. M. Blee, *Inside Organized Racism: Women in the Hate Movement*, Berkeley: University of California Press, 2002.
10. E. Goffman, *Frame Analysis: An Essay on the Organization of Experience*, Cambridge, MA: Harvard University Press, 1974; J. D. McCarthy and M. N. Zald, 'Resource Mobilization and Social Movements: A Partial Theory,' *American Journal of Sociology*, 1977, vol. 82, no. 6; D. A. Snow, E. B. Rochford,

Jr., S. K. Worden, and R. D. Benford, 'Frame Alignment Process, Micromobilization, and Movement Participation,' *American Sociological Review*, 1986, vol. 5.

11. D. A. Snow, and R. D. Benford, 'Master Frames and Cycles of Protest,' in A. D. Morris and C. M. Mueller (eds) *Frontiers in Social Movement Theory*, New Haven, Conn.: Yale University Press, 1992.

12. P. Ewick and S. S. Silbey, 'Subversive Stories and Hegemonic Tales: Toward a Sociology of Narrative,' *Law & Society Review*, 1995, vol. 29, no. 2; J. Davis (ed), *Stories of Change: Narrative and Social Movements*, Albany, New York: State University of New York Press, 2002.

13. C. Berlet, 'Christian Identity, The Apocalyptic Style, Political Religion, Palingenesis and Neo–Fascism,' *Totalitarian Movements and Political Religions*, 2004, vol. 5, no. 3; 'When Alienation Turns Right: Populist Conspiracism, the Apocalyptic Style, and Neofascist Movements,' in L. Langman & D. K. Fishman (eds) *Trauma, Promise, and the Millennium: The Evolution of Alienation*, Lanham, MD: Rowman & Littlefield, 2004; 'Mapping the Political Right: Gender and Race Oppression in Right-Wing Movements,' in A. Ferber (ed), *Home-Grown Hate: Gender and Organized Racism*. New York: Routledge, 2004.

14. E. Gentile, *The Sacralization of Politics in Fascist Italy*, Cambridge, MA: Harvard University Press, 1994.

15. The use of the term palingenesis apparently surface with Gentile, while Griffin has now cornered the franchise.

16. R. Griffin, ' "Shattering Crystals: The Role of "Dream Time" in Extreme Right-Wing Political Violence,' *Terrorism and Political Violence*, 2003, vol. 15, no. 1, pp. 57–95.

17. L. Quinby, *Anti-Apocalypse: Exercises in Genealogical Criticism*, Minneapolis: University of Minnesota Press, 1994.

18. E. Gentile, 'Fascism, Totalitarianism and Political Religion: Definitions and Critical Reflections on Criticism of an Interpretation,' *Totalitarian Movements and Political Religions*, special issue on Fascism as a Totalitarian Movement, 2004, vol. 5, no. 3, pp. 351–56.

19. Griffin (ed), *The Nature of Fascism*, New York: St. Martin's Press, 1991, pp. xi, 26.

20. N. Cohn, *Cosmos, Chaos and the World to Come: The Ancient Roots of Apocalyptic Faith*, New Haven: Yale University Press, 1970; ——, *The Pursuit of the Millennium*, New York: Oxford University Press, 1993; P. Boyer, *When Time Shall Be No More: Prophecy Belief in Modern American Culture*, Cambridge, MA: Belknap/Harvard University Press, 1992; C. B. Strozier, *Apocalypse: On the Psychology of Fundamentalism in America*, Boston: Beacon Press, 1994; S. D. O'Leary, *Arguing the Apocalypse: A Theory of Millennial Rhetoric*, New York: Oxford University Press, 1994; R. Fuller, *Naming the Antichrist: The History of an American Obsession*, New York: Oxford University Press, 1995; D. Thompson, *The End of Time: Faith and Fear in the Shadow of the Millennium*, Hanover, NH: University Press of New England, 1998; E. Pagels, *The Origin of Satan*, New York: Vintage, 1996. I first heard apocalypticism described as a type of frame by sociologist of religion Brenda E. Brasher at a conference. We later developed the idea in B. E. Brasher and C. Berlet, 'Imagining Satan: Modern Christian Right Print Culture as an Apocalyptic Master Frame,' paper

presented at the Conference on Religion and the Culture of Print in America, Center for the History of Print Culture in Modern America, University of Wisconsin-Madison, 10, 11 September 2004.

21. Here I disagree with Gentile's statement that apocalyptic political religions are not 'millenarian.' I think they are millenarian, but not necessarily millennialist. See E. Gentile, 'Fascism, Totalitarianism and Political Religion,' p. 356.

22. R. J. Lifton, *Superpower Syndrome: America's Apocalyptic Confrontation with the World*, New York: Thunder's Mouth Books/Nation Books, 2003, p. 21; Catherine Wessinger (ed), *Millennialism, Persecution, and Violence: Historical Cases*, Syracuse: Syracuse University Press, 2000.

23. Hofstadter, *Anti-Intellectualism*, p. 135.

24. D. Anthony and T. Robbins, 'Religious Totalism, Exemplary Dualism, and The Waco Tragedy,' in T. Robbins and S. J. Palmer (eds) *Millennium, Messiahs, and Mayhem: Contemporary Apocalyptic Movements*, New York: Routledge, 1997, pp. 261–84, quote from p. 267.

25. Ibid., pp. 264, 269.

26. G. W. Allport, *The Nature of Prejudice*, Cambridge, MA: Addison-Wesley, 1954: pp. 243–60; R. Girard, *The Scapegoat*, Baltimore: Johns Hopkins University Press, 1986.

27. J. A. Aho, *This Thing of Darkness: A Sociology of the Enemy*, Seattle: University of Washington Press, 1994, pp. 107–21; E. Pagels, *The Origin of Satan*; D. N. Smith; 'The Social Construction of Enemies: Jews and the Representation of Evil,' *Sociological Theory*, 1996, vol. 14, no. 3; L. Noël, *Intolerance, A General Survey*.

28. The sequence concept for generating hatred was suggested by K. S. Stern at the Conference to Establish the Field of Hate Studies, at the Institute for Action against Hate, Gonzaga University Law School, Spokane, Washington, 18–20 March. See also, K. S. Stern, 'The Need for an Interdisciplinary Field of Hate Studies,' *Journal of Hate Studies*, 2003/04, vol. 3, no. 1, pp. 7–35.

29. R. S. Wistrich (ed), *Demonizing the Other: Antisemitism, Racism, and Xenophobia*, London: Routledge [1999] 2003.

30. G. W. Allport, 'Demagogy,' in R. O. Curry and T. M. Brown (eds) *Conspiracy: The Fear of Subversion in American History*, New York: Holt, Rinehart and Winston, 1972, pp. 263–76.

31. J. Higham, *Strangers in the Land: Patterns of American Nativism 1860–1925*, New York: Atheneum [1955] 1972; R. Hofstadter, 'The Paranoid Style in American Politics,' in *The Paranoid Style in American Politics and Other Essays*, New York: Alfred A. Knopf, 1965, pp. 37–38; D. B. Davis (ed), *The Fear of Conspiracy: Images of Un-American Subversion from the Revolution to the Present*, Ithaca, N.Y.: Cornell University Press, 1971; D. H. Bennett, *The Party of Fear: The American Far Right from Nativism to the Militia Movement*, revised and updated, New York: Vintage Books [1988] 1995; G. Johnson, *Architects of Fear: Conspiracy Theories and Paranoia in American Politics*, Los Angeles: Tarcher/Houghton Mifflin, 1983, pp. 17–30; F. P. Mintz, *The Liberty Lobby and the American Right: Race, Conspiracy, and Culture*, Westport, Conn.: Greenwood, 1985; R. A. Goldberg, *Enemies Within: The Culture of Conspiracy in Modern America*, New Haven: Yale University Press, 2001; M. Barkun, *A Culture of Conspiracy: Apocalyptic Visions in Contemporary America*, Berkeley: University of California Press, 2003.

32. H. Arendt, *The Origins of Totalitarianism*, new edition, new prefaces, New York: Harcourt Brace Jovanovich [1951] 1973; Gentile, 'Fascism, Totalitarianism and Political Religion,' pp. 351–56.

33. Payne, *A History of Fascism*; R. Eatwell, 'Towards a New Model of Generic Fascism,' *Journal of Theoretical Politics*, 1992, vol. 4, no. 2; pp. 161–94, —— 'On Defining the "Fascist Minimum," the Centrality of Ideology,' *Journal of Political Ideologies*, 1996, vol. 1, no. 3; pp. 303–20, —— *Fascism: A History* New York: Allen Lane, 1997; R. Griffin (ed), *International Fascism: Theories, Causes, and the New Consensus*, London: Arnold, 1998; ——, *The Nature of Fascism*; R. O. Paxton, *The Anatomy of Fascism*, New York: Alfred A. Knopf, 2004; E. Gentile, 'Fascism, Totalitarianism and Political Religion,' pp. 342–43.

34. R. Griffin, *Nature of Fascism*, p. xi.

35. R. Eatwell, 'Reflections on Fascism and Religion,' and M. Barkun, 'Religious Violence and the Myth of Fundamentalism,' both in L. Weinberg and A. Pedahzur (eds) *Religious Fundamentalism and Political Extremism*, series on Totalitarian Movements and Political Religions, London: Frank Cass, 2004; M. Cristi, *From Civil to Political Religion. The Intersection of Culture, Religion and Politics*, On.: Wilfrid Laurier University Press, 2001.

36. R. Griffin, 'Introduction: God's Counterfeiters? Investigating the Triad of Fascism, Totalitarianism, and (Political) Religion,' *Totalitarian Movements and Political Religions*, 2004, vol. 5, no. 3.

37. Gentile, 'Fascism, Totalitarianism and Political Religion;' ——, 'The Sacralization of Politics: Definitions, Interpretations and Reflections on the Question of Secular Religion and Totalitarianism,' *Totalitarian Movements and Political Religions*, 2000, vol. 1, no. 1; Gentile, *The Sacralization of Politics in Fascist Italy*.

38. R. Eatwell, 'Reflections on Fascism and Religion', p. 163.

39. S. G. Payne, *A History of Fascism*, see the Table 1.2 on page 15 of that book.

40. C. Berlet, 'Christian Identity.'

41. D. Redles, *Hitler's Millennial Reich: Apocalyptic Belief and the Search for Salvation*, New York University Press, 2005; Klaus Vondung, *The Apocalypse in Germany*, Columbia and London: University of Missouri Press, 2000; R. Ellwood, 'Nazism as a Millennialist Movement,' in Wessinger (ed) *Millennialism, Persecution, and Violence: Historical Cases*; J. M. Rhodes, *The Hitler Movement: A Modern Millenarian Revolution*, Stanford, Calif: Hoover Institution Press, Stanford University, 1980; R. Wistrich, *Hitler's Apocalypse: Jews and the Nazi Legacy*, New York: St. Martin's Press, 1985; Nicholas Goodrick-Clarke: *The Occult Roots of Nazism: Secret Aryan Cults and Their Influence on Nazi Ideology*, reprint with new preface, New York University Press [1985] 2004; N. Cohn, *The Pursuit of the Millennium: Revolutionary Millenarians and Mystical Anarchists of the Middle Ages*, revised and expanded, New York: Oxford University Press [1957] 1970.

42. T. Gibbons, 'Shadows from a Black Sun,' review of Goodrick-Clarke's *Black Sun*, in *Quadrant*, 2004, vol. 48, no. 4, pp. 59–62. http://www.quadrant.org. au/php/archive_details_list.php?article_id=754 (accessed 17 February 2006); citing Cohn, *The Pursuit of the Millennium*; E. J. Weber, *Apocalypses: Prophecies, Cults, and Millennial Beliefs Through the Ages*, Cambridge, Mass.: Harvard University Press, 1999.

43. Redles, *Hitler's Millennial Reich*, pp. 4–5.
44. R. Steigmann-Gall, 'Nazism and the Revival of Political Religion Theory,' *Totalitarian Movements and Political Religions*, 2004, vol. 5, no. 3, pp. 376–96.
45. R. Griffin and I have been trying to sort out the proper terminology for writing about political religion, syncretism, and politicized religion. It is unfinished business. See the discussion in C. Berlet, 'Christian Identity,' pp. 494–96.
46. E. Voegelin, *The Political Religions*, in M. Henningsen (ed), The Collected Works of Eric Voegelin, vol. 5: Modernity Without Restraint, Columbia and London: University of Missouri Press, 2000; discussed in this book in the chapter by K. Vondung.
47. Arendt uses the term 'totalitarianism,' while Lifton uses 'totalism.' They are describing the same type of group. Arendt, *The Origins of Totalitarianism*; Lifton, *Thought Reform and the Psychology of Totalism*.
48. It may seem laughable to some that these leaders are 'charismatic,' but former members often use that term to describe their impressions of the leader (even LaRouche). What matters is how they are perceived by followers, rather than observers.
49. R. Boettcher, *Gifts of Deceit: Sun Myung Moon, Tongsun Park and the Korean Scandal*, New York: Holt, Rinehart and Winston, 1980; S. Diamond, *Spiritual Warfare: The Politics of the Christian Right*, Boston: South End Press, 1989, pp. 58–59, 68–70, 78–79; D. Junas, *Rising Moon: The Unification Church's Japan Connection*, Working Paper no. 5, Seattle, Wash.: Institute for Global Security Studies, 1989; Clarkson, *Eternal Hostility*, pp. 44–75, 135–36;
50. On the cult charges, see the book by former Unification Church member S. Hassan, *Combatting Cult Mind Control*, Boston, MA: Park Street Press; reprint edition, 1990. On the network of groups, see the official Family Federation for World Peace and Unification web site links page: http://familyfed. org/usa/links.htm (accessed 17 February 2006), as well as the main home pages, http://familyfed.org (accessed 17 February 2006), and http://www. unification.org (accessed 17 February 2006).
51. Clarkson, *Eternal Hostility*, pp. 45, 135.
52. Bellant, *Old Nazis*, p. 65.
53. D. Ignatius, 'Tension of the Times,' column, *Washington Post*, 18 June 2004, p. A29, online archive.
54. J. Gorenfeld, 'Hail to the Moon King,' 21 June 2004; and 'Bad Moon on the Rise,' 24 September 2003; both on Salon.com, online magazine, http://www. salon.com (accessed 17 February 2006).
55. For a look at the larger networks, see Bellant, *Old Nazis*, especially pp. 61–65.
56. S. Anderson and J. L. Anderson, *Inside the League: The Shocking Expose of How Terrorists, Nazis and Latin American, Death Squads Have Infiltrated the World Anti-Communist League*, New York: Dodd, Mead and Company, 1986.
57. Bellant, *Old Nazis*, p. 45.
58. S. Diamond, *Roads to Dominion: Right-Wing Movements and Political Power in the United States*, New York: Guilford Press, 1998, pp. 242–44, quote from p. 242.
59. Ibid., p. 242.
60. D. G. Racer, *Not For Sale: The Rev. Sun Myung Moon And One American's Freedom*, St. Paul, Minn.: Tiny Press, 1989.

61. D. E. Robinson, *Black Nationalism in American Politics and Thought*, Cambridge, UK: Cambridge University Press, 2001; R. Singh, *The Farrakhan Phenomenon: Race, Reaction, and the Paranoid Style in American Politics*, Washington, D.C: Georgetown University Press, 1997; M. Gardell, *In the Name of Elijah Muhammad: Louis Farrakhan and the Nation of Islam*, Durham: Duke University Press, 1996; Nation of Islam, 'A Brief History on the Origin of the Nation of Islam in America: A Nation of Peace & Beauty,' official website, http://www.noi.org/history_of_noi.htm (accessed 17 February 2006); Nation of Islam 'An Historical Look at the Honorable Elijah Muhammad,' official website, http://www.noi.org/elijah_muhammad_history.htm (accessed 17 February 2006).

62. C. Waldron, 'Minister Louis Farrakhan Sets the Record Straight about His Relationship with Malcolm X,' interview, *Jet* magazine, 5 June 2000, online archive.

63. C. Berlet and M. N. Lyons, *Right-Wing Populism in America: Too Close for Comfort*, New York: Guilford, 2000, p. 267. For extensive documentation of the ongoing ties between the LaRouchites and Farrakhan's movement, see Note 2 on page 393.

64. D. King, *Lyndon LaRouche and the New American Fascism*, New York: Doubleday, 1989; Berlet and Lyons, *Right-Wing Populism in America*, pp. 265–69, 273–76.

65. Berlet and Lyons, *Right-Wing Populism in America*, p. 265.

66. King, *Lyndon LaRouche*: Teamsters, pp. 335–62; UAW, pp. 239–40; UMWA, pp. 355–56.

67. Ibid., pp. 121–22.

68. U.S. Labor Party Investigating Team (K. Kalimtgis, D. Goldman, J. Steinberg), *Dope, Inc.: Britain's Opium War against the U.S.*, New York: New Benjamin Franklin House, 1978. On the *Protocols*, see pp. 31–33; on the Rothschilds, see the chart on pp. 154–55, consult index for page entries on the Rothschilds.

69. LaRouche in 2004, *Children of Satan, The 'Ignoble Liars' Behind Bush's No-Exit War*, http://larouchein2004.net/pdfs/pamphletcos.pdf (accessed 17 February 2006); *Children of Satan II: The Beast-Men*, http://larouchein2004.net/pdfs/pamphlet0401cos2.pdf (accessed 17 February 2006); *Children of Satan III: The Sexual Congress for Cultural Fascism*, http://larouchein2004.net/pdfs/040614beast3.pdf (accessed 17 February 2006); all published Leesburg, Virginia: by the author.

70. C. Berlet, 'ZOG Ate My Brains,' *New Internationalist* (London), 2004, no. 372, special issue on Judeophobia, http://www.newint.org/issue372/zog.htm (accessed 14 February 2006); see, for example, LaRouchite article listing Arab coverage in 2002, http://larouchein2004.net/pages/other/2002/020427arabcoverage.htm (accessed 14 February 2006).

71. K-G. Riegel, 'Marxism–Leninism as a Political Religion,' *Totalitarian Movements and Political Religions*, 2005, vol. 6, no. 1.

72. S. Vysotsky, 'Understanding the Racist Right in the Twenty First Century: A Typology of Modern White Supremacist Organizations,' paper presented at the annual conference of the American Sociological Association, San Francisco, 2004; G. Michael, *Confronting Right-Wing Extremism and Terrorism in the USA*, Routledge Studies in Extremism and Democracy, New York: Routledge, 2003; Dobratz, and Shanks–Meile, *White Power, White Pride!*

73. Lifton, *Thought Reform and the Psychology of Totalism.*
74. R. J. Lifton, *Destroying the World to Save It: Aum Shinrikyo, Apocalyptic Violence, and the New Global Terrorism*, New York: Metropolitan Books, 1999, p. 434.
75. Portions of this section were pilfered from my article 'Calvinism, Capitalism, Conversion, and Incarceration,' *The Public Eye*, Political Research Associates, 2004, vol. 18, no. 3, pp. 8–15. http://www.publiceye.org/magazine/v18n3/berlet_calvinism.html (accessed 17 February 2006).
76. A. Zakai, *Exile and Kingdom: History and Apocalypse in the Puritan Migration to America*, Cambridge, UK: Cambridge University Press, 1992.
77. Ibid., p. 7.
78. M. Weber, *The Protestant Ethic and the Spirit of Capitalism*, trans. T. Parsons, reprint, New York: Routledge [1930] 1999.
79. S. Diamond, 'Dominion Theology,' *Z Magazine*, February 1995, online archive.
80. N. O. Hatch, *The Democratization of American Christianity*, New Haven: Yale University Press, 1989.
81. W. Martin, *With God on Our Side: The Rise of the Religious Right in America.* New York: Broadway Books, 1996, p. 4.
82. Ibid.
83. J. Hutson, 'Faith of Our Forefathers: Religion and the Founding of the American Republic,' *Information Bulletin*, The Library of Congress, 1998, vol. 57, no. 5 (May), pp. 112–19, 121. http://www.loc.gov/loc/lcib/9805/religion.html (accessed 30 November 2004).
84. N. T. Ammerman, 'North American Protestant Fundamentalism,' in M. E. Marty and R. S. Appleby (eds) *Fundamentalisms Observed*, The Fundamentalism Project, vol. 1, Chicago: The University of Chicago Press, 1991.
85. Martin, *With God on Our Side*, p. 6.
86. Lyrics online http://www.cyberhymnal.org/htm/b/h/bhymnotr.htm (accessed 12 February 2006).
87. Northcott, *An Angel Directs The Storm*, p. 42.
88. A. R. Schaefer, 'Evangelicalism, Social Reform and the US Welfare State, 1970–1996,' in D. K. Adams and C. A. van Minnem (eds) *Religious and Secular Reform in America: Ideas, Beliefs, and Social Change*, New York: New York University Press, 1999.
89. P. Greven, *Spare the Child: The Religious Roots of Punishment and the Psychological Impact of Physical Abuse.* New York: Knopf, 1991.
90. G. M. Marsden, *Fundamentalism and American Culture: The Shaping of Twentieth Century Evangelicalism, 1870–1925*, New York: Oxford University Press, 1982; G. M. Marsden, *Understanding Fundamentalism and Evangelicalism*, Grand Rapids, MI.: William B. Eerdmans, 1991; K. Armstrong, *The Battle for God: A History of Fundamentalism*, New York: Ballantine Books, 2001; Ammerman, 'North American Protestant Fundamentalism.'
91. Martin, *With God on Our Side*, pp. 7–8.
92. D. M. Oldfield, *The Right and the Righteous: The Christian Right Confronts the Republican Party*, Lanham, Md.: Rowman & Littlefield, 1996. p. 14.
93. D. M. Oldfield, 'The Evangelical Roots of American Unilateralism: The Christian Right's Influence and How to Counter It,' *Foreign Policy in Focus*, Silver City, NM: Interhemispheric Resource Center, March 2004, http://www.fpif.org/papers/2004evangelical.html (accessed 11 February 2006).

94. N. Gibbs, 'Apocalypse Now,' *Time*, 1 July 2002.
95. T-shirts with the phrase are available: http://www.cafepress.com/magentastudios/781149 (accessed 17 February 2006).
96. M. Barkun, *Religion and the Racist Right: The Origins of the Christian Identity Movement*, revised, Chapel Hill, N.C.: University of North Carolina Press [1994] 1997.
97. Not all practitioners of Christian Identity adopt the neo-Nazi version, but all use a racialized reading of the Bible.
98. D. Levitas, *The Terrorist Next Door: The Militia Movement and the Radical Right*, New York: Thomas Dunne/St. Martin's, 2002; J. Kaplan, *Radical Religion in America: Millenarian Movements from the Far Right to the Children of Noah*, Syracuse, NewYork: Syracuse University Press, 1997, pp. 47–68; J. Ridgeway, *Blood in the Face*, rev. 2nd edn, New York: Thunder's Mouth Press, 1995; Barkun, *Religion and the Racist Right*.
99. Levitas, *The Terrorist Next Door*, p. 81.
100. Ibid., C. Berlet, 'Christian Identity.'
101. P. Minges, 'Apocalypse Now! The Realized Eschatology of the "Christian Identity" Movement,' *Union Seminary Quarterly Review*, 1995, vol. 49, pp. 83–107.
102. Berlet, 'Christian Identity.'
103. Clarkson, *Eternal Hostility*, pp. 78–96; B. Barron, *Heaven on Earth? The Social and Political Agendas of Dominion Theology*, Grand Rapids, Mich.: Zondervon, 1992. Note there is no connection with the Jewish Reconstructionist movement.
104. Barron, *Heaven on Earth?*, p. 10.
105. Chalcedon Foundation, http://www.chalcedon.edu (accessed 17 February 2006).
106. Martin, *With God on Our Side*, p. 354.
107. Diamond, *Spiritual Warfare*, 1989, p. 138, emphasis in the original.
108. Armstrong, *Battle for God*, pp. 361–62.
109. Berlet and Lyons, *Right-Wing Populism in America*, p. 249.
110. P. Boyer, 'John Darby Meets Saddam Hussein: Foreign Policy and Bible Prophecy,' *Chronicle of Higher Education*, supplement, 14 February 2003, pp. B10–B11; see also, W. Martin, 'The Christian Right and American Foreign Policy,' *Foreign Policy*, 1999, vol. 114 (Spring), pp. 66–80.
111. J.L. Himmelstein, *To the Right: The Transformation of American Conservatism*, Berkeley: University of California Press, 1990; S. Diamond, *Not by Politics Alone: The Enduring Influence of the Christian Right*, New York: Guilford Press, 1998; Martin, *With God on Our Side*; Diamond, *Roads to Dominion*.
112. C. Berlet, 'Religion and Politics in the United States: Nuances You Should Know,' *The Public Eye*, Political Research Associates, 2003, vol. 17, no. 2, http://www.publiceye.org/magazine/v17n2/evangelical-demographics.html (accessed 17 February 2006).
113. J. V. Hardisty, *Mobilizing Resentment: Conservative Resurgence from the John Birch Society to the Promise Keepers*, Boston: Beacon Press, 1999.
114. J. C. Danforth, 'In The Name Of Politics,' Op-Ed, *New York Times*, 30 March 2005, online archive.
115. F. FitzGerald, 'Reflections: The American Millennium,' *New Yorker*, 11 November 1985.

116. Oldfield, 'The Evangelical Roots of American Unilateralism.'
117. G. Gorenberg, *The End of Days: Fundamentalism and the Struggle for the Temple Mount*, New York: The Free Press, 2000.
118. A. Smith, *Bible, Gender and Nationalism in American Indian and Christian Right Activism*, dissertation, U. C. Santa Cruz, 2002.
119. Boyer, 'John Darby Meets Saddam Hussein.'
120. Oldfield, 'The Evangelical Roots of American Unilateralism'; see also, D. Wagner, 'Evangelicals and Israel: Theological Roots of a Political Alliance,' *Christian Century*, 4 November 1998, archived at, http://www.publiceye.org/christian_right/zionism/wagner-cc.html (accessed 17 February 2006); see also, C. Berlet and Nikhil Aziz. 'Culture, Religion, Apocalypse, and Middle East Foreign Policy,' IRC Right Web, Silver City, NM: Interhemispheric Resource Center, 2003, http://rightweb.irc-online.org/analysis/2003/0312apocalypse.php (accessed 11 February 2006).
121. C. Berlet, 'U.S. Christian Evangelicals Raise the Stakes,' (The Threats to Haram al Sharif/Temple Mount), *BitterLemons*, 2004, vol. 2, no. 34, http://www.bitterlemons-international.org/inside.php?id=226 (accessed 11 February 2006).
122. T. LaHaye and J. B. Jenkins, *Left Behind: A Novel of the Earth's Last Days*, Left Behind Series, vol. 1, Wheaton, Ill.: Tyndale House Publishers, 1995; J. B. Jenkins and T. F. LaHaye, *Tribulation Force: The Continuing Drama of Those Left Behind*, Left Behind Series, vol. 2, 1997, etc. through vol. 12, 2004, *Glorious Appearing: The End of Days*.
123. Visit the website: http://www.leftbehind.com (accessed 17 February 2006).
124. G. Gorenberg, 'Intolerance: The Bestseller,' book review of Left Behind series by T. LaHaye, J. B. Jenkins, *American Prospect*, 23 September 2002, http://www.prospect.org/print/V13/17/gorenberg-g.html (accessed 17 February 2006).
125. Ibid.
126. M. Harrington, *The Dream of Deliverance in American Politics*, New York: Alfred A. Knopf, 1986, pp. 17–18.
127. B. Woodward, *Bush at War*, New York: Simon & Schuster, 2002; S. Mansfield, *The Faith of George W. Bush*, New York: J. P. Tarcher, 2003; D. Frum, *The Right Man: the Surprise Presidency of George W. Bush*, New York: Random House, 2003.
128. M. Rothchild, 'The Hidden Passages in Bush's Inaugural Address,' *Progressive* website, 23 January 2005, reposted on Common Dreams http://www.commondreams.org/views05/0123-05.htm (accessed 17 February 2006).
129. Northcott, *An Angel Directs The Storm*, p. 9.
130. Ibid., p. 8.
131. A. Lieven, 'Bush's Choice: Messianism or Pragmatism?' Open Democracy, online essay, 22 February 2005, http://www.opendemocracy.net/articles/ViewPopUpArticle.jsp?id=3&articleId=2348 (accessed 17 February 2006); see also, Anatol Lieven, *America Right or Wrong: An Anatomy of American Nationalism*, New York: Oxford University Press, 2004.
132. Rothschild, 'Bush's Messiah Complex.'
133. Quinby, quoted in Rothschild, 'Bush's Messiah Complex.'
134. M. Gerson, *The Neoconservative Vision: From the Cold War to the Culture Wars*, Lanham, Md. and London: Madison Books, 1997.

135. Berlet and Lyons, *Right-Wing Populism in America*, pp. 243–44.
136. J. Mann, *Rise of the Vulcans: the History of Bush's War Cabinet*, New York: Viking, 2004; T. Barry and J. Lobe, 'U.S. Foreign Policy: Attention, Right Face, Forward March,' Foreign Policy in Focus http://www.fpif.org/papers/02right/index.html, (accessed 12 February 2006); K. Husain, 'Neocons: The Men Behind The Curtain,' *Bulletin of the Atomic Scientists*, 2003, vol. 59, no. 6., http://www.thebulletin.org/issues/2003/nd03/nd03husain.html (accessed 12 February 2006).
137. Neoconservatives have been in the forefront of pointing out these problematic issues; see J. Muravchik, 'The Neoconservative Cabal,' *Commentary*, September 2003, online archive.
138. For a collection of seminal writings, see M. Gerson (ed) *The Essential Neoconservative Reader*, Reading, MA.: Addison Wesley Pub. Co, 1996.
139. A. Norton, *Leo Strauss and the Politics of American Empire*, New Haven Conn.: Yale University Press, 2004; S. B. Drury, *Leo Strauss and the American Right*, New York: St. Martin's Press, 1997.
140. S. A. Halper and J. Clarke, *America Alone: The Neo-Conservatives and the Global Order*, Cambridge: Cambridge University Press, 2004, pp. 14, 103–5, 198, 205–06.
141. Halper and Clarke, *America Alone*, p. 11.
142. C. A. Johnson, *The Sorrows of Empire: Militarism, Secrecy, and the End of the Republic*, New York: Metropolitan Books, 2004; I. M. Wallerstein, *The Decline of American Power: the U.S. in a Chaotic World*, New York: New Press, 2003. For those who prefer their irony served hot, a number of millennialist Christian evangelicals suspect the neoconservatives are agents of the Antichrist because they see them as building a global New World Order.
143. S. S. Wolin, 'A Kind of Fascism Is Replacing Our Democracy,' *Newsday* New York: Long Island, 18 July 2003, archived online at, http://www.commondreams.org/views03/0718-07.htm (accessed 17 February 2006).
144. A. Etzioni, 'The Real Threat: An Essay on Samuel Huntington,' *Contemporary Sociology*, 2005, vol. 34, no. 5, pp. 477–85, quote from p. 485.
145. G. Monbiot, 'Religion of the Rich: There is a Precedent for the Bush Project, But It's Not Fascism,' 9 November 2004, Monbiot.com, archived at http://www.commondreams.org/views04/1109-24.htm (accessed 17 February 2006).
146. H. Urban, 'Bush, the Neocons and Evangelical Christian Fiction: America, "Left Behind,"' *Journal of Religion & Society*, 2006, vol. 8, pp. 1–15. http://moses.creighton.edu/JRS/2006/2006-2.html (accessed 17 February 2006).
147. Ibid.
148. J. Zogby, 'Understanding America's Right Wing, Part II,' *Washington Watch* (Arab American Institute), column, 3 June 2002, http://www.aaiusa.org/wwatch/060302.htm (accessed 17 February 2006).
149. Ibid.
150. Northcott, *An Angel Directs The Storm*, p. 41.
151. See, for example, L. H. Lapham, 'We Now Live in a Fascist State,' *Harper's Magazine*, October 2005, pp. 7–9. If true, Lapham's article could not have been published.
152. See, for example, L. W. Britt, 'Fascism Anyone?' *Free Inquiry* magazine, 2003 vol. 23, no. 2, http://www.secularhumanism.org/index.php?section=libr

ary&page=britt_23_2 (accessed 17 February 2006). For a better and more accurate list, see, U. Eco, '"Ur-Fascism" [Eternal Fascism],' *New York Review of Books*, 22 June 1995, pp. 12–15; excerpted as 'Eternal Fascism:Fourteen Ways of Looking at a Blackshirt' in *Utne Reader*, November–December 1995, pp. 57–9; the latter is online at, http://www.themodernword.com/eco/eco_blackshirt.html, (accessed 17 February 2006).

153. S. Power, 'The Anatomy of Fascism: The Original Axis of Evil,' review of Paxton, *New York Times*, Sunday 'Books' section, 2 May 2004; L. Miller, 'Who's a Fascist? The Ultimate Political Insult is Making a Comeback. But Does Anyone Know What it Really Means?' *Salon*, online magazine, 19 April 2004, http://www.salon.com/books/feature/2004/04/19/fascism/print.html (accessed 17 February 2006).

154. R. O. Paxton, *The Anatomy of Fascism*, p. 218.

155. N. Solomon, 'Dean Hopes and Green Dreams: The 2004 Presidential Race,' syndicated column, *Z Magazine*, archived at http://www.zmag.org/content/showarticle.cfm?ItemID=4086 (accessed 17 February 2006); see also, A. Shivani, 'Is America Becoming Fascist?' CounterPunch, online, 26 October 2002, http://www.counterpunch.org/shivani1026.html (accessed 17 February 2006).

156. Lieven, 'Bush's Choice.'

157. E. L. Tuveson, *Redeemer Nation: The Idea of America's Millennial Role*, Chicago: University of Chicago Press, 1968.

158. Lifton, *Superpower Syndrome*, p. 99.

159. Ibid., p. 123. See also, R. A. Horsley, *Jesus and Empire: The Kingdom of God and the New World Disorder*, Minneapolis, MN: Augsburg Fortress Publishers, 2002.

160. Ibid., pp. 123–4.

Appendix

What follows is an 'e-interview' which Stanley Payne (SP) gave to Roger Griffin (RG) in the summer of 2007. It is printed here as an integral part of his *Festschrift* in order to provide a biographical context to the remarkable range of topics he has addressed within an output sustained at the highest level of original scholarship for nearly 50 years. It is followed by a comprehensive Bibliography of his publications till December 2007.

Interview

RG *Is there anything in your background that predisposed you to becoming (a) a historian and (b) an expert in modern Spanish history or ultra-right wing politics?*

SP Working with history is a matter of being interested in the past, of reading about it, having imagination for it and imagining oneself in it, and at the same time probably of having a bookish and literary turn of habits. All those things characterised me from childhood. By the age of 12, if not earlier, I looked at the older buildings in Sacramento (California), built in the late nineteenth century, and imagined them to be houses of the seventeenth-century New England frontier, with Indians lurking behind the outlying trees.

Becoming a Hispanist had both a profound logic, and also an element of serendipity, to it. I grew up entirely in the territory of the old Spanish empire (Texas and California) and was exposed to the language from childhood, though I didn't really learn it properly till I was an undergraduate, when I did an undergraduate minor in Spanish. (The major, of course, was history.) But by my last two undergraduate years I lived increasingly in the world of classic Russian literature, and was oriented primarily to Russian history. In my small college Russian was not taught, which handicapped me, nor was I particularly well advised. For graduate study in Russian history I applied only to Berkeley and to the Russian Institute at Columbia. The former put me on the alternate list and the latter asked for further letters of recommendation. Since the Columbia letter was held up in the mail for three months, I couldn't meet their deadline and thus did not get into a Russian programme.

What I did end up with was a fellowship to the Claremont Graduate School (now Claremont University). In the intervening summer (1955) I read two books which first gave me the idea that Spain – rather than Latin America, which was then and remains the primary focus in the US – would be interesting and important to study. One was *The Spanish Temper*, by the British critic V. S. Pritchett (himself a first-rate avocational Hispanist) and the other a book on historic Spanish art and architecture. These two works powerfully fired my imagination. Then at Claremont the only Latin Americanist historian, Hubert Herring, happened to have had more contact with and knowledge of Spain than most American Latin Americanists, who can scarcely locate Spain on a map. He gave me strong encouragement, and that was crucial in my beginning research on Spain. Even so, between 1955 and 1957 I continued to look to some extent in the direction of Russia or Italy, and studied Russian for six weeks at Berkeley in the summer of 1956. I was not fully set in the direction of Spain until I matriculated in the doctoral program at Columbia in September 1957. I had selected Columbia over Harvard and Chicago, which also offered partial fellowships, because I calculated – correctly, as it turned out – that it, together with the ambience of New York City, had the most to offer someone trying to deal with Spain. The help of Francisco García Lorca (brother of the poet), who taught at Columbia, and his friend Joaquín Maurín (founder of the famous POUM), who lived in exile in New York, was fundamental in establishing the right contacts to do oral history in Spain.

Concentrating on the right was strictly the result of having the wit to follow a suggestion made by Herring. Before 1955 my own idea would rather have been to study the left, like the standard academic conformist. Then I found that I had a good thing going, and stayed with it. I became engaged in the longer run with the study of the Franco regime, because it lasted so long and bulked so large in Spanish affairs.

It is misleading to think that I am especially interested in the politics of the right, as distinct from fascist studies. Of my last four main Spanish books, one has dealt with the right, one with the left, and the two books on the Republic as much or more with the centre.

RG *Has academic/student life changed significantly since you were starting out at Pacific Union College or Columbia in the 1950s?*

SP Yes, but only in ways similar to most other things. The student culture now is much more materialist, as is society in general, and there is more emphasis on having a higher standard of living and constantly travelling round, even as a graduate student. I find this bewildering, though in the contemporary culture it is normal. In my time we expected to live modestly and to concentrate on our work, though most of my contemporaries did not concentrate as much as I did. And of course in those days academic life was both more simple and more formal, and much more traditionalist.

One of the biggest changes – though it began as early as the 1970s, but has remained semi-constant – is that most doctoral students in history, to some extent depending on field, can have no great confidence about landing a regular academic position on a permanent basis. In the late 1950s, we thought we had at least a fighting chance, rather better than 50 per cent. Soon afterward there began the great, but alas very temporary, history boom of the 1960s, which only lasted from about 1962 or 1963 until 1970. But those were heady days, brief as they were.

RG *Your first book (*Falange*) is presumably based on your PhD. What drew you to studying the Falange?*

SP This is explained in my answer to the first question. Nothing 'drew me', other than the fact that this was a potentially significant topic that no one else was working on. Just the standard scouting for a dissertation theme; I had no idea there might be any such thing as 'fascist studies'. No one talked of such things then in that form, and when I began I did not in any way have any more interest in fascism than in a number of other things.

RG *Franquism was still very much a historical reality when you started out on your academic career: what was it like to be studying Falangism in Spain as a 'liberal' historian? Were there any tensions at the time between your search for historical truth/academic objectivity and its 'lived history' in the experience of Spaniards and the life of the regime?*

SP Two factors helped a lot: The first was timing. I arrived in the fall of 1958, by which point the regime had been in its middle, more moderate, period, for several years. The second was being American, since the pact had been signed five years earlier and that provided Americans with somewhat better status. A third factor was simply being a foreign dissertator, which was accepted as a more 'objective' and 'professional scholarly' status than any Spaniard could have presumed to at that time. A fourth factor was that two decades had now passed, and old Falangists were now ready to talk. My most important research was done in oral history (though I didn't know it, since we didn't use the term then). The Spanish contacts were set up, first by Joaquín Maurín from New York and then by the premier ex-Falangist writer and official, Dionisio Ridruejo. They were both extraordinary personalities. The fact that Ridruejo was both an ex-Falangist and a generous person was key; he helped a very great deal, though I don't think he was that much impressed by the book. And since this was the quasi-liberal late Franco regime, the police never interfered, since the regime had long since given up pretensions to being totalitarian. So long as I didn't meddle in politics, it didn't meddle with me. I'm sure that I had a police file, but no one ever bothered me.

Nonetheless, everything was coloured by politics, and I dealt with people from all the opposition parties except the Communists, having already established some contact with them in New York. But the only Spanish person who had any 'intellectual' or historiographical influence was the great Catalan historian Jaume Vicens Vives, undoubtedly the greatest historian whom I have ever personally known in any country. He was then only 48, but would die of cancer two years later. He had more influence on me than any of my American professors, and the first book was appropriately dedicated to his memory. Political perspective did not seem much of a problem then, for most of the people I dealt with were opposed to Franco, at least platonically, and that included a fair number of the Falangists themselves.

RG *How did your interpretation of the Franco era and of Spanish fascism in books/ articles written in the 1960s/1970s (such as* Falange, Politics and the Military in Modern Spain, Franco's Spain) *conflict with prevailing orthodoxies during and after the Franco era?*

SP *Falange* caused comparatively little conflict; even Marxist historians sometimes adopted it for class use in the 1960s. Nearly every single review was (a) fulsome or (b) perfectly positive. *Franco's Spain* was less read, and perhaps unusual because of the emphasis on positive economic development. *Politics and the Military* was the most original and revisionist, not in giving a positive spin to pretorianism (it did not), but simply in 'complexifying' history a good deal, and showing that the standard left-liberal interpretations were ill-informed and quite incomplete.

RG *How were you seen by the Franco regime/Spanish academics working under Franco and how are you seen in Spain and Hispanic America now?*

SP That depended. To the ultra-right I was anathema, and thus could not publish in Spain, but the more liberal Francoists were relatively positive from the start, realising that an objective treatment that did not take sides was the best they could hope for and better than they usually got. The left in general was pleased, though the ultra-left always felt that I failed to denounce adequately.

This began to change with *The Spanish Revolution* (1970), still the only one-volume treatment of the whole revolutionary process of Spain in the 1930s. Its origins were serendipitous, once more, originally not my idea but that of the Americanist Jack Greene, who had sold W. W. Norton on his ten-volume series of *Revolutions in the Modern World*. (Remember, the 1960s were the decade of the great publishing boom in history.) The late 1960s were the time when I really learned Spanish history, because I had begun to teach it in 1964, was preparing my two-volume *History of Spain and Portugal*, and, for the *Revolution* book, did primary research on the left for the first time. The latter was much more of an eye-opener than any of the research on the right, for I had been raised on the myth of the Republic and of the (at least fundamentally) virtuous left. Discovering that the left, rather than the right, had initiated political violence, both small-scale and large-scale, and was responsible for the initial breakdown of democracy was the most radically new finding of my entire career, and changed my whole outlook. It also meant that my reputation among the left would begin to go into decline, though that varies a great deal depending on which leftist – some are more objective than others.

RG *What has the reception of your work on Spain and generic fascism abroad told you about the degree of mutual awareness, understanding, and collegiality that prevails in the international academic community?*

SP That just about anything is possible, for reactions have varied across the political, professional and international map. Some have been predictable, others not. Reception of my Spanish work ultimately came to depend partly on a kind of left/right split, but only to some extent. Some leftist historians have always been good friends and colleagues.

The reception of the historiography of fascism is yet more complex, because this is an area in which lots of different people think they have expert knowledge, or at least enough knowledge, to have firm and valid opinions of their own. There are firmly established notions, even though not determined by individual political ideology, to which must be added various schools of doctrinaire leftists. Thus the tendency for every man to be his own fascistologist. Beyond that in the continental European countries there are various national biases, as well. Yet I am not complaining; I have been fortunate that my work has been as well received as it is. And by the 1990s serious scholars began to agree on at least certain fundamentals with regard to generic fascism.

RG *When did you start being interested in the theory of fascism?*

SP As nearly as I can remember, about 1967. I taught general contemporary European history as well as Spanish history, and I became more intrigued by the puzzle of what was the real common denominator between Falangists and other European fascists – something that was not at all satisfactorily explained. My most important senior colleague at UCLA at that time was

Eugen Weber, who was publishing his works on French nationalism and his little *Varieties of Fascism*, which was a very original book, and one stimulated by the fact that its author was a Transylvanian Romanian who worked on France. This gave him a broader perspective. In 1965 he and Hans Rogger edited the volume of studies on *The European Right*, to which I contributed, which also played a role. But I had not made much progress on this score – mainly being focused on Spanish research – by the time that I left UCLA in 1968.

RG *Tell us about the role of Juan Linz in the genesis of* Fascism: Comparison and Definition

SP Juan José Linz Storch de Gracia has been since 1958 arguably the greatest single conceptual/analytic influence on my work, even more than Vicens Vives or George Mosse. He has been the outstanding analyst in the field of comparative historical European political sociology in my lifetime. His comparative grasp of political and social data is extraordinary and his analytic depth and originality unparalleled. We were both in Madrid together in 1958 on SSRC fellowships (mine pre-doctoral, his post-doctoral) and he wrote to me even before my arrival, so that I got in touch with him immediately. In the early years we talked more about Spanish politics generally and Falangism specifically, not much about generic fascism. My first two analytic essays on generic fascism were both deficient; neither was published, and appropriately so. Juan and I coincided at the Bergen conference in 1974. He presented his concept of the tripartite structure of fascist doctrine, as well as a good deal more. I included in my Spanish paper a brief but broad-ranging discussion of its relationship to the general problem of comparative fascism. This was the first time that I was able to deal with the latter in a coherent and convincing way. Juan strongly endorsed my analysis, while I in turn was stimulated by his newest work. By the time that conference was over the road to *Comparison and Definition* had begun to open, though there was still a long way to go.

RG *What sort of collegial relationship did you build up with George Mosse and how decisive was it for your involvement in fascist studies and Journal of Contemporary History?*

SP George Mosse was chair of the committee which hired me for Wisconsin in 1968, and from that time became the closest friend and most influential colleague I ever had among more senior colleagues in any department in which I taught. He did not originate my interest but he nourished and stimulated my work a great deal. Even though he was not involved in the direct writing of *Comparison and Definition*, and only made comments on it after it was complete, it is quite possible that without him the book would not have developed, or would have developed only much later. Moreover, it was George who particularly encouraged me to do the broader book that appeared in 1995. Another stimulus for *Comparison and Definition* was the encouragement of Tom Webb, director of the University of Wisconsin Press, since before finally undertaking the writing of the MS in 1978 I was still not entirely sure that I could make a coherent and successful book of it.

RG *What is about the University of Wisconsin-Madison that enabled it to become such a powerful international force in fascist and Nazi studies?*

SP First and above all the presence of George Mosse, who particularly in the 1960s was a towering campus figure. Then there was Bob Koehl in the History Department, who did two books on the SS and had many good graduate students, such as Chris Browning. The founding of the *JCH* was important, and then I added to the mix.

RG *How has your own theory of fascism evolved in the last 25 years?*

SP After the 1980 book, my thinking has changed for the most part only in marginal ways. This is partly dependent on new monographic research. By 1995 I came to the conclusion that the Spanish and Romanians should be considered rather more marginal than I had earlier thought. Even that was not new, but only added to the emphasis. In recent years the biggest changes have had to do with my understanding of the relationship of fascism with religion and the interaction with communism, though this last is partly simply due to the fact that I had not studied communism enough earlier. Then in recent years the biggest influences have been Emilio Gentile and Roger Griffin. Gentile has to some extent – perhaps not 100 per cent – brought me round to his understanding of the character and reality of Italian fascist totalitarianism.

RG *Do you see any narrative shape in the evolution of the debate about generic fascism?*

SP Not in the sense of a directly continuous narrative. The fascism debate of the 1960s and 1970s clarified a good deal, but exhausted itself without achieving consensus. *Comparison and Definition* thus became a kind of coda with regard to how far it had gotten. The 1980s were a drier decade, before the debate picked up again in the 1990s, by which time at least there was some agreement on some things, which one could hardly have said in the 1970s.

RG *How important is it for historians to be interested in the political science debate surrounding their specialism?*

SP I think it is quite important, but that is a hard idea to sell to many historians. Historians are great at generating data, but not always at thinking about it and analysing it. Then in the past 20 years many of the younger ones have been dominated by fairly simplistic so-called 'theoretical' approaches, though the scientific use of theory is largely unknown to these people. The political science debates have the advantage of framing things within a broader perspective that also opens new analytical dimensions. If it is true that a renewed emphasis is beginning to emerge on 'big issues' in history, as distinct from the micro-topics that have often promoted trivialisation in the past 20 years, this perspective may be more important than ever.

RG *What do you make of the growth of interest in political religion: How far is it a fashion driven by the concern with Islamic terrorism (like the explosion of nationalism studies after the collapse of the Soviet Empire) and how far a substantive issue for historians and political scientists to understand?*

SP It's too early to tell. In the 1980s there was first predicted a 'return of the religious' after the great secularisation of the 1960s and 1970s, but there was little sign of that in the 1990s. For scholars, PR is a heuristic device like generic fascism. There is a broader interest, however, in politics and religion and in the politicisation of religion. This is clearly stimulated by current events, and PR studies will also feed off that. Note also that Stanley Fish, the great guru of American postmodernism, published an article in the *Chronicle of Higher Education* in January 2005 flatly insisting that the fad of 'race, class, gender' studies would soon be replaced by that of 'religion' studies. Let's wait and see.

RG *Has the debate over political religion any relevance has it to your own interpretation of fascism and Francoism/would it have modified your interpretations had it been an issue in the 1950s?*

SP I always found the PR concept plausible but not indispensable and used it very little, and never prominently. In Spain the only genuine PRs were those of the revolutionary left. Falangism at no time proposed to become or became a PR, while Francoism merely relied on a massive politicisation of religion – and with great success, at least for the first quarter-century. But I think that PR analysis, as well as other new research, indicates that the relationship between fascism and religion, and as PR, requires deeper and more extensive study.

RG *Given the conflicting interpretations of the relationship of fascism to religion (e.g. the radical differences in the way Laqueur, Gentile, or Steigmann-Gall approach it), are there any observations you would like to make on the concept? Have you developed a distinctive 'position' on political religion?*

SP I decided last year that I should try to frame my own understanding of PR more precisely, and the result is the article published in *TMPR* in September 2005. Just as one of the most important aspects of fascist studies is generic fascism, PR studies simply point to the need for a broader, clearer, better informed framework for the understanding of the relationship between politics and religion, in general. Gentile has been pointing the way on this, but even his framework is not yet fully complete.

RG *Do the contrasting relationships to traditional Catholicism of Franco and the Falange have anything useful to contribute to clarifying some of the complex taxonomic issues surrounding political religion in the current debate (e.g. the distinction that Gentile makes between civic and political religion?)*

SP There are two dimensions here. One is the extraordinary depth and success of the Francoist politicisation of religion, the nearest thing to a Catholic equivalent of a sort of Islamism, and one that led to a genuine revival of traditionalist Catholicism for 20 years. Here the type was unusual only in its extent; what was singular was the degree of its practical success, at least for a while.

The second dimension is that of the relationship between Falangism and religion. Of the larger European fascisms, it was relatively the most orthodox, and identified with and challenged religion the least. That is why in my later *Fascism in Spain* I altered my analysis to place Falangism on the cusp between fascism and the radical right. It never became a fully fledged revolutionary fascism.

RG *In* Fascism: Comparison and Definition *published in 1980 you referred to the Romanian Iron Guard as 'a mystical, kenotic form of semi-religious fascism that represented the only notable movement of this kind in an Orthodox country and was* *also marginal to the species'. This implies a genuine hybrid between institutionalised religion and a modern secularised but sacralised nationalism. Has your position on the Iron Guard been modified by the subsequent debate on fascism and political religion?*

SP No, only confirmed and if anything carried farther. It was in some respects the most religious fascism, in some respects more than Falangism, but at the same time could not square the circle with religion. A few adherents admitted that their actions were heterodox, something that equivalent Falangists would never have done. But this also prevented it, also like Falangism, from becoming a full revolutionary fascism.

RG *You wrote a review of Gentile's* Le religioni politiche *for the journal Totalitarian Movements and Political Religions (TMPR) (Summer 2002, Vol. 3, no. 1, pp. 122–30(9)): Has your position on the value of his taxonomy (which you welcomed, though with some reservations) changed since?*

SP No, I think it is pretty valid as far as it goes, though it needs further refinement and development, which he continues to give it. As in the case of most heuristic concepts, it is easy to exaggerate it into something which it is not. What was most original and useful, perhaps, was the analysis of Islamism, which correctly took demolished the naturally popular but mistaken notion of 'Islamo-fascism' or of Islamism as a PR itself.

RG *What role do you attribute to 'political religion' in shaping the politics of contemporary America, and how far does it bear out Gentile's distinction between civic and political religion?*

SP None whatsoever. Here Gentile is right on. I think that his taxonomy does, however, contribute to thinking more seriously and precisely about religion and politics in America. The main qualification that I would mention is that, examining it more closely, there is more religion in the American civil religion than he may have thought. We correspond from time to time about this.

   The nearest thing to developing a kind of PR in the United States was, loosely, Wilsonism, when the liberal Protestant leaders took the lead in demanding war on Germany and making the United States the leader in the world struggle for democracy, etc. Richard Gamble's *The War for Righteousness* is the best account of that, though it passed quickly. The relationship between religion and politics in the United States is a huge and complex field which will provide opportunity for scholars for a long time.

RG *What is the significance of the collection of essays in this book?*

SP Their significance is to help to broaden considerably the study of PR and also of the relationship between politics and religion, generally. They are very illuminating on such diverse topics on Hitlerian Germany and PR, on Hindutva, on Cuba, Maoist China and on the merely candidate-PR of the contemporary west European left. They don't resolve all the comparative issues, but contribute considerably to their elucidation, as well as offering key case studies.

RG *What do you consider the main achievements of your academic life?*

SP To open new fields both geographically and thematically, and to try to revise several basic historical analyses and conclusions. In the 1950s and 1960s, it was very important to study Spanish history seriously, and it has been important to take a fresh and more objective look at all the key themes and developments. Later the same would be said for trying to make analytic sense of comparative fascism, and also the relation between fascism and communism.

RG *Can you distinguish a fundamental 'red thread' running through your academic life?*

SP Nothing in terms of a single dominant concept or theme per se. I would say rather that it has been an ability fairly persistently to 'think outside the box', and thus to come up with new analytic approaches. This may be related to having grown up in a minority religious culture, and, even though I abandoned that specific religion very early, I early became sceptical of predominant orthodoxies.

RG *Is there any historical issue/debate on which you have radically changed your mind?*

SP The biggest change came 35 years ago, when I saw that my research demonstrated that the standard mythic approach to Spanish affairs in the 1930s was fundamentally flawed.

RG *What are the highlights of academic career in the context of Anglophone academics and Hispanic academics? What book or article are you most proud of?*

SP That may be the toughest one of all. Though I am proud of several honours that have come my way, I do not rate any one above the others. The two individual books that gave me the greatest feeling of accomplishment were *Fascism: Comparison and Definition* – I remember that the day I finished that MS I went to bed with a rare feeling of satisfaction, thinking that I had finally accomplished the first fully coherent analysis of generic fascism – and more recently with *The Spanish Civil War, the Soviet Union and Communism*, which largely solved a problem that I had wrestled with for 35 years but usually thought I might never be able to resolve, or at least to write up coherently as a book. Subsequently, the American Association for the Advancement of Slavic Studies awarded the latter book its Marshall Shulman Prize for 2005. That a Hispanist has been given a Russian/Soviet studies prize rather astounds me. So those were perhaps the two highest points.

Strictly in Hispanism, perhaps my biggest feeling of accomplishment was the two-volume *History of Spain and Portugal*. There had never been a work quite like that, and I may have enjoyed it and learned more from it than from any other project. Two millennia of Iberian history was a heady experience.

Another high-point of Hispanism was my role as public intellectual and area expert on the peninsula during the era of democratisation (roughly 1973–1983). Here the activity that provided greatest satisfaction in retrospect was my testimony at a conference (not a formal hearing) in the US Congress in June 1975. This had been organised at the behest of the Junta Democrática, a bizarre coalition of the Spanish Communists and more moderate groups. Their burden was that the American government should take some initiative to promote democratisation (Franco would die within five months) and to keep the military from intervening. Otherwise military intervention was inevitable. Of all the people there, I was the only one to take exactly the opposite tack, and my analysis proved correct. My position was (a) the Spanish could and should do it on their own; (b) the military would not intervene if civilian politicians behaved responsibly. I was right on both scores. Since 'experts' often provide faulty testimony in these circumstances, this became a source of satisfaction, and in fact the entire proceedings were soon published as a small book, so there is a record. Most people predict on the basis of what is going on at present or has happened in the past. Having done a book on military politics, I thought it important in terms of expert analysis to be able to get straight when the military would probably *not* get involved in politics.

March 2005, was an usually good month: I received my first-ever front-page review in the *TLS*, and very apposite and positive indeed, then secondly a communication from Planeta, the largest publisher in the Spanish-speaking world, that they wanted to do a new edition of my *Spanish Catholicism* on extraordinarily generous terms. Both these developments quite astonished me.

In general I have been quite overwhelmed by all that has happened since April 2004, after I had initially announced my retirement set for 2005: the conference in Madison, this book, the possible of a Hispanist Festschrift by my Hispanist students and colleagues, the honorary doctorate in Valencia, the Shulman Prize, the scholarly excellence award named for me by the editors of *TMPR*. I'm simply very grateful to everyone who has been involved in these things.

RG *If you were starting out as a postgraduate now what discipline would you be drawn to and what subject would you be tempted to research for a PhD?*

SP I would not be able to imagine myself as anything but an historian. Curiously, if I were starting out in 2005 I might be drawn to Russian history even more than in 1954–1955. The kinds of new opportunities that once existed in Spanish history are simply not there, while the major area of Russian history – after all, one of the major world histories – is now becoming a neglected field. Moreover, to a limited degree one can now do research in Russia in a normal way, which was hardly possible half a century ago.

RG *Have you any tips for apprentices hoping to emulate your distinguished career and immense impact on your discipline?*

SP Work hard, don't fixate on whether other people in your department are making more money than you are, but concentrate on original research and writing. Try to think outside the box. Combine comparative analysis with history as much as possible. Be serious, but don't take yourself too seriously. Sometimes you're simply wrong. Remain humble, as in 'I'm simply a humble history professor', since no matter what we may think with our often-inflated egos, we'll never amount to more than that.

STANLEY G. PAYNE
AWARDS AND PUBLICATIONS
(as at January 2007)

Born September 9, 1934. Denton, Texas.

Education:
B. A., Pacific Union College, 1955
M. A., Claremont Graduate School and University Center, 1957
Ph. D., Columbia University, 1960

Professional Experience:
Lecturer, Columbia University, 1959–60
Lecturer, Hunter College, 1960
Instructor, University of Minnesota, 1960–62
Assistant Professor to Professor, University of California, Los Angeles, 1962–68
Vice-chairman, History Department, University of California, Los Angeles, 1966–67
Professor, University of Wisconsin-Madison, 1968–
Chair, History Department, 1979–82
Retired as Professor Emeritus, 2005

Awards:
a. Graduate Fellowship, Claremont Graduate School and University Center, 1955–57
b. Duryea Fellowship, Columbia University, 1957–58
c. Social Science Research Council Fellowship, 1958–59
d. SSRC Grants-in-Aid, 1961 and 1970
e. American Philosophical Society Grants-in-Aid, 1961 and 1967
f. Guggenheim Fellowship, 1962–63
g. ACLS Fellowship, 1971
h. ACLS Travel Fellowship, 1974
i. APS Travel Grant, 1975
j. ACLS Summer Fellowship, 1977
k. Multiple awards, Graduate School, University of Wisconsin, 1969–79
l. Jaume Vicens Vives Professorship, 1981–2005
m. Hilldale Professorship, 1982–2005
n. Fellow, Institute for Research in the Humanities, 1983
o. Hilldale Award for Social Studies, 1994
p. Senior Fellow, Institute for Research in the Humanities, 1995–2000
q. Elizabeth Steinberg Prize of the University of Wisconsin Press, 2004
r. Doctor honoris causa, CEU-Universidad Cardenal Herrera Oria, 2004
s. Marshall Shulman Book Prize of the American Association for the Advancement of Slavic Studies, 2005.

Member:
a. Corresponding Member, Real Academia Española de la Historia (elected 1987)
b. American Academy of Arts and Sciences (elected 1997)
c. The Historical Society
d. International Conference Group on Portugal (Co-founder, 1972)
e. Society for Spanish and Portuguese Historical Studies

PUBLICATIONS
Books:
 1. *Falange: A History of Spanish Fascism.* (Cloth and paperback: Stanford University Press, 1961).
    UK edition: Oxford University Press, 1961.
    French and Spanish editions: Paris: Ruedo Ibérico, 1965.
    First Spanish reprint edition: Madrid: Editorial SARPE, 1985.
    Second Spanish reprint edition: Madrid: Editorial Grupo, 1994.
 2. *Politics and the Military in Modern Spain.* (Stanford University Press, 1967).
    UK edition: Oxford University Press, 1967.
    Spanish edition: Paris: Ruedo Ibérico, 1968.
    Revised and expanded edition: *Ejército y sociedad en la España liberal, 1808–1936.* Madrid: Akal, 1977.
    Spanish reprint edition: Madrid: SARPE, 1993.
 3. *Franco's Spain.* (New York: Thomas Y. Crowell, 1967).
    UK edition: Routledge and Kegan Paul, 1968.
 4. *The Spanish Revolution.* (Cloth and paperback: New York: W. W. Norton, 1970).
    UK edition: Weidenfeld and Nicolson, 1970.
    First Spanish edition: Barcelona: Ediciones Ariel, 1972.
    Second Spanish edition (separate translation): Barcelona: Argos Vergara, 1977.
    Japanese edition: Tokyo: Heibon-sha, 1974.
 5. *A History of Spain and Portugal.* (Cloth and paperback: University of Wisconsin Press, 1973) 2 Vols.
    History Book Club edition, 1973.
    Revised and expanded Spanish edition: Madrid: Editorial Playor, 1985–88. 5 Vols.
    Spanish reprint edition: Madrid: Editorial Grupo, 1993. 5 Vols.
    Digital edition of Volume One: LIBRO, 2002.
 6. *Basque Nationalism.* (Reno: University of Nevada Press, 1975).
    Spanish edition: *El nacionalismo vasco desde sus orígenes a la ETA.* Barcelona: Dopesa, 1974.
    Digital edition: University of Nevada Press, 2000.
 7. *La revolución y la guerra civil española.* Gijón: Ediciones Júcar, 1976.
 8. *Fascism: Comparison and Definition.* (Cloth and paperback: University of Wisconsin Press, 1980.)
    Spanish edition: Madrid: Alianza Editorial, 1982.
    Spanish reprint edition: Madrid: Editorial Altaya, 1996.
 9. *Spanish Catholicism: An Historical Overview.* (Madison: University of Wisconsin Press, 1984).
    Spanish edition: Barcelona: Editorial Planeta, 1984.
    Revised edition: Barcelona, Editorial Planeta, 2006.
10. *The Franco Regime, 1936–1975.* (Madison: University of Wisconsin Press, 1988).
    Spanish edition: Madrid: Alianza Editorial, 1988. Reprinted, 2005.
    Paperback edition: London: Phoenix Press, 2000.
11. *Franco: El perfil de la historia.* (Madrid: Espasa-Calpe, 1992).
    Reprint edition: Barcelona: Planeta-DeAgostini, 1995.

12. *Spain's First Democracy: The Second Republic, 1931–1936.* (Cloth and paperback: University of Wisconsin Press, 1993).
    Spanish edition: Barcelona: Editorial Paidós, 1995.
13. *A History of Fascism 1914–1945.* (Cloth and paperback: University of Wisconsin Press, 1996.)
    UK world paperback edition: London: UCL Press Limited, 1995.
    Spanish edition: Barcelona: Editorial Planeta, 1995.
    Italian edition: Rome: Newton & Compton Editori, 1999.
    Digital edition: University of Wisconsin Press, 2000.
    German edition: Munich-Berlin: Propylaen Verlag, 2001. Reprint edition, 2006.
    Greek edition, 2002.
14. *El primer franquismo, 1939–1959: Los años de la autarquía.* ("Historia de España," Vol. 28.) Madrid: Historia 16, 1998. Reprinted, 2005.
    CD-Rom edition: Madrid: Ediciones Dolmen, 2002.
15. *Fascism in Spain 1923–1977.* (Cloth and paperback: University of Wisconsin Press, 2000.)
    History Book Club edition, 2000.
    Expanded Spanish edition: *Franco y José Antonio: El extraño caso del fascismo español.* Barcelona: Editorial Planeta, 1998.
16. *La época de Franco. La España del Régimen (1939–1975).* ("Historia de España," Vol. 13.) Madrid: Espasa-Calpe, 2000.
17. *The Spanish Civil War, the Soviet Union, and Communism 1931–1939.* (New Haven: Yale University Press, 2004).
    Spanish edition: *Unión Soviética, comunismo, y revolución en España, 1931–1939.* Barcelona: Random House Mondadori, 2003.
    Portuguese edition: Lisbon: Editora Ulisseia, 2006.
18. *The Collapse of the Spanish Republic, 1933–1936: Origins of the Civil War.* (New Haven: Yale University Press, 2006).
    Spanish edition: Madrid: La Esfera de los Libros, 2005.
19. *Cuarenta preguntas fundamentales sobre la Guerra Civil.* (Madrid: La Esfera de los Libros, 2006).

Co-authored book:
(with Enrique de Aguinaga) *José Antonio Primo de Rivera.* Barcelona: Ediciones B, 2003.

Textbook:
(with Otto Pflanze) *Modern Times: Europe since 1815.* (*A History of the Western World, Vol. 3.*) Boston: D. C. Heath, 1964. Third revised and illustrated edition, 1975.

Edited books:
Society and Politics in Twentieth-Century Spain. New York: New Viewpoints (Franklin Watts), 1976.
Reprint edition: New York: Marcus Wiener, 1982.
Expanded Spanish edition: Madrid: Akal Editor, 1978.
The Politics of Democratic Spain. Chicago: Chicago Council on Foreign Relations, 1986.
Identidad y nacionalismo en la España contemporánea: El Carlismo 1833–1975. Madrid: Editorial Actas, 1996.

Co-edited books:
(with Javier Tusell) *La guerra civil: Una nueva visión del conflicto que dividió España*. Madrid: Temas de Hoy, 1996.
(with Delia Contreras) *España y la Segunda Guerra Mundial*. Madrid: Universidad Complutense, 1997.
(with David J. Sorkin and John S. Tortorice) *What History Tells: George L. Mosse and the Culture of Modern Europe*. Madison: University of Wisconsin Press, 2004.

Edited book series:
Six monographs on Spain and Portugal in *Modern European History*. New York: Garland, 1991–1993.

ARTICLES, CHAPTERS AND NOTES

1. "Workers, Bankers, and Social Evolution in Franco Spain," *Claremont Quarterly*, 6:4 (Summer 1959), 27–36.
2. "El Carlismo en la preparación de la Cruzada de 1936," *Tradición* (Barcelona), no. 5 (November–December 1959). 12–19. Repr. *Siempre* (Palencia), nos. 29–30 (February–March 1969).
3. "José Antonio Primo de Rivera and Contemporary Spain," *Claremont Quarterly*, 9:1 (Autumn 1961), 31–50.
4. "Ledesma Ramos and the Origins of Spanish Fascism," *Mid-America*, 43:4 (October 1961), 226–41.
5. "Jaime Vicens Vives and the Writing of Spanish History," *Journal of Modern History*, 34:2 (June 1962), 119–34.
6. "Recent Studies on the Spanish Civil War," *Journal of Modern History*, 34:3 (September 1962), 312–14.
7. "The Second Spanish Republic, 1931–39," in Allen Guttman, ed., *American Neutrality and the Spanish Civil War* (Boston: D. C. Heath, 1963), 20–30. (Problems in American Civilization Series.)
8. "Twentieth-Century Spanish Nationalism," *Review of Politics*, 26:3 (July 1964), 403–22.
9. "Spain," in Hans Rogger and Eugen Weber, eds, *The European Right* (Berkeley and Los Angeles: University of California Press, 1965), 168–207.
10. "Falangism," in *Encyclopedia of the Social Sciences*.
11. "Unamuno's Politics," in J. Rubia Barcia and M. A. Zeitlin, eds, *Unamuno: Creator and Creation* (Berkeley and Los Angeles: University of California Press, 1967), 203–19.
12. "Catalan and Basque Natioinalism," *Journal of Contemporary History*, 6:1 (1971), 15–51.
13. "In the Twilight of the Franco Era," *Foreign Affairs* (January 1971), 342–54.
14. "The Army, the Republic and the Coming of the Civil War," in Raymond Carr, ed., *The Republic and the Civil War in Spain* (London: Macmillan, 1971), 79–107.
15. "Political Ideology and Economic Modernization in Spain," *World Politics* (October 1972), 155–81.
16. "Alfonso XIII en la perspectiva histórica de su tiempo," *Historia y Vida*, no. 56 (November 1972), 124–29.
17. "Il nazionalismo basco tra destra e sinistra," *Rivista Storica Italiana*, 85:4 (1973), 984–1043.

18. "Spanish Fascism in Comparative Perspective," *Iberian Studies*, II (1973), 3–12. Repr. in Henry A. Turner, Jr., ed., *Reppraisals of Fascism* (New York: New Viewpoints, 1975), 142–70.

19. "El nacionalismo vasco y la Segunda República," *Actualidad Económica*, 853 (July 1974), 36–44.

20. "La derecha en Italia y en España," *Boletín de Ciencia Política*, nos. 13–14 (August–December 1974), 65–82.

21. "El Ejército, entre el caos progresista y la reacción conservadora (1873–1874)," *Historia y Vida* (1974), 114–23.

22. "Possible Reigns in Spain," *Worldview* (November 1974), 31–35.

23. "Regional Nationalism: The Basques and the Catalans," in William Salisbury and James Theberge, eds, *Spain in the 1970s* (New York: Praeger, 1976), 76–102.

24. "Ejército y sociedad en la España liberal," *Historia 16*, 1:2 (June 1976), 131–35.

25. "España: Un futuro incierto" in J. Tusell, ed., *Actualidad Económica*, 958 (July 1976), 30–7.

26. "Recent Historiography on Modern and Contemporary Spain," *American Hispanist*, 2:10 (September 1976), 2–17.

27. "Intrigas falangistas contra Franco," *Historia 16*, 1:8 (December 1976), 35–41.

28. "Fascism in Western Europe," in Walter Laqueur, ed., *Fascism: A Reader's Guide* (Berkeley and Los Angeles: University of California Press, 1976), 295–311.

29. "Carlism – Basque or 'Spanish' Traditionalism?", in W. Douglass, R. Etulain and W. Jacobsen, eds, *Anglo-American Contributions to Basque History* (Reno: University of Nevada Press, 1977), 119–26.

30. "The Political Transformation of Spain," *Current History* (October 1977), 165–68.

31. "'Eurocommunism' and the PCE," *Problems of Communism*, 27:1 (January–February 1978), 77–80.

32. "La financiación del falangismo," *Historia 16*, 2:9 (March 1978), 44–51.

33. "New Political Literature of the Spanish Left," *The Washington Review*, 1:3 (July 1978), 95–104.

34. "1936: Calvo Sotelo y la Gran Derecha," *Nueva Historia*, 2:20 (September 1978), 88–95.

35. "Spain and Portugal," in Raymond Grew, ed., *Crises of Political Development in Europe and the United States* (Princeton University Press, 1978), 197–218.

36. "Spanish Conservatism, 1834–1923," *Journal of Contemporary History*, 13:4 (December 1978), 765–89.

37. "Epilogue," to L. Graham and R. Makler, eds, *Contemporary Portugal* (Austin: University of Texas Press, 1979), 343–50.

38. "ETA – Basque Terrorism," *The Washington Quarterly*, 2:2 (Spring 1979), 109–13.

39. "Asiocomunismo y eurosocialismo: El debate dentro del marxismo ruso (1906)," *Historia 16*, 4:38 (July 1979), 61–66.

40. "Terrorism and Democratic Stability in Spain," *Current History* (November 1979), 167–71, 182–83.

41. "The Concept of Fascism," in S. Larsen, *et al.*, *Who were the Fascists: Social Roots of European Fascism* (Oslo/Bergen/Tromso: Universitetsforlaget, 1980), 14–25.

42. "Social Composition and Regional Strength of the Spanish Falange," in *Ibid.*, 423–34.

43. "La transición española desde el punto de vista histórico," *Cuenta y razón*, 1:1 (November 1980), 5–8.
44. "Recent Research on Basque Nationalism: Political, Cultural and Socioeconomic Dimensions," *Society of Basque Studies in America*, II (1981), 9–22.
45. "Nacionalismo español y regionalismo nacionalista en España," in R. Morodo, ed., *Cultura, sociedad y política en el mundo actual* (Madrid: Universidad Internacional Menéndez Pelayo, 1981), 3–16.
46. "Navarrismo y españolismo en la política navarra bajo la Segunda República," *Príncipe de Viana*, 166–67 (May–December 1982), 895–905.
47. "Navarra y el nacionalismo vasco," *Cuenta y Razón*, 7 (Summer 1982), 21–32.
48. "Los nacionalismos," in J. Andrés-Gallego, ed., *Historia general de España y América*, Vol. 16:2, "Revolución y Restauración (1868–1931)," (Madrid: Ediciones Rialp, 1982), 109–30.
49. "The Authoritarian Century," *The New Republic* (11 October 1982), 32–37.
50. "Spain's Political Future," *Current History*, 81: 479 (December 1982), 417–22.
51. "Salazarism: 'Fascism' or 'Bureaucratic Authoritarianism'," *Estudos de história portuguesa: Homenagem a A. H. de Oliveira Marques* (Lisbon: Estampa, 1983), 512–31.
52. "Post-Franquist Historiography of the Franco Era," *Society for Spanish and Portuguese Historical Studies Bulletin*, 8:3 (October 1983), 5–10.
53. "Fascism, Nazism, and Japanism," *The International Historical Review*, 6:2 (May 1984), 265–76.
54. "Die spanischen Militaers wahren der Franco-Ara (1939–1975)," in P. Waldmann, *et al.*, eds, *Sozialer Wandel und Herrschaft im Spanien Francos* (Paderborn: Schoeningh, 1984), 195–210.
55. "Raíces del nacionalismo vasco," *The Journal of Basque Studies*, 6:1 (July 1984), 7–28.
56. "Navarra and Basque Nationalism," in W. A. Douglass, ed., *Basque Politics: A Case Study in Ethnic Nationalism* (Reno: University of Nevada Press, 1985), 21–39.
57. "Representative Politics in Spain: The Historical Background," in H. Penniman, ed., *Spain at the Polls* (Durham, NC: Duke University Press, 1985), 7–44.
58. "Fricciones entre los franquistas," in Diario 16, *Historia del franquismo* (Madrid 1985), 194–99.
59. "Los sucesos de Begoña," in *Ibid.*, 210–15.
60. "La Guerra Civil como lucha militar," *Cuenta y Razón*, 21 (September–December 1985), 113–24.
61. "Spain, Europe and NATO," in K. Maxwell, ed., *Spain's Prospects* (New York: The Spanish Institute, 1985), 19–22.
62. "De Teruel a la batalla del Ebro," in E. Malefakis, ed., *La guerra de España 1936–1939* (Madrid: El País, 1986), 194–208. Repr. in E. Malefakis, ed., *La guerra de España 1936–1939* (Madrid: Taurus, 1996), 385–418.
63. "El régimen de Franco en perspectiva," *Historia 16*, 11:122 (April 1986), 163–77.
64. "Fascism and Right Authoritarianism in the Iberian World – The Last Twenty Years," *Journal of Contemporary History*, 21:2 (April 1986), 163–77.
65. "The Concept of 'Southern Europe' and Political Development," *Mediterranean Historical Review*, 1:1 (June 1986), 100–16. Repr. in *Znamim*, 9:34–5 (Summer 1990), 62–72.

66. "The Foreign Policy of Democratic Spain," *AEI Foreign Policy and Defense Review*, 6:2 (1986), 29–36.
67. "O fascismo espanhol revisitado," *Ler História*, 8 (1986), 115–20.
68. "The Last Good Cause: 50 Years Later," *The World and I* (November 1986), 455–60.
69. "Modernization of the Armed Forces," in S. Payne, ed., *The Politics of Democratic Spain* (Chicago Council on Foreign Relations, 1986), 181–96.
70. "The Elections of June 1986," in *Ibid.*, 246–55.
71. "Una tragedia tra due guerre," *Storia Illustrata*, 344 (July 1986), 54–66.
72. "Francisco Franco: La mia mano non tremerà," *Ibid.*, 66–71.
73. "Spain, the Church, the Second Republic, and the Franco Regime," in R. Wolff and J. Hensch, eds, *Catholics, the State, and the European Radical Right, 1919–1945* (Highland Lakes, NJ: Atlantic Research, 1987), 182–98.
74. "Natural Evolution in Spanish Political Culture," in H. Binnendijk, ed., *Authoritarian Regimes in Transition* (Washington, DC, 1987), 186–92.
75. "Counterrevolution," in *Spain from Civil War to Democracy* (Harvard University Center for European Studies. Working Paper Series, no. 13, 1987), 1–13. Repr. in R. Fishman and C. Maier, eds, *1936–1986: From Civil War to Contemporary Spain* (Harvard, 1989).
76. "The Role of the Armed Forces in Transition," in R. Clark and M. Haltzel, eds, *Spain in the 1980s* (Cambridge, MA, 1987).
77. "A taxonomia comparativa do autoritarismo," *O Estado Novo* (Lisbon, 1987), I, 23–30.
78. "Recent Historiography on the Spanish Republic and Civil War," *Journal of Modern History*, 60:3 (September 1988), 540–56.
79. "Spanish Fascism," *Salmagundi*, 76–77 (Winter 1988), 101–12.
80. "Los estadounidenses y la guerra," *Cuenta y Razón*, 39 (September 1988), 25–36.
81. "Dictatorship and Democratization in Southern Europe: A Historian's Perspective," *Modern Greek Studies Yearbook* (1988), 1–13.
82. "Moderna historiografía sobre Carlismo y las guerras carlistas," *Aportes*, 9:3 (1988), 40–47.
83. "The Army," in R. W. Kern, ed., *Historical Dictionary of Modern Spain, 1700–1988* (Westport, CT: Greenwood, 1989), 39–50.
84. "Falange Española," in *Ibid.*, 199–204.
85. "Francisco Franco Bahamonde," in *Ibid.*, 223–31.
86. "Political Violence during the Spanish Second Republic," *Journal of Contemporary History*, 25: 2–3 (May–June 1990), 269–88.
87. "La oposición a las dictaduras en Europa Occidental: Una perspectiva comparativa," in J. Tusell, *et al.*, eds, *La oposición al régimen de Franco* (Madrid 1990), 51–64.
88. "Próleg: L'exèrcit espanyol i Catalunya," in J. M. Solé and J. Villarroya i Font, eds, *L'Exèrcit i Catalunya (1898–1936)* (Badalona, 1990), 9–18.
89. "La guerra de España," in *La guerra y la paz: Cincuenta años después* (Madrid 1990), 203–10.
90. "Nationalism, Regionalism and Micronationalism in Spain," *Journal of Contemporary History*, 26:3–4 (September 1991), 479–92.
91. "Die Kirche und der Uebergangsprozess," in W. Bernecker and J. Oehrlein, eds, *Spanien heute: Politik, Wirtschaft, Kultur* (Frankfurt am Main, 1991), 105–20.

92. "Foreword" to Burnett Bolloten, *The Spanish Civil War: Revolution and Counterrevolution* (Chapel Hill: University of North Carolina Press, 1991), xi–xv.

93. (with Burnett Bolloten) "The Flight of Negrín and the end of the Third Republic," in *Ibid.*, 726–43.

94. "Felipe González: Decisive Leader," *The World and I* (December 1991), 80–83.

95. "King Juan Carlos: El motor del cambio," *Ibid.*, 76–79.

96. "Fascism," in M. Hawkesworth and M. Kogan, eds, *Encyclopedia of Government and Politics* (New York: Routledge, 1992), I, 167–78.

97. "Franco: Cien años después," *Suplemento Semanal* (Madrid), 266 (29 November 1992), 24–34.

98. "Fascismo, modernismo e modernizaçâo," *Penélope*, 11 (1993), 69–75.

99. "Historic Fascism and Neo-Fascism," *European History Quarterly*, 23 (1993), 69–75.

100. "Stanley Payne: La historia, una vocación; España, un acierto," in A. M. González Martín, ed., *Historia abierta*, 13 (March 1994), 2–3.

101. "Nacionalismo español, nacionalismo vasco," in J. M. González, ed., *Aula de Cultura 1993–1994* (Bilbao, 1994), 109–23.

102. "Regional Historiography of the Spanish Civil War," *European History Quarterly*, 24:3 (July 1994), 403–10.

103. "Autoritarisme portugais et autoritarismes européens," *Revista de História das Ideias*, 16 (1994), 7–18.

104. "Fins a quin punt van ser 'feixistes' la Falange i el régim franquista," *L'Avenç*, 186 (November 1994), 30–33.

105. "Authoritarianism in the Smaller States of Southern Europe," in H. Chehabi and A. Stepan, eds, *Essays in Honor of Juan J. Linz: Politics, Society and Democracy* (Boulder: Westview, 1995), 183–96.

106. "Carlism in Spanish Politics, 1931–1939," in S. Payne, ed., *Identidad y nacionalismo en la España contemporánea: El Carlismo 1833–1975* (Madrid, 1996), 103–22.

107. "Antecedentes y crisis de la democracia," in S. Payne and J. Tusell, eds, *La Guerra Civil* (Madrid, 1996), 17–121.

108. (with J. Tusell) "Conclusions," in *Ibid.*, 635–46.

109. "Spanish Pretorianism Revisited," in B. Frankel, ed., *A Restless Mind: Essays in Honor of Amos Perlmutter* (London: Frank Cass, 1996), 227–43.

110. Part I. "Gobierno y Oposición (1939–1969)." Chapter 1. "De la posguerra a la tecnocracia (1939–1959)." Chapter 2. "De la segunda metamórfosis al caso Matesa (1959–1969)." In R. Carr, ed., *La Epoca de Franco (1939–1975)*, Vol. 41 of R. Menéndez Pidal and J. M. Jover, eds, *Historia de España* (Madrid: Espasa-Calpe, 1996), 5–142.

111. "Greek Democracy and the 'Southern Europe' Paradigm Revisited," *Modern Greek Studies Yearbook*, 12–13 (1996–97), 609–15.

112. "The History of Fascism Revisited," *Camôes Center Quarterly*, 6/7: 1–2 (Summer/Fall 1997), 40–44.

113. "La quiebra de la República," in F. Rosas, ed., *Portugal e a guerra civil de Espanha* (Lisbon, 1998), 107–21. Repr. in M. A. Baquer, ed., *La guerra civil española (Sesenta años después)* (Madrid, 1999), 17–32.

114. "The Defascistization of the Franco Regime, 1942–1975," in S. U. Larsen, ed., *Europe after Fascism 1943–1980s* (Boulder, 1998), II, 1580–1600.

115. "Existió realmente un fascismo catalán?," *La Vanguardia* (Barcelona), (2 October 1998), 6–7.

116. "Fascist Italy and Spain, 1922–1945," *Mediterranean Historical Review*, 13:1–2 (June–December 1998), 99–115. Repr. in R. Rein, ed., *Spain and the Mediterranean since 1898* (London, 1999).

117. "Prólogo," to X. Casals i Meseguer, *La tentación neofascista en España* (Barcelona: Plaza & Janés, 1999), 15–23.

118. "Prólogo" to J. Palacios, *La España totalitaria* (Barcelona: Planeta, 1999), 17–21.

119. "Historical Fascism and the Radical Right," *Journal of Contemporary History*, 35:1 (January 2000), 109–18.

120. "Orígenes de la guerra civil," *Historia 16*, 24:286 (February 2000), 54–73.

121. "Estado fascista," in A. Barreto and M. F. Mónica, eds, *Dicionario da História de Portugal*, (Porto: Figueirinhas, 2000), Vol. VII, 686–91.

122. "Catalan and Basque Nationalism: Contrasting Patterns," in S. Ben-Ami, Y. Peled, and A. Spektorowski, eds, *Ethnic Challenges to the Modern Nation State* (London: Macmillan, 2000), 95–107.

123. "La Política," in J. L. García Delgado, ed., *Franquismo: El juicio de la historia* (Madrid: Temas de Hoy, 2000), 233–85.

124. "PNV: Mentiras y verdades," *El Mundo*, "Crítica," 9 January 2000, 4–5. Repr. in *El Babazorro*, no. 30 (March–April 2000).

125. "Generic Fascism: An Epochal Phenomenon Only," *Ethik und Sozialwissenschaft*, 11 (2000), Vol. 2, 314–15. Repr. in W. Loh and W. Wippermann, eds, *"Faschismus" – kontrovers* (Stuttgart: Lucius & Lucius, 2002), 116–20. Vol. 3 of "Erwägungskultur" in, W. Loh, ed., Forschung, Lehre und Praxis.

126. (with Frank Schauff) "The NKVD in Spain: Questions by Stanley Payne, answers by Alexander Orlov. With an introduction by Frank Schauff," *Forum für osteuropäische Ideen- und Zeitgeschichte*, 4 (2000), Heft 2, 229–50.

127. "Fascism in Western Europe," in W. Laqueur, ed., *The Holocaust Encyclopedia* (New Haven and London: Yale University Press, 2001), 181–84.

128. "Fascism and Communism," *Totalitarian Movements and Political Religions*, 1:3 (Winter 2001), 1–15.

129. "Prólogo" to Elisa Chuliá, *El poder y la palabra. Prensa y poder político en la dictadura. El régimen de Franco ante la prensa y el periodismo* (Madrid: Biblioteca Nueva, 2001), 1–4.

130. "El misterio del último pronunciamiento finalmente resuelto," *El Mundo* (Madrid), 29 May 2001.

131. "ETA, entre el terrorismo y el fascismo," *El Mundo*, 4 June 2001.

132. "Terrorismo y fascismo," *El Mundo*, 27 June 2001.

133. "Spain Betrayed," *Los Angeles Times Book Review*, 15 July 2001, 1–3.

134. "El dieciocho de julio," *El Mundo*, 11 July 2001.

135. "La revolución que cambió el mundo," *La Aventura de la Historia*, 3:33 (July 2001), 42–43.

136. "La apertura de los archivos soviéticos y la guerra de España," *El Mundo*, 19 August 2001.

137. "La guerra de EEUU contra el terrorismo," *El Mundo*, 28 September 2001.

138. "El Islam visto desde los Estados Unidos," *El Mundo*, 26 October 2001.

139. "Introducción: Una España fratricida y heroica," in M. Platón, ed., *Imágenes inéditas de la Guerra Civil (1936–1939)* (Madrid: Agencia Efe, 2002), 11–31.

140. "El fascismo en su época (1919–1945)," in *La extrema derecha en Europa* (Barcelona: Mundo Revistas, 2002), 31–49.

141. "Elementi per una teoria del fascismo a posteriori," in A. Campi, ed., *Che cos'è il fascismo?* (Rome: Ideazione Editrice, 2003), 299–323.

142. "Soviet Anti-Fascism: Theory and Practice, 1921–1945," *Totalitarian Movements and Political Religions*, 4:2 (Autumn 2003), 1–62.

143. "Fascism and Racism," in T. Bell and R. Bellamy, eds, *The Cambridge History of Twentieth-Century Political Thought* (Cambridge, UK, 2003), 123–50.

144. "Mi encuentro con José Antonio Primo de Rivera," *Aportes*, 17:3 (no. 50, 2003), 5–11.

145. "Foreword," to Emilio Gentile, *The Struggle for Modernity: Nationalism, Futurism and Fascism*. Westport, CT: Praeger, 2003, pp. ix–xix.

146. "Prólogo" to Daniel Kowalsky, *La Unión Soviética y la Guerra Civil Española 1936–1939*. Barcelona: Crítica, 2003, 1–4.

147. "Mitos y tópicos de la Guerra Civil," *La Revista de Libros*, June 2003, 3–6.

148. "Franco y el Dieciocho de Julio," *El Mundo* (Madrid), 18 July 2003.

149. "¿Por qué vuelve a estar de moda la Guerra Civil?," *Clío* (December 2003), 17–19.

150. "La religión en la historia de España y de los Estados Unidos," in J. Pérez Vilariño, ed., *Religión y sociedad en España y los Estados Unidos: Homenaje a Richard A. Schoenherr* (Madrid: CIS, 2003), 3–12.

151. "Los Estados Unidos y España: Percepciones, imágenes e intereses," *Cuadernos de Historia Contemporánea*, 25 (2003), 155–67.

152. "¿Se pudo haber evitado la Guerra Civil?," *El Mundo*, 17 June 2004.

153. "Las ideologías del 18 de julio," *El Mundo*, 19 July 2004.

154. "History, Nation, and Civil War in Spanish Historiography," *The Journal of the Historical Society*, IV:3 (Fall 2004), 335–44.

155. "La Guerra Civil, ¿desmitificada?" *La Revista de Libros*, 96 (December 2004), 3–5.

156. "Los verdugos de Stalin," *La Revista de Libros*, October 2004.

157. "La herencia soviética," *La Revista de Libros*, 97 (January 2005), 8–12.

158. "*1934: Comienza la Guerra Civil*: En torno al libro de Pío Moa," *Cuadernos de Pensamiento Político*, 5 (January–March 2005), 187–92.

159. "La Gulag como historia," *La Revista de Libros*, 98 (February 2005), 17–19.

160. "El nacionalismo y el colapso de la Unión Soviética," *La Revista de Libros*, 100 (April 2005).

161. "La presidencia de Ronald Reagan: Evaluación histórica," *Boletín de la Real Academia de la Historia*, 202: 1, 99–117.

162. "On the Heuristic Value of the Concept of Political Religión and its Application," *Totalitarian Movements and Political Religion*, 6:2 (September 2005), 163–74.

163. "Prólogo" to Jesús Lainz, *"Adios, España": Verdad y mentira de los nacionalismos*. Madrid: Ediciones Encuentro, 2005.

164. "Prólogo" to Jesús Palacios, *Las cartas de Franco: La correspondencia desconocida que marcó el destino de España*. Madrid: La Esfera de los Libros, 2005.

165. "Prólogo" to José María Zavala, *En busca de Andreu Nin. Vida y muerte de un mito silenciado de la Guerra Civil*. Barcelona: Plaza & Janés, 2005.

166. "En busca de la identidad cultural rusa," *La Revista de Libros*, 114 (June 2006), 15–16.

167. "?Pudo evitarse la Guerra Civil?," *Clío* (July 2006), 14–15.
168. "El alzamiento del 18 de julio," *Historia de Iberia Vieja*, 13 (2006), 6–7.
169. "Culpables de la contienda," *Interviú* (29 July 2006), 48–51, 76–8.
170. "Memoria histórica," *El Mundo* (7 September 2006), 8–10. La
171. "Prólogo" to Isabel Durán and Carlos Dávila, *La gran revancha. La deformada memoria histórica de Zapatero.* Madrid: Temas de Hoy, 2006.
172. "Prólogo" to César Vidal, *Las Brigadas Internacionales.* Madrid: Espasa-Calpe, 2006.
173. "Prólogo" to A. de Lizarza Iribarren, *et al. Navarra fue la primera 1936–1939.* Madrid: Sahats, 2006.
174. "Stalin y el siglo soviético," *La Revista de Libros*, 119 (November 2006), 19–21.
175. "The NDH State in Comparative Perspective," *Totalitarian Movements and Political Religions*, 7:4 (December 2006), 409–15.
176. "Jacques Chirac tiene intención de descubrir América," *El Mundo*, 17 February 2007.
177. "Tardofranquismo o pretransición?," *Cuadernos de la España contemporánea_* (CEU. Instituto de Estudios de la Democracia), 2 (April, 2007), 5–15.
178. "Aprender la lección," *Revista de Libros*, 126 (June, 2007), 22–24.
179. "Franco, the Spanish Falange and the Institutionalization of Mission," in A. Costa Pinto, *et al.*, eds, *Charisma and Fascism in Interwar Europe* (London: Routledge, 2007), 53–63.
180. "Prólogo," to J. J. Esparza, *El terror rojo en España. Una revisión de la Causa General* (Barcelona: Ediciones Áltera, 2007), 15–18.
181. "Foreword," to W. H. Bowen and J. E. Álvarez, eds, *A Military History of Modern Spain* (Westport: Praeger, 2007), vii–viii.
182. "Visigoths and Asturians Reinterpreted: The Spanish Grand Narrative Restored?," in J. A. Corfis and R. Harris-Northall, eds, *Medieval Iberia: Changing Societies and Cultures in Contact and Transition* (Woodbridge: Tamesis, 2007), 47–56.

BOOKLETS AND PAMPHLETS

1. *Fascism and National Socialism.* St. Charles, MO.: Forum Press, 1975.
2. *Historia del Carlismo.* Madrid, 1996.

SHORT ENCYCLOPEDIA ARTICLES
Fifteen articles on personalities and topics in modern Spanish and Portuguese history in the third edition of the *Columbia Encyclopedia*, *Encyclopedia Britannica* and the *World Book Encyclopedia*, three articles in J. W. Cortada, ed., *Historical Dictionary of the Spanish Civil War 1936–1939* (Westport, CT: Greenwood Press, 1982), and the article on "Fascism" in the *Social Science Encyclopedia*.

SHORT NEWSPAPER ARTICLES
Several dozen, mostly in Spanish newspapers.

BIBLIOGRAPHICAL ANALYSIS
(with David T. Cattell) "Spain and the Spanish Civil War," in T. T. Hammond, ed., *Soviet Foreign Relations and World Communism: A Selected Annotated Bibliography* (Princeton, 1965), 585–94.

BOOK REVIEWS
Approximately 80 reviews published since 1960 in the *American Historical Review, American Political Science Quarterly*, Aportes, *Book Week, Book World, Bulletin of Hispanic Studies, Business History Review, Canadian Journal of History, Comparative Politics, Contemporary Politics, España Libre, Ethnic and Racial Studies, European History Quarterly, Foreign Affairs, Hispanic American Historical Review, Hispanic Review, The Historian, The History Teacher, Illes i imperis, International History Review, Journal of European Economic History, Journal of Interdisciplinary History, Journal of Military History, Journal of Modern History, Journal of Religion, Journal of Social History, Labor History, Los Angeles Times Book Review, Luso-Brazilian Review, Modernism, Modernity, New Oxford Review, New York Times Book Review, Oral History Review*, Orbis, *Political Science Quarterly, Red River Valley Historical Journal of World History, La Revista de Libros, Saturday Review, Social History Society Bulletin, Times Literary Supplement, Worldview*, and numerous others.

PUBLISHED INTERVIEWS
Personal interviews concerning my work have been published in such journals and magazines as *Clío, La Gaceta Ilustrada, Cambio 16, Actualidad Económica*, and *Blanco y Negro*, and in such newspapers as *ABC* (Madrid), *El Mundo* (Madrid), *La Razón* (Madrid), *La Vanguardia* (Barcelona), *Ya* (Madrid), *El Heraldo de Aragón* (Zaragoza), *El Correo Español* (Bilbao), the *Diário de Notícias* (Lisbon), and many others.

LECTURES AND INTERVIEWS ON RADIO AND TELEVISION
Lecture series for History 356, WHA (Madison).
Talks and interviews on Spanish affairs for National Public Radio and for various radio and television stations in Spain, and on other research for Rome television and a variety of media outlets in the United States.

EDITORIAL WORK
Co-editor, *Journal of Contemporary History*, 1999–
Co-editor, *Luso-Brazilian Review*, 1886–1991
President of Editorial Board, *Luso-Brazilian Review*, 1996–2004
Either in the past or at present member of the editorial or advisory board of the *American Historical Review, Aportes, Cuenta y Razón, Historia 16, Historical Abstracts, International History Review, Luso-Brazilian Review, Mediterranean Historical Review, Portuguese Studies Review, and Totalitarian Movements and Political Religion*.

Index

In this index figures and notes are indicated in italics, enclosed in parenthesis, following the page number. E.g. *Fiamma Nera*, 101*(fig.5.8)*. Notes are indicated by *n*. Figures by *fig*. Works are entered in italics.